Accessibility for Everyone

Authors, Developers, Managers, Trainers and More!

D1742160

Including A Complete

508 And WCAG Compliance Manual

For Websites, Applications

And Documents

Plus Complete Tutorials!

Ed Thrush

Edition 2, October 2016

What is in the Book:

- Guides for everyone at all levels who need to deal with some aspect of accessibility
- Tutorials that start with a simple introduction tutor and then lead to more detailed methods. All tutorials are very colorful and to the point.
- A more technical manual for every type of possible situation. Covering presentation of information in all formats. Includes general guides, more information links, and sample HTML code where it is useful.

Summary:

If you need to look up an accessibility issue, it is here. You can read through all or what is relevant and have a handy reference.

Includes:

- Extensive Table of Contents
- List of Figures
- Index to All Sections

Table of Contents

1 Introduction

1.1   Who Is This Book For?

It is for you of course! The very fact that you are reading this means you want to consider improving accessibility or you have been suddenly forced to by a contract or agency requirement. Even if you are not being forced to do this, increasing your user base and user understanding is always a good thing to do, for both society and business.

1.2   How Are You Approaching This?

We do have to cover a lot of material, but you can jump around of course for what is needed. I will employ colorful examples and even some humor (but not silly cartoons) where possible to keep this material from being too dry. The sad truth is most people are turned off from accessibility due to poor presentation. Being a little considerate, you have to understand that people start with technical requirements that are not easy to explain and apply to everyday office life.

1.3   History (Yes Boring I Know, But You Need At Least A Short Version Of Where This All Came From)

Section 508 was created in 1986 when Congress added this section to the Rehabilitation Act of 1973. It was revised In 1997 through the Rehabilitation Act Amendments of 1998, the Federal Electronic and Information Technology Accessibility Compliance Act was amended into the Workforce Investment Act of 1998, This requires that electronic and information technology that is developed or purchased by the Federal Government and those receiving Federal contracts and services is accessible by persons with disabilities.

The Americans with Disabilities Act (ADA) became law in 1990 and prohibits discrimination against people with disabilities. As a result of ADA, all state and local governments are required to offer reasonable services or tools to ensure that people are not discriminated against on the basis of disability.

Section 504, an amendment to the Workforce Rehabilitation Act of 1973, prohibits discrimination on the basis of disability.

So in accessibility, 504 and 508 both apply, not to mention the ADA itself.

Basically it all adds up to equal access and equal information. That my friends, means the disabled get the exact same information as the able-bodied person. Most importantly they will not be at any disadvantage due to lack of information or access when performance review time comes around. This is very serious stuff and it is less work to give equal access than to go to court. Having been through that experience, I can easily say it is a lot worse.

Many States and local governments have adopted these laws, in relation to federal contracts it has to be applied anyway. Private companies now have to comply as the Target case demonstrated. The National Federation of the Blind (NFB) sued the Target Corporation in 2006 as blind people couldn't use their website. The claim was asserted through the ADA using the equal access requirement for the disabled, specifically the requirement of "effective communication" with the blind and deaf. It cost Target a total of $9.7 million.

While a group like NFB above may gather a class action suit, a lone individual in an agency can utilize the Equal Employment Opportunity Commission (EEOC) to guide and support them. It all starts with one complaint that goes unresolved.

1.3.1 This Is All Old Stuff - How Do We Work With It Now?

The original technical standards are difficult to understand and even more difficult to implement without direction. The Access Board which is responsible for the standards has excellent guides, explanations and scenarios to help. However this only goes so far as the original standards were limited in their ability to help people. There are 75 Section 508 standards. Only 37 of those requirements apply to content, websites, and applications. Those being sections:

- Software applications and operating systems.

- Web-based intranet and internet information and applications

- Functional performance criteria

- Information, documentation, and support

Now of course these standards all being implemented around the year 2000, you can imagine we could use an update and a little more help. That is where WCAG comes in. Web Content Accessibility Guidelines 1.0 (WCAG 1.0) came into working life in 2001. This was replaced by WCAG 2.0 in 2008. It covers a huge range of recommendations for making Web content more accessible to a wider range of people with disabilities, including blindness and low vision, deafness and hearing loss, learning disabilities, cognitive limitations, limited movement, speech disabilities, photosensitivity and combinations of these. This was developed by The World Wide Web Consortium (W3C) and Web Accessibility Initiative (WAI). A wide range of public, private, and governmental participation helped to create the huge body of information.

The original 508 generally was interpreted (in practice) to favor blindness for content when in fact many other disabilities dominate.

1.4 Who Are We Talking About

56.7 million people in the United States have a disability (as of this publishing from US Census). Each of the disabilities described above has sub-categories. Vision impairment alone has multiple types of color blindness and levels of sight, Cognitive has huge categories that can affect ability to focus, follow reading order, and lose orientation without on-screen assistance.

It is also very important to realize that there is rarely any one type of disability people inherit or acquire; often there are multiple issues and combinations of disabilities. As a result one person may require many different types of tools to access your content and your content must be in a format that is receptive to these tools known as assistive technology.

1.5 In Brief What Laws Or Standards Apply?

- 508 which all Federal IT and many states and private companies have adopted

- 504 for discrimination in being treated different and affecting performance
- ADA which applies as equal access
- State Law which usually has provisions for the disabled to access information
- Your Project which itself should have made a commitment to the community that it would be accessible

2   First Steps

2.1   Okay, How Do I Get Started If I Have Not Done Any Accessibility Compliance?

It is rare that you would be starting totally from scratch, but if so we have you covered. Most private and definitely governmental agencies have polices and some checklists in place. What may be missing is what to do for all situations and what are the best practices. Having a dedicated 508 Compliance Officer or Manager is the best solution in the end. The reason is that research to solutions never ends, and the sheer workload cannot realistically be doubled up with another position. The best candidate will have some degree of application development, technical 508 background, authoring, and training. We will cover this more in detail later.

2.2   What Is Covered By 508?

First let us take a look at what is affected, so we see the bigger picture. What needs to be compliant?

We are looking from a user perspective, not the backroom technician.

- All Application and web or cloud software
    - Especially those made in house, products like MS office all have non-compliant modes but generally meet compliance for the basic tasks and they are heavily tested.
- Content Management Systems (templated databases for websites)
- Learning Management Systems (templated databases for training)
- Document Management Systems (storage, indexing, and version control for documents)
- Documents
    - All types, Word, PDF, Excel, PowerPoint (even plain text files must be formatted correctly)
- Training Materials
    - Video and Interactive Video (there are different solutions we will cover), documents, web pages

- Notifications, Messages
- Forms
  - Including employment applications, evaluations
- Reports (not just your reports, but data outputs)
- Collaboration Tools
  - Messaging, Forums, Databases, Dashboards, Project Issues
- Presentations
  - Including: handouts, email, and physical accommodations.

I could go on, but you get the point, basically anything that appears on the screen and by screen I mean any device the employee must use to do work that has a screen they read and interact with.

2.3 Other Little Things 508 Covers (What!)

508 also covers physical phones (also computer/internet integrated phones), computers, mobile devices, copiers, and essentially all basic office hardware. Yes even the prehistoric fax machine – all that falls under information technology hardware. We will not be covering that as those functional requirements are different from what we want to focus on here and that is the content you create (or publish on your website) and interactions via screen apps with your employees. Take my word for it; that will keep you busy enough.

2.4 Where Do I Focus?

Talking from experience again, I have seen two different agencies spent a lot of time trying to make a multi-function copier work for 508 requirements. They both succeeded after more than 2,000 hours each invested. In each agency, they were never used by the disabled. It took lots of training to learn how to operate the machine, and if there was a typical paper jam and you were disabled then you were stuck. The simple answer for most blind and limited vision users was to have their own printer. That way they knew only their own job was coming out.

Now while that was a hardware story, you can see that the effort was misdirected. Instead of following strict rules without ranking tasks, they should have been fixing the issues that the users were complaining about. In both of those cases, it was mandatory training that was completely inaccessible, and this had serious ramifications. So be warned, find out the real issues to address and get to work on them.

3 Very Condensed Guides

3.1 Fitting Accessibility Into Projects

First, there is no difference from accessibility requirements than security, business or any other requirements. So how does this work?

- 508 must be a stakeholder

- The lifecycle phases start with accessibility in the concept and design

- Agile is the preferred method as accessibility requires lots of rapid feedback and testing

- Create developer guides for making screens accessible to code guides

- Use known best practices such as WCAG and tailor known solutions to create your own best practices database

- Testing: Do spot checks, in-depth testing, and user testing. For the users or junior 508 testers, create a test script.

- Use professional issue tracking, if you can add requirements traceability all the better.

- Have frequent scrum like sessions to go back and forth on issues, if the developer is unclear on any point, the issue must be updated and more screen shots supplied with more clarity. The tester being a Subject Matter expert (SME) should provide best practice examples as a guide for solutions.

3.2   General Code Practice for Accessibility

Believe it or not the best simple thing you can do, is follow existing code standards and you will have less accessibility issues. What are we talking about?

- Follow the code standards and that means strict HTML format, and strict rules of code languages used

- HTML is what designs the screens, so careful code is always needed here most

- CSS solves a lot of issues, and that means a CSS file that you reference, not in-line styles
    - CSS can create messages, columns, block text, color separators and more

- Labels for fields are critical, they must be labeled and those labels and IDs are unique. You do not want multiple same name fields on a page unless you use a FIELDSET to group them (and if you do those FIELDSET names must be unique also)

- Use multiple navigation methods
    - Breadcrumbs
    - Expandable menus
    - Site Map
    - Search (one that really returns what is needed)
    - Index (by category or by alphabetic keywords or both)

3.2.1   Be Careful What You Buy!

Code libraries and widgets come in many types, some have no accessibility features, some have a few, and some have everything you need, but only if you turn on the features. Before you use a code library of functions read how much accessibility is supported by the vendor, and then read forums for how it works in the real world.

3.3   Testing Applications

I have to be very honest with you, there are no automated tools that will do the entire job. It requires a human. Now there are lots of software that can help you make sure code is written correctly, fields have names, tables are well formed. But there is no way to analyze an image description except by manually looking at it and determining if the image, chart, or screenshot, is correctly described than be examining the image. You must read the description and determining in the context of the page and the context of the section how much description is needed.

The other aspect of testing is user control and information. The reading order must be determined (generally a screen reader uses Tab key for link, fields, and tabable sections, and Arrow keys for all text and content.) This involves using the keyboard and using everything on the screen. A screen reader, (the most used is JAWS) can be the most helpful evaluation tool as it tells right away what is read and what controls work. But is also has element listing functionality, you can show a list of all links, fields, headings, buttons, images, and more. This is key to help identify issues and also acts as a documentation tool.

In the early days of web applications it was fairly easy to look at the screen code and determine the issue. While you can still do some of that today, a lot of source code is read from many other files and modules not available when you display the screen source. The way to compensate for this is rigorous manual testing and with some help from some other common tools we will discuss further on.

3.4   Testing Documents

This is a large category as there are many types of documents. There are commonalties among them all such as Word, PDF, or PowerPoint.

- Have unique titles
- Use built-in formatting for spacing, bullets, numbering
- Use links for footnotes and references
  - Use numbers or letters for links, not Roman numerals or symbols.
- Tables must be kept to a simple grid, no sub-headers or merged cells (there is much more on this later)
- For long manuals use numbers/letters with the headings
- Use correct heading levels H1, H2 followed by H3, do not skip or mix up
- Images are fully described
  - Use links to move complex data or explanations to an appendix

- Forms must meet the same requirements as applications

3.5   Recorded Webinars

One of the most complex issues is trying to make a recorded webinar accessible. We are talking after the fact, when the video of the training or demo session is put on the website. This being WebEx or similar, which can have a combination of slides, real-time application usage, notes, and dialogs. Do not forget that if you attach anything to event in the calendar or email then that attachment must also be accessible or have another format handy.

The main issue is that producing a transcript of the video after the fact is very difficult and extremely time consuming. Software that translates voice to text does not work in this situation as the voice needs to be one voice with consistent tone and volume and speed. Unless you have very clear or studio grade sound and control over all the sounds, you are not going down that road. It is possible your presenter is going to do all the talking in even paced and very clear speaking, announcer like, then your word accuracy would be very high and you could give it a shot. But that does not include other requirements.

What is required is a transcript that not only captures the voices, but also describes all the screens that were shown. This is a huge task. But you can tackle it faster, if approached at the time of creation rather than after the fact.

You can contract to have this work done after the fact or during the webinar. That is one solution.

You can also do this and save money and lots of time in publishing:

Have someone with a decent typing speed; take dictation of everything they hear at the webinar. The presenter needs to slow down a little and also must describe:

- The screens they are displaying
- The actions they are doing

The screen description can be a legitimate compromise. The first time the screen is described in detail (how much depending on familiarity), the second time state the name of the screen they are on, and what part they are going to select, and what actions. This is so that if somebody were only listening on the phone and had no image, they would have enough to go on (Example: "Go to the Contact page by selecting Personal Information on the Home page, go to the Address field located after the Name fields...")

One person types everything, the presenter describes a little more than usual and you can have it at minimal cost. Then you can post a transcript without little further effort except adding more descriptions where missed. The goal is equal information, what was communicated to visual is communicated via text.

Another positive is that non-disabled people like a well done transcript as they can look up what they need fast reference, rather than shuffling back and forth through an hour long video.

3.6   What Formats Should I Use?

3.6.1 Documents

If you created in Word or PowerPoint or InDesign, your final document should be a PDF. Now that is assuming you did proper styling and formatting in the original document. Once you convert there is always some cleanup to do in the PDF file. However once the cleanup is done, it is a better format for locking the document, for printing and for clear reading with JAWS. A PDF file has something called tags which are format tags to show how each word, table, list, and link is structured. Once they are cleaned up correctly, the file will pass any test (more on that later).

HTML that is well formed is the best overall, as all devices can use it easily and it also converts to other formats quite nicely. There are many document and help systems that can make mismanagement of large manuals and huge amounts of content easy to deal with and publish in HTML. Robohelp is one such product, there are others. You can also use a Content Management System to create different formats and retain easy editing.

3.6.2 Videos

These are the usual troublemakers. You have to have closed captions. You will also have to have a transcript – unless you have a video that is keyboard accessible and everything is described. There are several HTML5 packages that work quite well such as Elucidat that can do simulations. Captivate can produce a video that is accessible and also output a transcript if time is taken to learn how to do it correctly and format the screen right. If you do a transcript there are techniques for this, but the basic idea is that any screen must be described so there is the same information for the visual as there is for the limited vision user.

3.6.3 Warning – Other Formats You May Not Be Ready For

You may have to put your document in a different format if requested (that's the law). If Braille is all they can use, then braille it is. Or large print – this is tricky as you just cannot increase font size to 40 point, the format of everything may be unreadable if scattered all around, especially if you have columns, tables, block quotes or any other space aligned or restricted area formatting. Anything converted to audio needs to be organized so the reading makes sense.

3.6.4 Notes On Braille

Braille is for text only; you are not going to put a large table in Braille. There is Braille language for a very tiny table – as they have to memorize the columns and rows since it is printed out in words. So if your original is not text based, Braille will be a huge disappointment (to put it mildly). If you have a good document to begin with that has excellent descriptions of images and has easy to following headings, then it will succeed.

3.6.5 File Names

Accurate and usable/readable file names are needed when something goes wrong with an image and that file name is what is displayed or read to a screen reader. Giving a well described name such as "Beneficiary_Claim_Process" for both images and downloadable files (especially if downloaded) such as PDF or Word, will help everyone out. One technique with files is to put your descriptive name in front of the formal file name to combine both. In addition add as much meta data (title, author, keywords, description - information in the document properties) as the image or document format allows.

4 Class Training

4.1 These Checks Help With All Disabled Groups

- How effectively do the lessons gain and maintain the attention of the learner?
- How clear is the presentation of content? (Concise, focused, logical)
- How thought-provoking are the questions? Or can they confuse?
- To what degree does the learning system engage the learner?
- How useful are the analogies?
- How useful are the scenarios?
- To what degree are skills required explained?
- How relevant is the hands-on-guidance?
- Did you prepare accessible copies of everything covered?
- Did you provide self-guided tutorials?
- Did you get feedback? Do you have a process to quantify feedback?

4.2 Training Issues To Be Ready For With The Disabled

- Memory Difficulty
- Distractibility
- Inattention
- Difficulty staying on task, Many projects going on at one time and rarely completing any of them
- Understanding and remembering auditory instructions
- Differentiating between similar sounds, may hear inaccurately, or have challenges hearing one sound over a background noise.
- Resistant to change
- Ability to analyze written material
- Slow rate of reading, difficulty with spelling and written composition
- Difficulty taking notes.
- Trouble reading black text on white paper
- Difficulty with forming letters
- Writing within a defined space
- Problems doing arithmetic and grasping mathematical concepts

- Photosensitivity

- Positional sensitivity

- Difficult picking out an object from a background of other objects

- Seeing things in correct order.

- Lose their place frequently when reading

4.3   How To Deal With Some Of Those Training Issues

- Organize information with frequent headings and sections.

- Make sure content is visually separated from page borders or embedded images or graphics. Do not overlay anything or use semi-transparent images or text.

- Be aware of the use of color, make sure there is a high contrast between text and background and do not use a background image unless it has learning significance. If a background is used make sure it can be visually separated from other content.

- Sans-serif fonts should be used, such as Arial or Verdana. Minimize use of italics as these are also difficult for many to read.

- The reading order also called the logical reading order is the order in which the author intended the content to be read. Usually this is left to right and top to bottom. That is the general reading structure. The specific structure requires the reading to follow from the page title, section title, paragraph title and then any subsections and sub-paragraph titles. Numbering and lettering is the best practice as this makes the order explicit. Do not use Roman Numerals for anything (screen readers cannot interpret them).

- Titles, Fields, Section Names must be unique. Non-unique titles and names can cause issues for recognition and orientation.

- Make each page have unique identifiers for orientation and navigation, if a person landed on that page first or by accident, they should be able to tell where they are in the general document.

4.4   Basis For A Well Organized Training Document (And All Documents)

- Unique Page Title

- Unique Headings

- Heading Numbers

- Figure Numbers

- Table Numbers

- Footnote Numbers

- Table of Contents
- Index
- List of Figures

Examples:

1.0 Welcome to the 508 Users Guide

1.1 Introduction and Purpose of 508

4.5   Web Quick Training Check

- Make every control such as [Previous] and [Next] clear and consistent
- Links must identify the target by description. Do not use "Click Here" or "Click the Following".
- Let the user control the page, do not auto-initiate or auto-run anything.
- Everything that is a field, link, button or other control must have a unique name
- Consistency is critical, do not change the operation, name, or appearance of standard controls

5 Video Presentation Guide

No matter what type of video you are creating the following requirements will apply. This means all the 508 and WCAG forms and interaction standards apply. See the table at the end.

5.1   Voiceover

Voiceovers take the place of text instructions; as a result they must be very clear and descriptive. You cannot assume the user knows the locations or types of all items on the screen. Clearly give the location of each step. When describing the specific location; try to use more than one reference. Using only spatial references (up/down to the right/left) is not sufficient; add the shape, size, color, text, or icon description, and what the control or text is usually sitting next to or is after or before (this is best when next to a link or button as they can be more easily identified to screen readers, links, fields, buttons, and controls are tabbed items (Screen readers uses Tab key to jump to each active element).

The most frequent issue in 508 is navigation and orientation. Keep in mind how to describe where they are currently are and how the user to go back, forward, or receive help for the current task. If the user must leave the page temporarily, give instruction on how to return to complete the task.

Describe the type of event accurately when triggered by the user. For example if a button is selected, be precise as to what happens, distinguish between a pop-up windows, a drop-down menu, hover windows with multiple sub-hover windows, or panels/regions elsewhere on the page that update. The effect of selections is not always clear to all users, you must describe in detail what will occur and what is the expected range of results the user may experience.

5.2   Captions

As in closed captions which the user can control, not open captions which are printed on the video.

The captions must be accurate; you cannot have any difference between the audio and the captions. The captions must also be synchronized with the audio and video.

Software generated captions: these can be very inaccurate and can lead to complaints. Any auto-captioning must be reviewed and corrected. It is better to have someone dedicated who knows how to publish captioning.

5.3   Screen Shots, Screen in View

Use the full screen at first to get oriented, and then crop your screen to eliminate sections that are not relevant. If possible, crop out any blank space in all screens. The reason is that the resolution is very important for those who must magnify the image. Another reason is that by eliminating non-active areas, you can help users focus who may need help in doing so.

One technique is to have a magnified section of the screen in a window or box to help focus on the part that will require action and attention. Use arrows or lines (bold ones, not think ones) to show where it came from. Never assume it is obvious to make the connection, you must make the connections by visual and audio means.

5.4   Transcript

A transcript will be required for all videos (unless screen readers can access the captions and other text and that text describes everything visual). This can include the screen shots from the video, but each must be described fully. The current best practice is the put the description of images on the page itself instead of the alternative text of the image. The reason is that:

- All users can read at the same rate and get the same experience

- It will also print if needed

- In addition this will allow a quick method to convert to another format if needed for a request.

5.5   Titles

Divide the video into manageable chunks, give each section a title, and make that title unique. Particularly helpful is numbered titles. For example: 1. Introduction, 2. Getting Started with Your Profile…. Using a title screen will allow for easier searching if the user needs to rewind or advance.

5.6   Video of Classes, Instructors

These can be difficult to record accurately and also to describe. Anything written on a board must be clearly seen in the video. If an instructor points to something on the board, chart, or project screen, that action will have to be described. It is better for production purposes if the instructor themselves over-describes what they are doing to facilitate this (as if there were a blind person in the audience or they also are being heard over a conference line). If pointing to a list of steps projected on a screen, then announce for example: "From the 'Steps to Conduct a Project Checkpoint', let's look at number 3, 'Contacting the Stakeholders'". If a text of the presentation is given out before the class (a best practice), this will be useful for a later transcript but will not be sufficient as everything said and demonstrated must be written down in text.

The test of the final video is if the same information in its entirety is available by audio, visual, captions, and text transcript. They must be equal in information or it fails. If one medium is updated, the others must be updated also to keep equality of information.

One method of preparing for making a course accessible is to imagine (and sometimes in reality) making the presentation as if were to be packaged as a self-paced learning course. The will help guide that all information is very clear.

5.7   Items Viewed in Video Screen

Text must be readable to an equivalent of 10pt and with good contrast/color as a general guide.

Subject must be in focus or zoomed to indicate target of instruction. Highlights or circling objects can be helpful, back this up with text as to what is being highlighted.

The video itself should never autoplay (automatically start when loading or landing on a web page with the video), but equally important is a video within the video or animated demos should also not autoplay. The user must have the ability to start and stop anything associated with the video and the video itself.

Do not use transition effects that are more than a fraction of a second (such as slow fades) as these can cause many issues with assistive technology.

Learning games can be done but do not use drag and drop, instead use basic form controls in a colorful screen with different sized checkboxes, radio buttons, select lists and other standard HTML-type controls.

5.8   Language

Technical terms, abbreviations, and acronyms need to be explained.

5.9   Video Section 508 Checks In Non-Tech Talk

Keyword	Description
Animation	When animation is displayed, the information is displayed in text or audio with captions at the option of the user.
Disrupt AT	You cannot disable or use software that disables accessibility features of any assistive technology.

Keyword	Description
Focus	A well-defined on-screen visible indication of the current focus must be provided that changes as the input focus changes. The focus must be accessed and controlled by assistive technology. If the user can move keyboard focus to a place then they must be able to move focus away from that place (you cannot trap the keyboard in any spot).
Forms	Assistive technology must access the information, field elements, and functionality required for completion and submission of forms, including all instructions and status.
Image Controls, Icons, Status	Images used to identify controls, status indicators, or other elements must have consistent meaning throughout an application's performance. The information conveyed by the image must also be available in text.
Keyboard	All functions must work with a keyboard.
Media Alt	Text alternatives must be synchronized with the video.
Text Only	If you cannot make the video give text, then you must make a transcript. The content of the transcript must be updated whenever the video changes.
Timed Response	When a timed response is required, the user shall be alerted with an accessible message and given sufficient time to indicate that more time is required.

5.10   WCAG 2.0 for Video (Not All But What You Need To Know)

Tag	Description
Change Meaning	When a user is focused on a control or field the meaning or type of that item being focused does not change without alerting the user and giving the option to turn off changes.
Controls, Consistent	Controls that have the same function within a set video pages or sections are identified consistently.
Errors, Identified & Prevented	If the user inputs an error it is automatically detected, and that error is identified and described to the user in text, instructions for correction are given.

Tag	Description
Images, Charts	All images that are presented to the user must have a text alternative (or text is presented to assistive technology – it can be visually hidden) that contains the same information.
Moving, Blinking, Scrolling, Updating	There must be a method for the user to pause, stop, or hide moving, blinking, scrolling, or updating content.
Sensory	Content cannot rely solely on sensory characteristics such as shape, size, visual location, orientation, or sound.

6 PowerPoint

6.1 Description

When PowerPoint is formatted correctly, the file can be made mostly accessible. However, it is easy to render a presentation unreadable by assistive technology. It is also not as easy to convert to other formats as HTML, Word or PDF is. Except for conversion to PDF, a PDF version of a well-structured PowerPoint will actually perform better with assistive technology. Consider PDF as the final version for distribution or to reside on a website. Since PowerPoint can cause issues if not created properly and is difficult to edit later on for 508, it is very important to get it right the first time. Reducing the number of text boxes and images on a single page will make that task easier. Logical reading order is top to bottom, left to right. The objects on a PowerPoint page can lose logical reading order very easily due to editing. The order of objects on a page is determined by the order of placement – this is why editing can cause issues. The order is critical to assistive technology to render the content so it is understood and is presented as the author intended.

6.2 Template

Create a template or slide to copy from that contains a simple structure. This structure should look like a Title text box and a main content text box. It is crucial to keep the number of text boxes small due to issues with logical reading order.

6.3 Provide Copies Before Presentations Or Online

Provide a printed and a digital copy before or during the presentation. This will also allow users to request any special versions needed.

To format an easier-to-read printout than the built-in PowerPoint print layouts, move the final version to Word. There you can increase the page size and use more of the border space. This option is only in Word 2007 and higher. To package the Word-formatted version for a print service, convert it to PDF. You can convert directly to PDF from PowerPoint, but you will not have as many edit options to control size and margins. You want to maximize content space on the page, not small windows of your slides.

6.4   Fonts

Use fonts and charts that can be read from the back of the room. Go look at it from the users seat.

Use Sans-Serif fonts such as: Arial, Calibri, Verdana, Corbel, and Tahoma.

Provide strong contrast between foreground text and objects and background. If text is packed too tightly for reading at a distance, break it up into multiple slides.

6.5   Tab Order (If Keeping As PowerPoint Final Format)

Set TAB order by moving objects to the front and back (Send to Back, Bring to Front). This can be difficult to perform if there are many text boxes and objects. Keep the number of text boxes small, 3 or less if possible, to make the logical order easier to control.

6.6   Image Description

Verify all images and charts with information have text descriptions that contain the same information as the image or chart does.

Verify any audio or video clips have text descriptions. Check when audio descriptions of images, charts, or relationships are provided that they are in text somewhere (slide, notes, link) or are captured by someone taking notes and made available.

6.7   Notes

The notes section can be useful for additional information, make sure the notes are available in the users version in some format. If converting to PDF, the notes will appear as a Text Annotation (similar to a comment bubble) – this is accessible and the best method to retain notes for everyone.

6.8   Audio

Check that slides and any additional material describes any audio embedded. If audio is given there must be a text version somewhere. You must supply a contact is given for additional information and format alternatives.

6.9   Tables

Check that tables have column headers and if applicable, row headers. The table headers should be visually distinguished with sharp contrast. You can have images or tables or actual dynamic tables from Excel or Word. If images there must be a real table somewhere that is screen readable.

6.10   Additional Materials

Check that all handout and additional resource material formats are accessible; refer to other checks that are applicable to documents.

6.11 Presentation

Provide the largest projection possible with clear edge definition (edges around text is crisp). Many projectors have an adjustable setting; use it to increase edge definition to make text more readable.

Pay attention to obstacles that prevent a clear view of the presentation. Tables, chairs, and height of computers monitors may need to be adjusted. In some cases you may need to move all furniture around to provide a clear view for everyone. Allow ample time for setup.

Be prepared to provide extra descriptions of slides, if some people in the audience are not able to fully understand the visual information.

If possible, reduce any background noise as this can interfere with many who rely on hearing for comprehension.

Do not rely solely on the slide presentation. Give equal time to strong explanations and handouts. Providing further reading and extended guides via printouts, online documents, and links, give additional options for comprehension.

Makes notes in a paper copy of the presentation where people get confused, or something is difficult to see or needs more text to explain.

6.12 Conversion

The best conversion as mentioned is PDF. If you do convert, be sure to have high resolution for all images and do not optimize the PDF by having it reduce the quality of the images. This is very important as 508 requires that the material be comprehensible when magnified. You can use 10X magnification as a guide.

7 VPATs

7.1 What *Are* These Things And Why Should I Care?

A VPAT is simply a table of Section 508 requirements that a vendor or contracting agency fills out to say:

- If they are meeting the 508 standards

- How they are meeting them

- If not meeting the standards, what the workaround is

- What measures to fix issues, if there are any

However this is not a huge report, it is all condensed to fit in the table. Some VPATs are beefy for huge complex systems, this can make it hard to read in a table. The VPAT can have added notes or attachments depending on complexity of the item. The Voluntary Product Accessibility Template is not voluntary when a contract mandates it. Filling out a VPAT requires a degree of technical ability to determine by testing if a document or application meets all the standards. And it is not "all" standards, it is the applicable ones. Web and Software usually apply to documents (there is not universal agreement on which ones so different places will have different guidelines). GPATs are the same thing for a government in-house document or application. The standards cover all IT, but we are not dealing with hardware such as phones, computers, tablets, copiers, kiosks, monitors, or any IT physical device.

It stands to reason that if you are going to get your car inspected, it must be done by somebody actually trained and experienced in the standards to make sure you do not die on the road. Likewise, you just do not grab any IT staff to do 508 testing to fill out a VPAT. This is speaking from the vendors (or if you are creating software for the government or state) side as that is where it comes from. To understand how to apply the 508 technical standards to anything, you have to have experience. That experience includes how to expertly use assistive technology, various analysis tools, and lots of manual inspection of the visual, and user process order of what is be evaluated. The tester may also have to do some code inspections which for web applications will involve at least HTML, CSS, and JavaScript. There are many other skills involved as this is not a simple cut and dry examination. The tester needs to address how the application author intends the user to read, learn, or complete a task.

Given all this, that same experience must be on the delivery side in order to be able to evaluate and accept the product whatever form it takes.

7.2   How Do I Apply These Standards?

Selecting the applicable standards and particularly the software and web-based standards confuses many people as they were originated in 1988, when there was clearly distinct software and website but now the two mix and both standards apply to web applications. In fact the 508 guidance from section 508.gov and the access board - who implements and updates the standards note that any application that is software or databased built and has web delivery requires both set of standards. This is also true of documents and mobile apps. You would be hard pressed to locate any major software only or web (HTML) only product today. However you will find utilities, modules, and simple informational websites that could fit into those categories.

Some federal agencies combine a VPAT structure with a test plan to see not only if 508 is met, but to say how they will test that it complies. In addition many also include a condensed set of WCAG 2.0 standards. A well trained 508 person can determine right away whether the VPAT is thorough enough or even is accurate for the product in question.

There is a built-in dilemma with these. As mentioned the vendor must really have a 508 expert on site to determine how to answer every technical requirement. The receiver of the VPAT must be familiar enough on a technical level with the document or application to determine if the VPAT is correct or not.

To add more difficulty to this, many texts and applications require able-bodied people to execute them. For instance this book requires visual determinations as part of testing and remediation.

Below are a few rows of the typical blank VPAT table. As mentioned these are often supplemented with additional columns of information, footnotes, exceptions, or addendum of testing results.

There are many sources to help you fill and interpret these VPATs.

More Help:

GSA hosted, Section 508 VPAT help:

> http://www.section508.gov/tags/vpat-gpat

GSA Buy Accessible Wizard, this helps in documenting your project and creating one:

> http://buyaccessible.gov/

You can download a Word Version from this page:

> https://www.itic.org/policy/accessibility/

Section 1194.21 Software Applications and Operating Systems - Detail Voluntary Product Accessibility Template		
Criteria	**Level of Support & Supporting Features**	**Remarks and explanations**
(a) When software is designed to run on a system that has a keyboard, product functions shall be executable from a keyboard where the function itself or the result of performing a function can be discerned textually.		
(b) Applications shall not disrupt or disable activated features of other products that are identified as accessibility features, where those features are developed and documented according to industry standards. Applications also shall not disrupt or disable activated features of any operating system that are identified as accessibility features where the application programming interface for those accessibility features has been documented by the manufacturer of the operating system and is available to the product developer.		

Figure 1: Part of a blank VPAT.

8 Who Are All These Accessibility Groups, How Are They Different?

The easy one is the GSA Section 508 website. They host the current standards; utorials, FAQs, and lots of discussion on how to implement and manage 508, and how to evaluate them.

www.section508.gov

Next is the U. S. Access Board. This is an independent federal agency that promotes accessibility. They create and revise the standards with federal and public input. Here is where you can get all types of accessibility standards for anything you can imagine (yes those iconic wheelchair ramps too), including 508 of course.

https://www.access-board.gov

Next I would put the W3c, The World Wide Web Consortium (3 "W"s and a "c" you got that right?). This is where WCAG 2.0 is hosted (the Web Content Accessibility Guidelines – this started a long time ago as 1.0 and like 508 covers many mixed elements like web applications and documents).This is where you can get a ton (literally if you ever would try to print out the website) very light and very intense tutorials. This is the ultimate place for solutions to accessibility. W3c covers a wide breath from giving a presentation to code level samples for many types of issues. It also contains a killer list of tools for testing accessibility, you cannot go wrong here, and this *is* the place. The accessibility coverage is breathtaking – as in, huge:

https://ww.w3.org

Directly related to the W3c is the WAI (Web Accessibility Initiative – they make guidelines) W3schools, Here is where you can get the final word on strict HTML, CSS, and full website design and management. There are tutorials (some very high level and some code level) and live code you can modify.

http://www.w3schools.com/website/web_wai.asp

WebAim is all about accessibility and has checklists and tutorials but does not go as heavy as the W3c:

http://webaim.org/

The Trace website is an endless (take a look!) supply of web accessibility and usability references and design guides:

http://trace.wisc.edu/world/web/

How to Search for Good Accessibility Material

In addition to the above sites, there is a wealth of material in the UK and Australia. You can find excellent tutorials for documents and websites in particular.

One good source is the BBC, they have extensive materials:

http://www.bbc.co.uk/accessibility/guides/allguides_index.shtml

There are also good links here:

http://webguide.gov.au/accessibility-usability/accessibility/

http://www.mediaaccess.org.au/web/policy-and-web-accessibility

Some vendors have excellent libraries, while some have issues with some of the large Mega-companies, they actually do produce some excellent tutorials. Adobe is a great source, Microsoft also has a knowledgebase. There are a lot of great forums also, but be careful that a solution you found is aligned with the 508 or WCAG 2.0 standard. WCAG is particularly good about how to check for being compliant when different methods are applied.

9 Litigation (When They Take You To Court, It Happens...)

Avoid at all cost, I mean it. If you get a complaint that something is not accessible, put that on an escalation path right away. Have procedures in place to handle it. Going to court means:

- Lots of your people will be in unplanned meetings on the court preparation for entire days and may not have any plannable end in sight - really

- There will be months of creation of documents, maybe audio, video

- You will need to have lawyers or your inside counsel to understand the technical issues

- You will need to convince a judge who is not technical of what the best technical solution is

- If you do end up in court, it means you did not solve the issue, the judge will make you solve the issue on the judge's timetable, you will lose the case as almost all plaintiffs win (look up the history, or maybe not, you may get nightmares)

- And not to be left out, it will cost you tons of unbudgeted money

Note the Target case, $9.7 million and tons of time, when they could have made the website accessible for much less to begin with.

Then there is the SSA (yes the Social Security Administration). They only produced printed benefits notices in the past and had no other format due to antiquated equipment, they lost that case. Then when they figured out how to get the information online, the online version was not accessible. So they were sued again for the same basic issue and lost again. Millions of dollars and countless lost hours, over years, years!

Please take my advice and make the dedicated effort to go accessible, court is not where you want to end up.

9.1   But What Am I Responsible For?

Anything you create of course that falls into the above "What is covered" list. Here is where it gets surprising to some, you are also responsible for what you post on your website or deliver to employees. Nobody cares if somebody else wrote the document; you are responsible once it is posted. And that goes for any applications you contracted out (we will cover contracts in more detail later). If it is not accessible then do not put it up.

Now, dealing in the real world, many outside authors and small time (or new) vendors are not experienced in creating accessible output. You may have to fix some documents. For applications you must have the vendor fix, and fix any issues right away – the lesson here is you should not have accepted it without rigorous testing. But given nothing is perfect, you still may have to work with the vendor to identify issues and remediate them. And for goodness sakes, if anything requires a trail of documentation, this is surely it.

9.2   How to Build Your Castle To Avoid Court

Here are your defenses:

- An accessibility page on your website, and I mean a very robust one that would answer any possible issue and provide all possible contacts

- Support lines. There must be support available (as announced on your accessibility page) and they must be trained to handle issues and how to process them

- You need an SOP (Standard Operating Procedures) to have basic scripts and answers for the majority of issues. This will also have the process of escalation so that you capture and solve the issue. Avoid vague boilerplate and have very concise answers or steps for solutions.

- For internal employees, your ticket system must have a 508 path or routing system to the 508 people who will be a 508 SME (Subject Matter Expert) handle in a timely manner – and announce that time period to the user

- List of services at the ready to produce formats you are not capable of creating yourself

- List of services at the ready to provide sign language interpreters, or real time captioning

- A 508 plan that address current issues and future ones. This can be an important defense to show you are already on top of the situation (you had better be)

- Be communications sensitive, if the user is blind, then be prepared to describe accurately in text. If your documents and website and applications all have unique named/numbered/lettered sections, this makes what you are talking about go easier.

  - Be very careful to stay on the same page in responses to users – a sure fire way to upset somebody looking for a solution is to give competing or confusing answers "First I was told to do it one way…but *now* you're telling me…"

- Catch issues before the user does, conduct regular testing and checks

- Set priorities and risk factors, you need to triage to manage time and effort

- A full featured help system that is context sensitive can save a lot of heartache by doing the work for you.

    o A help system that allows different levels of detail is very good for this type of user; you can have a short sentence that could expand to a paragraph that could expand to a full page depending on how deep the user chooses or needs to go. The more user options and control, the better.

10   Accessibility as a Stakeholder

One of major mistakes, and I mean a mistake that results in a catastrophe is because 508 and WCAG are not part of the stakeholders in a project. What does this mean? It means there is equal standing as business, security, enterprise, and anybody else that has requirements that must be met.

This works as any other stakeholder. You have a set of requirements; you are at every checkpoint and particularly at the design and concept stage. You cannot incorporate accessibility requirements at a later date as that often means a rebuild. So to keep everything moving smooth, have accessibility at every step of the way.

10.1   What Could This Mean?

- Training

    o This may involve managers, developers, clerical, authors, anybody producing or controlling content, they need to know what to do as many people are unfamiliar with the perspective and approach.

- Requirements

    o These are the technical standards; if you want to prepare for the future and expansion you should not only do 508 but include WCAG. You may need to breakdown the requirements into sub-requirements as you will have someone test against them.

- Guides and SOPs

    o These are the higher level methods for non-technical staff that need to create content that will be assessable. Easy to follow steps should be outlined.

- Checklists

- Based on the requirements, you can rephrase the long winded original requirements and get them on one page if possible. The shorter the better as a developer can keep that pinned on the board and glance to see if all is covered.

- Manuals

  - These are for the managers and technical staff to cite how to handle issues specifically, that way you get consistent fixes.

- Resources

  - Here we mean people, software, contracting. Do not go under the often misguided notion of adding to an existing employee's responsibilities, I have never seen it work.

- Knowledgebase

  - Here you should store your best practice solutions for everything that comes along. This should be in database format with search options that cover many different methods such as keyword, categories, issue, formats, and as many different ways someone might look for the solution. There are some systems you can purchase and add your own material to.

11 Risk Assessment

You have to have some idea of the measure of risk that the accessibility issues add up to. It is difficult to have a one size fits all for this because it depends on your deliverables. With documents such as PDF files we can have some general guidance, and web applications you can also rate. First you will probably want some kind of scale.

First what is risk in this area?

- The primary risk is being dragged into court which involves lots of hours on your part in preparation, and if it makes it into court, more than likely you must also prepare for satisfying a judge's order to fix the accessibility problem.

- The other risk is impact to project schedules by not having a well laid out plan to have documents or applications meets compliance early in their creation.

- There are also several peripheral but costly risks, such as support lines being bombarded with issues, help tickets needing resolution, and assigning resources to deal with disabled users having trouble, and authors/clerical remediating documents. It all adds up to money and time, so you need to have a handle on what the situation is.

I have used red yellow green traffic light based evaluation and that works well for these types of accessibility issues.

- [ ] Red for show-stopper, issues and number of issues are so severe, the disabled user simply cannot use the document, or get the same information out of it as an able bodied person.

- [ ] Yellow for the document can proceed to be used, but there are workarounds for minor issues, alternative formats or extra descriptions may be needed, it is not as easy for a disabled person to use, but it can be used with minimal effort.

- [ ] Green for no issues whatsoever, 100% compliant.

Words are fine also, such as Blocker, Difficult, and Compliant.

You may wish to use a grading system where there a numerical value, as much as I like to quantify systems, it can be a little difficult with accessibility. There are so many factors such as the capability of your users, the impact of the specific accessibility issues, the number of occurrences, the number of users, actual effect on comprehension of information, the effect on reading ability. Not to mention how critical the document is to the user's job. So if you want a highly defined grading system, go ahead, but do not leave anything out that could affect the disabled user and their ability to use the product for comprehension or to complete a task.

Note: Some offices solely base risk on the number of users affected. However this is not good solid science since it only takes one user to bring legal action. Obviously 60 million versus 10 people will expose you to more scrutiny and a larger disabled population, still your assessment should be based on more knowledge of the issues and the impact.

11.1   Fallacies in Risk Assessment

- This will only be used by managers so we do not need to worry.

  - Especially in Federal/State/County/City there are programs to encourage and help the disabled get management positons. I personally had a blind manager in charge of my department in one position.

- This is all being produced for systems administration and technical operators, so we are clear.

  - Nope, believe it or not there are lots of disabled application testers, analysts, requirements and project specialists and on and on. And there are managers or other people will need to see the system documents. Think of how many project stakeholders there are and you realize you cannot predict who will need to look at what you produce.

- We were certified by a third party, so we can relax.

  - No relaxing at all. There is no recognized certification program you can apply, and for some certifications, they are valid only for certain aspects. There are technical companies that have their own certification, there are federal agencies that have certification but they only apply to that agency and even then are not bullet-proof. Why? Because there are so many factors involved. Look at PDF files, depending on how thorough your requirements are depends on the accessibility. I have seen acceptance criteria that read, "Tagged PDF" and that was it. As you will see from this book, that is only a small start. If you have someone else evaluate your materials, make sure you have a technical analyst to review their methods.

- All our authors had training, so no more effort is needed.

  - Most of the training I have seen (and I have seen a lot) is not good enough, meaning some critical or important elements were left out. In one case a very big well-known contracting technical agency made online 508 training and it had to all (as in all of it) be rewritten by a team of well-seasoned 508 analysts (for one of the biggest private agencies). Most authors do not practice accessibility every day; some may only do a major document once a month. So you need very good training, quick guides, online help, templates, and style handbooks. If you cannot have accessibility experts on call (recommended) then adding more extensive training to create a group of leaders or coordinators who can play that role, will help fill that void.

- We already have a great accessibility document expert, nothing more to do.

  - Just like all areas, you must have redundancy. If you can only afford one body, then that body must produce materials, online or otherwise to allow quick assessment, creation, or remediation when they are not there. If they are truly great then they have produced highly useable training, guides, and best practices that everyone can easily use.

11.2   So What Do I Apply Risk Factors to?

With applications and websites it is issues. Issues discovered through testing, or if you are unlucky, a complaint – which is why you need to catch it first! The types of issues are the ones that will fail 508/WCAG testing. A serious issue is one that the disabled user cannot complete a task at all. A difficult issue is one that may take more keystrokes and time, but eventually works. Remember there are a lot of requirements, you do not just want to test for the screen reader, you also need to test for magnification, and voice control. In addition to other requirements such as: good contrast, reading order, and unique names and titles, tables have cell associations. See the other guides in this book for more details.

With documents, it is the ability to actually read the content with assistive technology in the same fashion as visual. With headings, links with text targets and complete image descriptions. Some are similar to the above requirements, but in context some documents have unique requirements such as a PDF which must be tagged, and the tag structure must be tested. With the visual group but who have cognitive issues, you need to make sure the text is organized with headings, sub-headings, sections and reference links.

11.3   Where Do I Focus If I Have Too Much To Fix?

There are some areas you may need to change. You might want to contract out some work to a place that does the fixes all the time. You also might need to change the process in which you produce material; this is usually needed with documents, as getting accessibility upfront requires training and different checks. There is also the possibility you need new software. If you create training, there are new packages that create compliant and gee-wiz training with very little effort and also let you customize. A lot of these are HTML5 based which can do many creative interactive and flashy presentations that are accessible. You also may have to hire an expert in the areas you need to be fixed.

11.3.1   Get An Idea From User Tests

Early on for websites you can try out basic navigation and home page designs. For documents, it can be the organization, the headings. It is very important to get feedback along the process, the decreases the risk of major changes later on.

There is a danger here. Small samples in any study are not valid. If you rely on one person, they may represent the views of nobody else or have impractical recommendations. The larger the number or people in the test or review group the better. Statistically speaking accuracy occurs after around 1,200 people, obviously unless you are a really big company that is not going to happen. But what you can do is maybe round up a dozen people or more and that will show the issues where you need to focus on.

11.3.2   How Do I make A User Test?

One easy method for an application is to simply have a list of instructions for each type of task. If they have difficulty with the task, then they should give feedback (if you number the steps, they can cite the exact issue). You should however control the format of the feedback. For example, a simple format:

- Issue Title

- Location of Issue

- Details

- Any Screen Shots

This will allow you to easily enter the issue into the most popular issue tracking systems. You can also just put them on a spreadsheet or table. You may have to paraphrase some feedback as some users are not used to a strict testing environment and can easily become too verbose or repetitive.

11.3.3   What About Issues I Cannot Fix or Control?

You must have an alternative. You have no choice, in the area of accessibility you cannot offer nothing if the application, document or training cannot be used by an individual. Unless you enjoy court battles you will lose. The smart thing to do with parts of your project that you have little control over is try to find some way of converting whatever it is to text or a transcript. Training is harder as you may have to describe screens, not the screen title, but actually describe what is on the screen and where the focus of the lesson is located on that page you just described.

You never really want two versions as they must be synchronized. The 508 rule is equal information. You are always better off with the original products working for everyone.

As mentioned earlier, you may need to contract out work. One way of handling information is on as "as needed" basis. Meaning you create the accessible format as you get requests. This works great if you have thousands of files. But make sure you have a system in place that can create the accessible version rapidly.

11.3.4   Do Your Research And Add The Time Into Your Schedule

It's a really big world out there, with many products to choose from. For example when I was reviewing training software, I downloaded 50 applications and tried them all and tested for accessibility. Might you think that should be put in your plan for time and resources?

The lack of product research is a major weak point in accessibility. Not only are there major application environments that are accessible, but also add-ons, converters, editing tools, all sorts of relevant choices for whatever you are making. There is no getting around it, you must put the time in.

Now if you are pressed for time in your schedule, there are many top ten lists out there by well-established IT websites and accessibility experts. This will help a great deal. I used these to help narrow my field of selections down.

11.3.5   Part Of Risk Mitigation Is Having A Plan

If you want to keep the complaints from burning the place down, a good first step is to have a plan to fix whatever the issue is. First actually make a remediation plan. Announce you have one in place and announce the targeted schedule. Guess what, this is what they make you do if you go to court, but not in any manner you can fit into current schedules. While you have the opportunity, create a specific plan (it can be a spreadsheet of issues and fix dates) and stick to it. You know by now what the "or else" is.

12   Quickly What Are Some Common Mistakes You Should Avoid For Applications?

- Error Messages

    - It cannot be emphasized enough how important error messages and error handling is. For some disabilities, this is their only guide as they make more mistakes. The error messages must tell what exact error was made, how to fix it, and give an example. Afterwards the focus should be in field to be corrected. If you are not doing this dynamically and only on Submit, then make sure the focus goes right to the error messages and provide a link to jump to the field with multiple fields.

- Keyboard Access and Screen Reader Access

    - While similar, they are not exactly the same. Keyboard access is required for all assistive technology. Screen reader access means that the screen reader can access all parts of the screen and identify the area it is in. In some cases, dynamic routines may block the screen reader or trap it in an area.

- Unique Labels

    - Buttons, icons, links, fields, menus and select options all need unique names. This makes it easy to obtain orientation, but also makes it easy for voice control software. If duplicate names are required, then either number them or put inside a FIELDSET tag.

- Contextual Instructions

    - This can be dynamic on directly on the screen but users need instructions for the specific field or field group. You can hide this with an icon link and have it pop-up. Letting the user decide whether to see it or not is the best practice, always default to an option.

- Visible and Tracking Focus

    - Often lost in the details of menus and options, is the requirement for a visible focus.

13   Big Strategies That Can Save You With Accessibility

- Content Management System (CMS)

    - Depending on the product, you can make an accessible template that allows authors to publish accessible web pages and retain creativity.

- Learning Management System (LMS)

    o A centralized training management system is a good way to also set policy for how the content is presented, and is consistent.

- Issue Tracking

    o A system that specifically records (or routes) the accessibility issues, and notifies all people you list will help with professional resolutions. With bigger systems you can also match to requirements (Traceability) with select lists.

- Support

    o This is where a lot of accessibility complaints first arrive. As a consequence you really want to be prepared. That is where the SOPs come in handy – and I mean a complete one, that is updated all the time. You can have templated responses for many issues and allow space for a personal response. I cannot stress enough that this is where you can prevent complaints from escalating.

- Remediation Services

    o If the user needs Braille, you better be able to produce it, or audio, or a transcript. That is why you need to keep a service at the ready. If you cannot fix a PDF to make it accessible, then have a service that can, but it is best if you have someone trained, and a backup person and can turn it around in a day.

- Regular Reviews

    o Many who should, do not do frequent checks (speaking from observed experience here). You do not want to wait for a complaint to start evaluating issues. Web pages, Applications, Documents, Media, all should be spot checked on a regular basis. A spot check is when you only spend a minute checking the critical items, and items that are repeated elsewhere (global repetitions of same operations).

14 Dealing With The Vendor For Development of Changes

14.1 Collaboration

Keep this in check. You can certainly collaborate on solutions, but the testing must be your testing, independent of the vendors. Only you can decide if requirements are being meet. Do not let the vendor sit in on your testing, certainly go to them if there are questions about some function, but otherwise keep a wall to stay true to un-influenced test results. This does not take away the fact that you need steps on how the application works.

14.2 Issues Scrums

Scrums are quick daily (or as needed) updates as to where issues are, who is handling them, and what should people focus on. These are not presentations – these are in the weeds details in summary, for example: you fixed issue 343 you are now working on 344 and will have that done by tomorrow and you need to make sure the application is up and running early morning for testing.

14.3   Keeping Firm on Requirements

Requirements are just that – required, especially if you doing Section 508 or if you have WCAG and other requirements in the contract. They must be met. Some places like to have one solution for each – that works for consistency and support but kills creative design and sometimes usability. There are many ways to meet the requirements. For example buttons require that they be labeled as to what they do and be keyboard accessible. There a huge array of techniques and designs to do that. You can actually make buttons that will turn into growing balloons as you mouse over them and still work with screen readers. Today there is really little limit on design as long as it meets the accessibility requirements.

14.4   Training Must Be Carefully Examined

Training can be in numerous formats, and the accessibility issues are mostly with video type self-guided modules (see above guide on training). These can be made accessible; however some items are not worth the trouble. One of those is Drag and Drop. Yes you can make it work with the keyboard, but it in no way compares to the mouse experience due to difficulty of re-reading and remembering the screen as options are presented. Many of the newer HTML5 authoring packages like Elucidat are quite good and appear animated and colorful. You can do similar in in software such as Captivate.

14.5   Ensure All Standards And Best Practices Were Followed

- HTML, CSS, ARIA (code to the standards)

- Section 508

- WCAG 2.0

- Usability

- Coding Guides

- Version Control

- Issue Tracking

- Code Comments

- System Design Documents

- Metatags

- Clear Process Rules

14.6   Stick to the Contract Because The Vendor Will

If you did not put enough specifics in the contract, that is your fault. You can specify not only the accessibility requirements, but also:

- How they will test for it

- How they will deliver the test results to you

- How you will accept the product – putting them on notice about how you will be evaluating for acceptance

A lot of companies do not have dedicated or even well-trained accessibility testers, your contract will find that out very quickly. When you issued an RFP or RFI they may have said they could do it, but with the contract you will actually have to see results. This is where samples, demos, and site visits pay off.

On a big project it is essential to visit the company and actually meet the people (not just the managers) who really make the application work and question their background to get a feel for what to expect. Prototypes are great for getting your message across when looking at a design, you can issue comments on what you expect (allowing for documenting your early requirements). You really cannot be specific enough, you do want any conversation to start with "Well…we understood that to mean…" Vendors need to know what you expect <u>exactly</u> and you need to know the vendor capabilities of achieving that expectation. If a verbal meeting follow up with good meeting notes, send them out and makes sure everyone agrees to what was said. Yes that means you need someone dedicated to the note taking and not talking.

15   So You Bought 508 Compliant Software, Mission Accomplished?

15.1   The Real Deal

There are many great applications out there, but the real danger lies with authoring or development software. Take for example Adobe Captivate, you can make extremely accessible videos, documents, if you produce them the correct way – in this case it pays to read the manual and visit support forums. Otherwise you can make a complete mess. The same is true for newer HTML5 based packages; they have all you need to make it work for the disabled, on any device – if you produce it correctly. This is particularly true of creating documents with Microsoft Word or Adobe Acrobat Pro. With Acrobat many people think the rule of adding tags to the document solves the issue of accessibility. If only this were true, the tags are an approximation after interpreting whatever the document was converted from. They have to be edited and tested. Word itself is not bad for textual based, but lacks the ability to fully support tables or complex forms – which Acrobat can. Better than both of these is HTML which can do it all.

Take another example, a little heavier like Flash. If coded correctly (and most do not) this can be made accessible and used to make training courses. However HTML5 will gradually move that out of the market as Flash is more limited in its accessibility features and has a higher learning curve even with authoring tools.

What is new, is that you can make an accessible Flash based training video in Captivate and publish that as a self-running PDF that can be distributed – the only requirement being a Flash player on the user's machine.

16 What Will Really Cause Me Trouble, And What Do I Do About It?

16.1 Webinars

Webinars are the big problem. If all people did was talk, a transcript would do. But if you are showing screens – they must be described. This must be described with equal information that the visually able person got out of the screen shot or active applications demo screen. One way out of this is to add the descriptions to your speaking part, that way the transcript will contain what you need and maybe require a little editing. You may wish to have someone transcribe while the webinar is live as that will save time. Talking from experience here, trying to decipher what someone is saying from a recording that may contain sidebar discussions, phone distortion, low volume questions, and room noises, takes a great deal of time especially in proportion to the length of the webinar. An hour can take many days to transcribe after the fact.

Note: If you record the webinar and put it on your website, you will need closed captioning. A complete alternative to this is a pictorial transcript, where you capture everything and provide descriptions.

16.1.1 How to Make a Pictorial Transcript From A Recorded Webinar

Capture each of the screens used in the recording. You can use a tool, but for low cost I just use ALT+PrtScn (pause the video) and paste the captured screen into a paint program where you can trim and add arrows or circles. If the audio is clear and consistent you can use a speech to text program to help type up the text – this does not work well if several people are talking, there are volume changes, and room or phone noise. Once you have the screen shots and text, if the screen shot is not fully described in the text, you must describe it. Now you can limit this to what is focused on, but you still must orient the blind reader. A good rule of thumb when a screen is used over several pages and steps, is to fully describe the screen the first time then refer to the screen name thereafter and describe the element on the screen that is the current topic. To complete the document, add a table of contents and do this by giving headings to each major section and change of topic. This allows easy searching for everyone.

16.2 Old Training

These are often inaccessible. So what do you do? Upgrading can be a lot of money for a major agency. Plus there is the learning curve for a new tool and worse the conversion of the old material. Even worse many courses are required, and they are tied to performance ratings, so we are dealing with very hot fire here. You must provide the information somehow. If there is any way to access the text you may be able to start a transcript, but remember to describe any image that has information. Moving to some form of HTML will help a lot. But also be wary of sample files like spreadsheets, or PDF file with charts or tables. If no solution can be found, you must provide a person to read all screens to the user – seriously that is what is done. The disabled user must access the required training in some manner.

16.3   Handwritten Forms, Notes And Miscellaneous Documents

If everything you had was a standard form, there would be little trouble as scanning technology is quite accurate to recreate a paper form into a digital form. Even tables can be captured quite well. But if we are talking about handwriting in pencil and messy ink or faxes, that is a whole different ballgame. The lowest effort (and this is almost a lie) is to scan each page, and fully describe it. With medical and legal papers, this can present a nightmare as they often have text in the margins or Post-It notes, or even crossed out and writing over other words, along with patient or client initialed parts located anywhere. It will require transcription if you cannot use scanner software to decipher that page. Adobe Acrobat Pro has built in scanning that is quite accurate and there are many fine products that should cut down some of the typing. The truly minimal effort is to scan the document as an image and then describe it fully. Realistically with a large agency the only way to do this is on a as needed basis. But you can start the scanning and index the files with keywords and ID numbers and other meta tags (identifiers such as keywords, author, summary description, dates etc.) so you can locate specific documents.

The real answer of course is a centralized formatted digital system. But there are always the existing and archival files. If you have a large number you can again produce on an as needed basis. Also it is not the total number but how big the paper file is. If your files are claims for medical disability, the individual file could be over 600 pages of mixed types of sensitive documents.

16.4   Guest Presentations

Whether the presentation is online or in person, if you have any disabled attendees, you need to be prepared. The last thing you need is someone to feel left out of an important demo, training, software support, or vendor selection. Let the visitor know ahead of time what they need to produce for you. It could be large print, accessible documentation, close captioned videos, or descriptions for charts. PowerPoint is good if done correctly, it can also be converted to PDF including the notes (yes the notes are accessible in a PDF).

16.5   Mainframe OR Similar Text Output in Large Amounts

The key to making the information accessible is two steps. One is making it digital of course. Printing to a file will do that. The next step is to make the database information usable. If separated by some delimiter like a tab, space or comma, it is easy to import into a spreadsheet and then manipulate it. You could also import into a modern database and make a web lookup page. This is easy with Microsoft Access or if it is a real heavy load of data you can move it to a SQL server. Keep it text based with simple HTML and also provide multiples ways of looking up the information such as keyword, title, category, issue or type.

16.6   Output From Applications That Create Data

SAS or similar data crunching programs can be written to output very clean HTML with accessible markup for column and row headers, then that can be imported into a PDF to produce accessible tables.

Other complex applications can use software to create accessible PDF output using modules like iText. This can produce final outputs or temporary dynamic files within the application. Just like anything else the settings must be correct to produce the accessible file.

17 Vendor Is A Small Company With Nobody To Handle 508

Surprisingly this happens with large vendors also, as they may be in the middle of a huge development cycle and cannot afford the resources. The key is to make sure you have someone on your staff that can correctly identify and log issues and transfer these issues to the vendor. Work with the vendor to give best practices and methods to deal with the issues. It may be worth a training session, if the vendor has no knowledge of accessibility then a good intro course will do. If they are familiar but lacking accessible methods, then training for developers and authors may be warranted.

Another solution is to contract another company to evaluate what the vendor is producing.

18 When Do You Call It Quits, How Many Issues Must Be Fixed

If you have one application that does not change dramatically, then you can have a continuous issue fixing process.

There are several ways to looks at this, here we look a little more granular at accessibility issues:

Blocker issues are ones so serious that the user cannot complete the task. These must in all cases be fixed and fixed first, and the timing must be like - Right Now. Examples would be:

- Where a screen reader gets stuck and cannot continue

- The keyboard cannot access a table or other region.

- Error messages are not receiving focus and are not screen reader accessible

Critical issues are those that will allow the user to complete the task, but are so confusing and designed incorrectly (or just plain have errors) that they waste the user's time by requiring them to re-loop throughout a form or to continue trying with variations until the function finally works. These must be resolved also as they pose a significant risk to understanding and completing in a timely fashion. So the risk is high with these also. Examples would be:

- Tables cannot be read with a screen reader's table reading keys

- Fields and the field names are not in the same area for screen reading

- A continue button takes you back to the home screen and stops the process, so you must keep re-entering

Major Issues these tend to be informational items that are crucial but are mostly text corrections. Examples would be:

- Button or links that are not named correctly

- Fields that are not identified

- Pages with wrong titles.

- Incorrect order of items to complete a task

All of these issues must be fixed, but if the project deadline is forcing a decision, you can fix the Major issues over time and cover them by adding the steps to work around them in training guides until you do fix them.

Of course any new feature added to an application will have to start the evaluation from scratch:

- Test

- Log Issues

- Fix Issues

- Retest

19 Cheat Sheets

19.1 WCAG 2.0 (by WCAG keywords)

Guide-line	Keyword	Requirement
1.3	Adaptable	Create content that can be presented in different ways (for example simpler layout) without losing information or structure.
4.1	Compatible	Maximize compatibility with current and future user agents, including assistive technologies.
1.4	Distinguishable	Make it easier for users to see and hear content including separating foreground from background.
2.2	Enough Time	Provide users enough time to read and use content.
3.3	Input Assistance	Help users avoid and correct mistakes.
2.1	Keyboard Accessible	Make all functionality available from a keyboard.
2.4	Navigable	Provide ways to help users navigate, find content, and determine where they are.
3.2	Predictable	Make Web pages appear and operate in predictable ways.
3.1	Readable	Make text content readable and understandable.
2.3	Seizures	Do not design content in a way that is known to cause seizures.
1.1	Text Alternatives	Provide text alternatives for any non-text content so that it can be changed into other forms people need, such as large print, Braille, speech, symbols or simpler language.
1.2	Time-based Media	Guideline 1.2 Time-based Media: Provide alternatives for time-based media.

19.2 508 (by my keywords & condensed)

Section	Keyword	Requirement
1194.41(b)	Accessibility Page	Access to a description of the accessibility features of products in alternate formats.
1194.21(h)	Animation	Animation is available in non-animated presentation mode at the option of the user.
1194.31(c)	Audio	Does not require user hearing or support for assistive technology.
1194.31(d)	Audio	Support for enhanced auditory fashion, or assistive hearing devices shall be provided.
1194.22(c)	Color	All information conveyed with color is also available without color.
1194.21(i)	Color	Color coding shall not be used as the only means of conveying information.
1194.21(b)	Disrupt AT	Applications shall not disrupt or disable activated accessibility features
1194.21(k)	Flashing	No elements having a flash or blink frequency greater than 2 Hz and lower than 55 Hz.
1194.22(j)	Flashing	No screen flicker with a frequency greater than 2 Hz and lower than 55 Hz.
1194.21(c)	Focus	Focus provided that moves among interactive interface elements as the input focus changes.
1194.21(l)	Forms	Assistive technology must access the information, field elements, and functionality required for completion and submission of the form, including all directions and cues.
1194.22(n)	Forms	Assistive technology to access the information, field elements, and functionality required for completion and submission of the form, including all directions and cues.
1194.22(i)	Frames	Frames shall be titled with text that facilitates frame identification and navigation.
1194.21(e)	Image Controls	Bitmap images as controls, status or other elements, meaning shall be consistent.
1194.22(e)	Image Map	Redundant text links shall be provided for each active region of a server-side image map.
1194.22(f)	Image Map	Client-side image maps shall be provided instead of server-side image maps except where the regions cannot be defined with an available geometric shape.
1194.22(a)	Images	A text equivalent for every non-text element shall be provided.
1194.21(a)	Keyboard	Functions shall be executable from a keyboard.
1194.22(b)	Media	Equivalent alternatives for any multimedia presentation shall be synchronized with the presentation.
1194.31(f)	Motor	At least one mode of operation and information retrieval that does not require fine motor control.
1194.21(d)	Name, State	Elements require the identity, operation and state of the element to assistive technology.
1194.22(m)	Plugin	Required Applet, plug-in or other application, the page must provide a link to a plug-in or applet
1194.22(l)	Scripting	Information provided by the script shall be identified with accessible functional text.
1194.22(o)	Skip Nav	A method shall be provided that permits users to skip repetitive navigation links.
1194.31(e)	Speech	Do not require user speech or support assistive technology.
1194.22(d)	Style Sheet	Documents shall be readable without requiring an associated style sheet.
1194.41(a)	Support	Support documentation provided in alternate formats upon request, at no additional charge.
1194.41(c)	Support	Support services accommodate the communication needs of end-users with disabilities.
1194.22(g)	Tables	Row and column headers shall be identified for data tables.
1194.22(h)	Tables	Associate data and header cells for tables with two or more rows or column headers.
1194.22(k)	Text Only	A text-only page, with equivalent information or functionality when compliance cannot be accomplished in any other way and updated whenever the primary page changes.
1194.21(f)	Text OS	Textual information shall be provided through operating system for text content, text input caret location, and text attributes.

1194.22(p)	Timed Response	When a timed response is required, the user shall be alerted and given sufficient time to indicate more time is required.
1194.21(g)	User Color Contrast	Applications shall not override user selected contrast and color selections and other individual display attributes.
1194.21(j)	User Color Contrast	When a product permits a user to adjust color and contrast settings, a variety of color selections capable of producing a range of contrast levels shall be provided.
1194.31(a)	Visual	Information retrieval not require user vision, or support for assistive technology.
1194.31(b)	Visual	Do not require visual acuity greater than 20/70 or provide in audio and enlarged print output , or support for assistive technology.

19.3   Applications Checks

Keyboard	Navigation, tab order, controls, access to text regions.
Code	Code review: common are fields LABEL ID FIELDSET, ALT heading levels, tab stops
Visual	Visual observation: of screen elements for focus, consistency, descriptions, process
Magnification	ZoomText, MAGic: Screen magnification (an intermediate solution is to utilize the Zoom feature in the browser or Windows combined with keyboard tabbing)
Screen Reader	JAWS: Screen reader common keys: TAB, ARROW, INS+F3 (lists)
Speech Recognition	Dragon: Ability to gain focus and dictation box

The purpose for using multiple test methods is that there is no single method applicable to the testing of every element. Automated 508 testing tools are valuable for catching some accessibility code errors in large applications but they cannot substitute for human inspection to verify accessible behavior of screen elements. Field LABEL, link text, ALT text, and logical reading or form TAB order all must be clearly descriptive and consistent. Human interpretation is required for this.

19.4   Cognitive Checks

Key Item	What To Look For
Focus	Visual focus is very clear and tracks to active items. Highlighting can be used to help in addition to enhancing visual focus lines.
Task Item	It is clear what action is to be take, what button to select or information to input. Guide the user with steps.
Orientation	User can tell where they are if they landed only on that page. The best method is a type of breadcrumbs to show where they are in the pages or in a process.
Help	Context sensitive help, for the input field give an example, indicate specific errors.
Messages	Instructions or related messages and alerts can be short but also have a link to more information which can be a pop-up.
User Control	User can control all actions, next, previous, save for later, cancel – but return to last step.

Chart Description	Summary on screen description with link to more info for data tables and explanations.
Titles	Generous use of unique page titles, headings, sub-headings, section titles with numbering or lettering but not with Roman numerals.

20   Tutorials

20.1   Section 508 Introduction

Section 508
Introduction
By
Ed Thrush

508 Intro: Topics

- Law & Standards
- Applying Accessibility to Training
- Reference Materials

508 Intro: Section 508 - Law

Section 508 is a Federal Law that Requires:

ALL Electronic Information & Technology be Accessible to People with Disabilities
Applies to:

ALL Federal Agencies & Contracts
Any Contract with 508 Requirements
Many States, Cities, and Counties Duplicate the Law.

Section 508 Covers Information in All Online Formats: Web, Documents, Video, Audio
Section 504 Covers Discrimination with Disabled
In Training This Means for The Disabled Trainee:

✦ **Did Not Get the Same Information**
✦ **Took Much Longer to Learn**
✦ **Inhibited Ability to Excel at Job or Move Up**

First There is a Complaint/Issue to You or Support

- If Unresolved, EO Office or Lawyers Take Over
- If Goes to Court, Disabled Usually Win
Court Fight and Court Forced Solution Will Cost You

Beyond Anything You Can Imagine – Really!

508 Intro: Section 508

Technical Categories Subsections

- ⇒ **Software** Applications & Operating Systems
- ⇒ **Web** Information and Applications
- ⇒ Functional Performance Criteria
- ⇒ Information, Documentation and Support
- ⇒ Telecommunications
- ⇒ Video and Multimedia
- ⇒ Self-Contained, Closed Products
- ⇒ Desktop and Portable Computers

508 Intro: Section 508 - Standards

1194.21(a) When Software is Designed to Run on a System that has a Keyboard, Product Functions Shall be Executable From a Keyboard

1194.22(a) A Text Equivalent for Every Non-Text Element Shall be Provided

WCAG
Web Content Accessibility Guidelines

- **Methods and Alternatives to Implement 508**
- **Covers Content Types After year 2000**
- **There is no Book, it is Wiki like with 15,000 Pages**

WCAG

Examples:
- **How to Make Presentations Accessible**
- **How to Make Word and PDF Accessible**
- **All Aspects of Web and Applications**
- **Complete Tutorials for Novice and Developers**
- **Links to Reliable Test Tools and References**

508 Intro: Assistive Technologies

Screen Reader	Voice Control	Screen Magnifier

JAWS	Dragon	MAGic & Zoom-Text

508 Intro: Assistive Technology Types

→ **Screen Readers (JAWS)[and others]**

Software Reads Text & Markup/Code Using Speech Synthesizer, Some OCR Signs, Menus

→ **Screen Magnifiers (Magic, ZoomText)**

Increase Screen Image with Contrast/Color Options, Key is the Screen Follows the Focus

→ **Paper Magnifiers**

TV with Video Magnifiers, Table Top or Hand Held

→ **Speech Recognition (Dragon)**

Input Device is a Microphone Rather Than Keyboard, Everything on Screen Must be Unique

→ **Braille Displays**

Tactile Outputs. Braille Displays are Unable to Output Graphics & Tables - Rely on Text Alternatives

→ **Adaptive Hardware And Input Devices**

Alternative Keyboards, Mouth Wands, Pointing Devices, Handheld OCR

508 Intro: Disabilities

56.7 Million People

Have a Disability in the US

(2012 Census Data)

508 Intro: People Who Made It With A Disability

Richard Branson **Billionaire**	**Dyslexic**	
John Nash **(Beautiful Mind)** **Nobel Prize** **Economics**	**Schizo-** **phrenic**	
Harriet Tubman **Underground** **Railroad**	**Impaired** **Vision** **Seizures**	
Albert Einstein **Nobel Prize** **Physics**	**Learning** **Disabled**	

Da Vinci = Epilepsy & Dyslexic

John Lennon = Learning Disabled

Tesla = Severe OCD & Speech Impaired

The following table shows those tasks which have been completed (**X**) and those which have not (**X**):

Task	Due Date	Completed
Task 1	January 3, 2013	X
Task 2	February 9, 2013	X
Task 3	March 4, 2013	X

What is the Issue ? In Black & White View?

Task	Due Date	Completed
Task 1	January 3, 2013	X
Task 2	February 9, 2013	X
Task 3	March 4, 2013	X

The following table shows those tasks which have been completed (Y) and those which have not (N):

Task	Due Date	Completed
Task 1	January 3, 2013	Y
Task 2	February 9, 2013	N
Task 3	March 4, 2013	Y

See How Color Does Not Matter If There Or Not

Task	Due Date	Completed
Task 1	January 3, 2013	Y
Task 2	February 9, 2013	N
Task 3	March 4, 2013	Y

508 Intro: Images & Alt-Text

Best Practice for Images is:

If Fully Described in Body Text there is No Need for Alternative Text. You Do NOT Want the Screen Reader to Waste Time on Alt-Text When the Description Already Exists.

Secret to Good 508 is Concise Accurate Descriptions

Law Requires Equal Information for Images –
Fundamental 508 Requirement

508 Intro: Link Solutions – Front Loading

Front-Loading

Place the Most Relevant Words at the Beginning Of The Phrase, so that Screen Reader Users Can Understand the Meaning of the Content Immediately. If it is Not Relevant, They can Skip to the Next Section.

- **Titles, Section Names**
- **Instructions**
- **Links**
- **Captions**

	Day	Week	Year
Group A	11	22	33
Group B	22	33	44
Group C	33	44	55
Group D	44	55	66

Keep Tables Simple and Small

All You Can Set in Word is The First Header Row

(1) SELECT Top Row

(2) [Table Tools]>[Layout]>[Repeat Header Rows]

Spatial References

Issue: Spatial (positional) references cannot be used <u>alone</u> as they have no meaning without vision. Examples: "Near the top of the page", "The right hand corner", "Middle of the form"

Solution: Use specific locations on the page such as "The second field in the Home Address form section", "The settings drop down menu, next to the search input among the first fields at the top right of the form".

Best: Number/Letter all sections and fields, then refer to that number, "See login example 4."

Transitions, Animations

Issue: These can cause accessibility problems for various types of people.

Solution: Do not use any transitioning effects such as fades, or animation such as text appearing slowly or moving.

Titles, Field Names, Section Names

Issue: Non-unique titles and names can cause issues for recognition and orientation.

Solution: Make every page title, field name, and section name highly unique and specific. Numbering/lettering will help with this and is a best practice.

Color Contrast

Issue: Many users cannot distinguish among colors that are close on the color chart.
Solution: Use high contrast colors that are opposite each other on the color wheel. Print in black and white to see how much contrast there is.

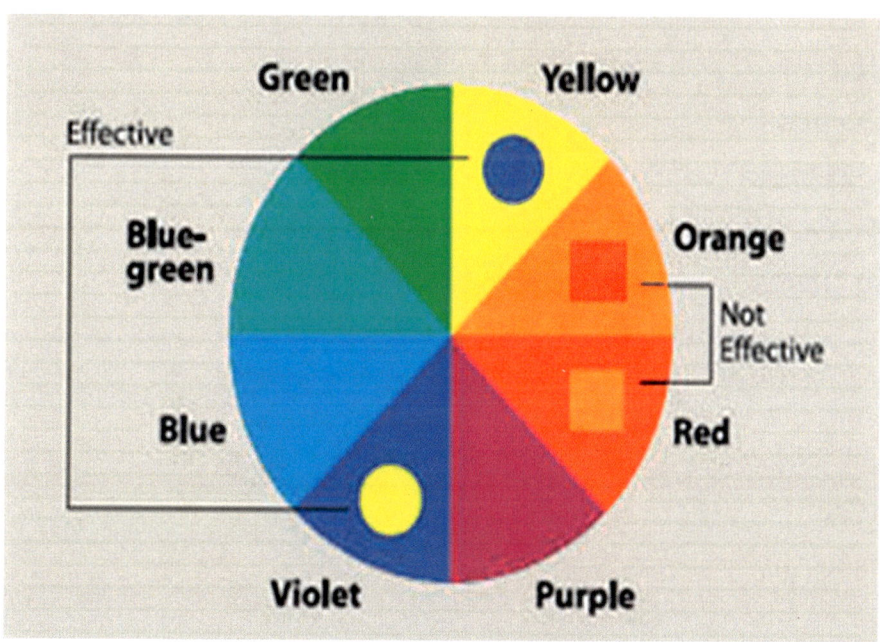

Do Not Use Roman Numerals
    Screen Readers Cannot Understand Them

Do Not Use Abbreviations
Limit Use of Quotes, Brackets, Braces, Parenthesis
Avoid Symbols, But Use Standard Known Ones
    Use Text Instead, For Charts Use Text Legend

Do Use Unique Descriptive Names of:
- ✪ **Titles**
- ✪ **Sections**
- ✪ **Tables**
- ✪ **Captions**

Do Use Numbers and Letters for:
- ✪ **Chapters**
- ✪ **Sections**
- ✪ **Sub-Sections**
- ✪ **Captions**

Arial

Arial Black

Bell Gothic

Berlin Sans

Calibri

Candara

Comic Sans

Consolas

Eras

Franklin Gothic

Gill Sans

Kozuka Gothic

Lucinda Sans

Myriad Pro

Tahoma

Trebuchet

TW Cent MT

Verdana

If You Convert Word to PDF, There is Still Work to Do.

- A PDF File Must Be Tagged (In the Settings When Converted)
- The Tags are Like HTML Code that Produce a Web Page, with Headings, Tables, Lists and So On.
- The Tags Must Be Tested and Edited In Acrobat Professional.

WHY?

- Because Tags Tell The Screen Reader What Is on The Page.
- PDF Files Are Pages of Sophisticated Layers of Images.
- Tags Contain The Actual Text And How It Is Formatted.
- No Tags = No Screen Reader Access At All
- Tags with Poor Format = Out of Order, Unformatted, And Unreadable Text.
- Somewhat Similar To Setting Styles In Word, Each Tag Must Tell What Kind of Text It is.
- It Does Take Some Skill, But the Simpler You Keep Your Document, the Better.
- Want To Create Lots of Work For Yourself?
- Add Complex Tables, Images With Text in Them, Lots of Text Boxes, Sectional Columns,
- And Inset Quotes.

508 Intro: PDF Files

Here we will show only one type of tag edit to give an idea, moving an image <Figure> to where it should be located from where it should not. Tags are for screen readers only, they do not affect what is on the page. It is just Drag & Drop.

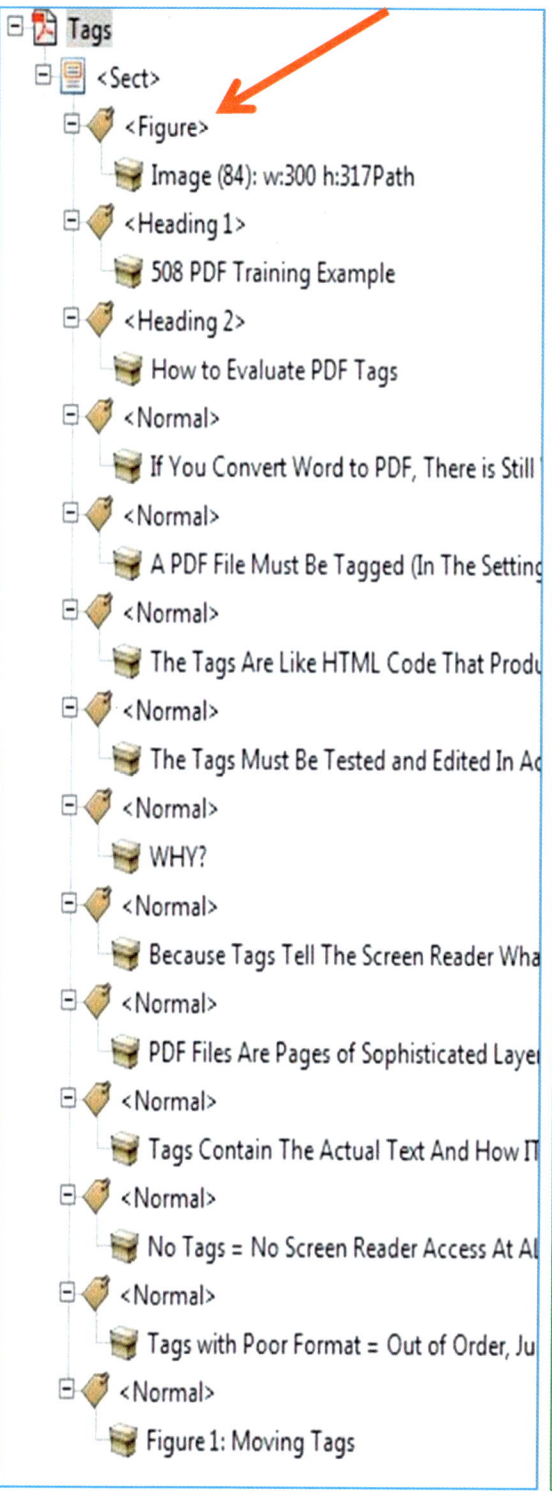

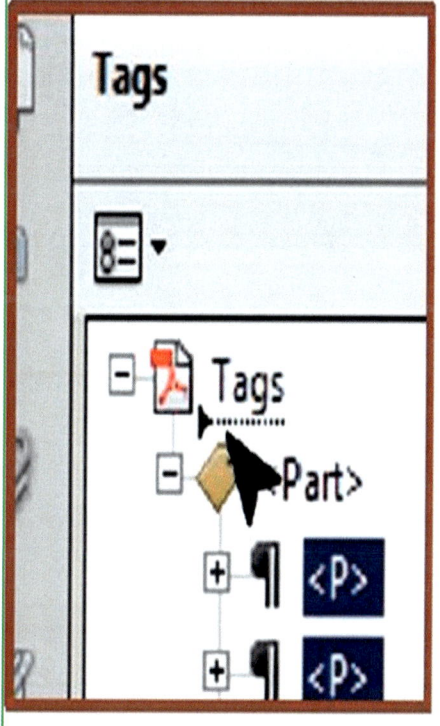

508 PDF Training Example

How to Evaluate PDF Tags

If You Convert Word to PDF, There is Still Work to Do.
A PDF File Must Be Tagged (In The Settings When Converted).
The Tags Are Like HTML Code That Produce A Web Page, With Headings, T
The Tags Must Be Tested and Edited In Acrobat Professional.

WHY?

Because Tags Tell The Screen Reader What Is On The Page.
PDF Files Are Pages of Sophisticated Layers of Images.
Tags Contain The Actual Text And How IT Is Formatted.
No Tags = No Screen Reader Access At ALL
Tags with Poor Format = Out of Order, Jumbled , And Unreadable Text.

Figure 1: Moving Tags

508 Intro: PDF Files

This is what is involved, some tags such as this image need to be moved to reflect the reading order. Other tags may be incorrect types, for example you may need to change a Normal to a Heading. Conversions always have issues.

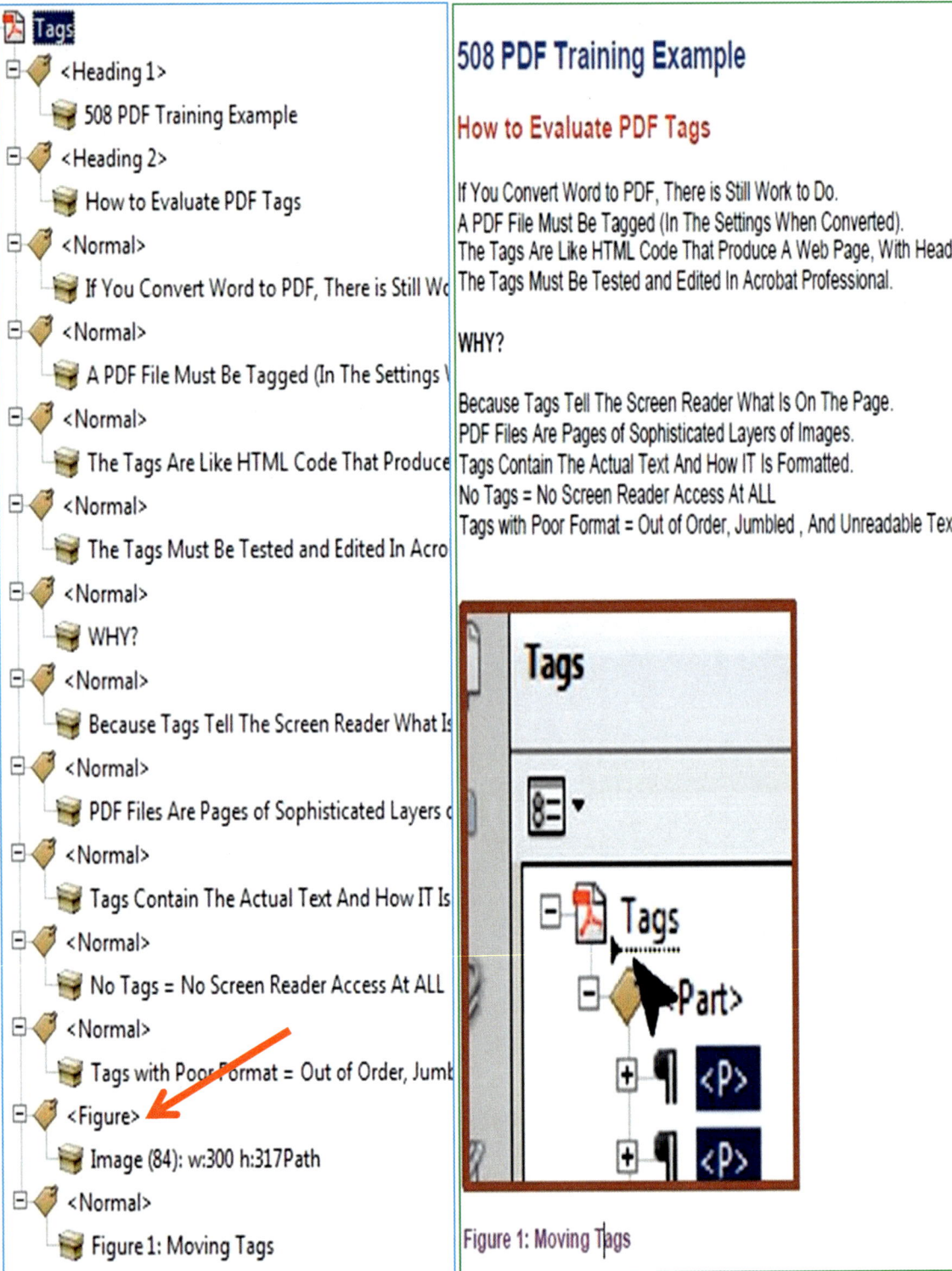

Tags
- `<Heading 1>`
  - 508 PDF Training Example
- `<Heading 2>`
  - How to Evaluate PDF Tags
- `<Normal>`
  - If You Convert Word to PDF, There is Still Wo
- `<Normal>`
  - A PDF File Must Be Tagged (In The Settings
- `<Normal>`
  - The Tags Are Like HTML Code That Produce
- `<Normal>`
  - The Tags Must Be Tested and Edited In Acro
- `<Normal>`
  - WHY?
- `<Normal>`
  - Because Tags Tell The Screen Reader What Is
- `<Normal>`
  - PDF Files Are Pages of Sophisticated Layers
- `<Normal>`
  - Tags Contain The Actual Text And How IT Is
- `<Normal>`
  - No Tags = No Screen Reader Access At ALL
- `<Normal>`
  - Tags with Poor Format = Out of Order, Jumb
- `<Figure>`
  - Image (84): w:300 h:317Path
- `<Normal>`
  - Figure 1: Moving Tags

508 PDF Training Example

How to Evaluate PDF Tags

If You Convert Word to PDF, There is Still Work to Do.
A PDF File Must Be Tagged (In The Settings When Converted).
The Tags Are Like HTML Code That Produce A Web Page, With Headings, Tables, Li
The Tags Must Be Tested and Edited In Acrobat Professional.

WHY?

Because Tags Tell The Screen Reader What Is On The Page.
PDF Files Are Pages of Sophisticated Layers of Images.
Tags Contain The Actual Text And How IT Is Formatted.
No Tags = No Screen Reader Access At ALL
Tags with Poor Format = Out of Order, Jumbled , And Unreadable Text.

Figure 1: Moving Tags

Use Built-In Formatting Features

TABLES
[Insert] > [Table]

HEADINGS
[Home] > [Styles] > [『 』 (Styles Menu)]
{Heading 1 to Heading 6} (Not 7 – 9)

SPACING (Not Carriage Returns to Create Space)
[Home] > [Paragraph] > {Line and Paragraph Spacing}

LISTS
[Home] > [Paragraph] > {Bullets/Numbers}

FOOTNOTES, ENDNOTES, REFERENCES
Use Links

COMPLEX IMAGES & CHARTS
Adjacent Text or Link to Full Description MUST be Equal to Image Info

Making Word Documents Accessible and Preparing Word Documents for Conversion to PDF

By
Ed Thrush

Word: Topics

- Headings
- Lists
- Charts & Color Usage
- Tooltips
- Link Issues & Solutions
- Footnotes, Endnotes, Captions, & Links
- Tables
- Fonts
- Word Tricks

Word: Headings

Style {Header} Converts To <P> Or Paragraph Text

In PDF & HTML This Equals Plain Text

It is Meant For Header/Footer

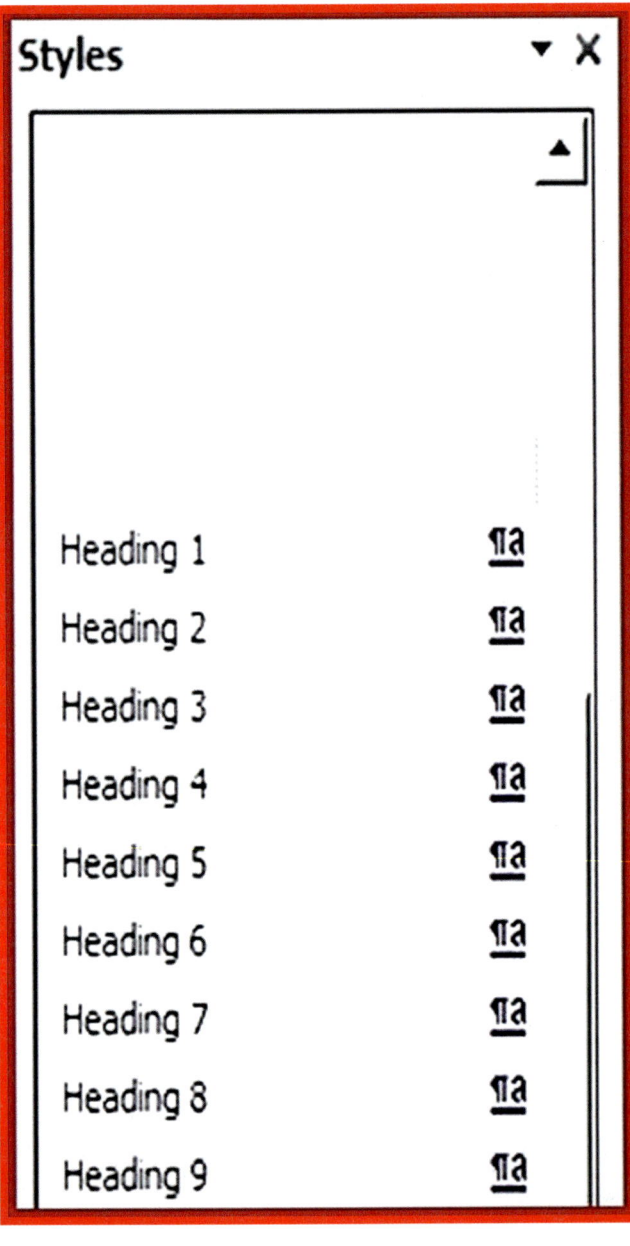

Always use {Heading 1 – 6}

{Heading 7 – 9} is Not Supported in PDF or HTML

SHIFT-ENTER In A List Or Outline Creates Paragraph Space Without Inserting Additional Markup Codes . Use It With Bullets When You Do NOT Want the Next Line to Have a Bullet. This is a **Soft-Break**.

For The Screen Reader This Keeps it as a Sub-Text After #1 & Does Not Break the List. You Will Not See the Text In The PDF Tags as it is Joined Directly to #1 Text.

As Long As You Use **Built In Number & Bullets** You Can Substitute Any Image or Symbol for Numbers & Bullets.

 **Use Built in Functions**

 **Use Headings**

1) Use Lists

2) Use a TOC with Links

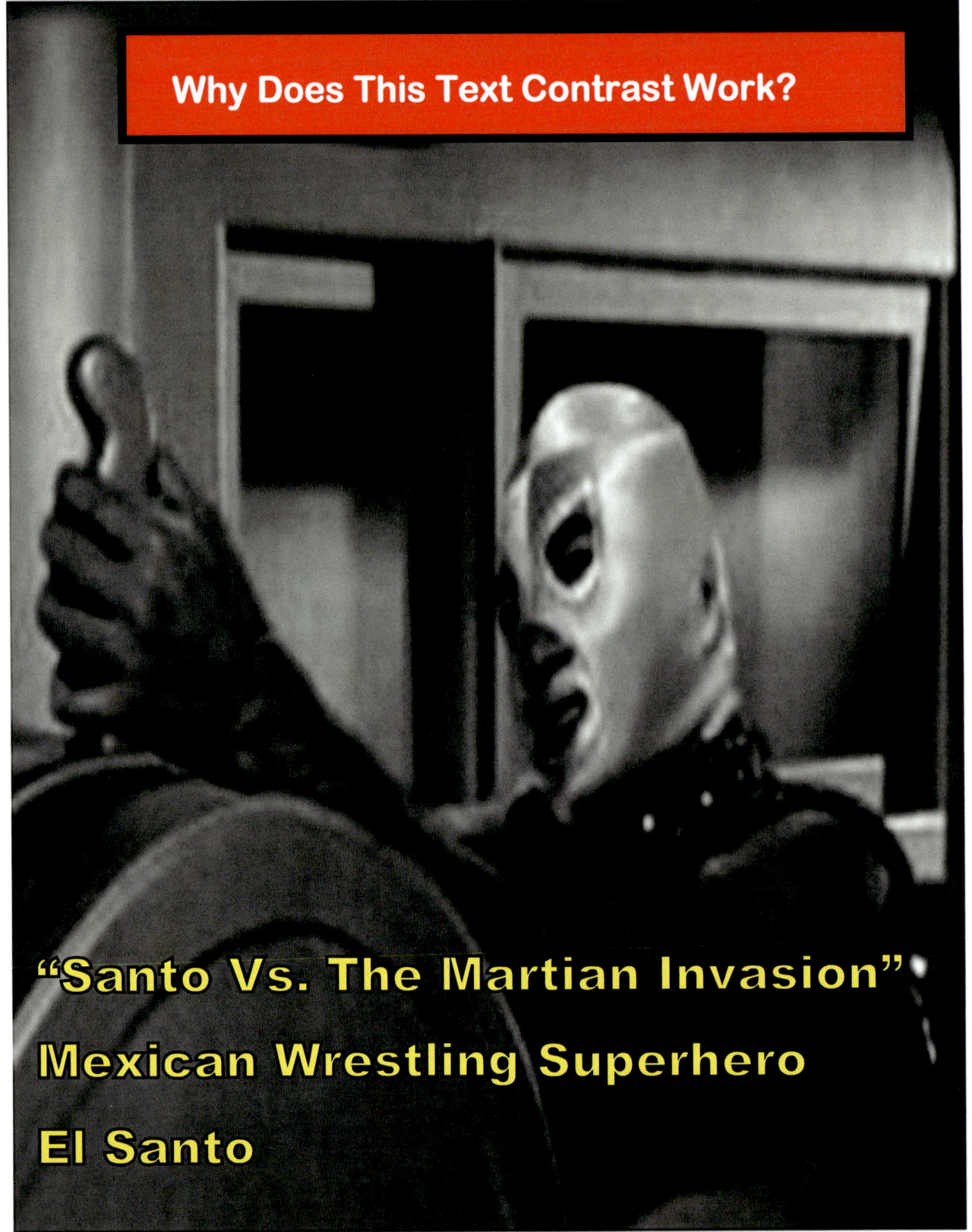

Why Does This Text Contrast Work?

"Santo Vs. The Martian Invasion"

Mexican Wrestling Superhero

El Santo

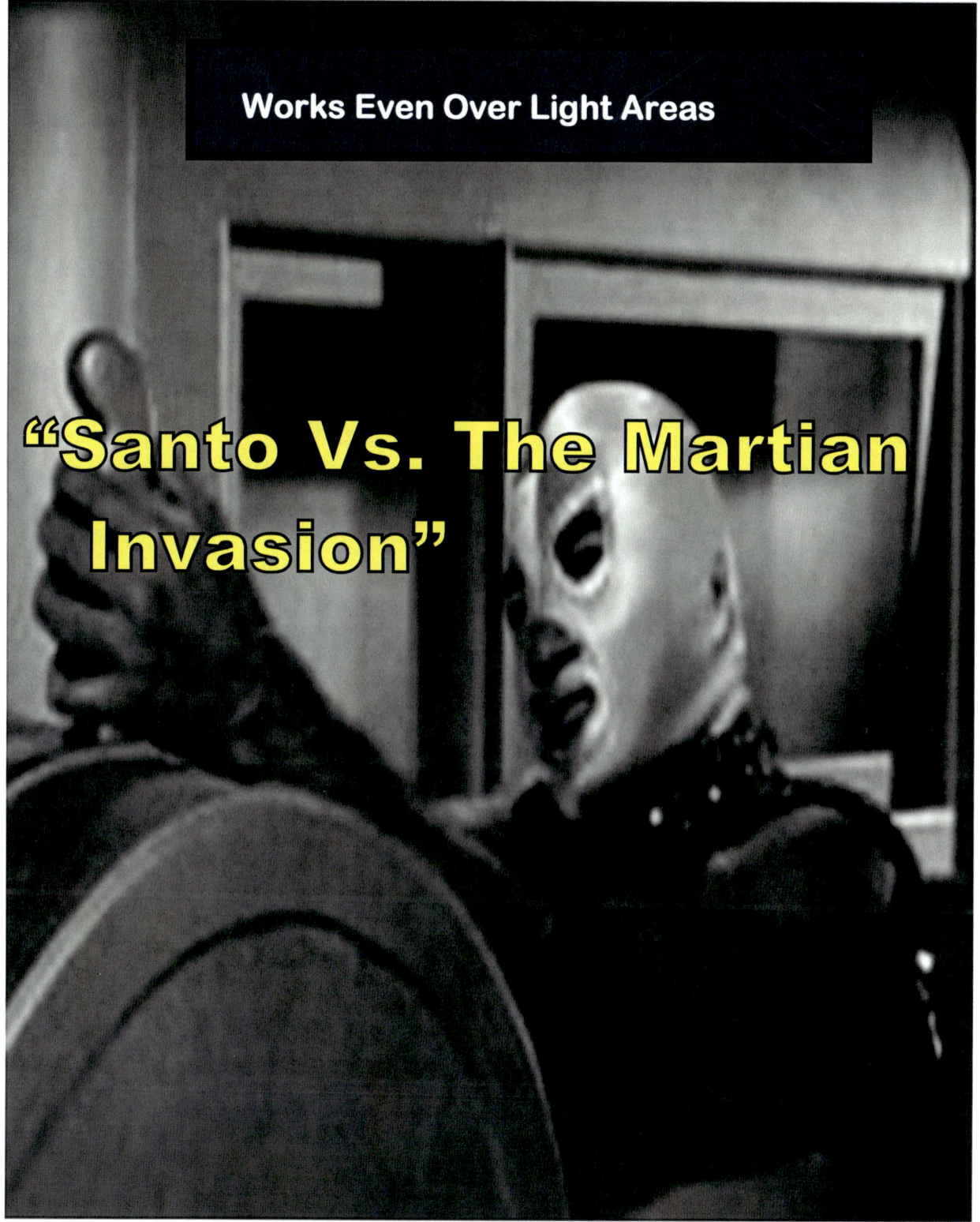

Word: Charts

Before Recon	Initiate Recon	Finalize Retirees	Finalize Costs
Host Kick-Off Meeting	Step 1: Initiate Application Reconciliationnti on	Step 3: Request Covered Retiree	Step 5: Prepare Recon Pavment
Prep Time-line & Plan	Step 2: Review Payment Setup & Mark 'Complete'	Distribute CRL	Prepare Final Costs
Assign User Roles		Compare CRL to Previous	Report Final Costs
Interim Pay Stop 90 Days Prior		Resolve CRL Dis-crepancies	Coordinate Cost Threshold & Cost
Process All Response & Notify Files		Step 4: Finalize CRL	Step 6: Manage Submissio n of Final Costs
Submit Retiree Updates			
Download Covered Retiree List			
Obtain Final Rebate Info			

Here is the Full Chart We Will Try to Create an Alternative For – We Only Need to Do Part to Show a Start

Word: Charts – Solution 1 Table Method

Before Recon	Host Kick-Off Meeting	Prep Time-line & Plan	Assign User Roles	Interim Pay Stop 90 Days Prior	Process All Response & Notify Files	Submit Retiree Updates	Download Covered Retiree List	Obtain Final Rebate Info
Initiate Recon	Step 1: Initiate Application Reconciliation	Step 2: Review Payment Setup & Mark Complete						
Finalize Retirees	Step 3: Request Covered Retiree	Distribute CRL	Compare CRL to Previous	Resolve CRL Dis-crepancies	Step 4: Finalize CRL			
Finalize Costs	Step 5: Prepare Recon Payment	Prepare Final Costs	Report Final Costs	Coordinate Cost Threshold & Cost	Step 6: Manage Sub-mission of Final Costs			

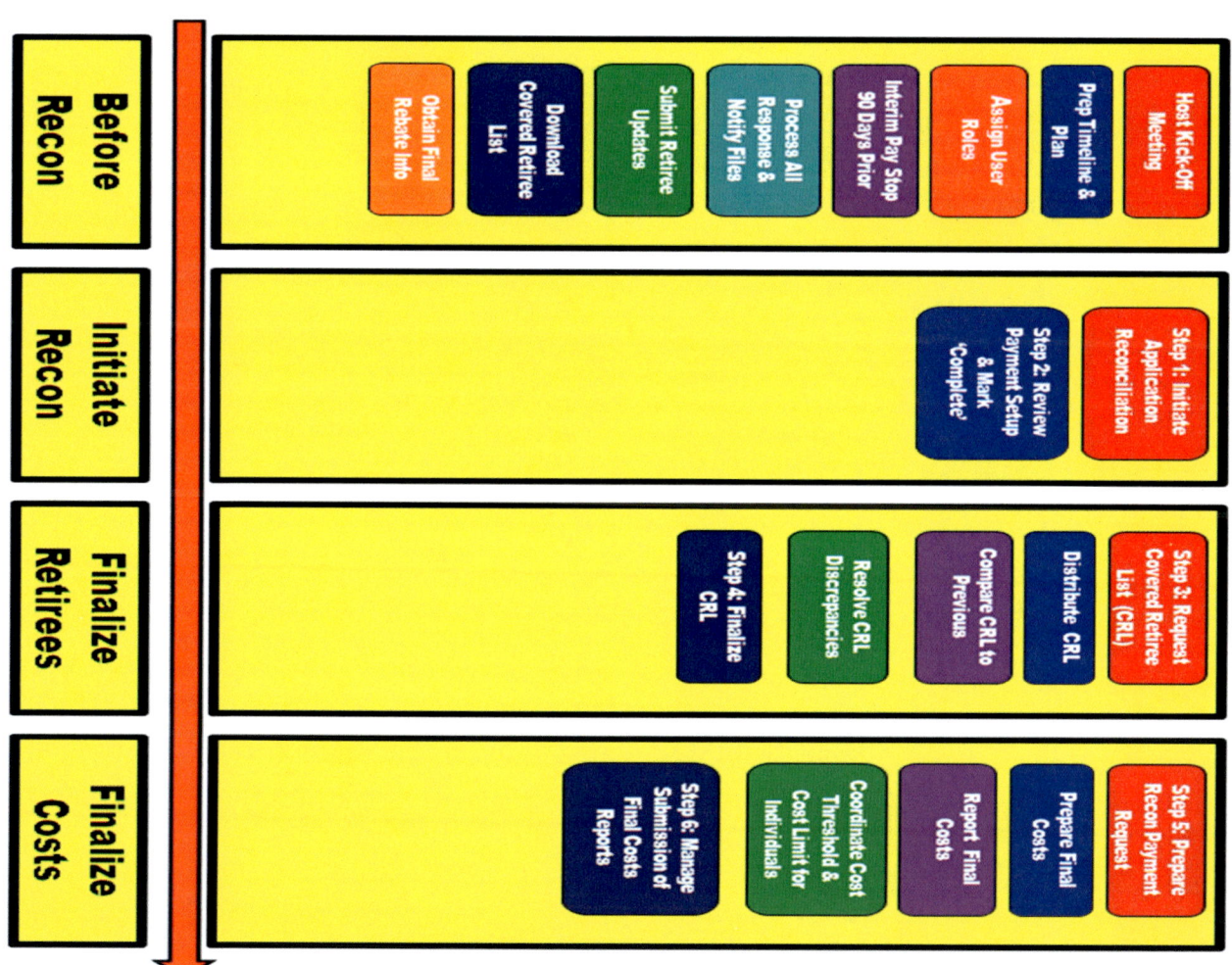

68

Word: Charts – Solution 2 Outline Method

1. **Before Recon**
   A. **Host Kick-Off Meeting**
   B. **Prep Timeline & Plan**
   C. **Assign User Roles**
   D. **Interim Pay Stop 90 Days prior**
   E. **Process All Response & Notify Files**
   F. **Submit Retiree Updates**
   G. **Download Covered Retiree List**
   H. **Obtain Final Rebate Info**
2. **Initiate Recon**
   A. **Step 1: Initiate Application Recon**
   B. **Step 2: Review Payment Setup & Mark 'Complete'**
3. **Finalize Retirees**
   A. **Step 3: Request Covered Retiree Lists (CRL)**
   B. **Compare CRL to Previous**
   C. **Resolve CRL Discrepancies**
   D. **Step 4: Finalize CRL**
4. **Finalize Costs**
   A. **Step 5: Prepare Recon Payment Request**
   B. **Prepare Final Costs**
   C. **Report Final Costs**
   D. **Coordinate Costs Threshold & Cost Limit for Individuals**
   E. **Step 6: Manage Submission of Final Costs Reports**

You Can Add More Descriptions & Notes Around Either of These Solutions – But be Concise

Reconciliation cannot be initiated when there is an Interim Payment in process. Identify that the date of the last Interim Payment request is at least 60 days before the date you want to initiate Reconciliation. If you have an Interim Payment request in process, check the RDS Secure Website to find the status of the request. It is recommended that Interim Payments are stopped 90 days prior to initiating Reconciliation.

If you have received any retiree files from the CMS' RDS Center, you should process them in the order in which they were received, updating internal subsidy records in the process. This will help make sure your records are in sync with the CMS' RDS Center before you work on the Covered Retiree List (CRL).

Communicating with Cost Reporters is essential to resolve any discrepancies with retiree data. Since the Covered Retiree List (CRL) includes the Plan Sponsor's full array of Benefit Options, in many cases it will need to be divided and communicated to multiple Cost Reporters. The cost data prepared and submitted by these Cost Reporters must not include data for anything outside the Qualifying Covered Retirees (QCR), Benefit Options, and corresponding subsidy periods listed in the Covered Retiree List.

In this task, the drug manufacturer usually communicates the rebates to the Pharmacy Benefit Manager (PBM) or Plan Sponsor. The Cost Preparer must receive the rebate information and incorporate it into the final cost figures.
Because the Final Cost Reports must include rebate information, they may take longer to prepare than interim costs. Be sure to pay close attention to coordination of individual retiree cost data as well. Starting early will leave you plenty of time to clear up any discrepancies.

Make any changes to Payment Setup that was not completed in the pre-Reconciliation process. Communicate those changes to the affected people.
Consider assigning Designees to Vendors who report Mainframe cost data so Vendors may monitor the receipt and processing of their Mainframe Cost Reports. For information about setting up a Vendor Designee in Payment Setup, go to: Set Up A Vendor Designee In Payment Setup.

Work with your Vendor to establish the proper Cost Reporter relationships in Payment Setup. Vendor Designees are frequently setup incorrectly as Plan Sponsor Designees. If possible, consider assigning only one source to report cost data for each Benefit Option to eliminate the possibility of duplicate Cost Reporting. If changing sources for Final Cost Reporting, you will not be permitted to remove a Vendor or individual Plan Sponsor Cost Reporter if they previously reported interim costs. In this case, you may need to assign multiple sources to the Benefit Option.

Communication is critical if multiple sources are assigned to assure duplicate cost data are not included in the Final Reconciliation Request. Cost data from multiple sources for the same Benefit Option will be accepted during Final Cost Reporting. The Account Manager and Designee with the Request Payment privilege must review cost data carefully in Step 7: Review Final Costs and if necessary, reject a duplicate Cost Report.

Best Practice for Charts/Images is:

If Fully Described in Body Text there is No Need for Alternative Text.

You Do NOT Want the Screen Reader to Waste Time on Alt-Text When the Description Already Exists.

On the PDF Side Make Sure Fully Described Images are NOT in the Tags or are Made [Background] with the TouchUp Tool. No need to announce image since described.

Word: Concise Tooltips (ScreenTips in Word)

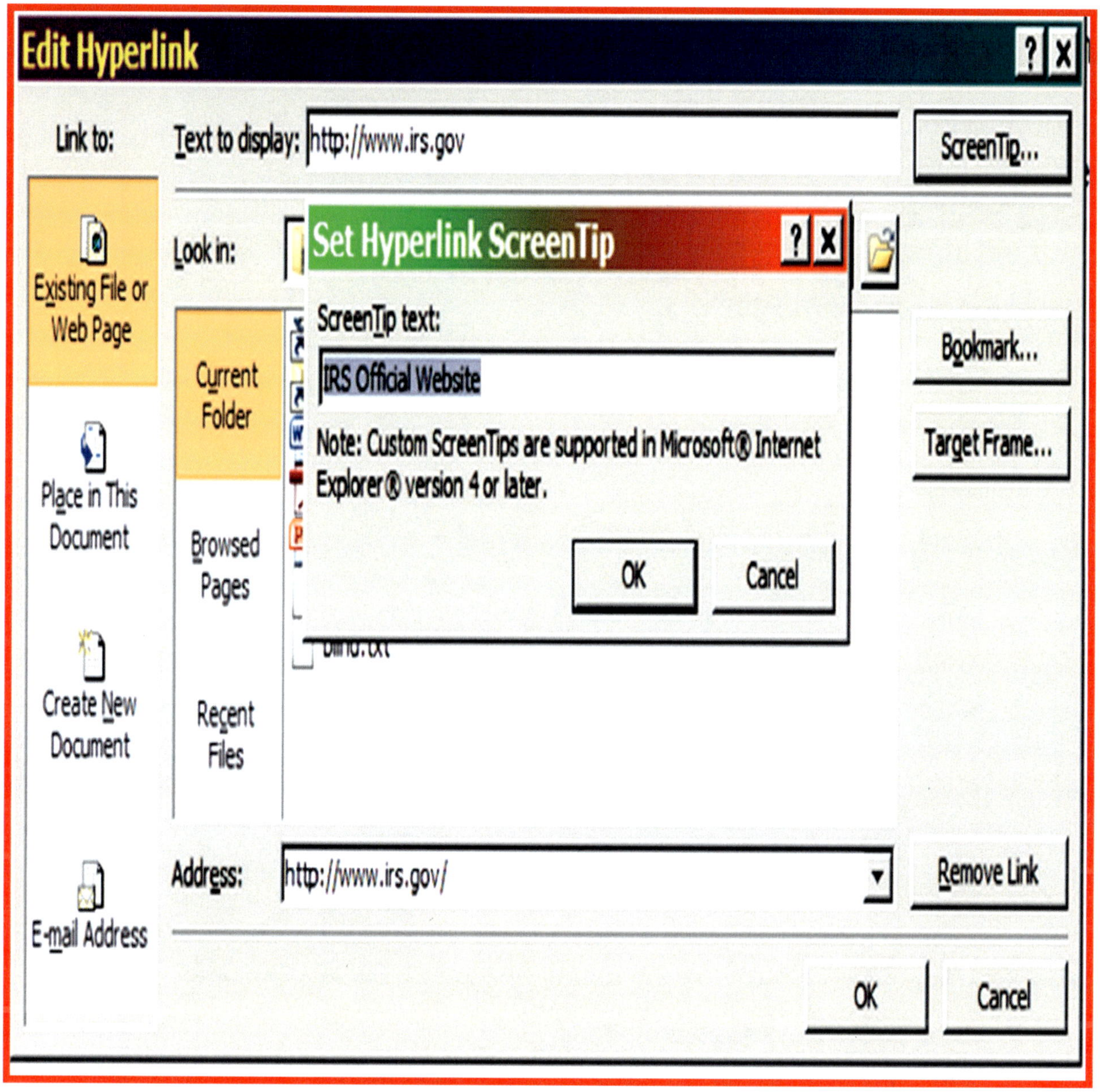

Edit Hyperlink ? X

Link to: Text to display: http://www.irs.gov   ScreenTip...

Existing File or Web Page

Look in:

Set Hyperlink ScreenTip ? X

ScreenTip text:

IRS Official Website

Note: Custom ScreenTips are supported in Microsoft® Internet Explorer® version 4 or later.

OK   Cancel

Current Folder

Place in This Document

Browsed Pages

Create New Document

Recent Files

Bookmark...

Target Frame...

E-mail Address

Address: http://www.irs.gov/   Remove Link

OK   Cancel

Summarize the Target of the Link

Word: Link Issues

HOW TO...

Click a topic for more information.

- Submit Costs And Request Payment

  - Extract Certain Medicare Part B Costs From RDS Payment Requests Updated 07/23/2007

  - Complete Payment Setup Updated 01/31/2008

  - Change Payment Setup Updated 11/16/2007

  - Prepare RDS Cost Data For Submission To The RDS Center Updated 03/25/2008

  - Submit Interim Cost Data Updated 03/25/2008

  - Submit An Interim Payment Request Updated 12/21/2007

  - Submit Final Cost Data Updated 10/22/2007

  - Access Payment History New 09/27/2006

Just Put the Date, or Revised, Updated with the Date

- **Page of Links, Accessed with TAB**
  Text Right of Link is NOT Read – Not Part of Link

- **"New" with Year 2006 Connotation**
  Out of Service Web Site, Not Maintained

- **Make Description Part of Link**
- **Give More Info in Tooltip**
- **Expand Links So They Look More Like Search Results**

Word: Footnotes, Endnotes, Captions, & Links

1. In the text, click where you want the raised reference mark to go, and then on the **References** tab, **Footnotes** group, click the **Insert Footnote** (or **Insert Endnote**) button [1].

2. Type your supplementary information at the flashing insertion point beneath the separator line, and then click back in the document to continue typing. Repeat the process for additional notes[i].

3. To change the footnote text, click the **Show Notes** button in the **Footnotes** group [2].

4. To remove a footnote, select the raised reference mark in the body of text and press **Delete**.

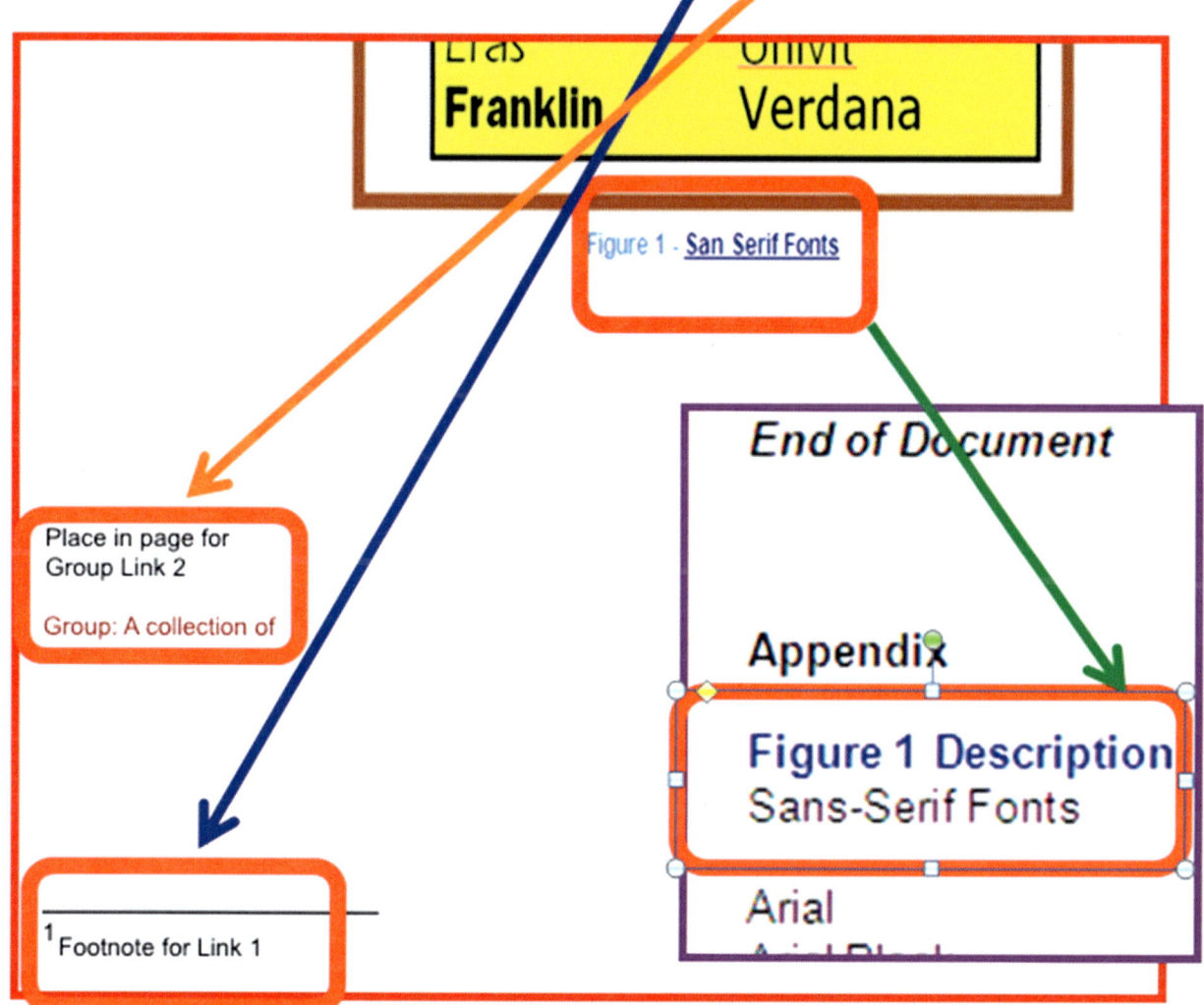

Eras   Univt
Franklin   Verdana

Figure 1 - San Serif Fonts

Place in page for Group Link 2

Group: A collection of

End of Document

Appendix

Figure 1 Description
Sans-Serif Fonts

Arial

_____
[1] Footnote for Link 1

Word: Link Solutions - Large List of Links

Pipeline Volume 5 Issue 1 **January 5, 2011**, New Resources: *DODD Priority Work Plan Series* Online; *Health & Safety Toolkit*, APSI Premieres Achievement Awards, *Connect Ohio* Launches "Every Citizen Online", New Library Services for Ohioans with Visual Impairments, "Resolve to be Ready" in 2011, CMS Expands, Upgrades Healthcare Provider Directory, Community Connections at Northwest Ohio Developmental Center

Pipeline Volume 4 Issue 26 December 22, 2010, Advocacy & Protective Services, Inc. (APSI) Names Karla Rinto Executive Director, Scioto County Board of Developmental Disabilities Superintendent Brenda Benson Retires, *Special Feature: 2010 – The Year in Review, Month to Month*

Pipeline Volume 4 Issue 25 **December 8, 2010**, Ohio Association of County Boards Conference Looks to 2011, Sharpens Focus, Southwest Ohio Developmental Center (SODC) Celebrates 25 Years of Service, Department of Aging Requesting Caregiver Stories, Ohio Public Images Announces 2011 Developmental Disabilities Awareness Theme, "Together ...", *PostScripts* – Noteworthy News Briefs & Calendar Items.

Pipeline Volume 4 Issue 24 November 23, 2010, Interagency Autism Coordinating Council Draws on Ohio Expertise, Family Advisory Council Members Look Ahead to 2011, Special Feature: Giving Thanks ... Thoughts from Across the State.

Pipeline Volume 4 Issue 23 November 10, 2010, National Family Caregivers Month Honors Many, Tenth Annual Ohio SIBS Conference Draws Diverse Group, Celebrates Progress, DODD Priority Work Plan, Progress Report & Update, Disability Housing Network Launches Housing Corporation Self Assessment, Ohio Public Images Announces Developmental Disabilities Awareness Events for 2011, *PostScripts*: Timely News Briefs and Calendar Items.

Pipeline Extra! November 3, 2010, Results of November 2 Election, County Board Levy Issues, Across the State

Pipeline Volume 4 Issue 22 October 27, 2010, Self Empowered Life Funding Waiver Submitted to CMS Today; National Disability Employment Awareness Month – Potpourri of Progress & Work Yet to be Done; Ohio Provider Resource Association (OPRA) Conference Reflects Partnership Approach; OSU Nisonger Center Receives $2.5 Million Grant to Benefit Students; Belmont County Hosts Kathie Snow, "Disability is Natural" Program; Tuscarawas County to Take Ownership, Consolidate Campus; DODD Website Upgrades to Enhance Interaction; Access, Election Information in Preparation for November 2; *PostScripts*: Timely News Briefs and Calendar Items.

Featured Reports and Other Publications

EPA Research Focus Health Effects of Near-Roadway Air Pollution (PDF) (5 pp, 162KB, About PDF)

This article appears in the August 2009 issue of EM Magazine, a publication of the Air & Waste Management Association (A&WMA; http://www.awma.org). To obtain copies and reprints, please contact A&WMA directly at 1-412-232-3444.

Ambient Air Quality Monitoring and Health Research: Summary of April 16-17, 2008 Workshop to Discuss Key Issues (PDF) (2 pp, 625KB, About PDF)

Emission and Air Quality Modeling Tools for Near-Roadway Applications (PDF) (80 pp, 635KB, About PDF)

Integrated Science Assessment (ISA) for Oxides of Nitrogen and Sulfur - Ecological Criteria

Particulate Matter Research Program: Five Years of Progress (PDF) (208 pp, 4MB, About PDF)

Word: 2 Link Solutions - Large List of Links

Current Sort Criteria is: Publication Title

Search Documents

Support Information

Publication Number	Publication Title	Publication language	Publication Subject	DWD Division	Revision Date	Content Contact
DWSI-15567-E-P.pdf	2006 Registered Nurse Survey	English	Labor Market	DET	3/1/2007	Sandra Fike
UCD-8303-P	2009 Wisconsin Acts 1, 11, 28, 287, 288, and 292, Amendments to Wisconsin Statutes Chapter 108, Unemployment Insurance Law	English	Unemployment	UI	8/1/2010	Unemployment Insurance Staff
DETJ-9517-P	80% of Job Search Success Depends on Research	English	Job Search	DET	10/1/2009	Wisconsin Job Center
DETV-14702-P	A Wisconsin guide to employment services and benefits	English	Veterans	DET	10/1/2009	Wisconsin Job Center
DETJ-5694-S-P	¿No consiguió el trabajo que quería?	Spanish	Job Search	DET	12/1/2003	Wisconsin Job Center
DETJ-9482-P	Ability to Follow Directions	English	Job Readiness	DET	10/1/2009	Wisconsin Job Center
SEC-6895-P	Access to Public Records	English	Records Management	ASD	2/20/2009	Eugene F. Lillge
ERD-7334-S-PWEB	Acosamiento en el Trabajo	Spanish	Fair Employment Law	ER	9/1/2005	Equal Rights

Sortable Table Plus Search
Gives Disabled User Multiple Options of Control

Front-Loaded Links

Place the Most Relevant Words in the Link Text At The Beginning Of The Phrase, So That Screen Reader Users Can Understand The Meaning Of The Link Immediately. If it is Not Relevant, They can Skip to the Next One.

Front-Load Instructions & Requirements Anything Important Before Link Selection Must Be Read First

Word: Tables

	Day	Week	Year
Group A	11	22	33
Group B	22	33	44
Group C	33	44	55
Group D	44	55	66

Keep Tables Simple and Small

All You Can Set in Word is The First Header Row

(1) SELECT Top Row

(2) [Table Tools]>[Layout]>[Repeat Header Rows]

Word: Tables Complex

		2006		2007	
		Paper	Toner	Paper	Toner
Contract A	Tom	A1	B2	C3	D4
	Ted	E5	F6	G7	H8
Contract B	Jane	I9	J10	K11	L12
	Jill	M13	N14	O15	P16

> If This is the Table Layout → Try to Simplify it
> Merged Header Cells Do Not Work in Word to PDF
> Using CommonLook with Acrobat You Can Edit the
> Tables and Keep Sub-Headers But It Takes Work

	2006 Paper	2006 Toner	2007 Paper	2007 Toner
Contract A Tom	A1	B2	C3	D4
Contract A Ted	E5	F6	G7	H8
Contract B Jane	I9	J10	K11	L12
Contract B Jill	M13	N14	O15	P16

The Word For Text Effects To Test = Outline

Fails

The Word For Text Effects To Test = Shadow

Works

The Word For Text Effects To Test = Reflection

Works

The Word For Text Effects To Test = Glow

Works

The Word For Text Effects To Test = Pick List Outline

Fails

Wildcards:

Settings

    Use Wildcards

    No Formatting

    Search > All

    Reading Highlight > Highlight All

    Find In > Find in Main Document

Enter the Following in Find What

[_____]

All Acronyms

  (<[A-Z]@>)

Big Words - 14 Characters or More

  <[0-9A-Za-z]{14,}>

All Words in Parentheses

  \(*\)

Word: Search Wildcard Options

?   Any single character, s?t finds "sat" and "set".
*   Any string of characters, s*d finds "sad" and "started".
<   The beginning of a word, <(inter) finds "interesting" and "intercept", but not   "splintered".
>   The end of a word, (in)> finds "in" and "within", but not "interesting".
[ ]   One of the specified characters, w[io]n finds "win" and "won".
[-]   Any single character in this range, [r-t]ight finds "right" and "sight". Ranges   must be in ascending order.

^p   Paragraph mark ( ) (doesn't work in the Find what box when wildcards are on)   or type ^13
^t or ^9   Tab character ( ) **^+**   Em dash (—)
^=   En dash (–)
^^   Caret character
^l or ^11   Manual line break ( )
^n or ^14   Column break
^12   Page or section break (when replacing, inserts a page break)
^m   Manual page break (also finds or replaces section breaks when wildcards are on)
^s   Nonbreaking space ( )
^~   Nonbreaking hyphen ( )
^-   Optional hyphen ( )

Codes that work in the Find what box only (when wildcards are off)

^f or ^2   Footnote mark
^e   Endnote mark
^d   Field
^19   Opening field brace (when field codes are visible)
^21   Closing field brace (when field codes are visible)
^a or ^5   Comment
^b   Section break

How to Make PDF Documents Accessible
By Ed Thrush

PDF: Topics

- ⊕ **How a PDF Works**
- ⊕ **See What a Screen Reader Speaks**
- ⊕ **View Tags & See How They Work**
- ⊕ **Text & Headings Structure**
- ⊕ **Role Maps for Tags**
- ⊕ **Images**
- ⊕ **Methods of Tag Cleaning**
- ⊕ **Logical Reading Order**
- ⊕ **Tables**
- ⊕ **Corrupt Files**

PDF: How a PDF Works

- MS Word Uses Actual Text with Format Codes
- PDF Uses Image Objects With Structural Codes = Tags

In a PDF The Actual Text or "Content" is Stored Elsewhere and is Indexed to the Image Objects on the Page.

- PDF is a Scanned Document with Markup Codes
- PDF Actual Text is Contained in Content
- PDF Structure of Text is Contained in Tags

Tags are Not Needed at ALL for the PDF, They are Required for 508 so Screen Readers Can Interpret the Document.

The PDF Word Conversion is a Software Only Version of OCR (Optical Character Recognition) This is a Primary Support and Works Well With Physical Scanners.

Styles are carried over to define heading levels, however due to so many Word codes and format complexities, conversions are rarely without errors.

For example, adding an image with captions to the inside of a numbered list often does not convert well.

PDF: A PDF Main Parts

A PDF is Made Up of:
- **Image Objects** (What You See on the Page)
- **Content** (Actual Text Stored Elsewhere)
- **Tags** (Structural Formatting Codes)
- **Forms** (Form Markup Format)
- **Hidden Text** (Transparent, Covered Up, Same Color as Background, OCR Text)
- **Layers** (Color, Signature, [Visible by User Action])
- **Media, JavaScript (Menus, Actions), Flash**

PDF: Composition Tags

Structure in a PDF:
- **Images <Figure>**
- **Tables <Table>**
- **Lists <L>**
- **Body Text <Normal> <P>**
- **Headings <H1>**
- **Links <Link>**
- **Captions <Caption> <P>**
- **Form Elements**
- **Buttons**
- **Logical Reading Order**

About PDF:
- Open Standard
- Views & Prints Everywhere
- More Accessible Than Word
- Based on PostScript Printer Language
- Archive Format - Not Meant to Be Edited

- Not a Word Processor – Designed to Preserve an Image of a Publication

Bad Example of a PDF File

JAWS

Projects	2009	2010	2011
Completed	43	78	56
Outstanding	25	62	37
Out of State	2	4	7

Customer Requesting Support ↑ 67%

Customers Rejected ↓ 89%

Bad PDF Jaws Screen Reading Text

Bad example of a PDF file, blank table with four columns and four rows, Projects 2009 2010 2011, Completed, 43 78 column 4 row 2 56, Outstanding 25 62 column 4 row 3 37, Out-of-state 2, 4, column 4 row 4, 7, table end, blank, graphic 88, customer requesting support 67%, customers rejected graphic 98, 89%

- *The column headings are not associated, so it is hard to follow and the graphics are not described, meaning is lost.*

Good Example of a PDF File

JAWS

Projects	2009	2010	2011
Completed	43	78	56
Outstanding	25	62	37
Out of State	2	4	7

Customer Requesting Support ⬆ 67%

Customers Rejected ⬇ 89%

Good PDF Jaws Screen Reading Text

Good example of a PDF file, black, table with four columns and four rows, Projects 2009, 2010, 2011, Completed 43, 78, column 3 2010, 78, 56, Outstanding 62, 37, Column 4, 2011 37, Out of state column 2, 2009 2, 4, column 4 row 4 2011 7, blank, customer requesting support graphic increase 67% customers rejected graphic decrease 89% decreased 89%

- *Column headers are associated and can be spoken on request with screen reader, graphics are described.*

Visual Page is Just Image Objects

Tags:
- Determine Structure of a PDF
- Define the Objects on the Page
- Are What the Screen Reader Uses
- Are Order of Reading, Not the Screen
- Define the Conversion to HTML

All Types of Tags

Plain paragraph text = body text with no special markup.

- Bullet List One
- Bullet List Two

1. Number List One
2. Number List Two

Here is a Link

Here is a Footnote [1]

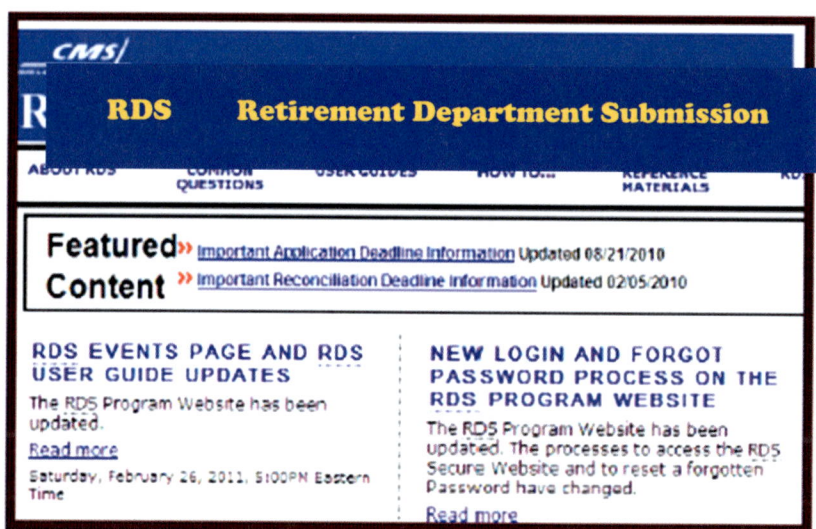

Figure 1 Example Caption

Projects	2009	2010	2011
Completed	43	78	56
Outstanding	25	62	37
Out of State	2	4	7

Here we have a sample PDF with various types of formatting of the content.

[1] A Footnote for the Everything Document.

PDF: 2 View Tags in a PDF – How to Find

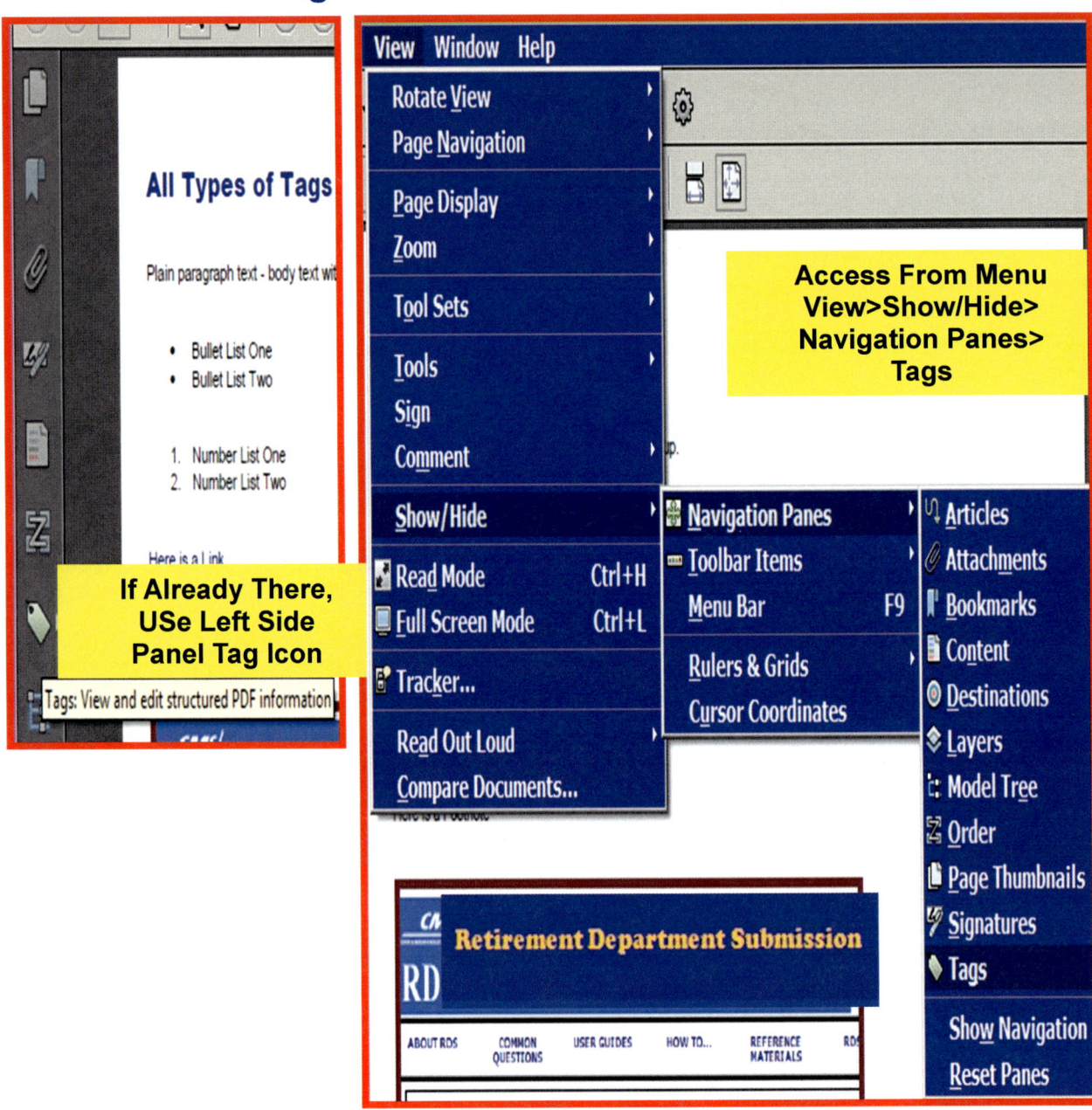

All Types of Tags

Plain paragraph text - body text wit

- Bullet List One
- Bullet List Two

1. Number List One
2. Number List Two

Here is a Link

If Already There, USe Left Side Panel Tag Icon

Tags: View and edit structured PDF information

View Window Help

Rotate View
Page Navigation

Page Display
Zoom

Tool Sets

Tools
Sign
Comment

Show/Hide

Read Mode   Ctrl+H
Full Screen Mode   Ctrl+L

Tracker...

Read Out Loud
Compare Documents...

Navigation Panes
Toolbar Items
Menu Bar   F9

Rulers & Grids
Cursor Coordinates

Access From Menu View>Show/Hide> Navigation Panes> Tags

Articles
Attachments
Bookmarks
Content
Destinations
Layers
Model Tree
Order
Page Thumbnails
Signatures
Tags

Show Navigation
Reset Panes

Retirement Department Submission

RD

ABOUT RDS COMMON QUESTIONS USER GUIDES HOW TO... REFERENCE MATERIALS RDS

PDF: ❸ View Tags in a PDF

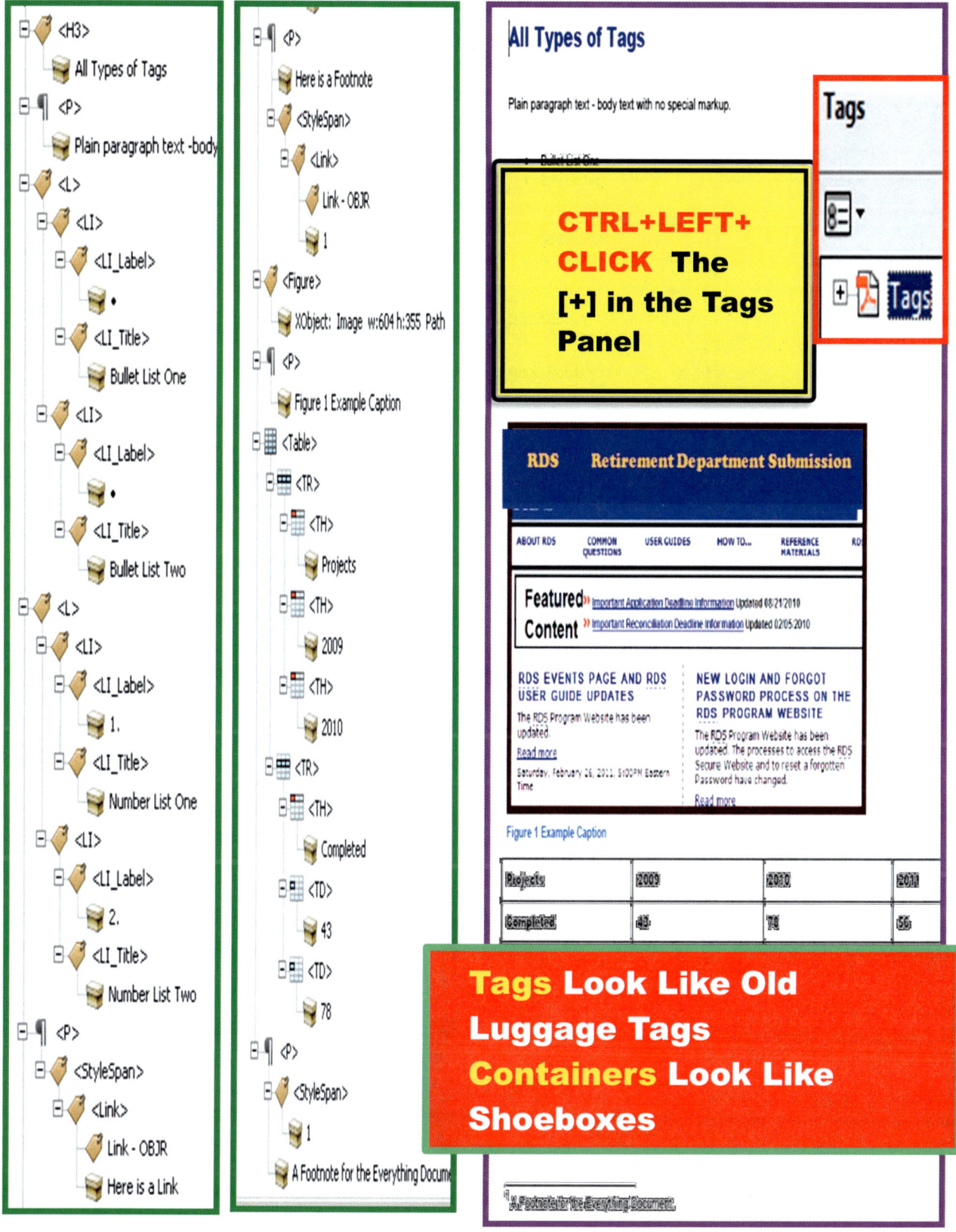

- <H3>
  - All Types of Tags
- <P>
  - Plain paragraph text -body
- <L>
  - <LI>
    - <LI_Label>
      - •
    - <LI_Title>
      - Bullet List One
  - <LI>
    - <LI_Label>
      - •
    - <LI_Title>
      - Bullet List Two
- <L>
  - <LI>
    - <LI_Label>
      - 1.
    - <LI_Title>
      - Number List One
  - <LI>
    - <LI_Label>
      - 2.
    - <LI_Title>
      - Number List Two
- <P>
  - <StyleSpan>
    - <Link>
      - Link - OBJR
      - Here is a Link

- <P>
  - Here is a Footnote
  - <StyleSpan>
    - <Link>
      - Link - OBJR
      - 1
- <Figure>
  - XObject: Image w:604 h:355 Path
- <P>
  - Figure 1 Example Caption
- <Table>
  - <TR>
    - <TH>
      - Projects
    - <TH>
      - 2009
    - <TH>
      - 2010
  - <TR>
    - <TH>
      - Completed
    - <TD>
      - 43
    - <TD>
      - 78
- <P>
  - <StyleSpan>
    - 1
  - A Footnote for the Everything Docum

All Types of Tags

Plain paragraph text - body text with no special markup.

- Bullet List One

CTRL+LEFT+CLICK The [+] in the Tags Panel

Tags

RDS   Retirement Department Submission

| ABOUT RDS | COMMON QUESTIONS | USER GUIDES | HOW TO... | REFERENCE MATERIALS | RD |

Featured Content
» Important Application Deadline Information Updated 08/21/2010
» Important Reconciliation Deadline Information Updated 02/05/2010

RDS EVENTS PAGE AND RDS USER GUIDE UPDATES
The RDS Program Website has been updated.
Read more
Saturday, February 26, 2011, 5:00PM Eastern Time

NEW LOGIN AND FORGOT PASSWORD PROCESS ON THE RDS PROGRAM WEBSITE
The RDS Program Website has been updated. The processes to access the RDS Secure Website and to reset a forgotten Password have changed.
Read more

Figure 1 Example Caption

Projects	2009	2010	2011
Completed	43	78	56

Tags Look Like Old **Luggage Tags** **Containers** Look Like **Shoeboxes**

A Footnote for the Everything Document

PDF: 4 View Tags in a PDF

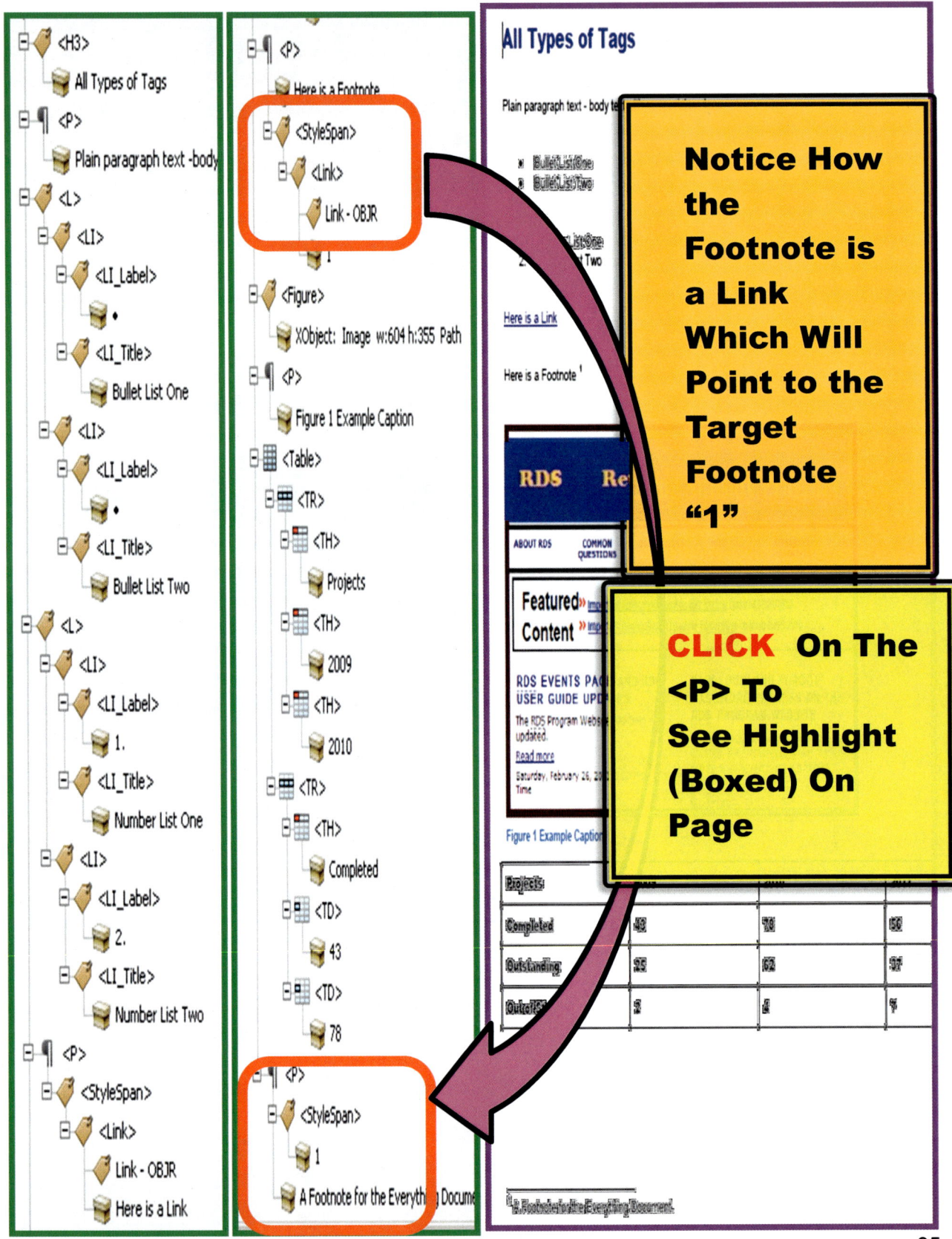

<H3>
All Types of Tags
<P>
Plain paragraph text -body
<L>
<LI>
<LI_Label>
•
<LI_Title>
Bullet List One
<LI>
<LI_Label>
•
<LI_Title>
Bullet List Two
<L>
<LI>
<LI_Label>
1.
<LI_Title>
Number List One
<LI>
<LI_Label>
2.
<LI_Title>
Number List Two
<P>
<StyleSpan>
<Link>
Link - OBJR
Here is a Link

<P>
Here is a Footnote
<StyleSpan>
<Link>
Link - OBJR
1
<Figure>
XObject: Image w:604 h:355 Path
<P>
Figure 1 Example Caption
<Table>
<TR>
<TH>
Projects
<TH>
2009
<TH>
2010
<TR>
<TH>
Completed
<TD>
43
<TD>
78
<P>
<StyleSpan>
1
A Footnote for the Everything Docume

All Types of Tags

Plain paragraph text - body te

- BulletListOne
- BulletListTwo

1. BulletListOne
2. d Two

Here is a Link

Here is a Footnote [1]

RDS   Re

ABOUT RDS   COMMON QUESTIONS

Featured » Imp
Content » Imp

RDS EVENTS PAG
USER GUIDE UPD
The RDS Program Websi
updated.
Read more
Saturday, February 26, 20
Time

Figure 1 Example Caption

Projects			
Completed	43	78	150
Outstanding	95	62	97
Outro RDS	9	4	4

A Footnote for the Everything Document.

Notice How the Footnote is a Link Which Will Point to the Target Footnote "1"

CLICK On The **<P>** To See Highlight (Boxed) On Page

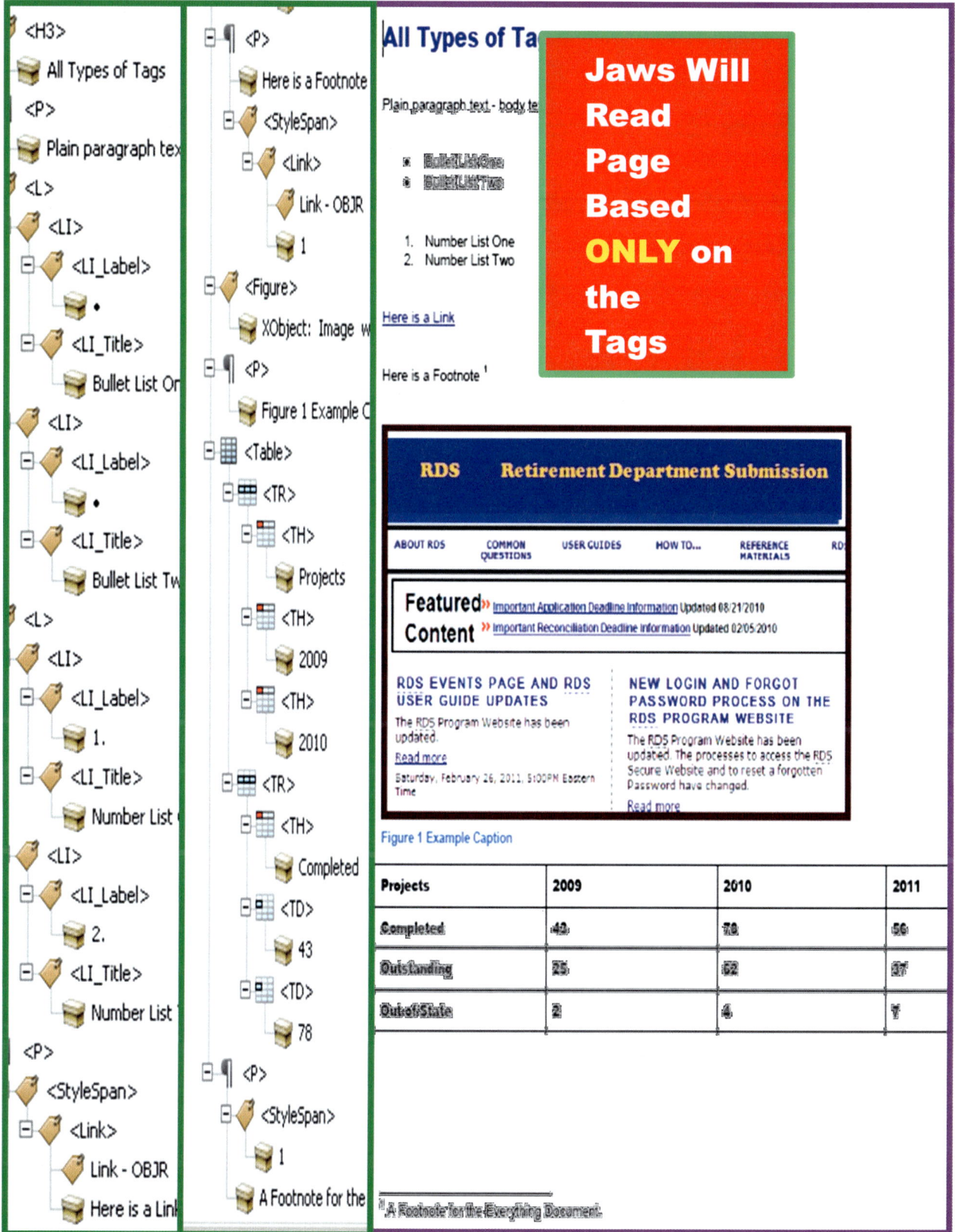

2 Major Components of Text in a PDF:

- **Plain Body Text or Paragraph Text <P>**
- **Headings <H1> - <H6>**

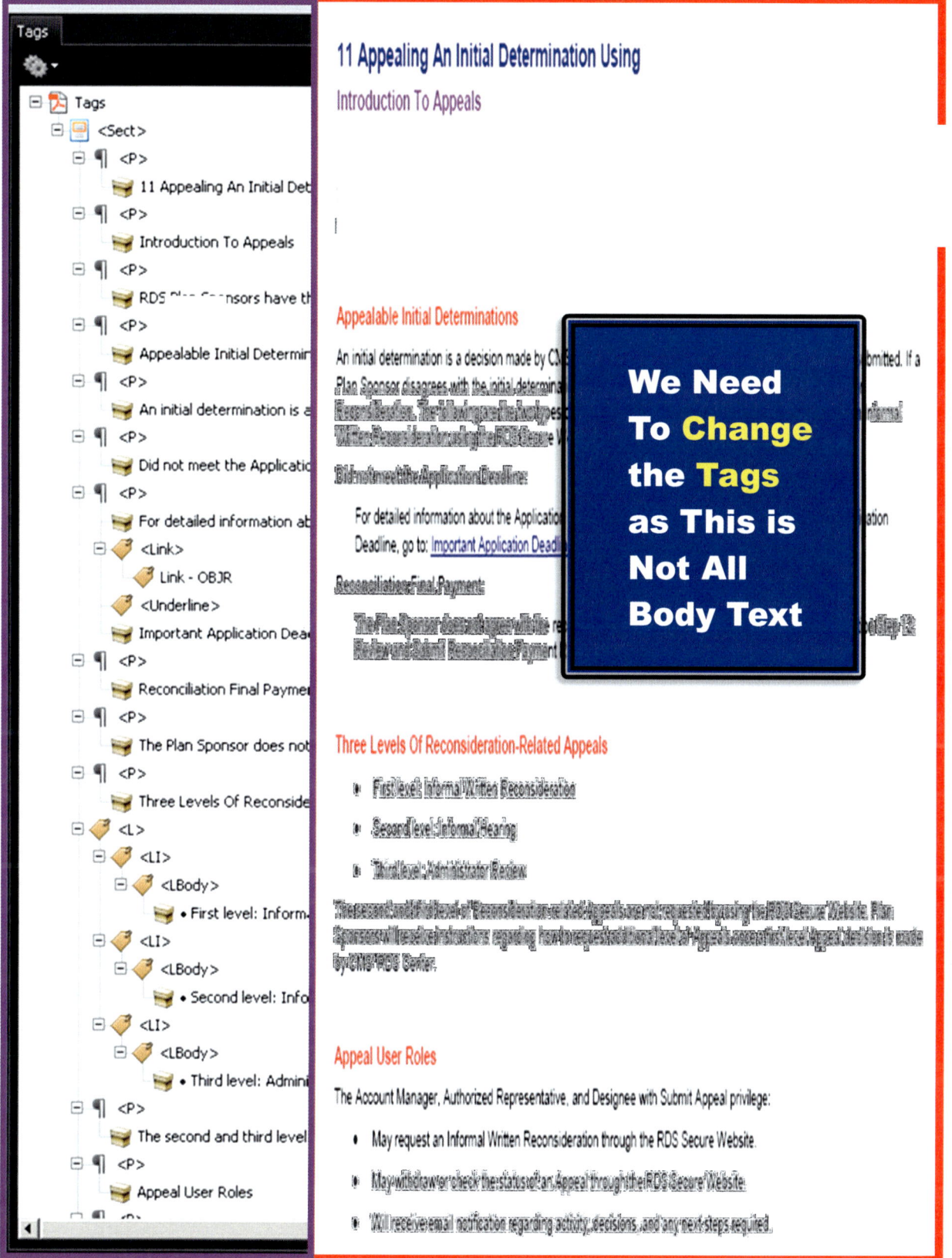

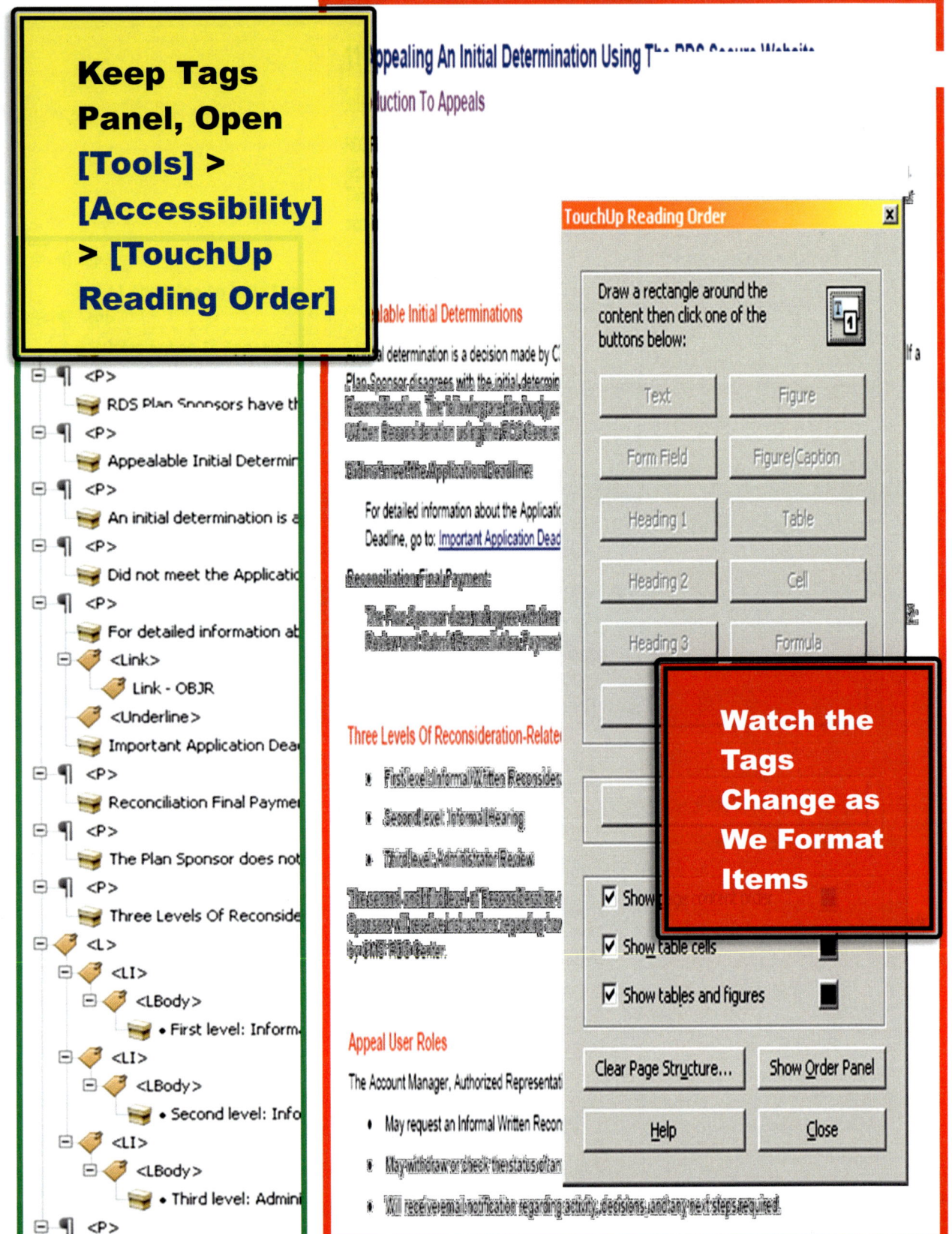

Keep Tags Panel, Open [Tools] > [Accessibility] > [TouchUp Reading Order]

Watch the Tags Change as We Format Items

TouchUp Reading Order

Draw a rectangle around the content then click one of the buttons below:

Text | Figure
Form Field | Figure/Caption
Heading 1 | Table
Heading 2 | Cell
Heading 3 | Formula

☑ Show ...
☑ Show table cells
☑ Show tables and figures

Clear Page Structure... | Show Order Panel
Help | Close

99

PDF: 4 Body, Paragraph Text & Headings

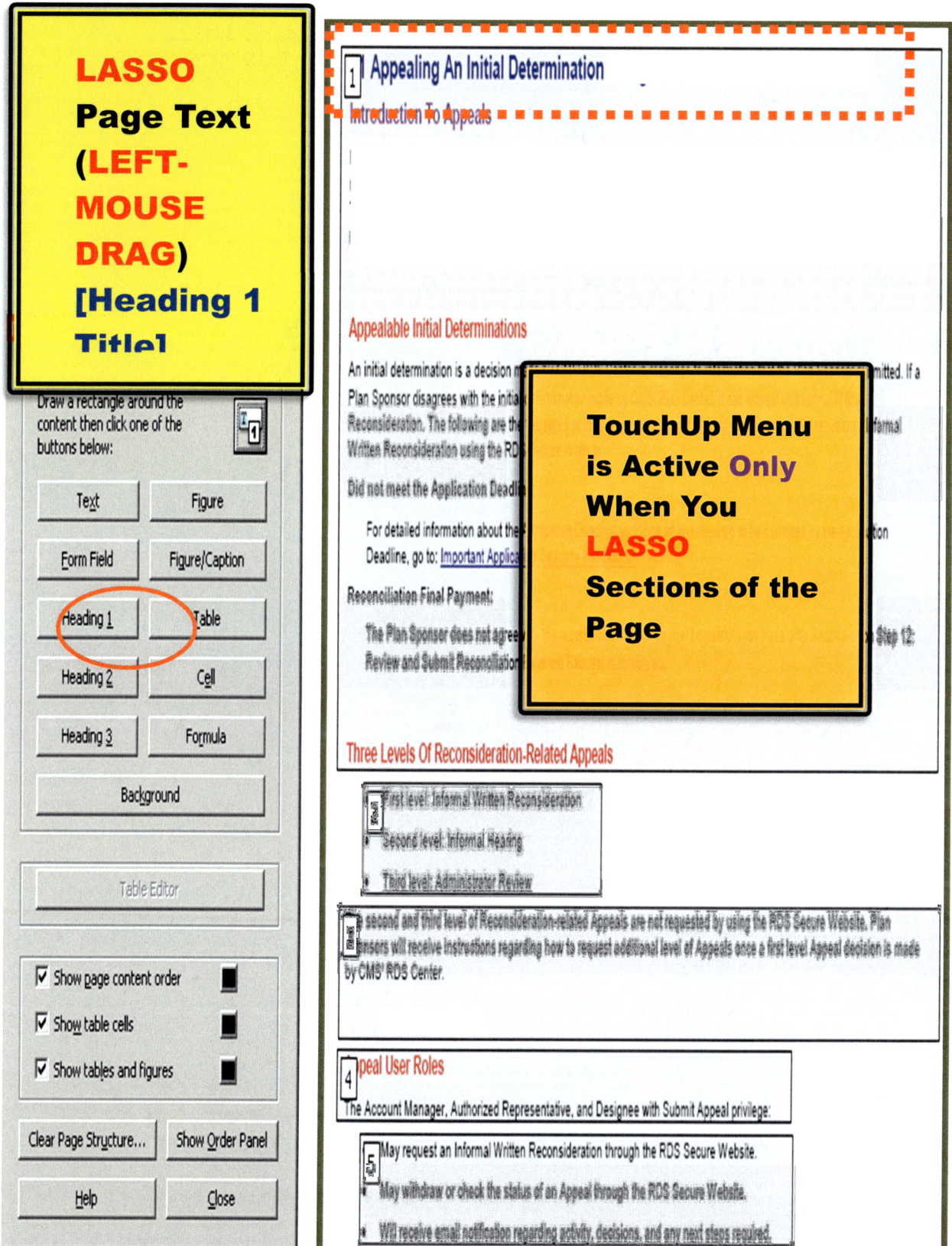

LASSO Page Text (LEFT-MOUSE DRAG) [Heading 1 Title]

TouchUp Menu is Active Only When You LASSO Sections of the Page

Draw a rectangle around the content then click one of the buttons below:

Text	Figure
Form Field	Figure/Caption
Heading 1	Table
Heading 2	Cell
Heading 3	Formula
Background	

Table Editor

☑ Show page content order ⬛
☑ Show table cells ⬛
☑ Show tables and figures ⬛

Clear Page Structure...	Show Order Panel
Help	Close

Appealing An Initial Determination

Introduction To Appeals

Appealable Initial Determinations

An initial determination is a decision m_____mitted. If a Plan Sponsor disagrees with the initial_____Reconsideration. The following are the_____formal Written Reconsideration using the RD

Did not meet the Application Deadli

For detailed information about the_____tion Deadline, go to: Important Applica

Reconciliation Final Payment:

The Plan Sponsor does not agree_____Step 12: Review and Submit Reconciliation

Three Levels Of Reconsideration-Related Appeals

First level: Informal Written Reconsideration

Second level: Informal Hearing

Third level: Administrator Review

The second and third level of Reconsideration-related Appeals are not requested by using the RDS Secure Website. Plan Sponsors will receive instructions regarding how to request additional level of Appeals once a first level Appeal decision is made by CMS' RDS Center.

Appeal User Roles

The Account Manager, Authorized Representative, and Designee with Submit Appeal privilege:

May request an Informal Written Reconsideration through the RDS Secure Website.

May withdraw or check the status of an Appeal through the RDS Secure Website.

Will receive email notification regarding activity, decisions, and any next steps required.

It Should Look Like This When Done Selecting Headings

Some Will Auto-Complete But they Will Often be Incorrect – So Do Them All
"Appealing" is <H1>
"Introduction" is <H2>
"Appealable" is <H3>
"Three Levels" is <H3>
"Appeal User" is

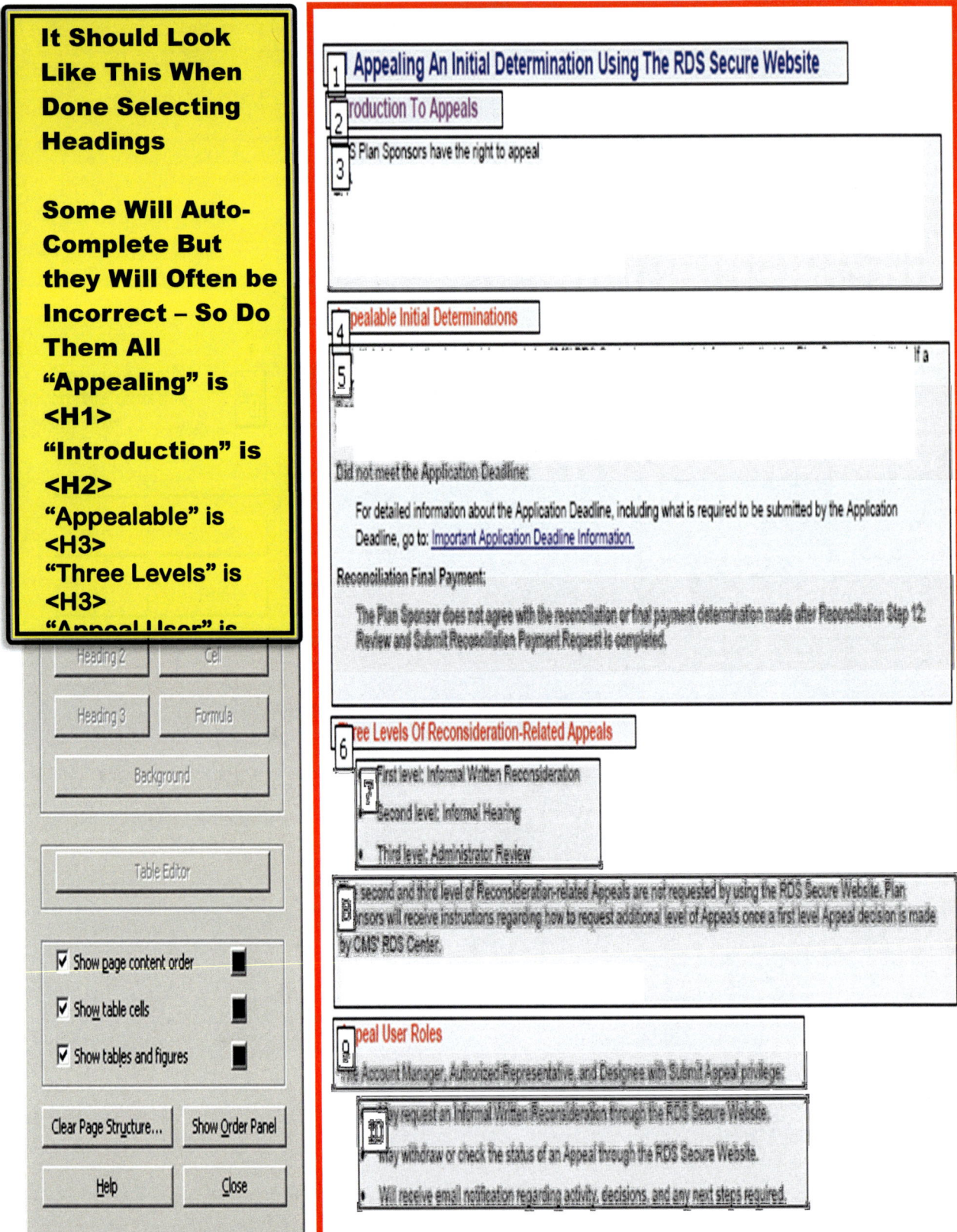

Heading 2   Cell

Heading 3   Formula

Background

Table Editor

☑ Show page content order   ■

☑ Show table cells   ■

☑ Show tables and figures   ■

Clear Page Structure...   Show Order Panel

Help   Close

1 Appealing An Initial Determination Using The RDS Secure Website

2 Introduction To Appeals

3 RDS Plan Sponsors have the right to appeal

4 Appealable Initial Determinations

5 If a

Did not meet the Application Deadline:

For detailed information about the Application Deadline, including what is required to be submitted by the Application Deadline, go to: Important Application Deadline Information.

Reconciliation Final Payment:

The Plan Sponsor does not agree with the reconciliation or final payment determination made after Reconciliation Step 12: Review and Submit Reconciliation Payment Request is completed.

6 Three Levels Of Reconsideration-Related Appeals

7 • First level: Informal Written Reconsideration
• Second level: Informal Hearing
• Third level: Administrator Review

8 The second and third level of Reconsideration-related Appeals are not requested by using the RDS Secure Website. Plan Sponsors will receive instructions regarding how to request additional level of Appeals once a first level Appeal decision is made by CMS' RDS Center.

9 Appeal User Roles

The Account Manager, Authorized Representative, and Designee with Submit Appeal privilege:

10 • May request an Informal Written Reconsideration through the RDS Secure Website.
• May withdraw or check the status of an Appeal through the RDS Secure Website.
• Will receive email notification regarding activity, decisions, and any next steps required.

PDF: 7 Body, Paragraph Text & Headings

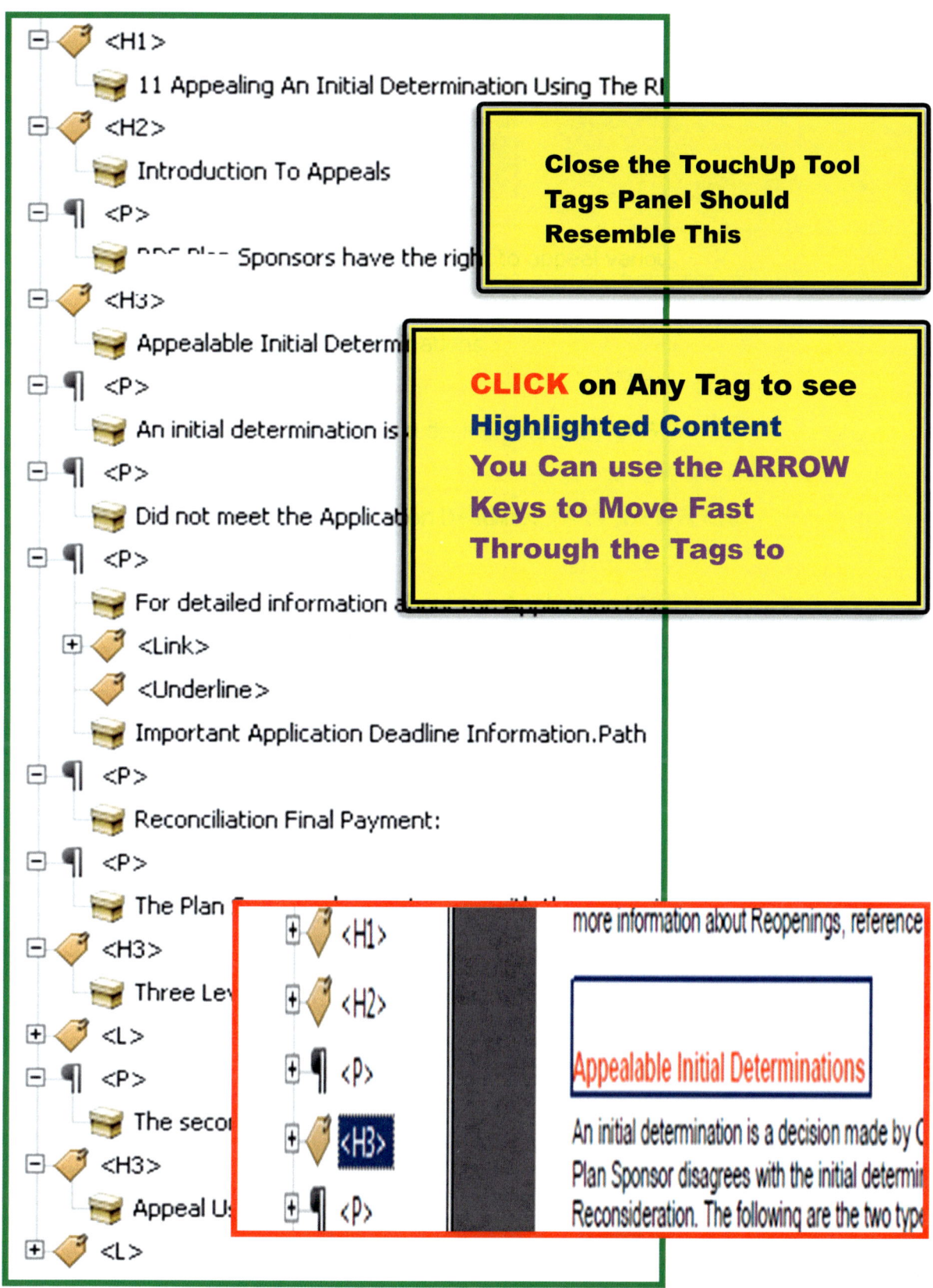

- <H1>
  - 11 Appealing An Initial Determination Using The RI
- <H2>
  - Introduction To Appeals
- <P>
  - PDS Plan Sponsors have the right
- <H3>
  - Appealable Initial Determin
- <P>
  - An initial determination is
- <P>
  - Did not meet the Applicab
- <P>
  - For detailed information a
  - <Link>
  - <Underline>
  - Important Application Deadline Information.Path
- <P>
  - Reconciliation Final Payment:
- <P>
  - The Plan
- <H3>
  - Three Lev
- <L>
- <P>
  - The secon
- <H3>
  - Appeal U
- <L>

Close the TouchUp Tool Tags Panel Should Resemble This

CLICK on Any Tag to see Highlighted Content You Can use the ARROW Keys to Move Fast Through the Tags to

- <H1>
- <H2>
- <P>
- **<H3>**
- <P>

more information about Reopenings, reference

Appealable Initial Determinations

An initial determination is a decision made by C
Plan Sponsor disagrees with the initial determin
Reconsideration. The following are the two type

A Single **CLICK** on the [+] After Collapsing (**CTRL-LEFT-CLICK** Again to First Collapse) Gives Just the Main Tags. Easy to See Issues Rather than Details.

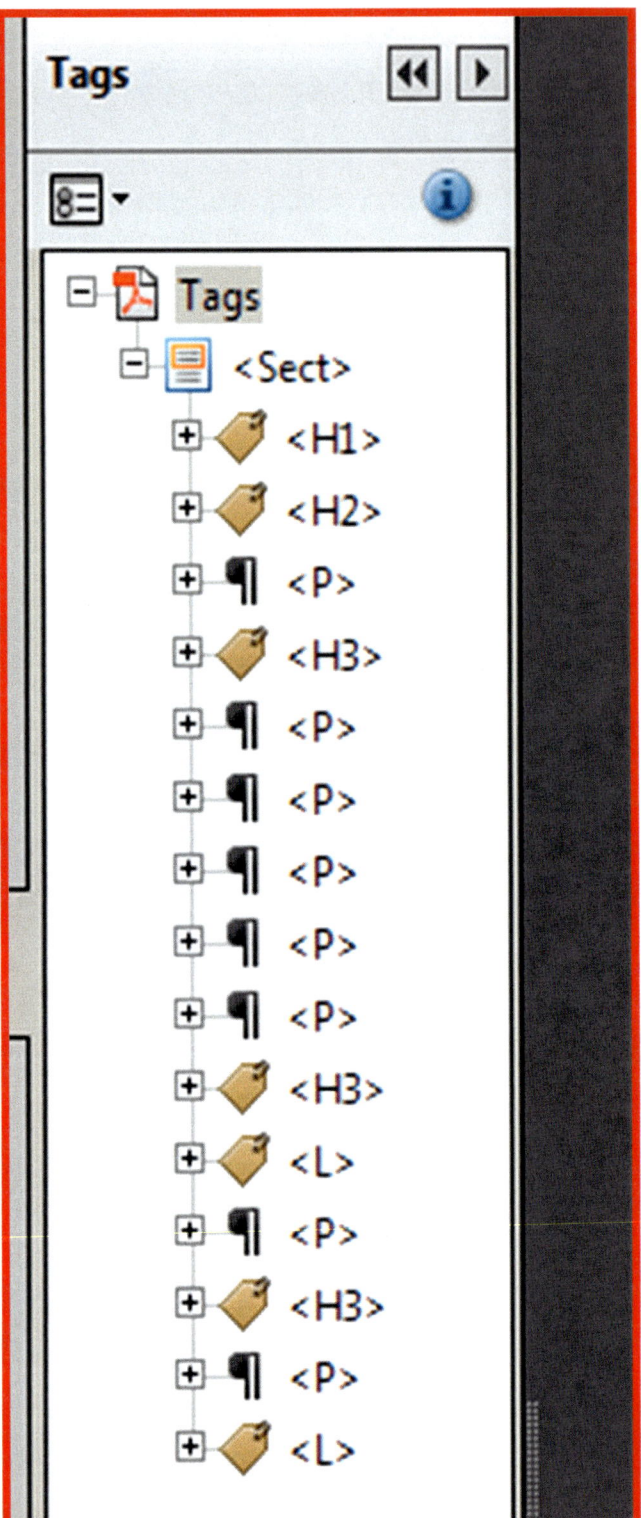

Simply Select the Tag to Edit and CLICK Again to Edit. Type What the Tag Should be.
Can Also Copy Paste When Doing Many.

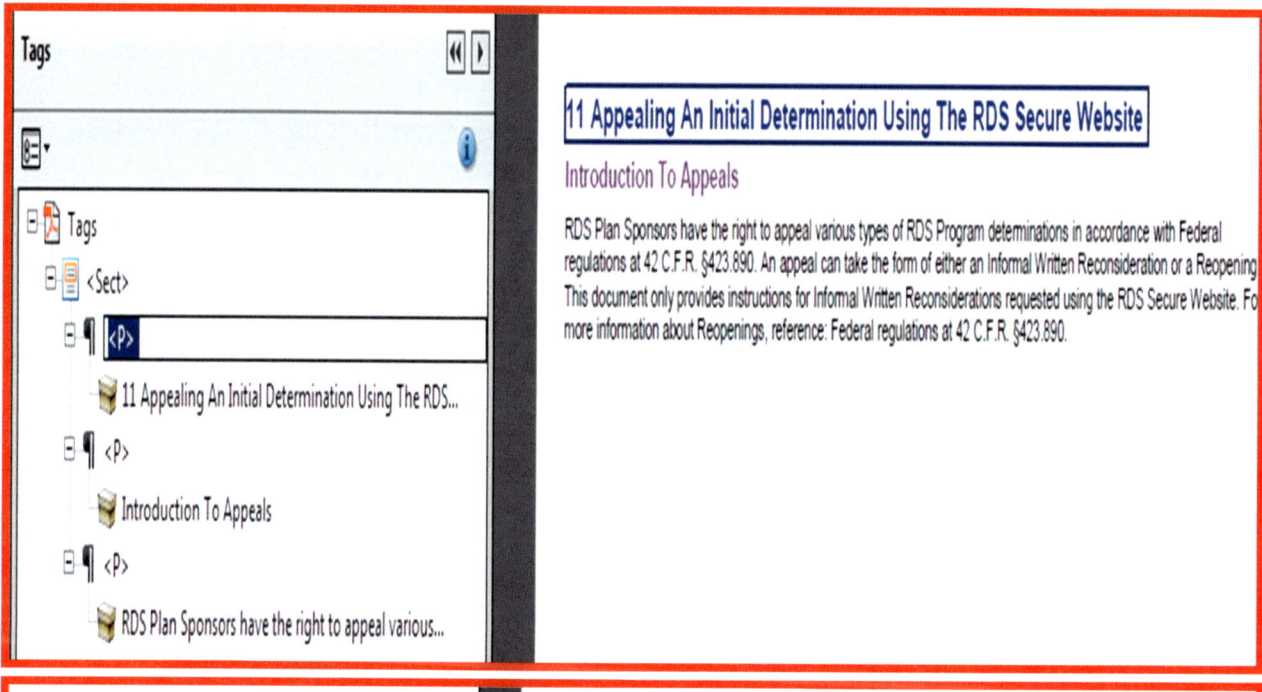

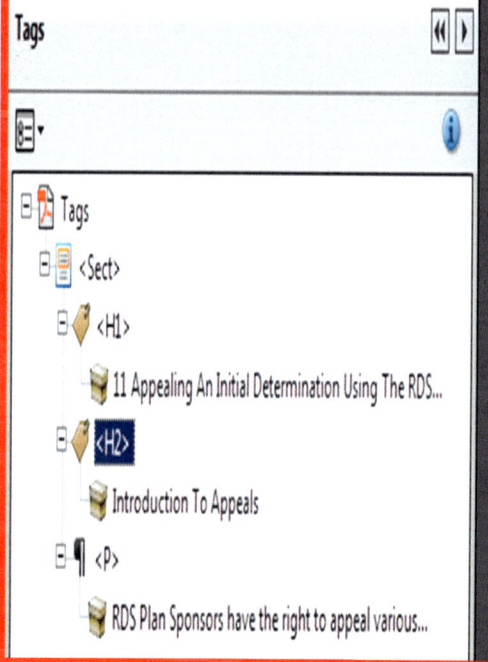

PDF: **2** Separate Text Into Tags

But Direct Tag Edit Does Not Work When Text Combined Into One Tag

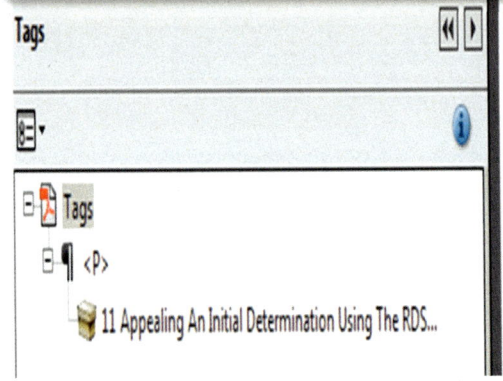

Use The TouchUp Tool to Lasso Each Section and Select What it is (One at a Time), Heading 1, Heading 2 & Text (which is <P>) – This Will Break it Up Into the Correct Sections

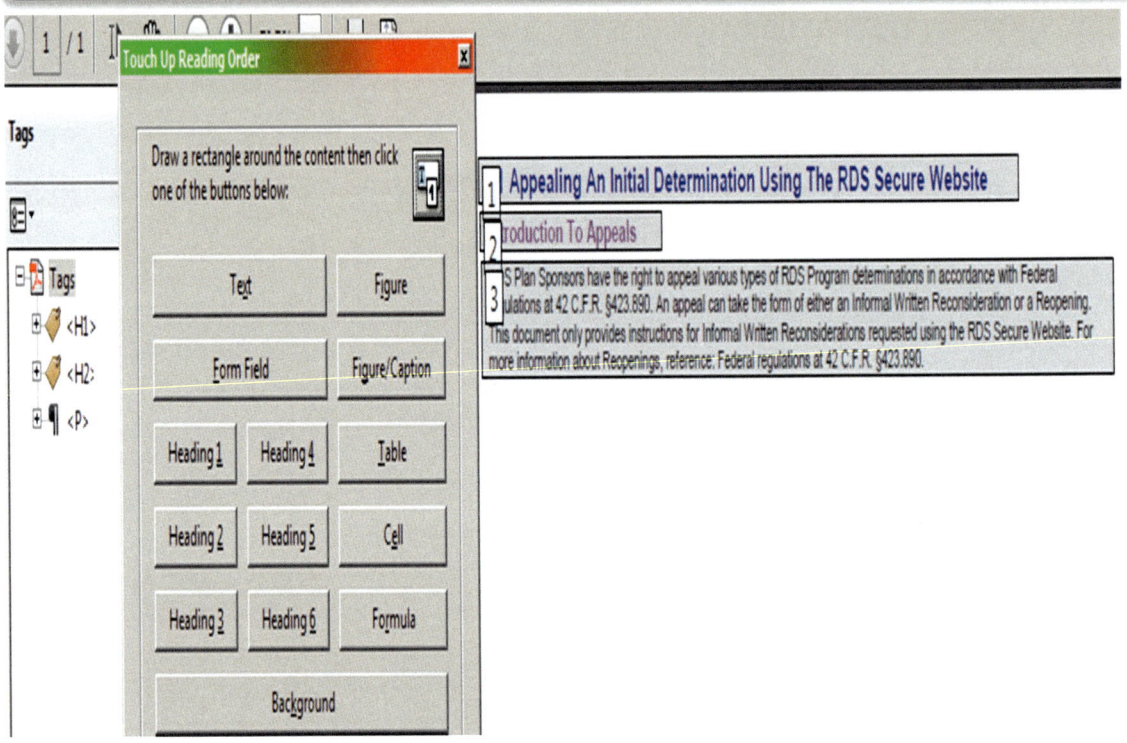

✗ **Acrobat Supports Heading Levels 1-6 on the TouchUp Tool**

✗ **Acrobat Supports Heading Levels 1-6 in the Tags**

✗ **Word Headings Levels 1-9 are Converted Correctly to PDF Bookmarks**

✗ **Word Headings Levels 7-9 are NOT Supported on the Acrobat Page or Tags (Only the Style)**

✗ **HTML Headings Levels 7-9 are NOT Supported**

✗ **The Screen Reader will NOT Read Them (7-9) as Headings and they CANNOT be Used for Screen Reader Navigation (Through the JAWS Headings List Function)**

PDF: 2 Headings Support

Word Document Created with Headings 1 – 9, You Can See How They Are Converted in the PDF Tags, Does Not Look Too Bad. But...

However They Can Actually be Undefined & End Up With an Incorrect Tag or Function & Cause Serious 508 Concerns. Let's See How This Works

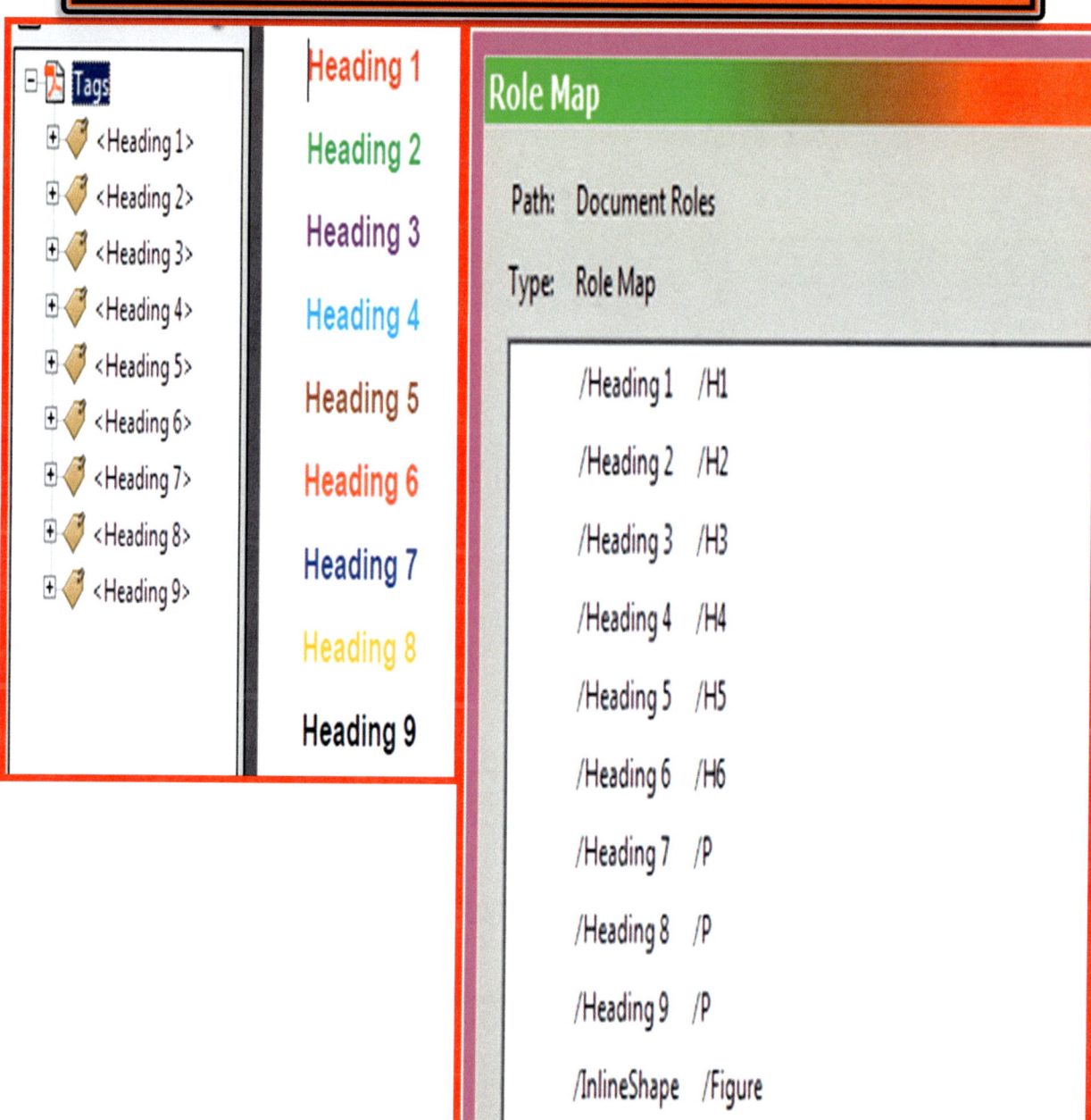

PDF: 1 Read a Role Map

Note: Tags Can be Redefined in Word (Style Modifications) or Other Applications.
You May End Up with Something Like <BodyText>
Which Was Assigned to <P>
You Have to Look at the Acrobat Role Map to See What is Referenced to What.

Select Text "Checking for Reflow" then the Drop Down Menu Icon Under "Tags" [Find Tag From Selection]

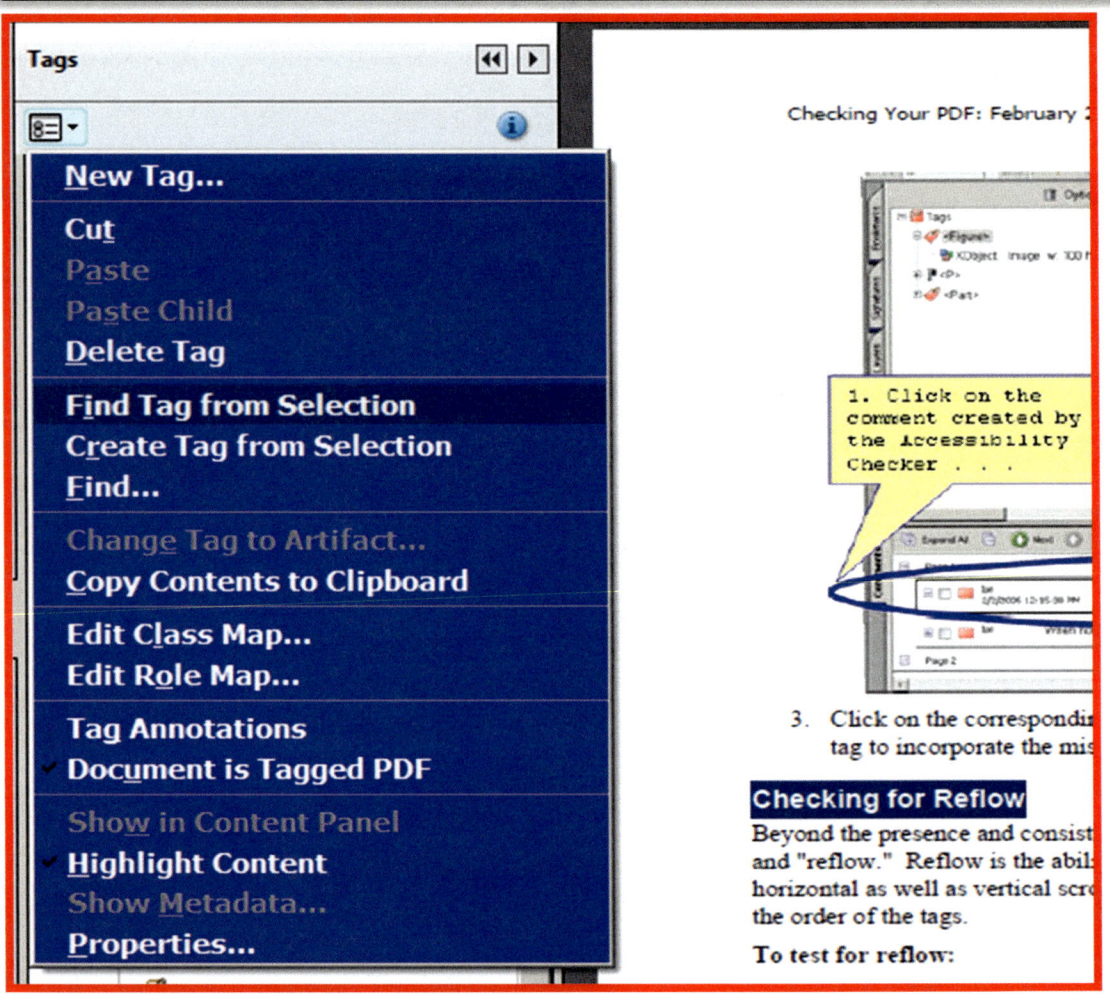

**Note Type of Tag for "Checking for Reflow"
We Will Need to See What
<Heading 2, Heading 3 Char> is Mapped to.**

**Note: Conversion From Word Often Result in
Incorrect Tags, That is Why You Must Check
Them.**

What Do You Think it Should it Be?

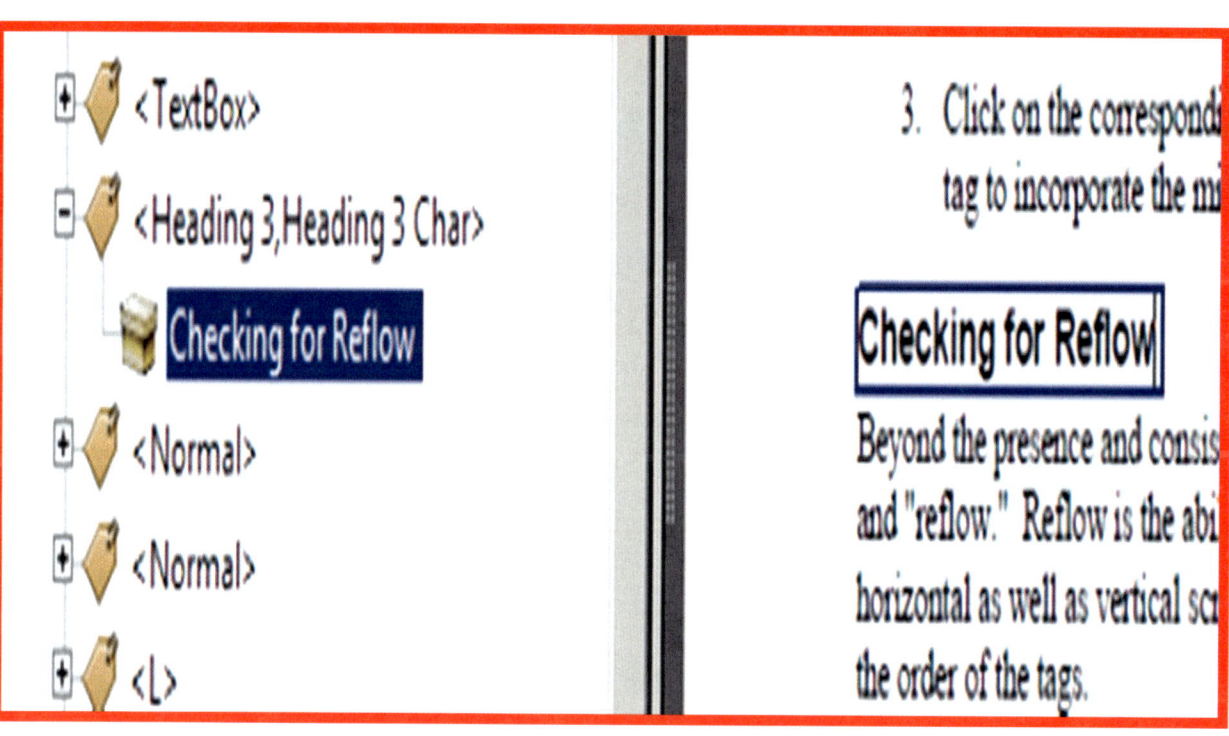

PDF: 3 Read a Role Map

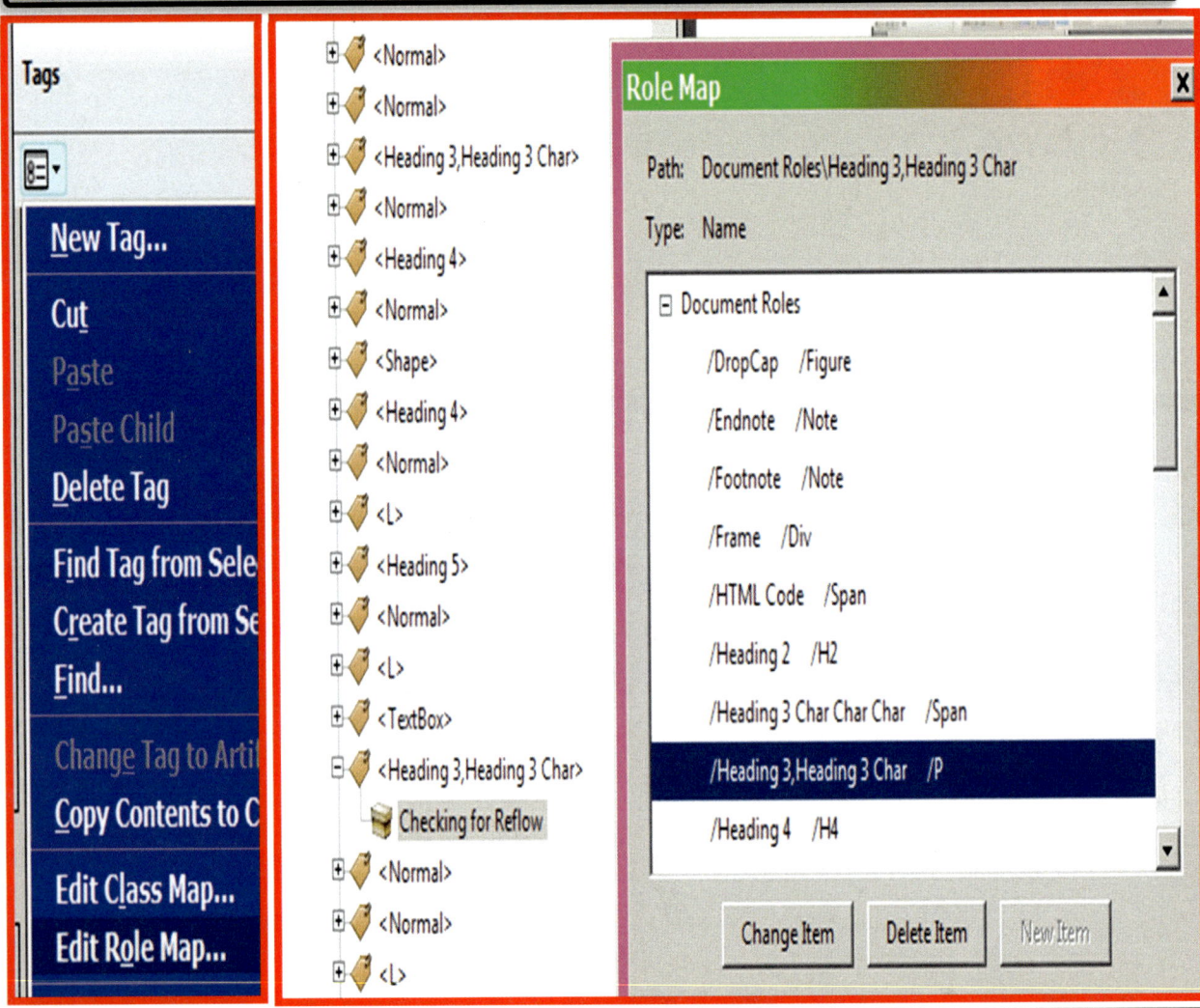

Images Noted as <Figure> in a PDF Can Either be an Intended Image Such as a Screen Shot

OR

Bad Conversions that Captures Artifacts – Image Items Not Meant for Screen Readers: Background Lines or Decoration

✦ Table Lines
✦ Bullets (Usually Kept as Text)
     -Might be Okay if Character in Actual Text or Tag
✦ Section Icons, Lines, Dividers
✦ Control Characters (Carriage Returns, etc...)
✦ Borders of Images
✦ Pieces of Highlighted Areas
✦ Parts of Text Boxes or Framed Areas

These Items Cause No Problem When Joined With an Image With Alt Text, But Sitting By Themselves They Should Not be in the Tags

PDF: 1 Images & Tag Cleaning

**[Tags]
CTRL-
CLICK [+]**

Learn More

At the bottom of the **VA Allergies and Adverse Reactions Summary** and **Details** page is a yellow information box. To get more information on VA Allergies and Adverse Reactions select the link to **Learn More**.

For information about Allergies and Adverse Reactions, Learn more▸

The **Learn More** page gives you a brief summary of what **VA Allergies and Adverse Reactions** is and the benefits of using **VA Allergies and Adverse Reactions**.

If you select **Learn More**, this is what you will see.

To leave the **Learn More** page, select the **Close** button at the bottom of the page.

PDF: 2 Images & Tag Cleaning

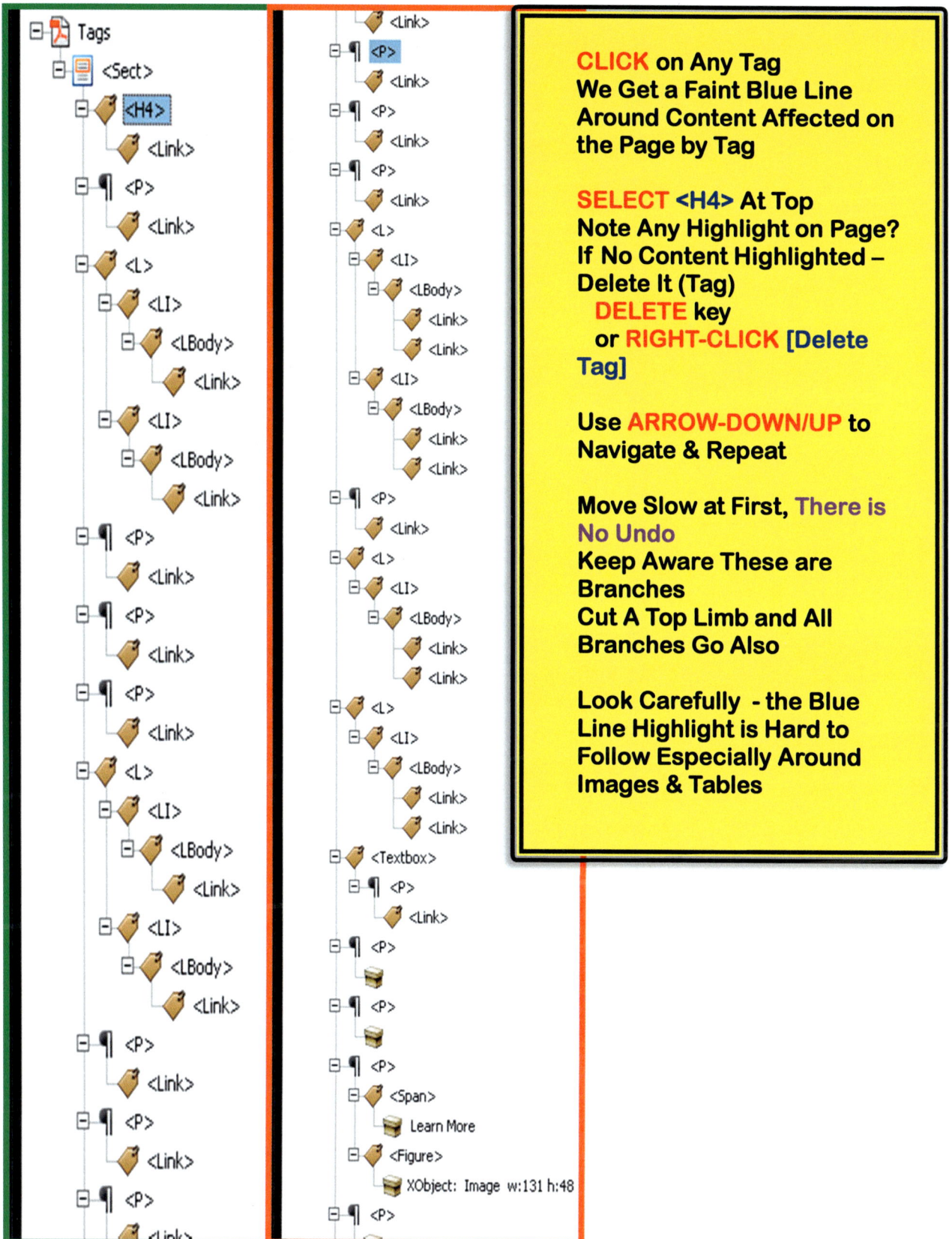

CLICK on Any Tag
We Get a Faint Blue Line Around Content Affected on the Page by Tag

SELECT <H4> At Top
Note Any Highlight on Page?
If No Content Highlighted – Delete It (Tag)
  DELETE key
  or **RIGHT-CLICK** [Delete Tag]

Use **ARROW-DOWN/UP** to Navigate & Repeat

Move Slow at First, There is No Undo
Keep Aware These are Branches
Cut A Top Limb and All Branches Go Also

Look Carefully - the Blue Line Highlight is Hard to Follow Especially Around Images & Tables

PDF: 3 Images & Tag Cleaning

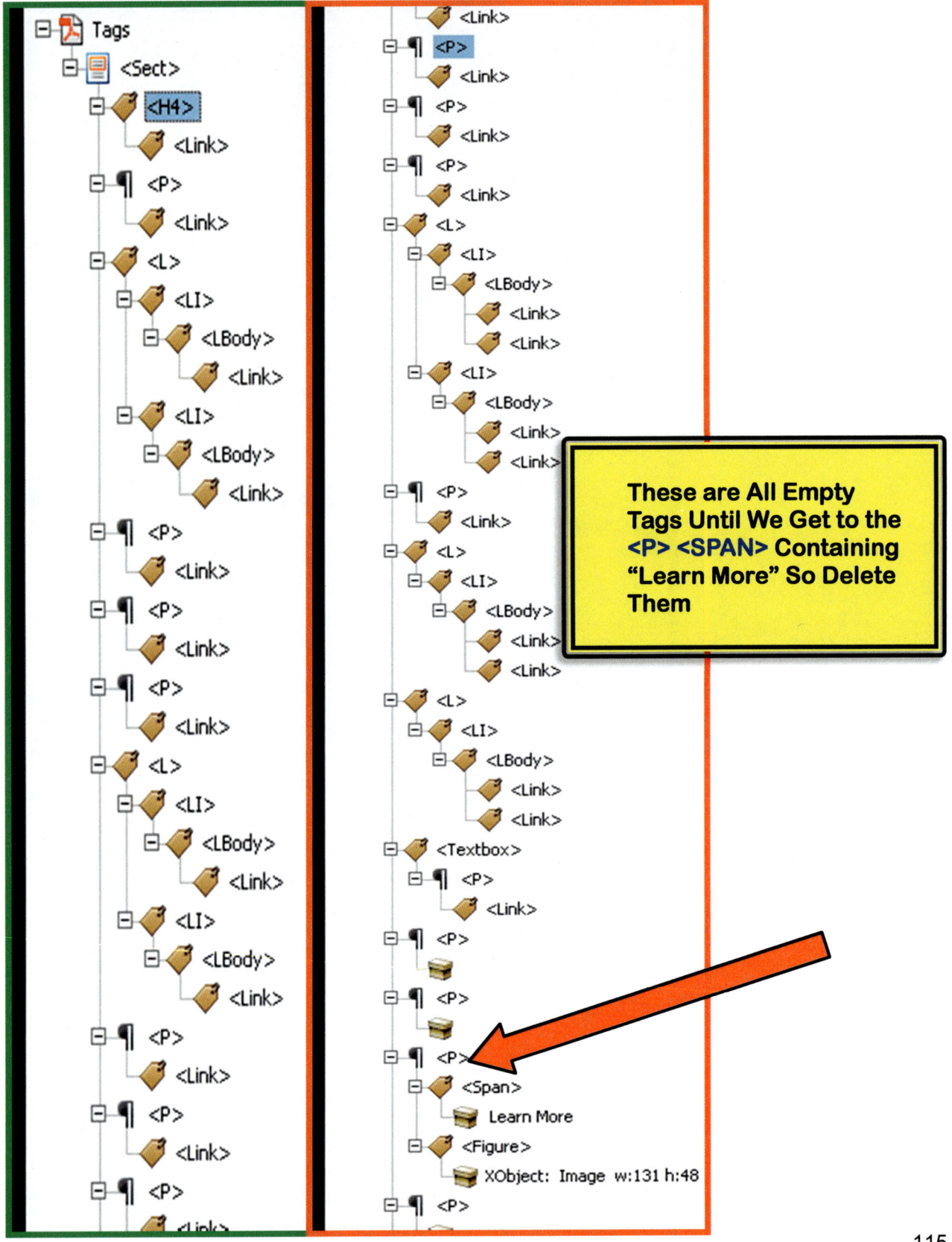

These are All Empty Tags Until We Get to the **<P> <SPAN>** Containing "Learn More" So Delete Them

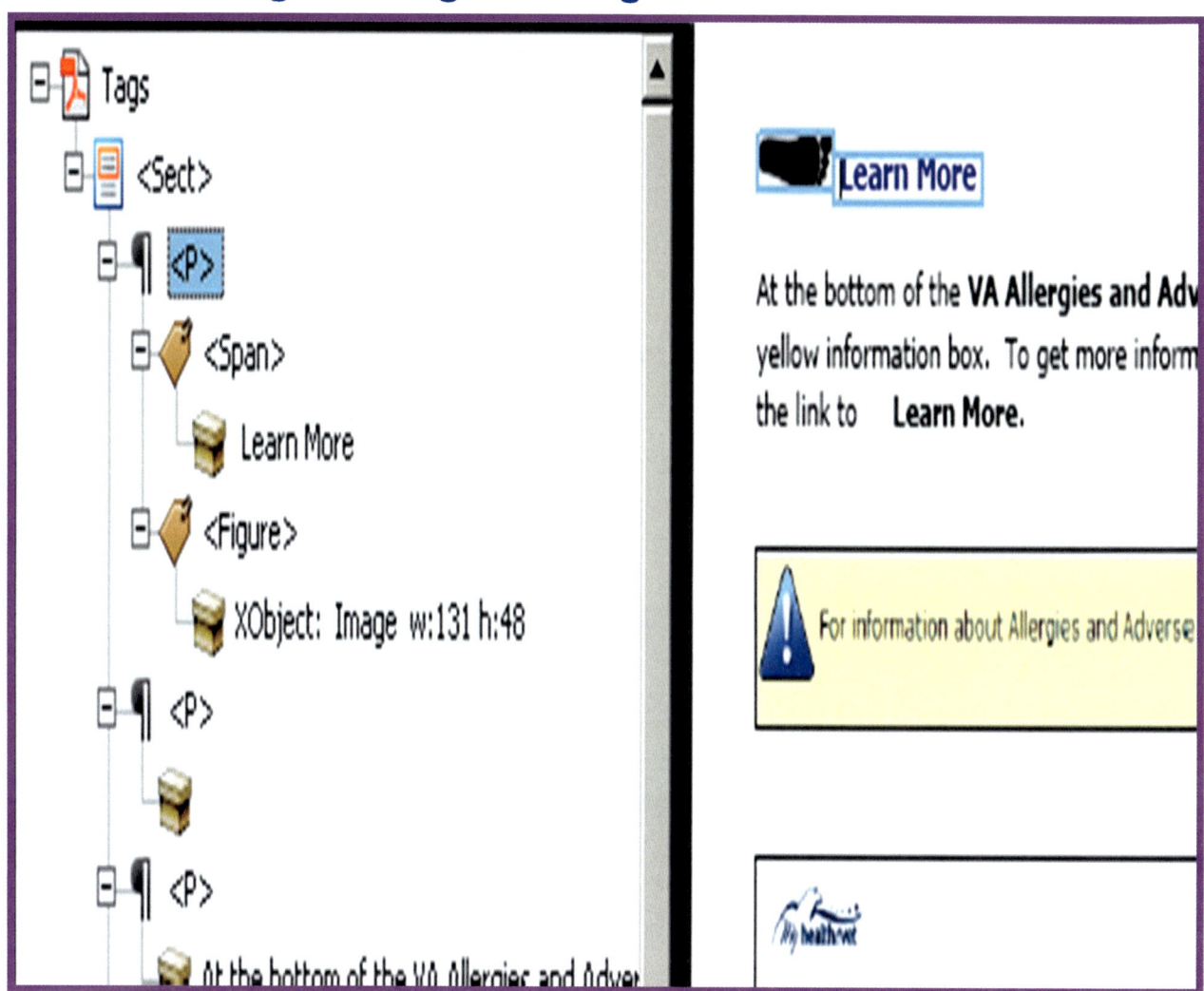

At This Point All the Bad Tags Should be Gone and Your Tags Should Look Like This.

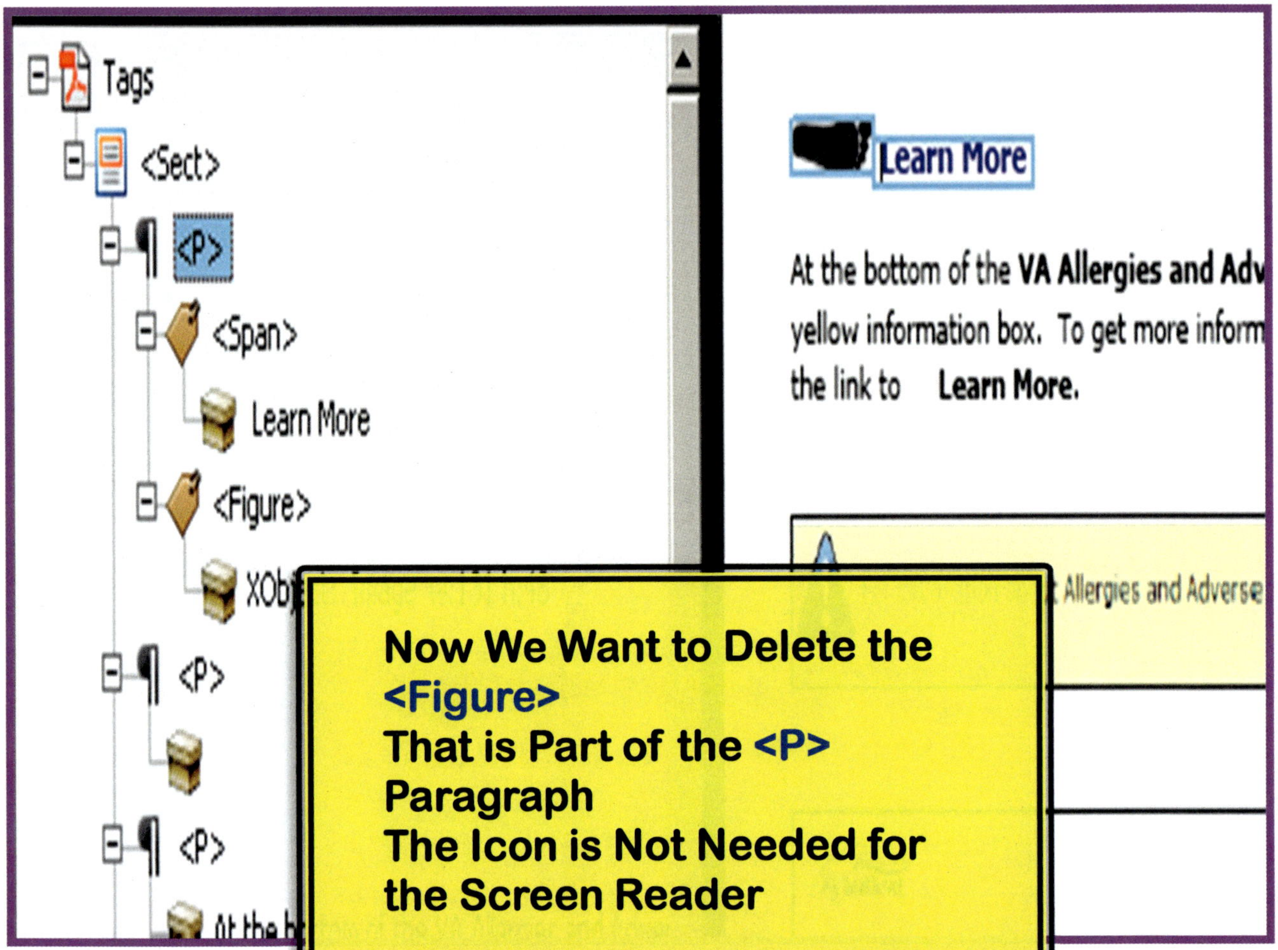

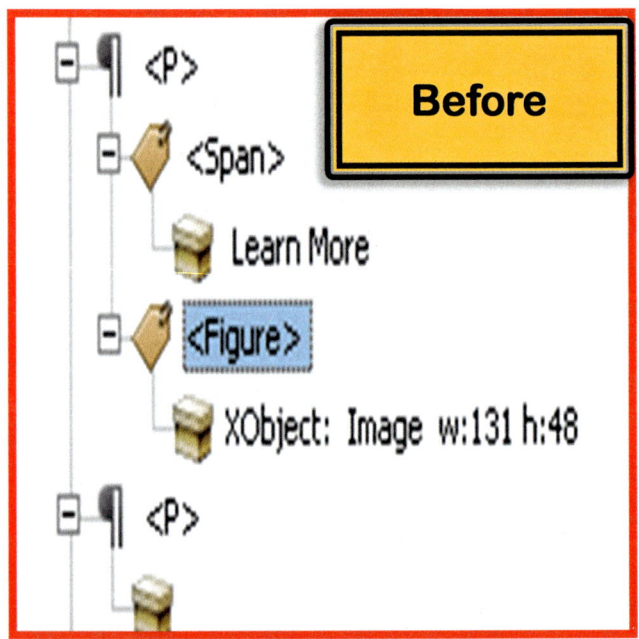

Tags
<Sect>
<P>
<Span>
Learn More
<Figure>
<P>
<P>
Learn More
At the bottom of the VA Allergies and Adv
yellow information box. To get more inform
the link to Learn More.

Now We Want to Delete the <Figure>
That is Part of the <P> Paragraph
The Icon is Not Needed for the Screen Reader

Before
<P>
<Span>
Learn More
<Figure>
XObject: Image w:131 h:48
<P>

After
<P>
<Span>
Learn More
<P>

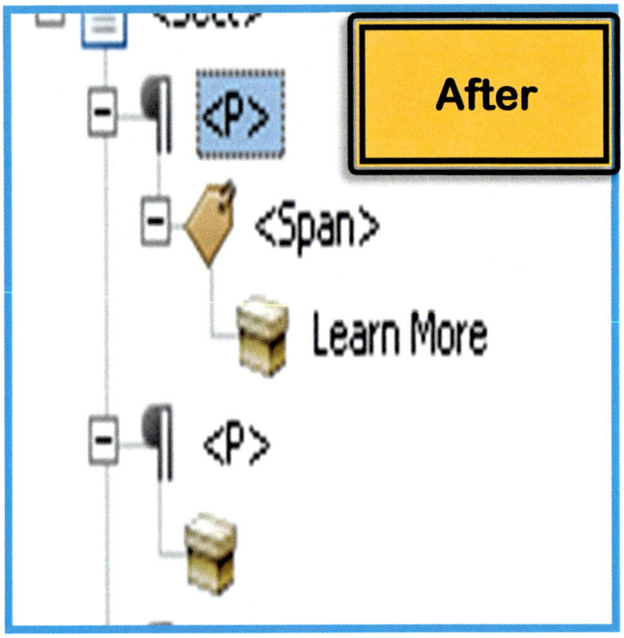

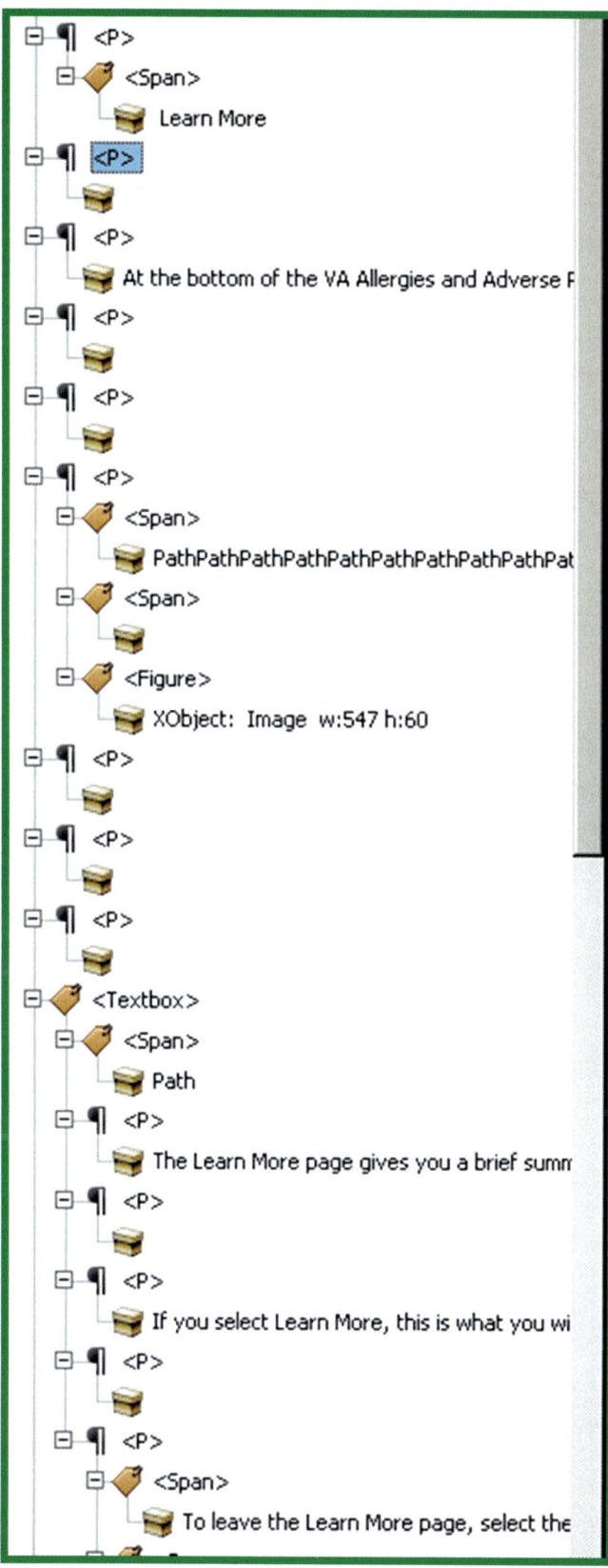

Continue Down and DELETE All Empty Tags
Leave the Other <Figure> They are Good
We Will Go Back and Correct Other Issues

Try to Stay on the Lower Branches

When Doing a Lot of This:
Save Many Different Named Versions of the Document

PDF: 7 Images & Tag Cleaning

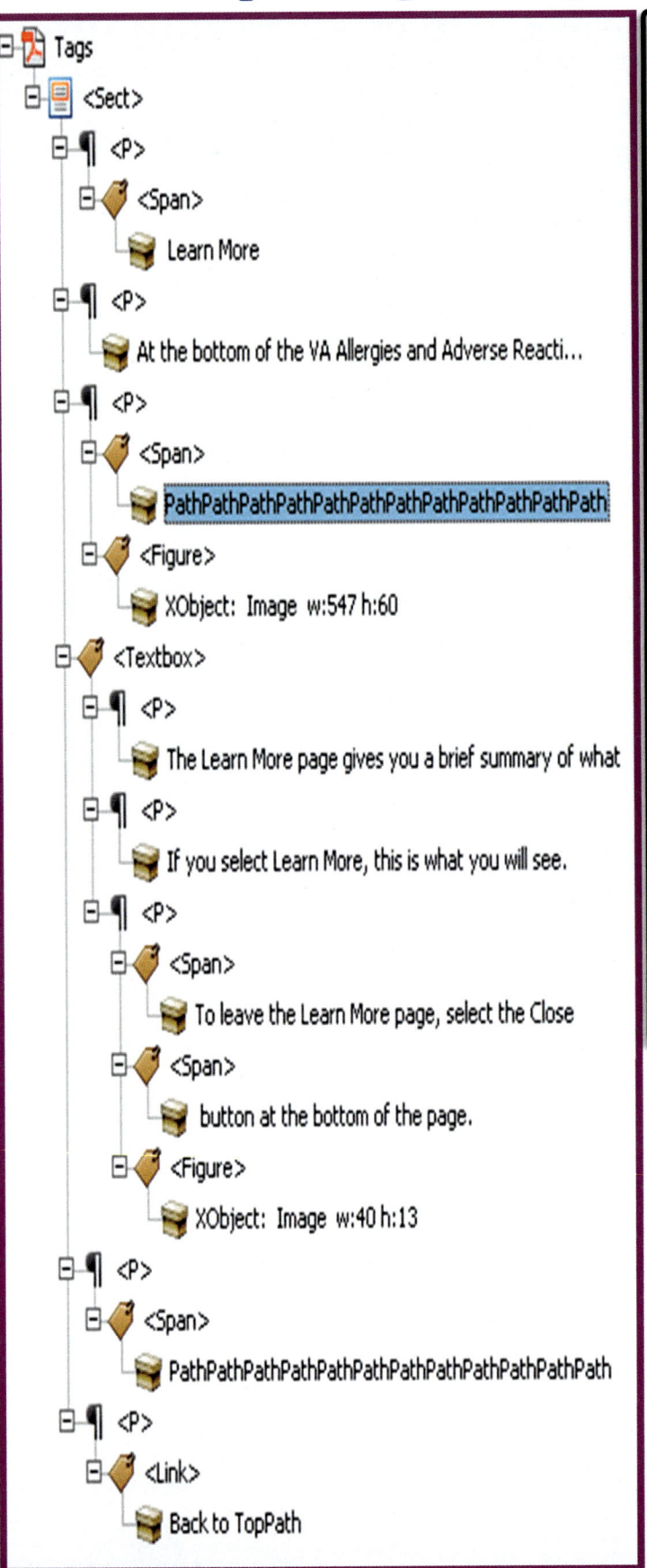

The Entire Tag List Should Look Like This Now

SELECT the PathPathPath…
Then SELECT the Xobject: Image w:547
OBSERVE Only What is Highlighted

They Appear to be the Same Image
BUT PathPathPath…
Is Just The Lines of the Box Around the Image (Okay When Inside the Image)

DELETE the <Span> Above the PathPathPath… Or Else You Leave an Empty <Span>

When You Do That on the One Below, it Will Leave an Empty <P> So DELETE that Also

PDF: Images & Tag Cleaning Good Tags

The Line Image "Path" is Embedded with the Content and Not on its Own, So the Screen Reader Only Reads the Text

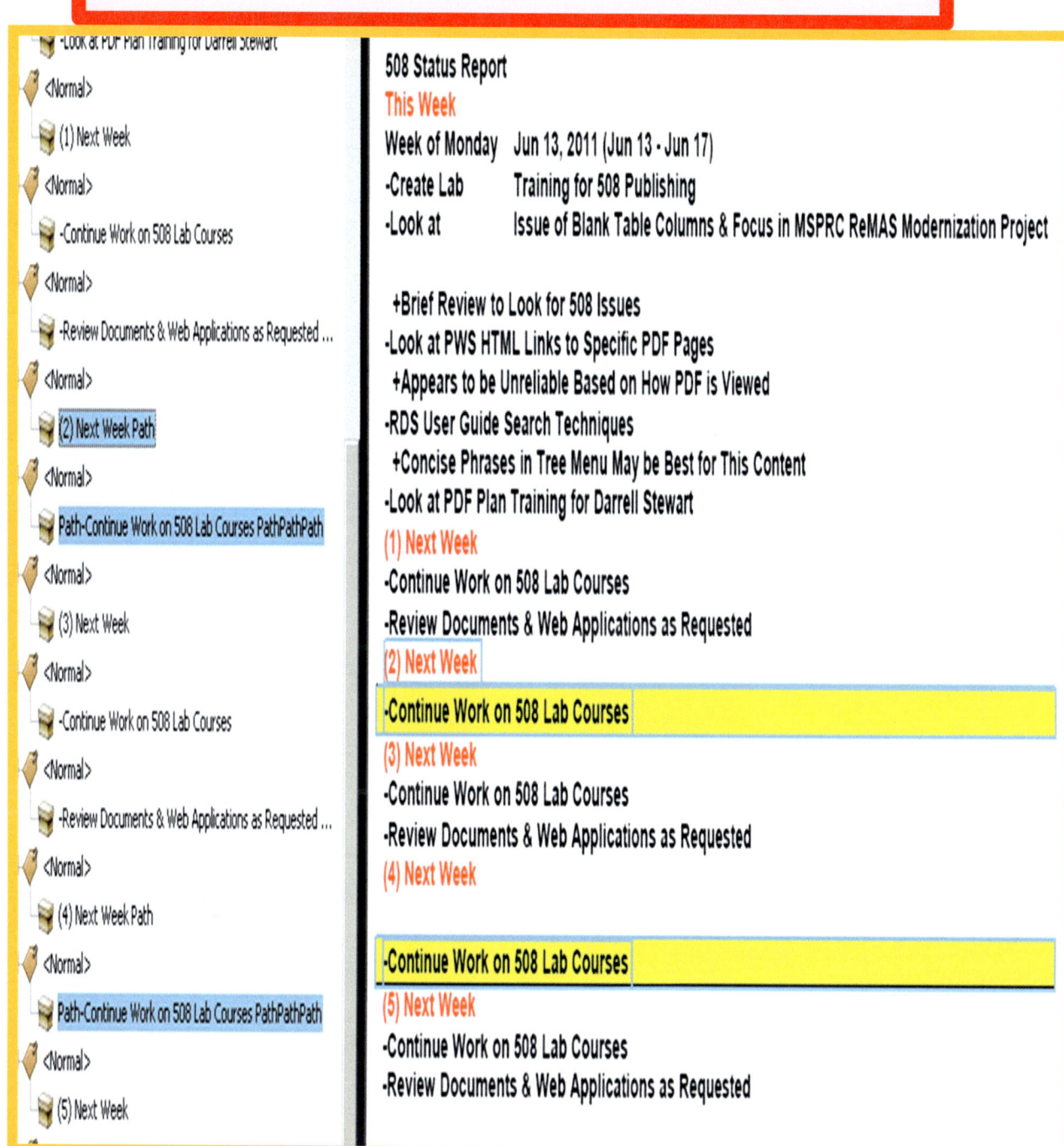

PDF: 1 Tag Cleaning Alternate Method

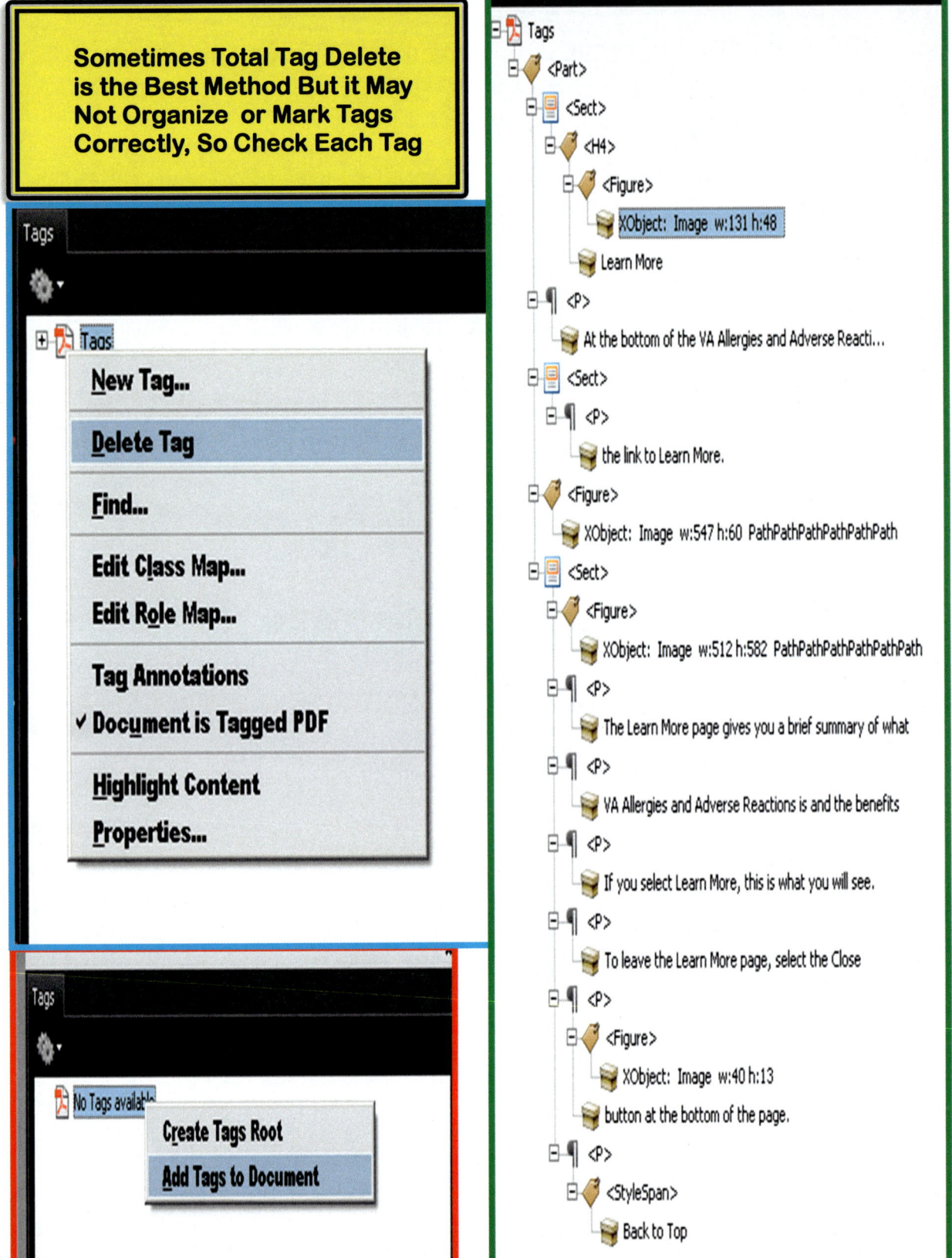

Sometimes Total Tag Delete is the Best Method But it May Not Organize or Mark Tags Correctly, So Check Each Tag

Tags

New Tag...

Delete Tag

Find...

Edit Class Map...

Edit Role Map...

Tag Annotations

✓ Document is Tagged PDF

Highlight Content

Properties...

Tags

No Tags available

Create Tags Root

Add Tags to Document

Tags
- ⊟ Tags
  - ⊟ <Part>
    - ⊟ <Sect>
      - ⊟ <H4>
        - ⊟ <Figure>
          - XObject: Image w:131 h:48
        - Learn More
    - ⊟ <P>
      - At the bottom of the VA Allergies and Adverse Reacti...
    - ⊟ <Sect>
      - ⊟ <P>
        - the link to Learn More.
    - ⊟ <Figure>
      - XObject: Image w:547 h:60 PathPathPathPathPathPath
    - ⊟ <Sect>
      - ⊟ <Figure>
        - XObject: Image w:512 h:582 PathPathPathPathPathPath
      - ⊟ <P>
        - The Learn More page gives you a brief summary of what
      - ⊟ <P>
        - VA Allergies and Adverse Reactions is and the benefits
      - ⊟ <P>
        - If you select Learn More, this is what you will see.
      - ⊟ <P>
        - To leave the Learn More page, select the Close
      - ⊟ <P>
        - ⊟ <Figure>
          - XObject: Image w:40 h:13
        - button at the bottom of the page.
      - ⊟ <P>
        - ⊟ <StyleSpan>
          - Back to Top

PDF: 2 Tag Cleaning Alternate Method

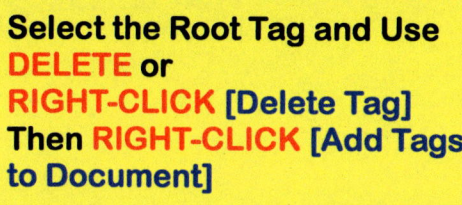

Select the Root Tag and Use DELETE or RIGHT-CLICK [Delete Tag] Then RIGHT-CLICK [Add Tags to Document]

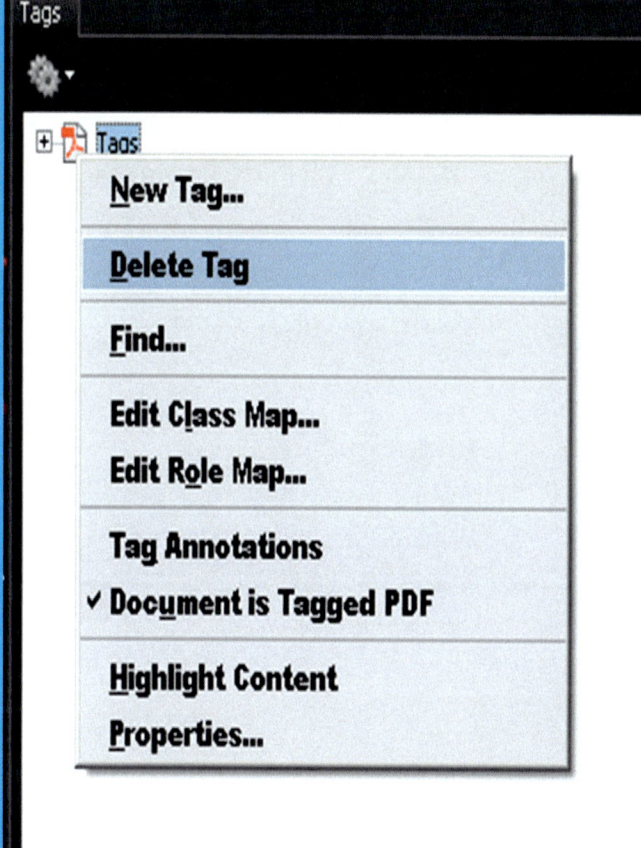

Tags

- Tags
  - New Tag...
  - **Delete Tag**
  - Find...
  - Edit Class Map...
  - Edit Role Map...
  - Tag Annotations
  - ✓ Document is Tagged PDF
  - Highlight Content
  - Properties...

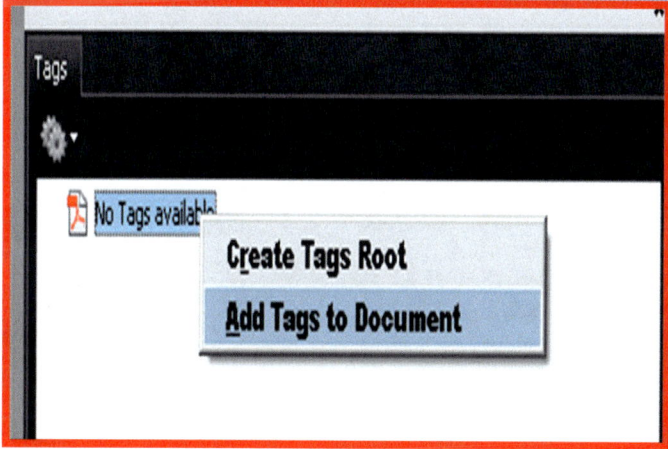

Tags

- No Tags available
  - Create Tags Root
  - **Add Tags to Document**

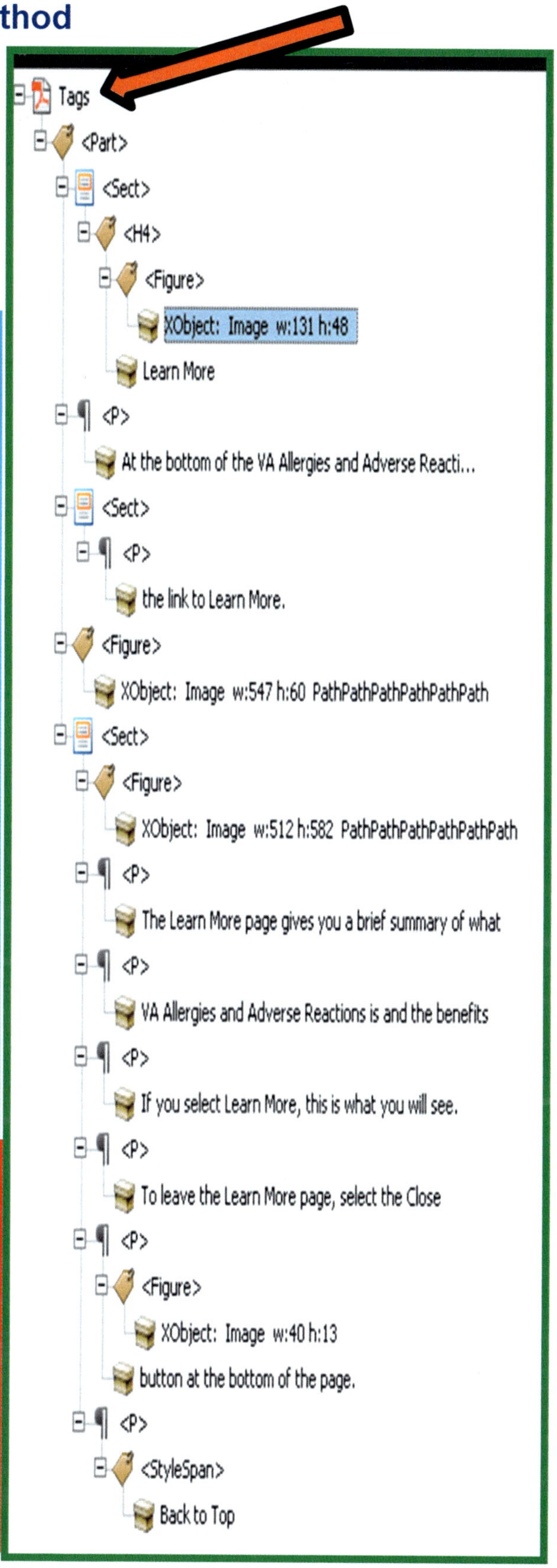

Tags
- Tags
  - `<Part>`
    - `<Sect>`
      - `<H4>`
        - `<Figure>`
          - XObject: Image w:131 h:48
        - Learn More
      - `<P>`
        - At the bottom of the VA Allergies and Adverse Reacti...
    - `<Sect>`
      - `<P>`
        - the link to Learn More.
    - `<Figure>`
      - XObject: Image w:547 h:60 PathPathPathPathPathPath
    - `<Sect>`
      - `<Figure>`
        - XObject: Image w:512 h:582 PathPathPathPathPathPath
      - `<P>`
        - The Learn More page gives you a brief summary of what
      - `<P>`
        - VA Allergies and Adverse Reactions is and the benefits
      - `<P>`
        - If you select Learn More, this is what you will see.
      - `<P>`
        - To leave the Learn More page, select the Close
      - `<P>`
        - `<Figure>`
          - XObject: Image w:40 h:13
        - button at the bottom of the page.
      - `<P>`
        - `<StyleSpan>`
          - Back to Top

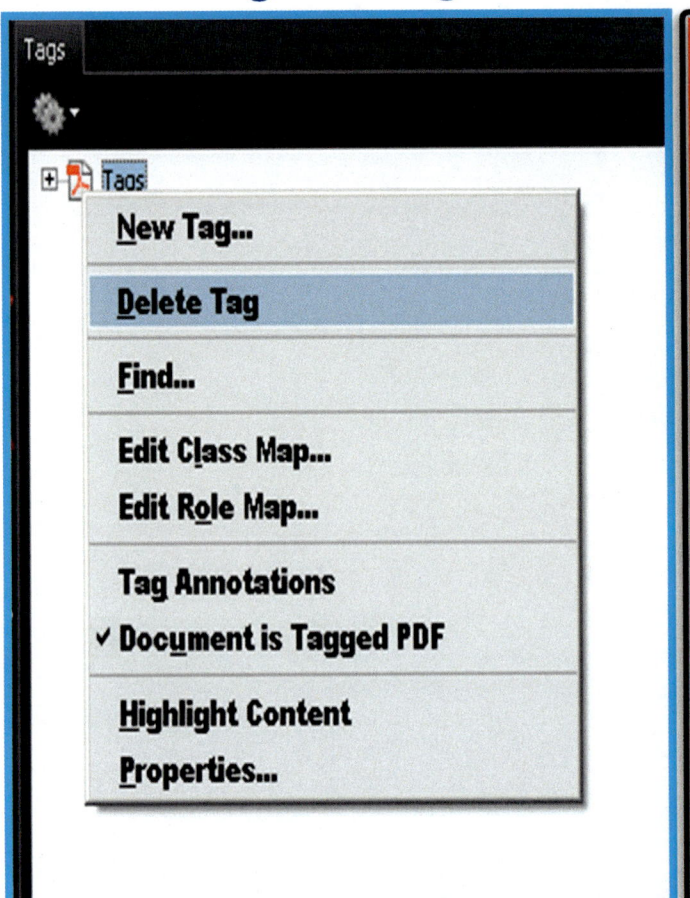

BEFORE You Do Any Major Work on a Large Number of Messy Tags Try This Option First – Deleting All Tags and Then Adding Tags, It May Fix Large Areas for You and Save Time Save a Different Version

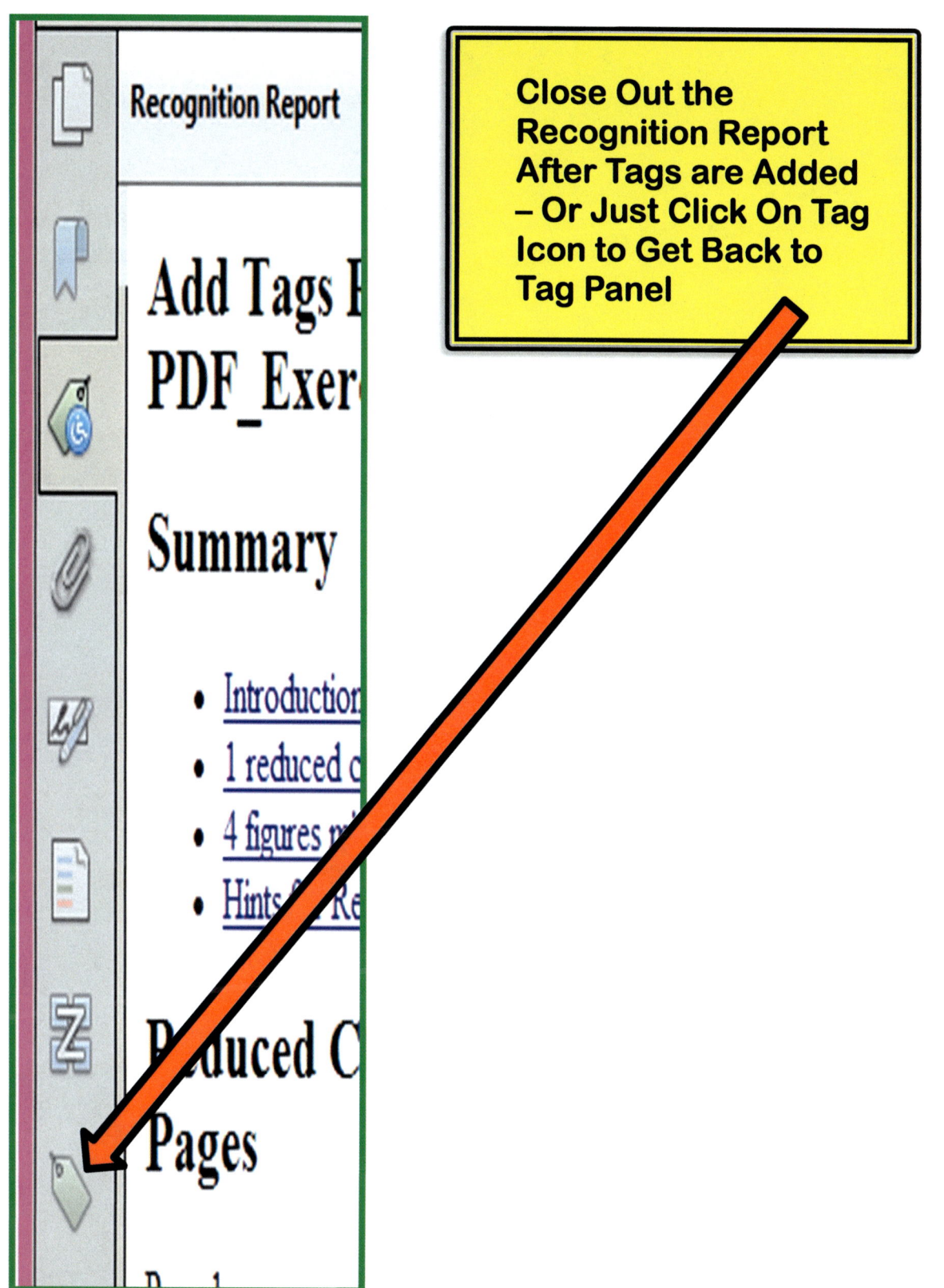

Close Out the Recognition Report After Tags are Added – Or Just Click On Tag Icon to Get Back to Tag Panel

PDF: 5 Tag Cleaning Alternate Method

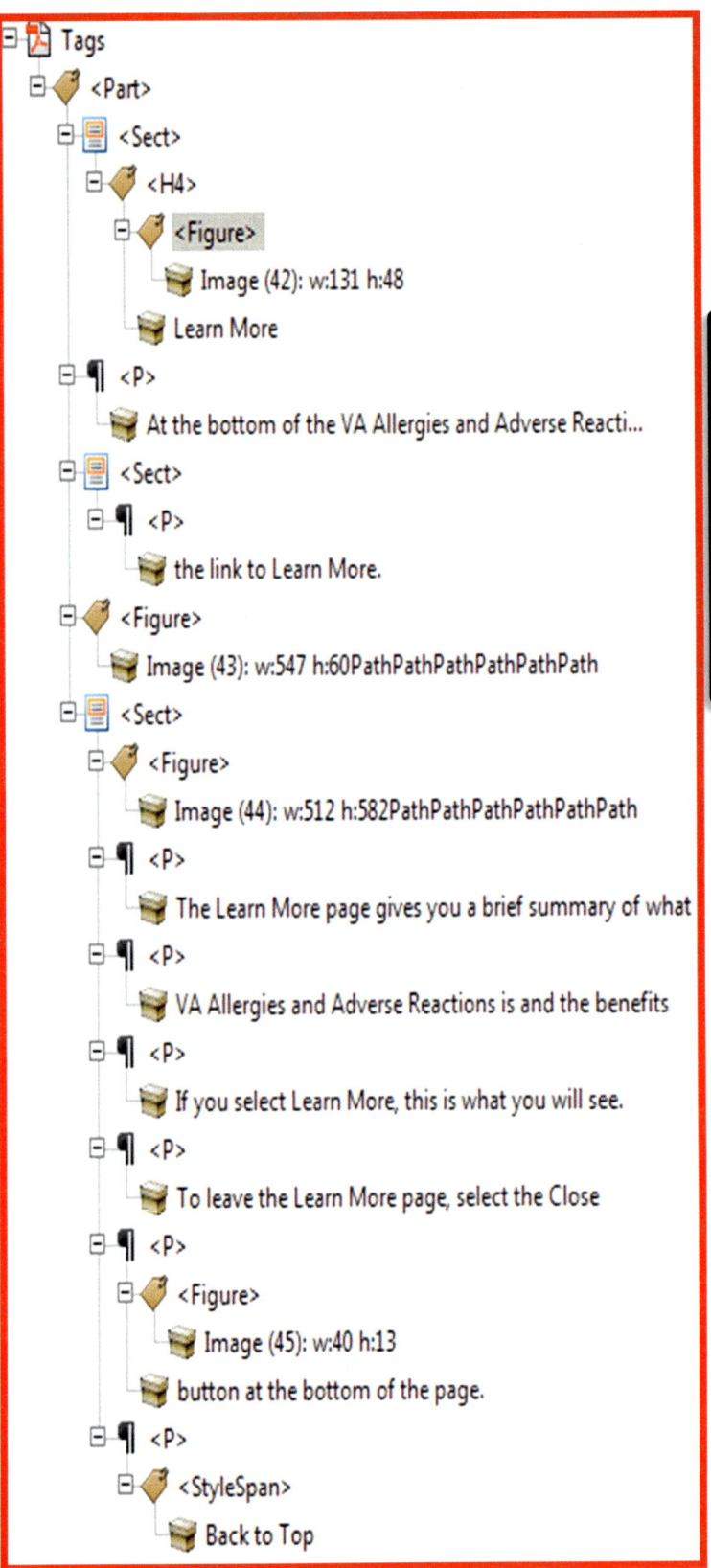

[Tags]
CTRL-CLICK
[+]
Should Look
Like This Now

PDF: **6** Tag Cleaning Alternate Method

We Can Remove The First Figure , The Foot Icon

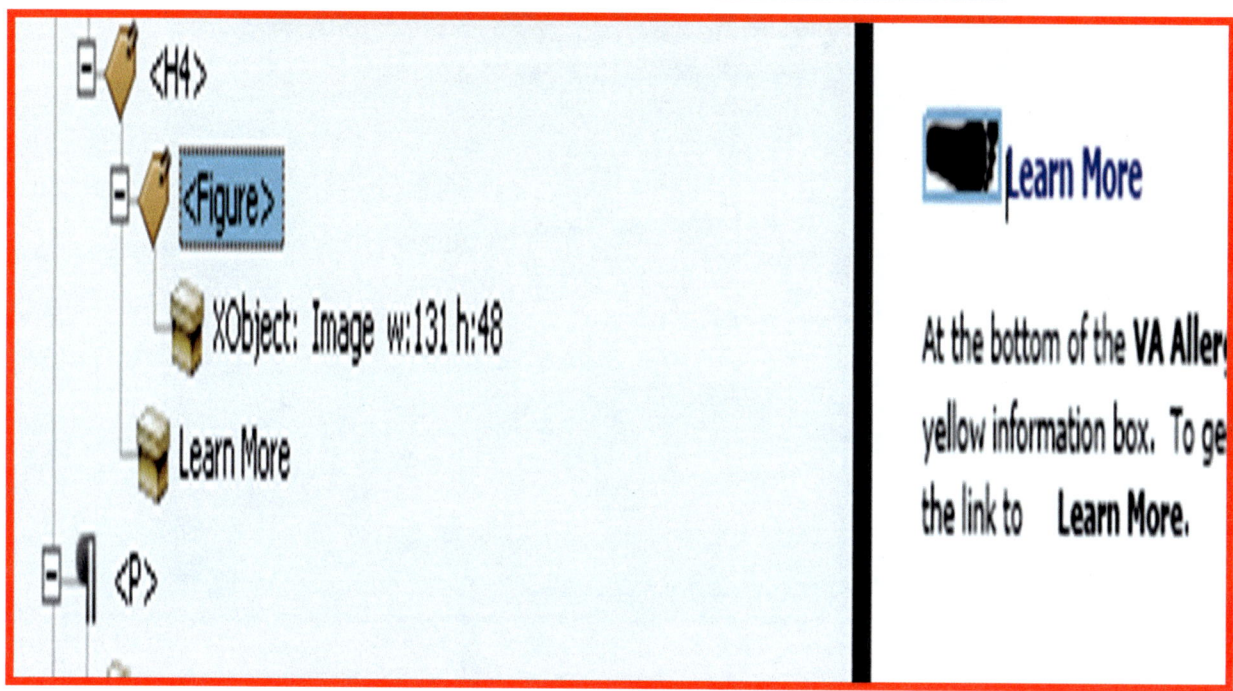

You Can See Part of the First Paragraph Was Moved to Create Another Section <Sect>

This Particular Separation Does Not Affect the Screen Reader as They are Both <P> Paragraph Body Text Markup
BUT This May Make Complex Documents Hard to Manage
AND Some Text Could Be Incorrectly IN or Out of a List or Other Formatting

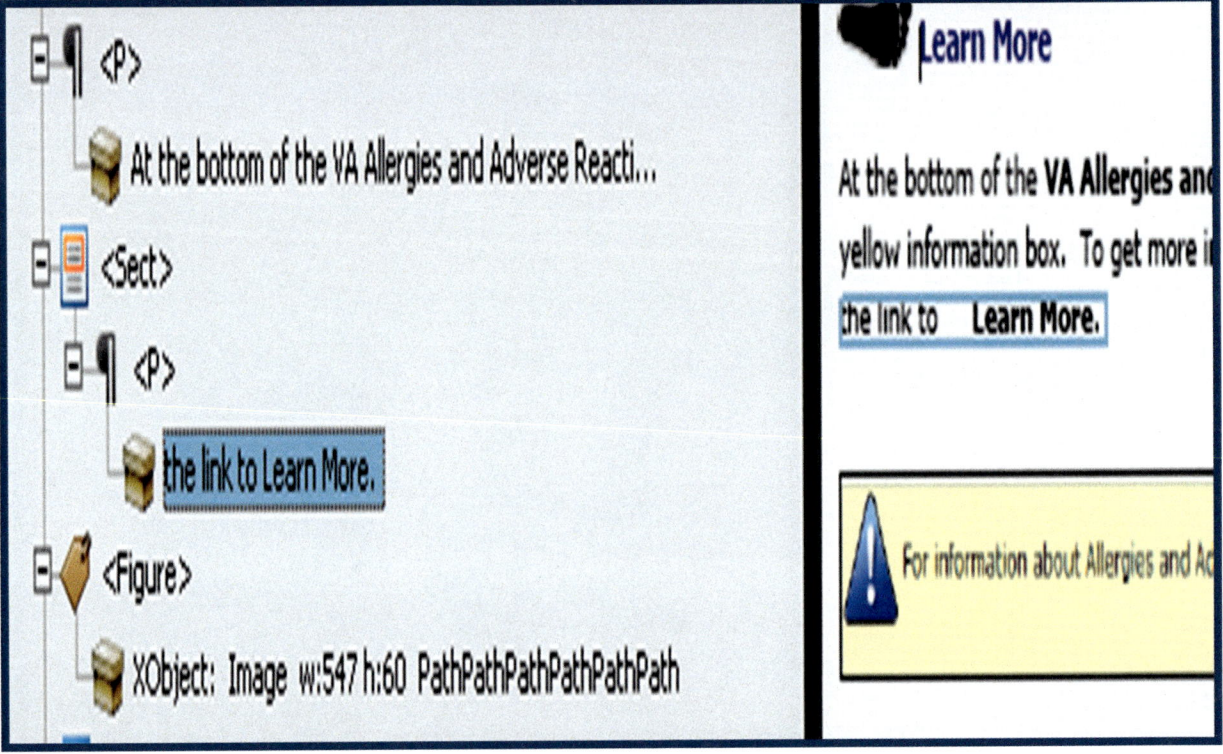

PDF: 8 Tag Cleaning Alternate Method

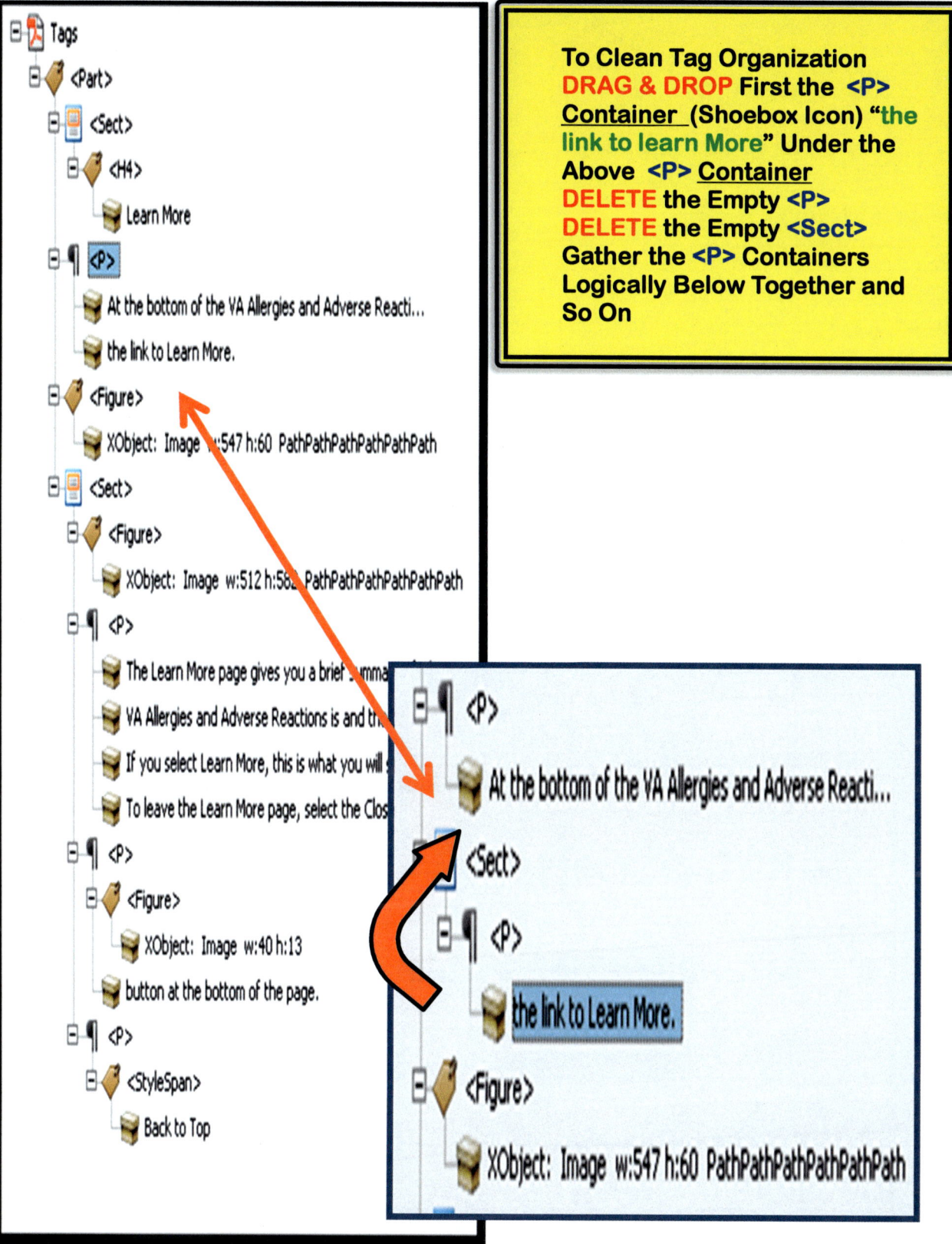

To Clean Tag Organization DRAG & DROP First the <P> Container (Shoebox Icon) "the link to learn More" Under the Above <P> Container DELETE the Empty <P> DELETE the Empty <Sect> Gather the <P> Containers Logically Below Together and So On

PDF: Document Properties

Be Careful What You Put into the Document Properties As Google and other Search Engines Will Use it

Gordon - I made a few additions to your report

Review the implementation of any new **SSA** initiatives such as QDD, ... but it makes it difficult for examiners to meet Incentive **Plan** criteria. .... The Disability Case Processing System (**DCPS**) continues to move along. The vendor who will build the new system will be **Lockheed** Martin. At this time, **SSA projects** implementing ...

www.usor.utah.gov/.../Annual%20Report%20DDS%20Advisory%20Council%202011.pdf - Similar

General+dynamics Senior director profiles |LinkedIn

Specific **Project** Experience Highlights: ARMY IMOD, Army TAC-SWA, Census ... NOAA ESPDS, **SSA DCPS**, SEC ISS, State of Texas-DCS, UK MOD Training • Over ... Title: Sr. Director, Strategic **Planning** and Business Development at GDIT ...

www.linkedin.com/title/senior+director/at-general+dynamics/ - Cached - Similar

1 2 3 4 5 6 7 8 9 10   **Next**

Document Properties ✕

Description | Security | Fonts | Initial View | Custom | Advanced

Description

File: Annual%20Report%20DDS%20Advisory%20Council%202011[1].pdf

Title: Gordon - I made a few additions to your report

Author: gordon

Subject:

Keywords:

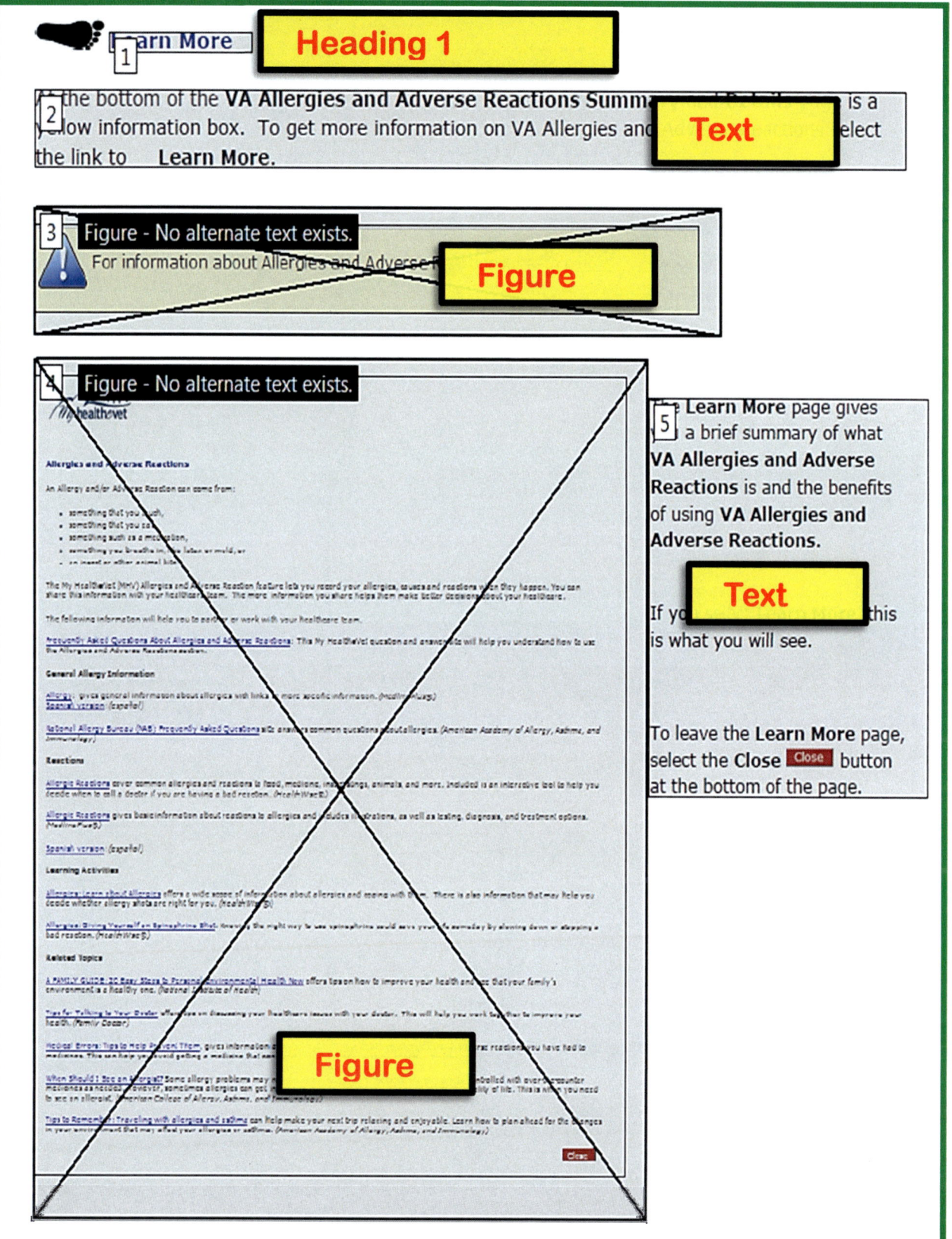

Heading 1

1 Learn More

2 At the bottom of the **VA Allergies and Adverse Reactions Summary** ... is a yellow information box. To get more information on VA Allergies and ... select the link to **Learn More**.

Text

3 Figure - No alternate text exists.
For information about Allergies and Adverse ...

Figure

4 Figure - No alternate text exists.

Figure

5 The **Learn More** page gives a brief summary of what **VA Allergies and Adverse Reactions** is and the benefits of using **VA Allergies and Adverse Reactions**.

If yo... this is what you will see.

To leave the **Learn More** page, select the **Close** Close button at the bottom of the page.

Text

PDF: 2 Tag Cleaning TouchUp

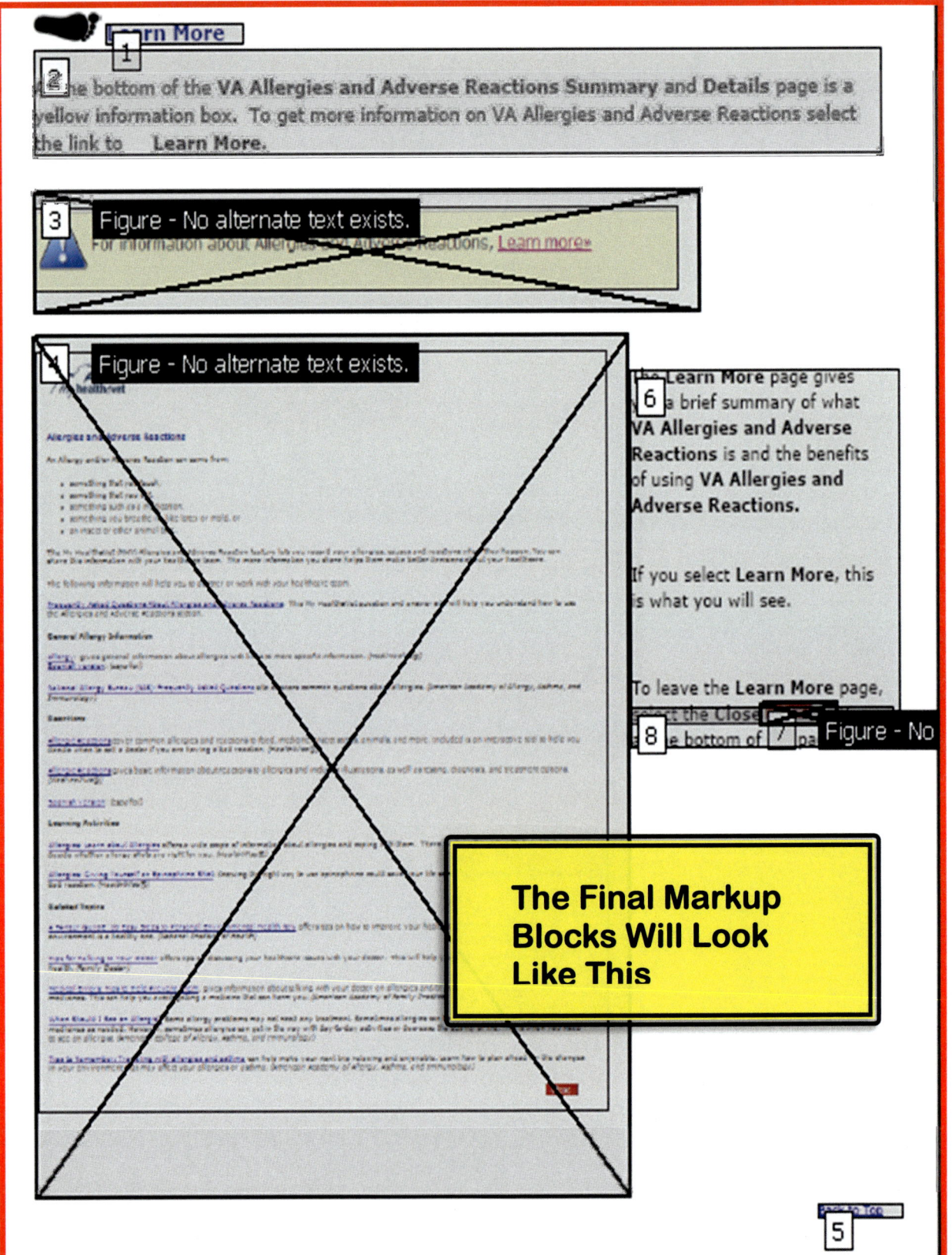

1 Learn More

2 At the bottom of the **VA Allergies and Adverse Reactions Summary and Details** page is a yellow information box. To get more information on VA Allergies and Adverse Reactions select the link to **Learn More.**

3 Figure - No alternate text exists.

4 Figure - No alternate text exists.

6 The **Learn More** page gives you a brief summary of what **VA Allergies and Adverse Reactions** is and the benefits of using **VA Allergies and Adverse Reactions.**

If you select **Learn More**, this is what you will see.

To leave the **Learn More** page, select the Close **7** at **8** the bottom of the page. Figure - No

The Final Markup Blocks Will Look Like This

5 Back to Top

PDF: ❸ Tag Cleaning TouchUp

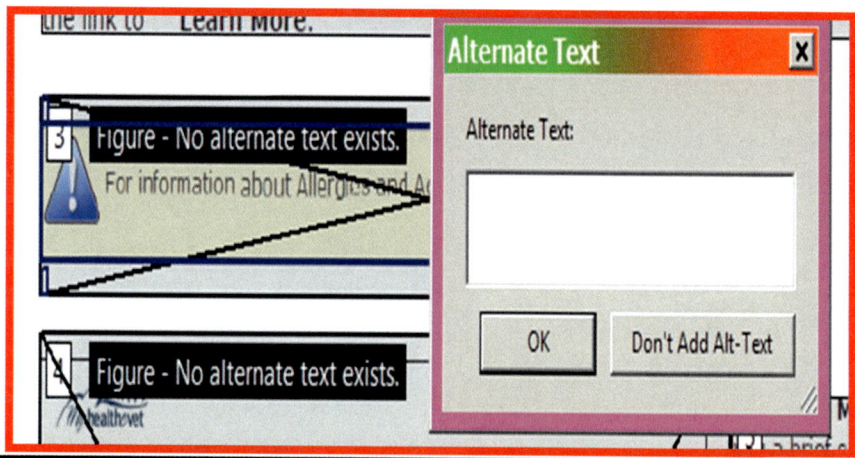

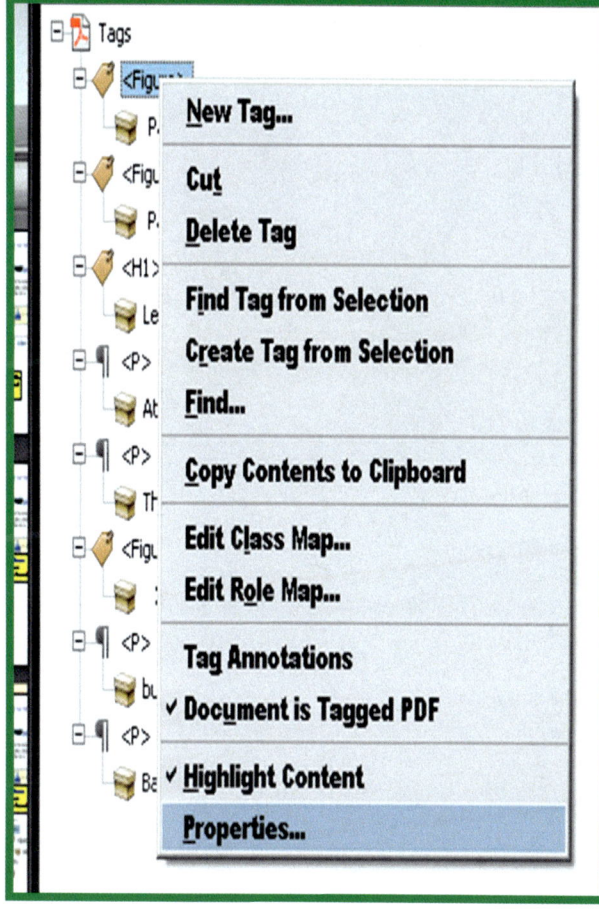

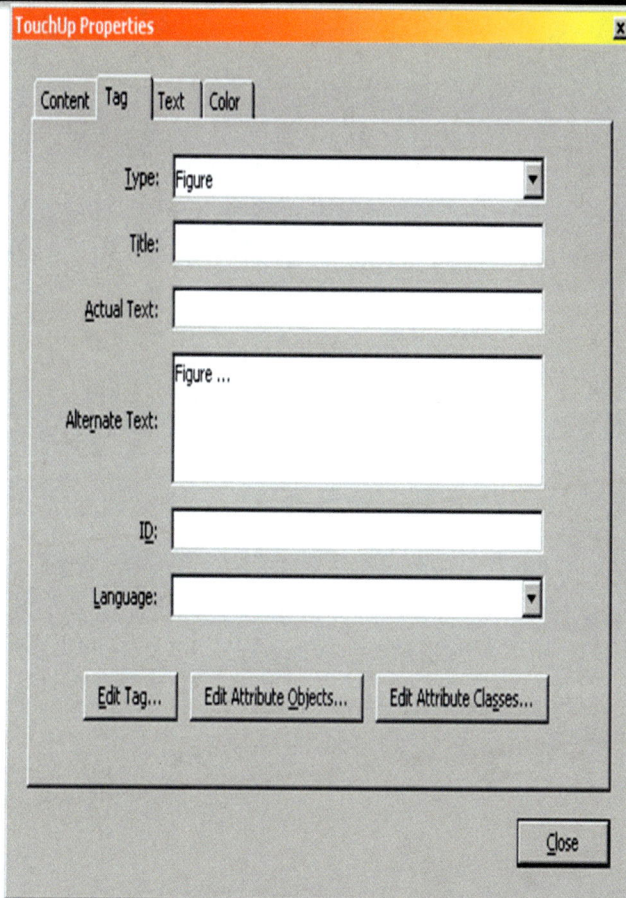

Logical Reading Order is

✿ **Generally Top to Bottom, Left to Right**
✿ **Intent of the Author**
✿ **Logical Sequence of the Content**
✿ **Order in Which to Fill a Form or Quiz**
✿ **Order & Groupings of Similar Items**
✿ **Order of Steps in a Process**

Logical Reading Order is Also

Tab Order on a Page (TAB Key)
✿ **Links**
✿ **Form Fields**
✿ **Controls**
✿ **Frames & Panels**
✿ **Required Instructions**

NOTE

The Tags are the Screen Reader Order

Acrobat Has an Order Panel That Summarizes Groups of Tags and Their Order and Can be Moved Around like Tags

Any of the Methods May Fail Due to Complexities or Partial Corruption in a Particular Document. If That Happens Just Move on to Another Method. Tags is the Most Stable.

PDF: 3 Logical Reading Order

This is What the Order Panel Looks Like, Are There Issues?

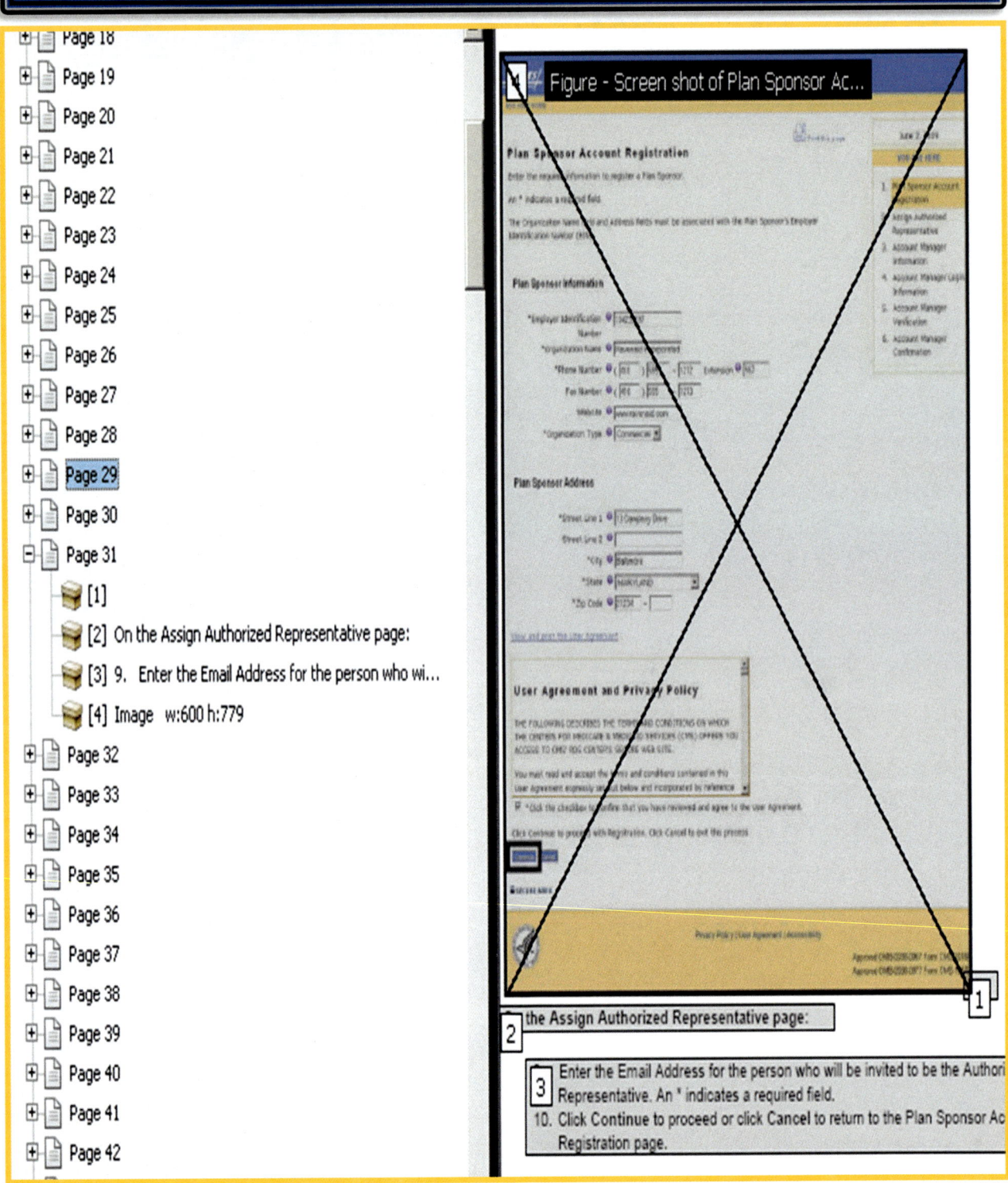

There are Cases Where all Document Images Can be Stacked in the Front of the Document in the Tags – When You Look at the Specific Page they are Missing However the Order Panel View Will Often Retain the Correct Image on the Page But it Often is in Reality Out of Order – **Tags Tell True Story**

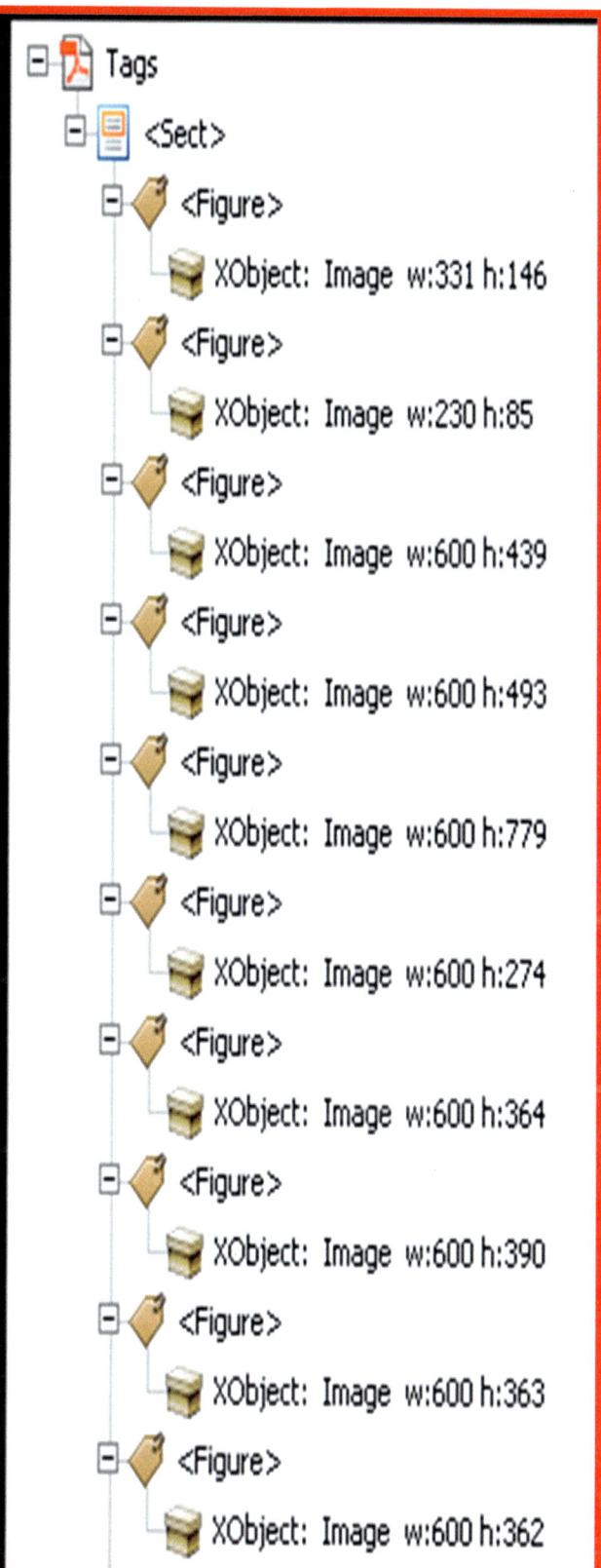

PDF: **5** Logical Reading Order

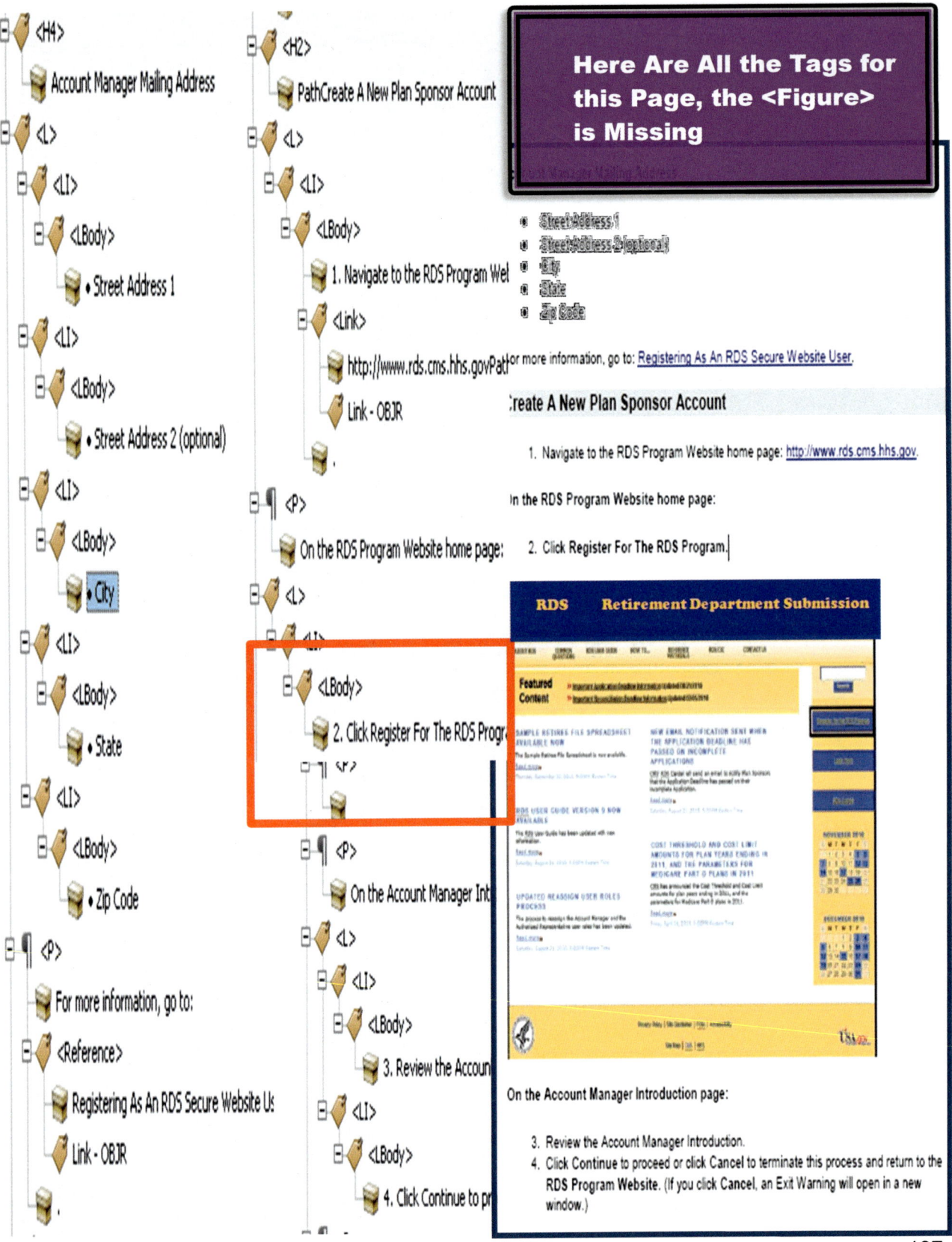

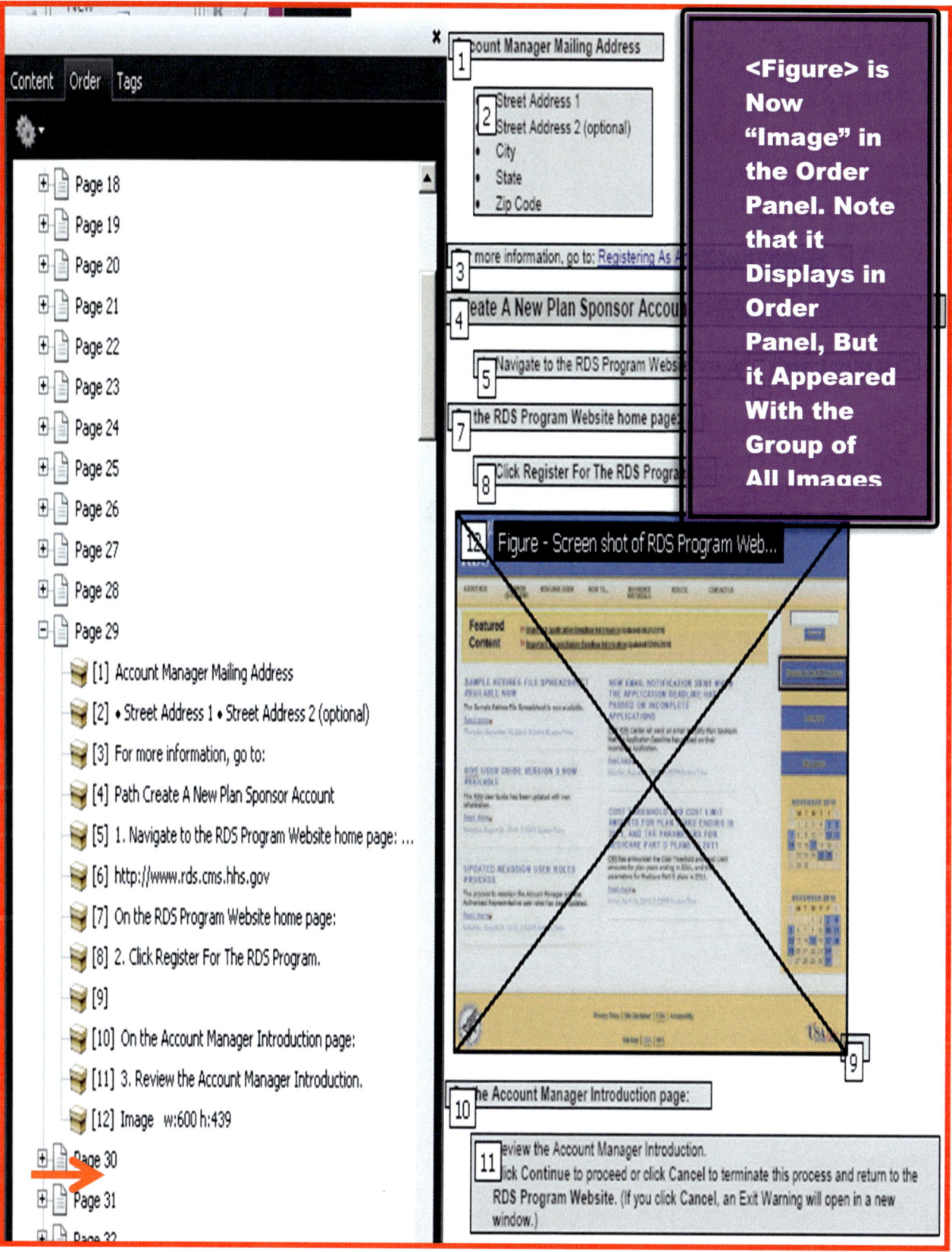

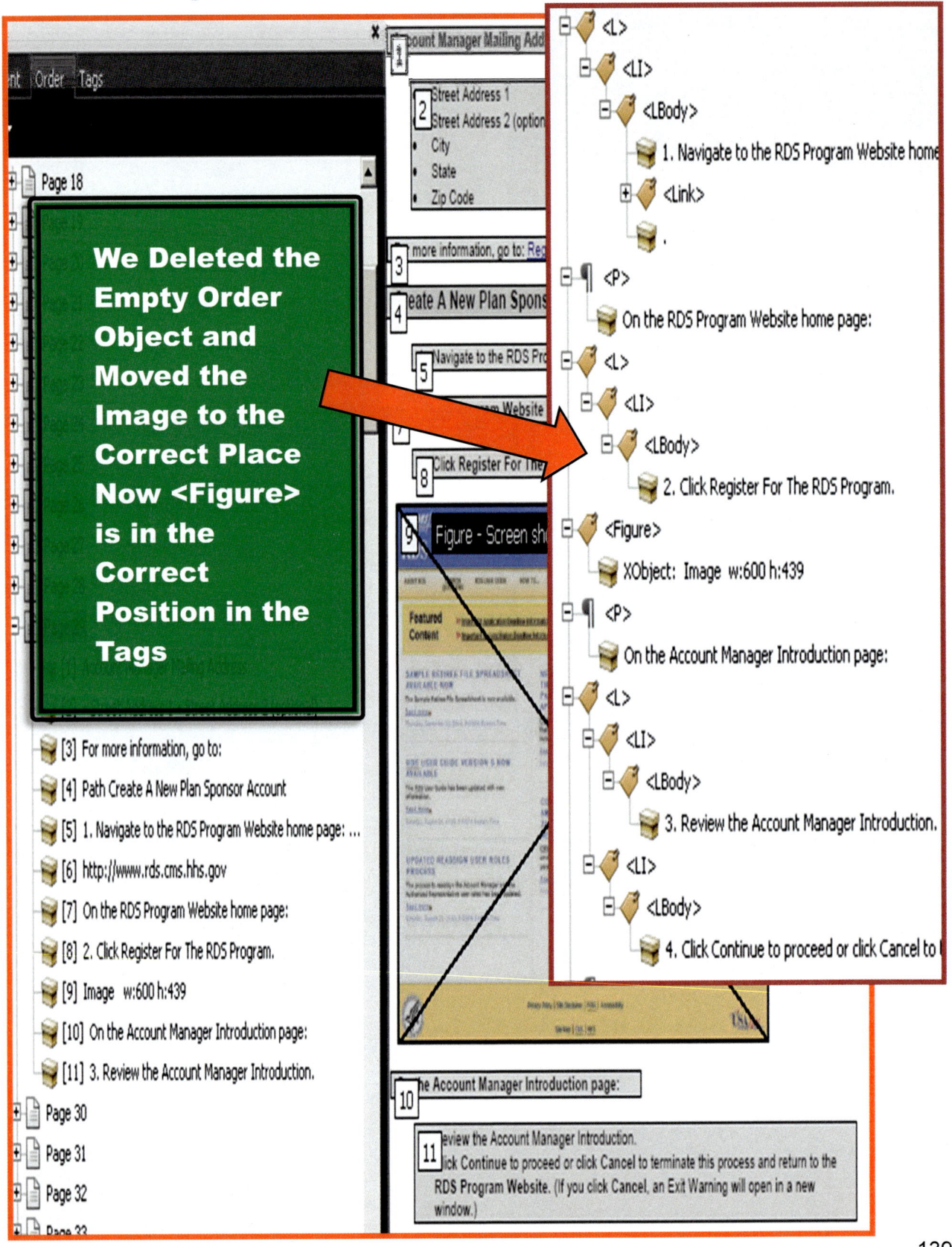

We Deleted the Empty Order Object and Moved the Image to the Correct Place Now <Figure> is in the Correct Position in the Tags

[3] For more information, go to:

[4] Path Create A New Plan Sponsor Account

[5] 1. Navigate to the RDS Program Website home page: ...

[6] http://www.rds.cms.hhs.gov

[7] On the RDS Program Website home page:

[8] 2. Click Register For The RDS Program.

[9] Image w:600 h:439

[10] On the Account Manager Introduction page:

[11] 3. Review the Account Manager Introduction.

Page 30

Page 31

Page 32

Page 33

Notice the Image is Not Where it Should Be in the Tags

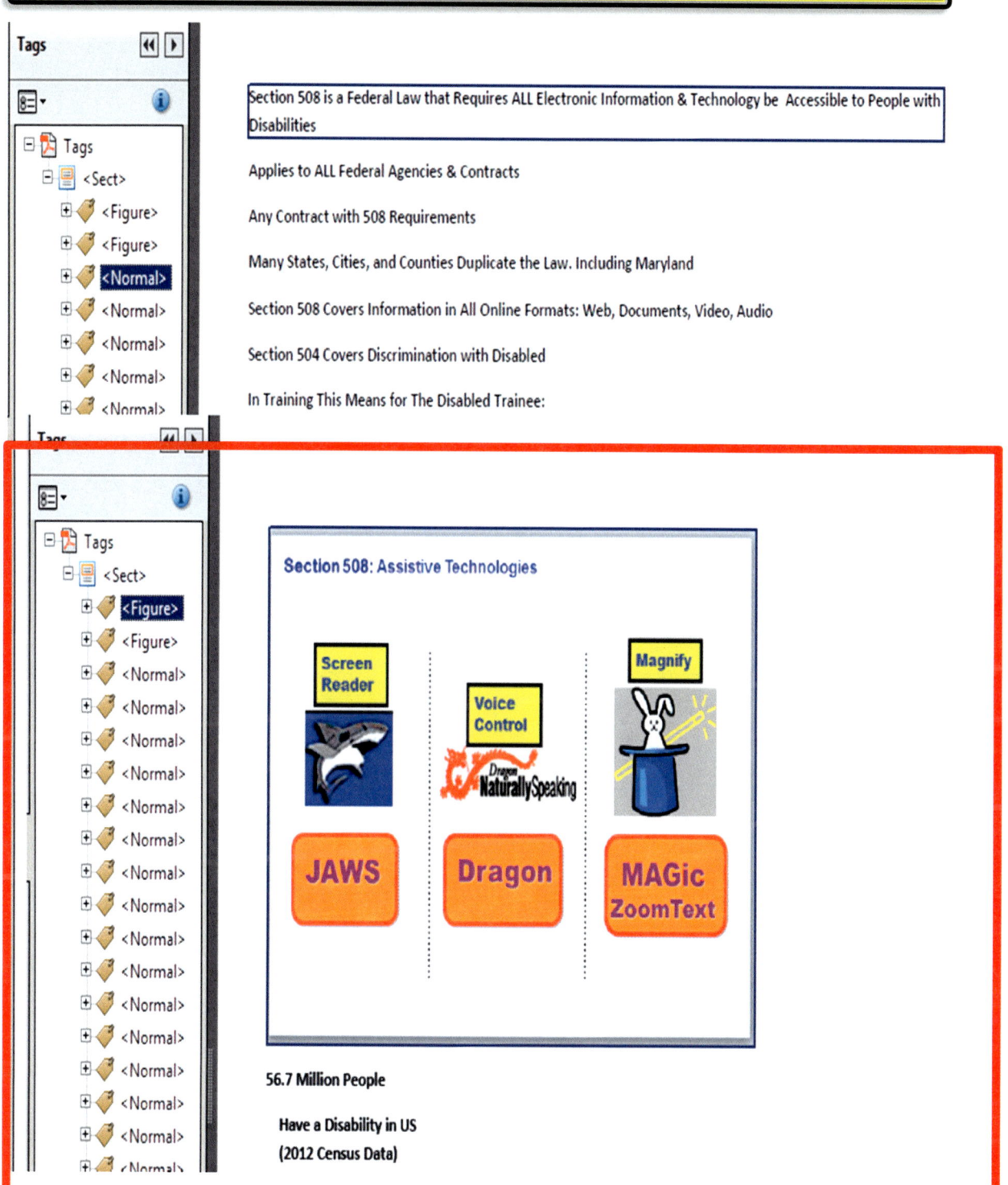

PDF: 2 Logical Reading Order: Order Panel

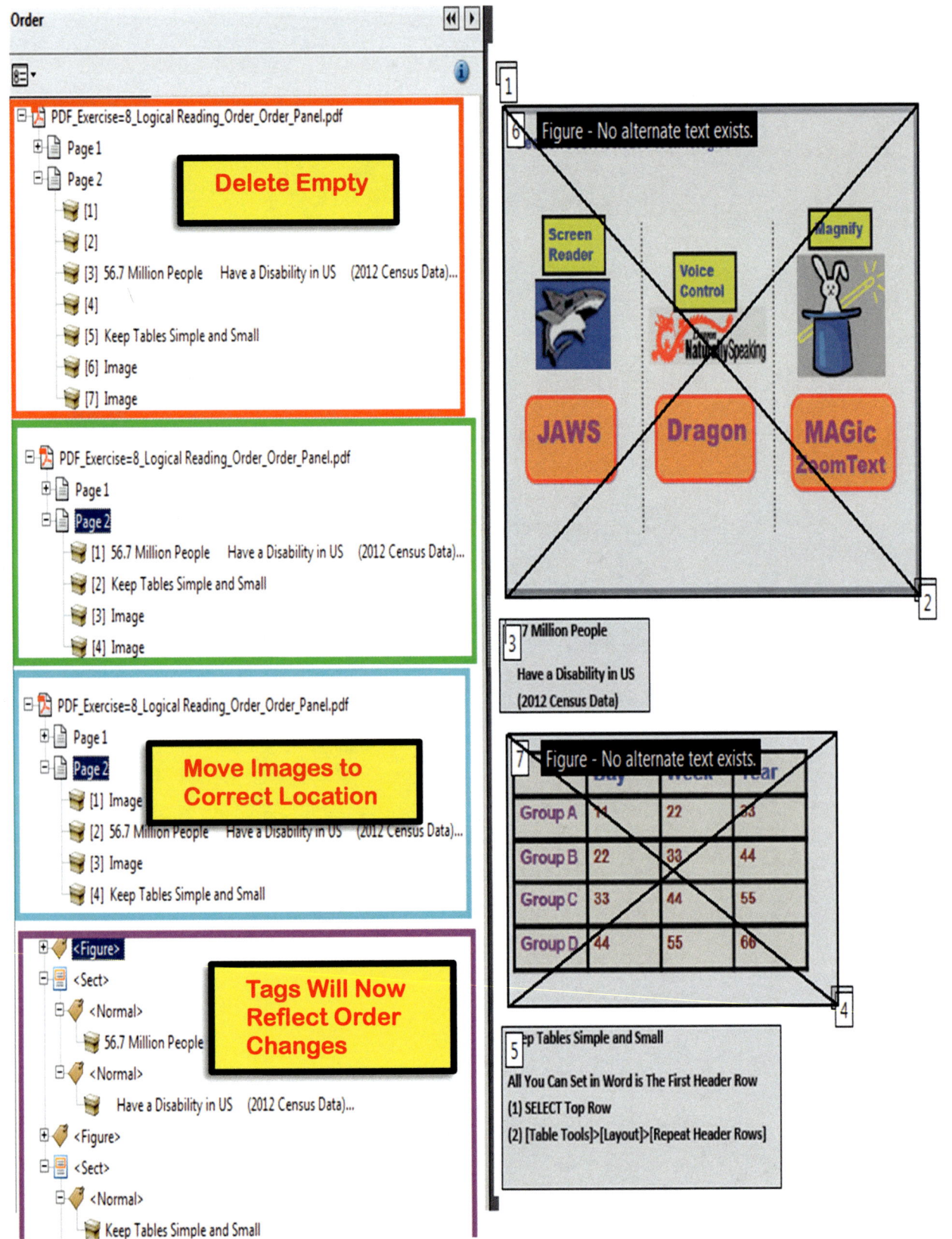

Order

PDF_Exercise=8_Logical Reading_Order_Order_Panel.pdf
- Page 1
- Page 2
  - [1]
  - [2]
  - [3] 56.7 Million People   Have a Disability in US   (2012 Census Data)...
  - [4]
  - [5] Keep Tables Simple and Small
  - [6] Image
  - [7] Image

Delete Empty

PDF_Exercise=8_Logical Reading_Order_Order_Panel.pdf
- Page 1
- Page 2
  - [1] 56.7 Million People   Have a Disability in US   (2012 Census Data)...
  - [2] Keep Tables Simple and Small
  - [3] Image
  - [4] Image

PDF_Exercise=8_Logical Reading_Order_Order_Panel.pdf
- Page 1
- Page 2
  - [1] Image
  - [2] 56.7 Million People   Have a Disability in US   (2012 Census Data)...
  - [3] Image
  - [4] Keep Tables Simple and Small

Move Images to Correct Location

- <Figure>
- <Sect>
  - <Normal>
    - 56.7 Million People
  - <Normal>
    - Have a Disability in US   (2012 Census Data)...
- <Figure>
- <Sect>
  - <Normal>
    - Keep Tables Simple and Small

Tags Will Now Reflect Order Changes

PDF: 1 Logical Reading Order Tags

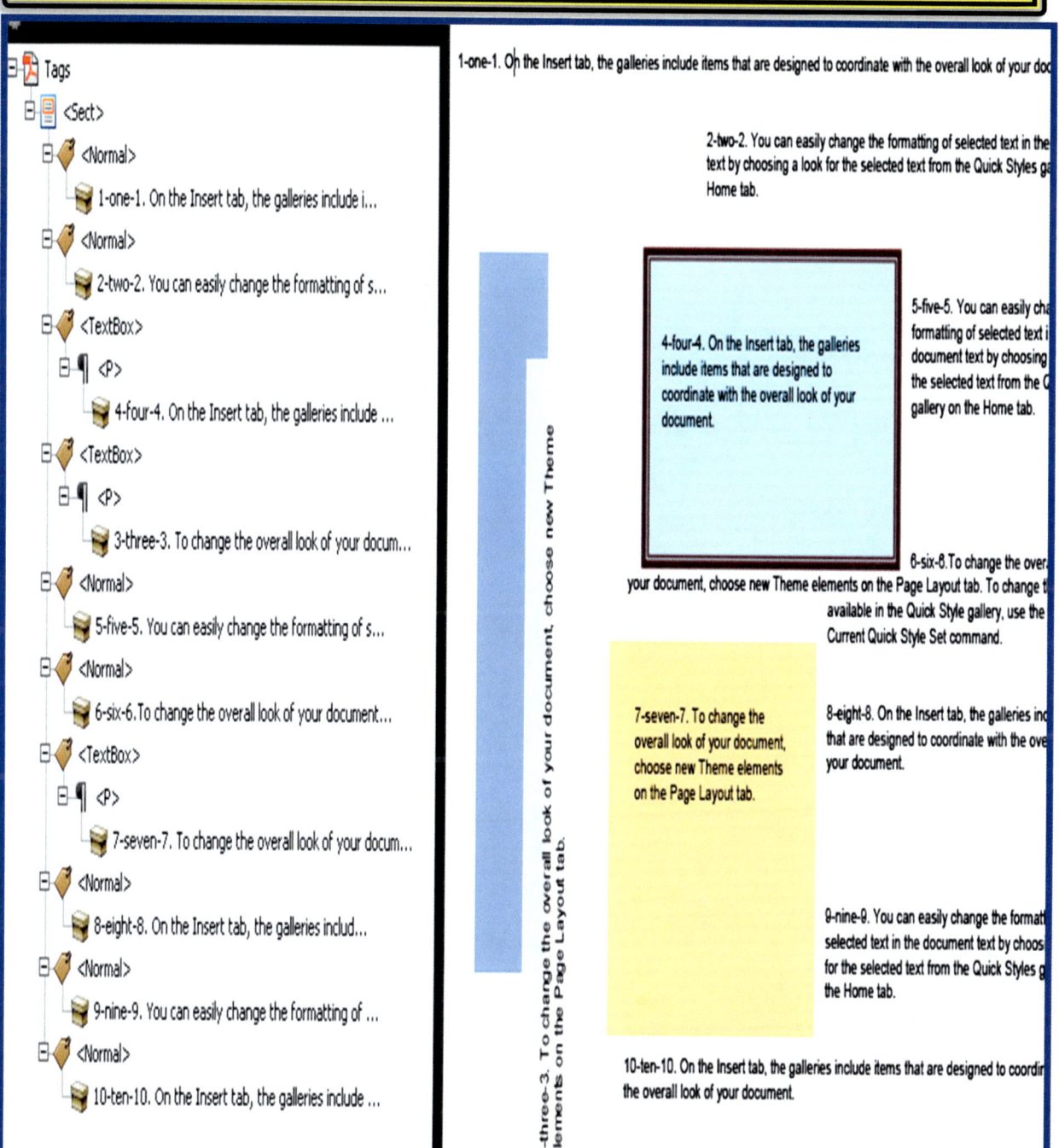

1-one-1. On the Insert tab, the galleries include items that are designed to coordinate with the overall look of your document.

2-two-2. You can easily change the formatting of selected text in the text by choosing a look for the selected text from the Quick Styles gallery on the Home tab.

4-four-4. On the Insert tab, the galleries include items that are designed to coordinate with the overall look of your document.

5-five-5. You can easily change the formatting of selected text in the document text by choosing a look for the selected text from the Quick Styles gallery on the Home tab.

6-six-8.To change the overall look of your document, choose new Theme elements on the Page Layout tab. To change the available in the Quick Style gallery, use the Current Quick Style Set command.

7-seven-7. To change the overall look of your document, choose new Theme elements on the Page Layout tab.

8-eight-8. On the Insert tab, the galleries include items that are designed to coordinate with the overall look of your document.

9-nine-9. You can easily change the formatting of selected text in the document text by choosing a look for the selected text from the Quick Styles gallery on the Home tab.

10-ten-10. On the Insert tab, the galleries include items that are designed to coordinate with the overall look of your document.

3-three-3. To change the overall look of your document, choose new Theme elements on the Page Layout tab.

142

DRAG&DROP
<Textbox> 3-three-3 to
<Normal> 2-two-2
   Specifically:
Put Mouse on <Textbox> TAG 3-three-3, Keep LEFT-MOUSE Depressed
Slide Until You See the Drag Pointer Under <Normal> TAG 2-two-2
Always DRAG to the Left Side or You Get a 'No' Symbol

Requires Careful Mouse Control

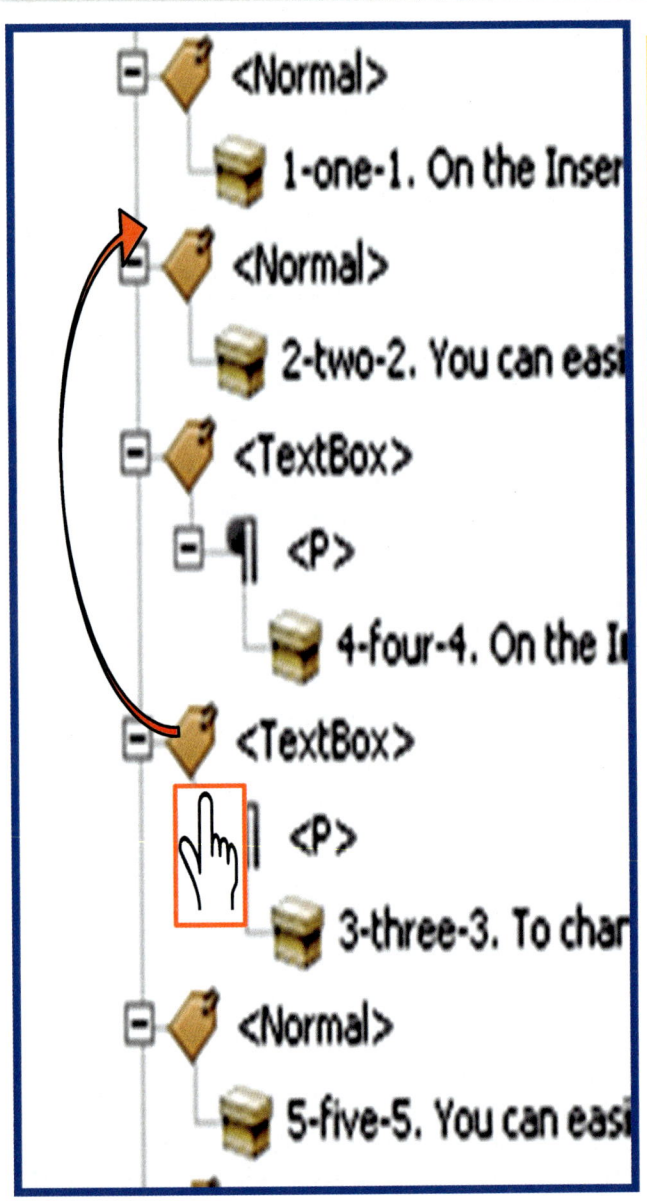

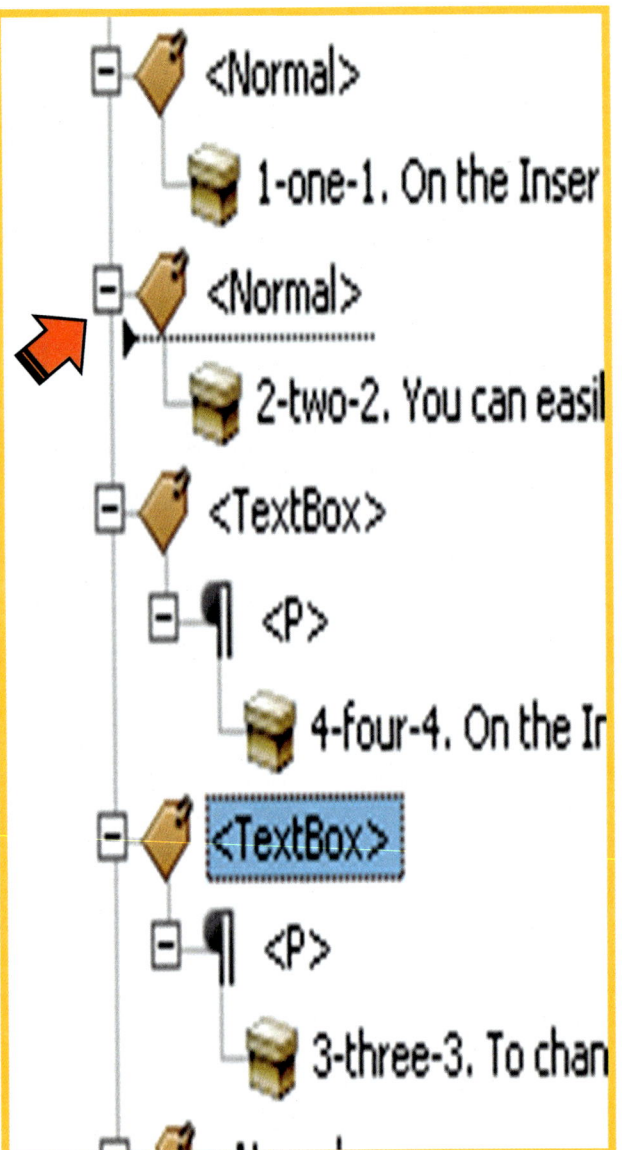

PDF: 3 Logical Reading Order Tags

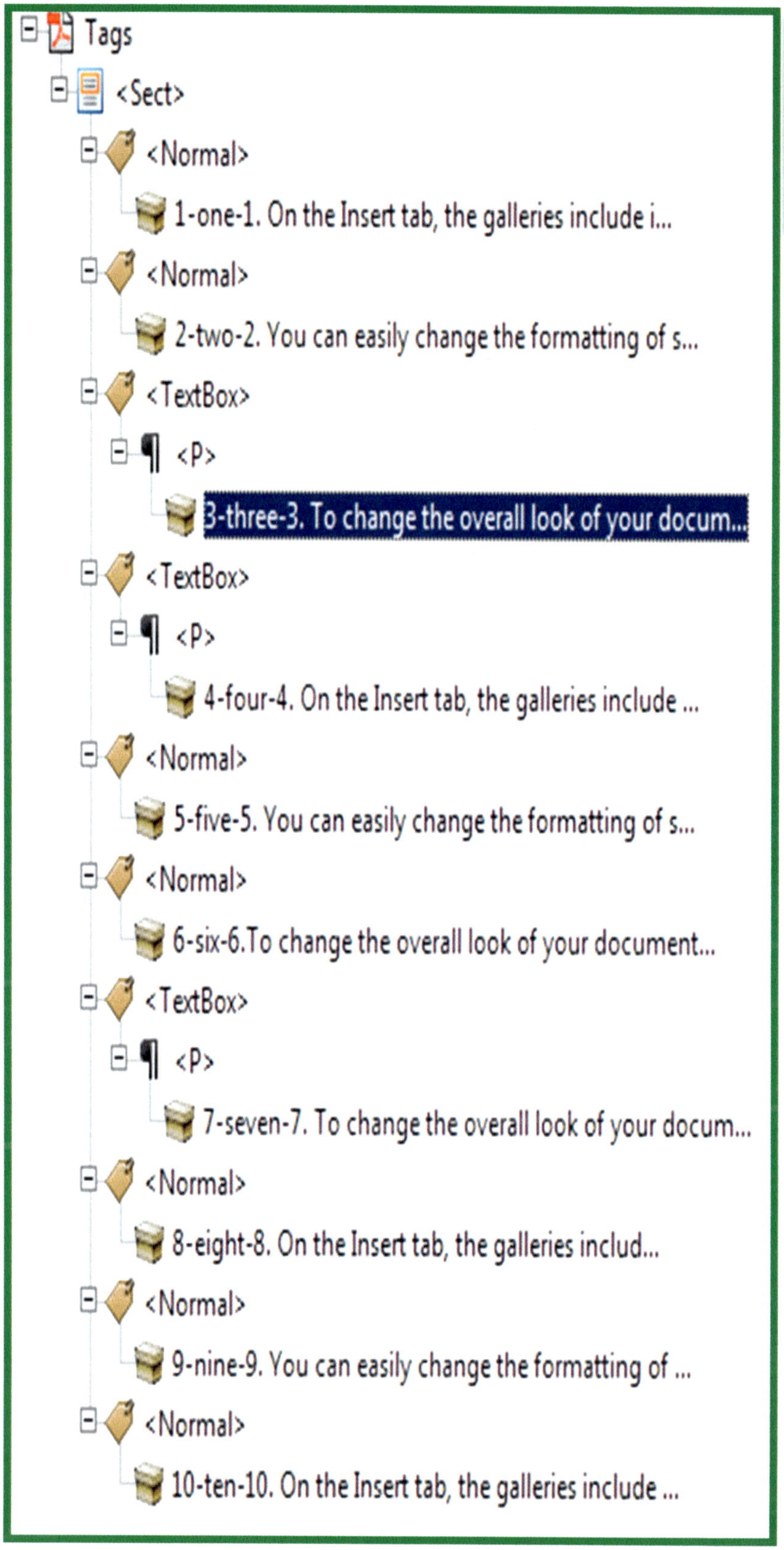

Tags
<Sect>
<Normal>
1-one-1. On the Insert tab, the galleries include i...
<Normal>
2-two-2. You can easily change the formatting of s...
<TextBox>
<P>
3-three-3. To change the overall look of your docum...
<TextBox>
<P>
4-four-4. On the Insert tab, the galleries include ...
<Normal>
5-five-5. You can easily change the formatting of s...
<Normal>
6-six-6.To change the overall look of your document...
<TextBox>
<P>
7-seven-7. To change the overall look of your docum...
<Normal>
8-eight-8. On the Insert tab, the galleries includ...
<Normal>
9-nine-9. You can easily change the formatting of ...
<Normal>
10-ten-10. On the Insert tab, the galleries include ...

Drag to the Base of the "2-two-2…" Main Tag

<Normal>
2-two-2. You can
<TextBox>
<P>
3-three-3. To c
<TextBox>
<P>
4-four-4. On th

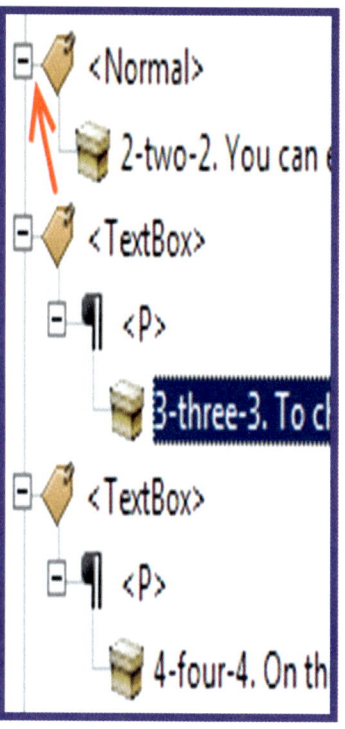

There is a Way in Acrobat to Make Merged Cells Work. BUT it is Tedious and the Conversion From Word is Prone to Errors.
Avoid always. CommonLook Allows Easier Table Corrections.

Red	Blue	Yellow	Green
11	22	33	44
55	66	77	88

You Would Need to Edit Each Cell Property to Indicate the Table Header

Orange		Violet	
11	22	33	44
55	66	77	88

AND Then Test It

Orange	Orange	Violet	Violet
11	22	33	44
55	66	77	88

skip to main content

Expanding the web's potential for people with disabilities

- Products
- Services
- Articles
- Resources
- Community

Search Terms   Search

Getting Started

Introduction to web accessibility

From the Blog

- Upcoming WebAIM Events
  February 25, 2011
- ADA ANPRM Response
  January 31, 2011
- Progress on Focus Indicators
  January 5, 2011
- WebAIM's 2010 Year In Review
  December 22, 2010
- The Ghosts of ARIA Present and Future
  November 30, 2010

Community

- Newsletter
- Blog
- Email Discussion List
- RSS/News Feeds

You are here: Home > Articles > JavaScript > Page 2: JavaScript Event Handlers

Open the Tags, Figure Out the Next Way to Look at it.

PDF: **2** Find the Tag Issue

skip to main content

Expanding the web's potential for people with disabilities

- Products
- Services
- Articles
- Resources
- Community

Search Terms Search

Getting Started

Introduction to web accessibility

From the Blog

- Upcoming WebAIM Events
  February 25, 2011
- ADA ANPRM Response
  January 31, 2011
- Progress on Focus Indicators
  January 5, 2011
- WebAIM's 2010 Year In Review
  December 22, 2010
- The Ghosts of ARIA Present and Future
  November 30, 2010

Community

- Newsletter
- Blog
- Email Discussion List
- RSS/News Feeds

You are here: Home > Articles > JavaScript > Page 2: JavaScript Event H

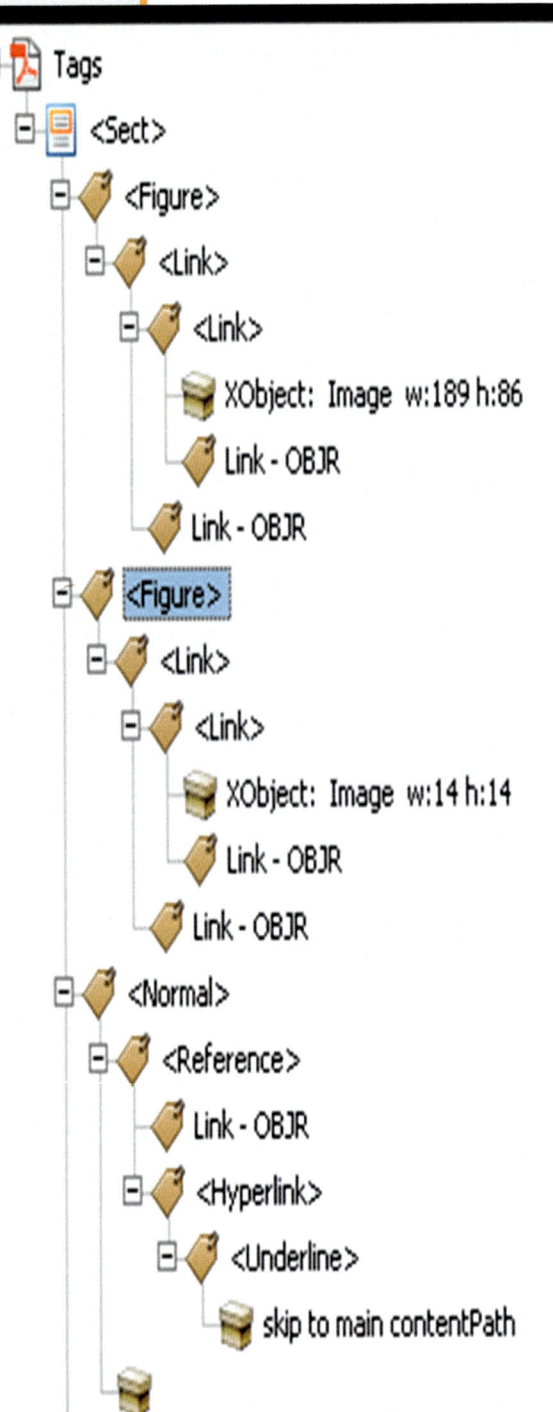

1-DELETE Second Figure As It Is Just an Icon

PDF: 3 Find the Tag Issue

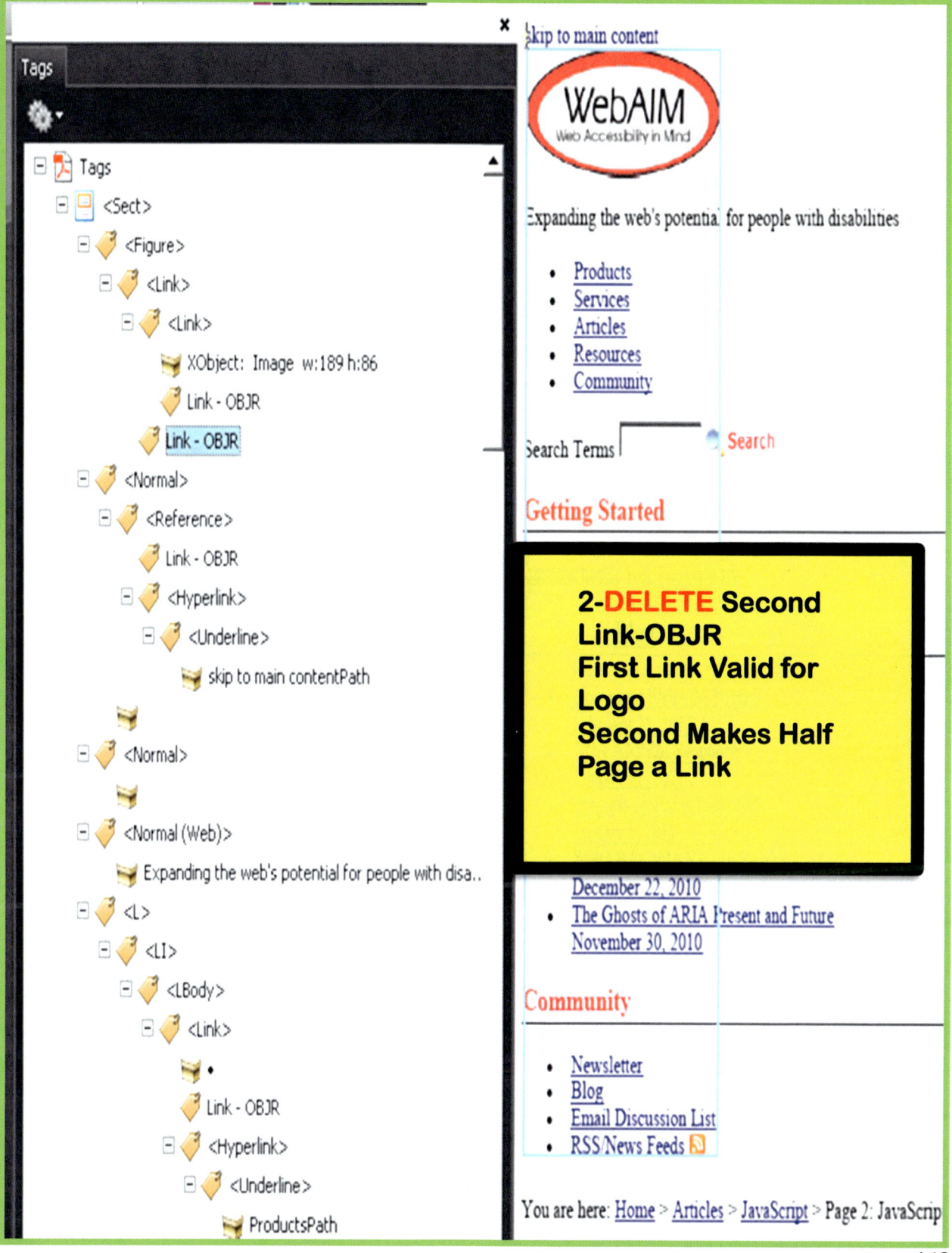

**2-DELETE Second
Link-OBJR
First Link Valid for
Logo
Second Makes Half
Page a Link**

148

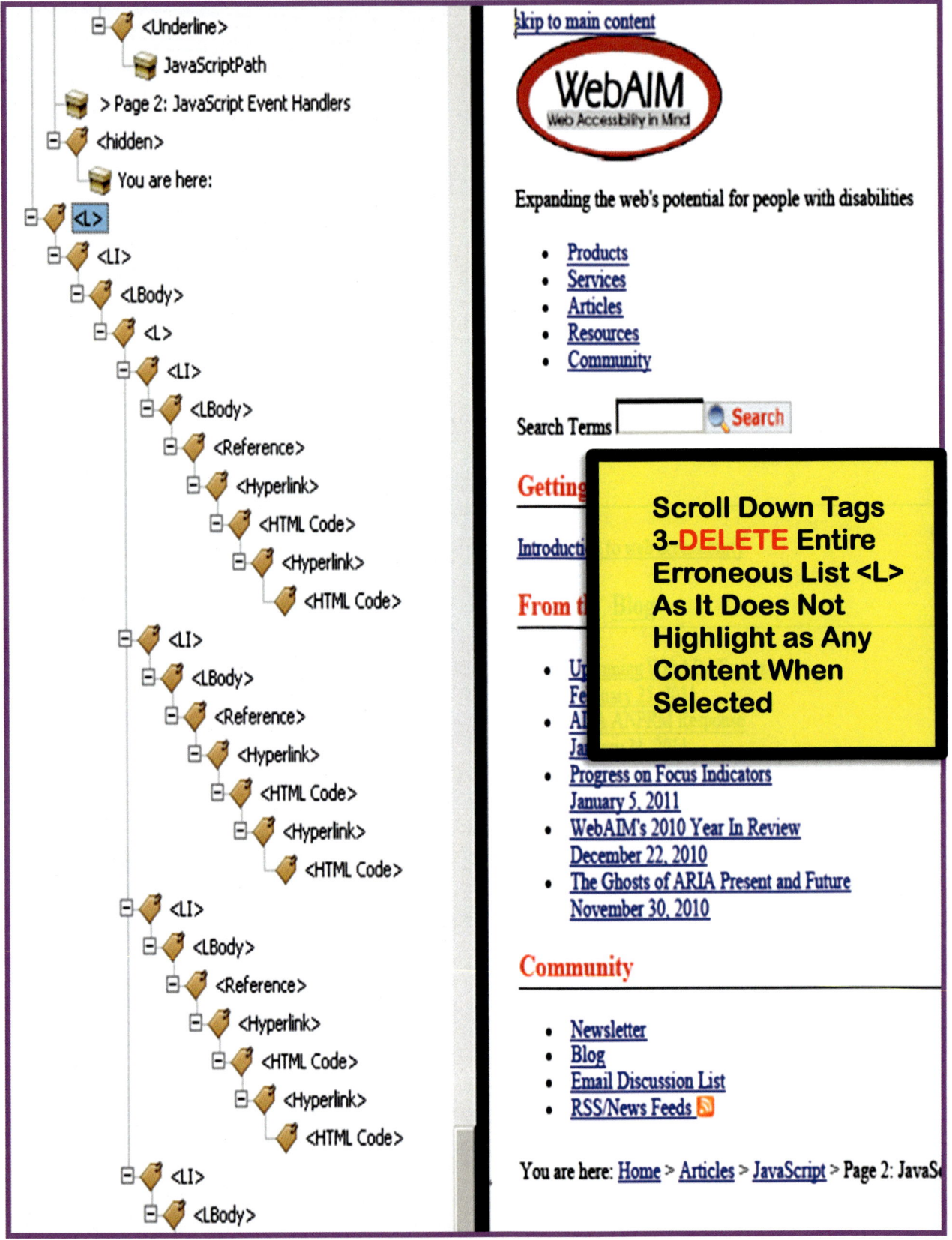

4-DELETE The 2 <InLineShape> After the Search Terms (Just Image for Search Box)
The Field is Not Active Here, If Active Then It Would Be a Button Link
The Rest of the Cleanup Would Involve Deleting Empty Tags

PDF: Example: Most Tags You Will See

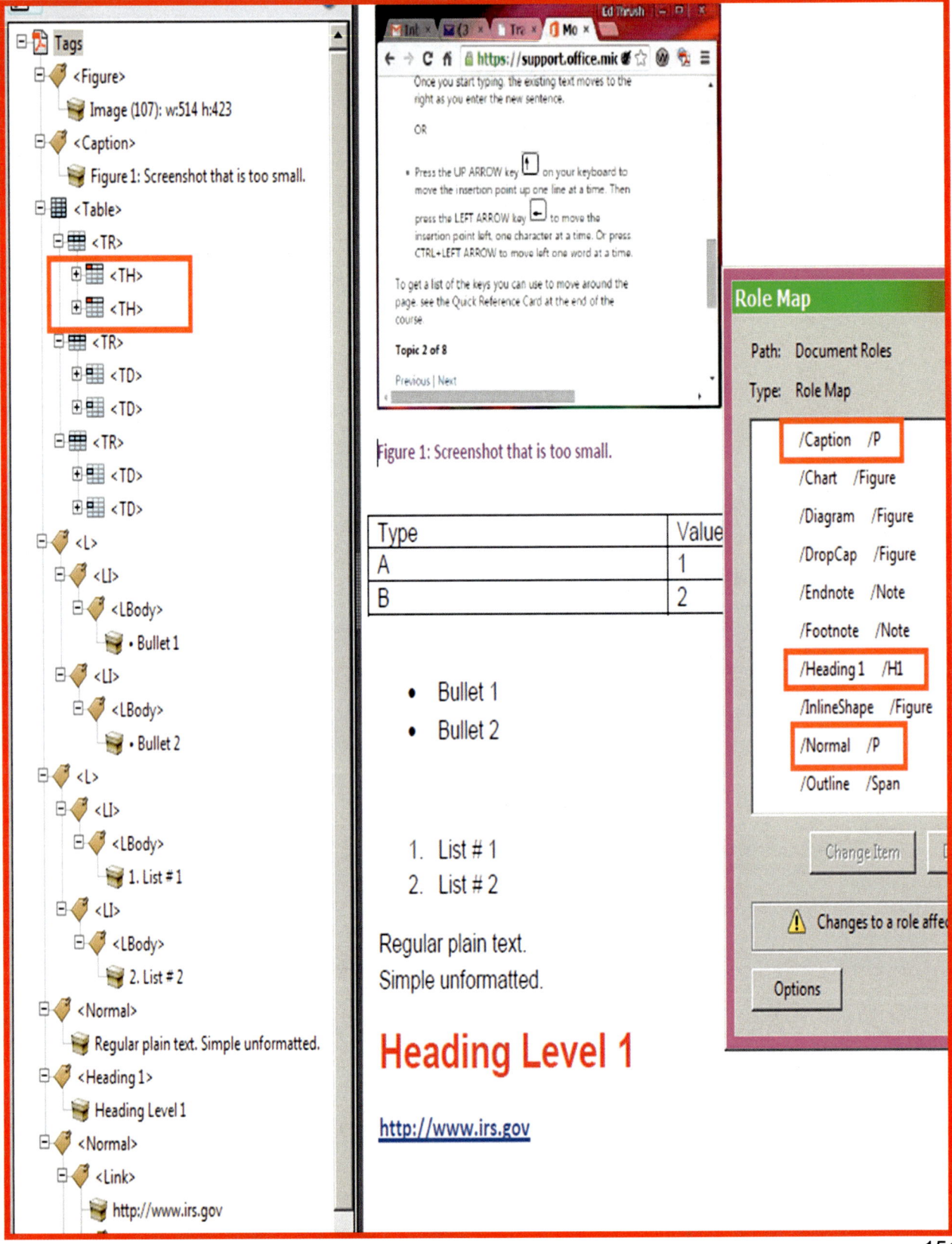

PDF: Corrupt Files

Word Files Can Become Corrupt Without Visual Indicators
- Bullets, Lists, Numbering & Headings May Need To be Redone
- Convert to HTML & Back
- Convert to RTF & Back
- Clear All Styles in Suspect Area in Word & Reset Carefully
- Reduce Complexity & Styles

PDF Files Can Inherit Issues From Word & Have Conversions Errors
- May Need to Delete All Tags (Alt Text Will be Lost) & Re-Add Tags
- Reduce File Size or Optimize [Tools] > [Save & Export]
- Extract Pages to Break Up Document [Tools] > [Pages] > [Extract] ✲
- Use TouchUp Tool to Group Similar Items if There Are Too Many Gray Structure Boxes for the Number of Content Areas

Additional PDF Techniques
- [Tools] [Print Production] > [Preflight] Examine Document Issues - Extensive & Requires Time
- Convert to HTML and Examine, Note: Tags & Role Map are Used to Filter Conversion

General Reminders For PDF Accessibility

OCR: Verify Tags Content

Logical Reading Order

Label Form Fields

Tag Structure

Delete Empty Tags

Alternative Text or Describe

Tables Have Headers

Sharp Contrast

Delete Tag Artifacts

Footnotes & Ref As Links

Linked TOC & Bookmarks

Headings Each Page

153

Adding Accessibility to the
Enterprise Life Cycle
508-ELC

508-ELC: ELC Process With 508

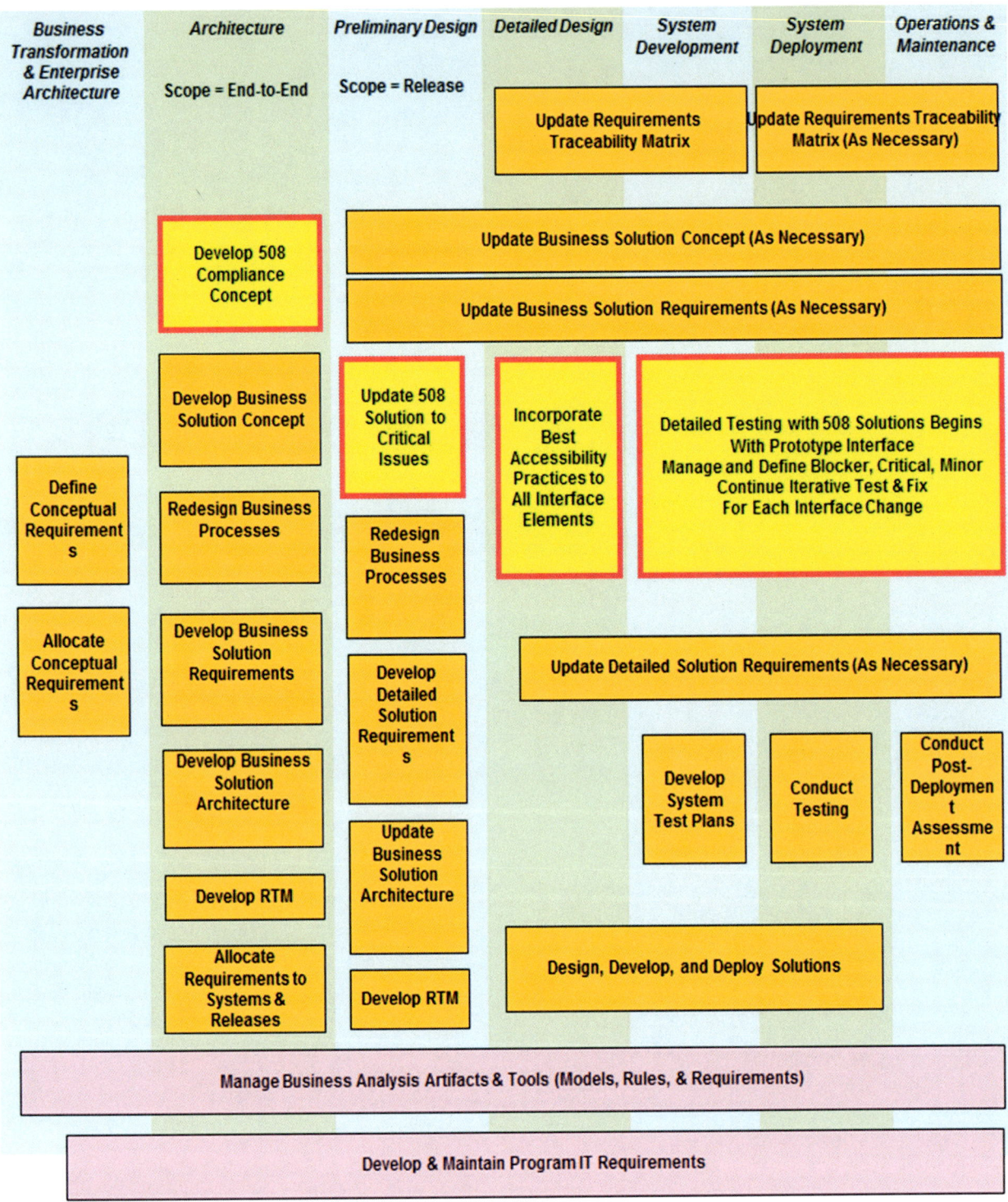

508-ELC: Typical Process Areas & Stakeholders

◆ **Acquisition Management**
◆ **Configuration Management**
◆ **Contract Management**
◆ **Cost and Schedule Estimation**
◆ **Enterprise Architecture**
◆ **Enterprise Life Cycle Protocols**
◆ **Governance**
◆ **Section 508 Compliance & Coordination**
◆ **Integrated Master Schedule**
◆ **Infrastructure Management**
◆ **Reporting Systems**
◆ **Program Performance Management**
◆ **Quality Assurance**
◆ **Release Management Integrated Test & Deployment**
◆ **Requirements Management**
◆ **Risk Management**
◆ **Transition Management**
◆ **Resource Tracking System**

508-ELC: Process Environment

Note: Managers must proactively identify the appropriate stakeholders; must apprise stakeholders of the nature, timing, and degree of the desired participation; and must ensure that these commitments are fulfilled through active and consistent participation.

Levels of Project Work and Involvement That Shapes The Specific Environment

Stakeholders
EA, Infrastructure, Business, Security, etc…
Can also be others outside

Documentation
ELC as determined what is needed

Requirements
Procedures, Certifications, Contracts, Laws

Coordination
Other projects, teams, and contractors

Detail Work
Sub-projects can have thousands of tasks

508-ELC: What We Need to Know

- Milestone Readiness Review - Satisfy conditions in checklists
- Milestone Exit Review – See if allowed to continue
- Customer Technical Review - Early stakeholder feedback as well as early identification and resolution of issues
- Life Cycle Stage Review - Technical and business aspects of the entire solution approve the solution for baselining. LCSRs occur at the end of life cycle stages.
- Enterprise Architecture certification - Conformance with the higher-level design, standards, and intent of the Enterprise Architecture
- Milestones

--- Phases (may span milestones)

--- Stages (segment within a phase, moves to a new level (logical/physical)

508-ELC: Tailoring

- Tailoring is modification of a standard approach to customize it for a specific situation
- Based on standard methods but that has been modified, if necessary, to take into account the specific needs and unique conditions
- Any component of the ELC may be tailored if protocol allows

508-ELC: Releases

When a project has multiple releases, design, development, and deployment usually occurs for a single release.

↳

The project then cycles back and again goes through design, development, and deployment for the next release.

↳

This cycle is repeated until all project releases have been deployed. It is also possible that work on releases is not strictly sequential - that is, that work on more than one release may be in progress at the same time.

Note: You may be responsible for multiple testing during overlapping time frames

508-ELC: Work Products

Accessibility Documentation

Explains the approach and tests to be used to ensure the solution being developed will be accessible to users with disabilities, and demonstrates compliance via actual test results.

Sample Types of Documents

- ❑ Domain Architecture
- ❑ Accessibility Compliance
- ❑ Preliminary Design
- ❑ Detailed Design
- ❑ System Development
- ❑ System Deployment
- ❑ Business System Architecture

508-ELC: Typical ELC Section 508 Requirements for Projects

Milestone 1 *Architecture*	Milestone 2 *System Requirements*	Milestone 3 *Application Requirements*	Milestone 4 *Detailed Design*	Milestone 5 *Development*	Milestone 6 *Deployment*
508 Provisions	♦ 508 Provisions Compliance Approach Risk Report	♦ 508 Provisions ♦ Compliance Approach ♦ Risk Report Accessibility Plan Test Plan	♦ 508 Provisions ♦ Compliance Approach ♦ Risk Report ♦ Accessibility Plan ♦ Test Plan	♦ Risk Report ♦ Accessibility Plan Test Results	♦ Risk Report ♦ Accessibility Plan ♦ Test Results

► Identify the Applicable 508 Provisions

► Create a Test Plan

► Identify 508 Issues and Make Corrections

508-ELC: Requirements & Applicable Provision Evaluation

Applicable Provision Evaluation ➜ [INITIAL]

- **Identify which set of provisions will apply**
  - This can be refined later

- **Project description**
- **User interface description**
- **Applicable 508 provisions**
- **Contact information**

Technical Provisions Example, fill out VPAT style		
1194.21 Software Applications and Operating Systems		
Provision	**Applies? (Y/N)**	**Description of Requirement**
1194.21a	Y	When software is designed to run on a system that has a keyboard, product functions shall be executable from a keyboard where the function itself or the result of performing a function can be discerned textually.
1194.21b	Y	Applications shall not disrupt or disable activated features of other products that are identified as accessibility features, where those features are developed and documented according to industry standards. Applications also shall not disrupt or disable activated features of any operating system that are identified as accessibility features where the application programming interface for those accessibility features has been documented by the manufacturer of the operating system and is available to the product developer.

508-ELC: Next Checkpoint Requirements

Applicable Provision Evaluation
➔ [RECERTIFY]

Provisions should be more specific, which specifically apply

Accessibility Compliance (Remediation Method) Approach
➔ [INITIAL]

Accessibility Risk Report Informational Document
➔ [INITIAL]
- Unmet provisions
- AT issues
- Interoperations with other systems
- Laws that affect the accessibility
- Description of potential impact
- Description of user base
- Risk Assessment
- Mitigation

508-ELC: Accessibility Compliance Approach

Accessibility Compliance Approach
➔ [INITIAL]
- List 508 documents, training procedures, and test plans
- Outline responsibility to remediate 508 issues and the process involved
- Testing process involving users who are disabled – if any
- Contact information
-

Purpose:
▶ Document how the project intends to ensure that the components provided by the contractor or internal effort meets 508

162

508-ELC: Next Checkpoint Requirements

Applicable Provision Evaluation

➔ [RECERTIFY]

- This should be locked in place now for testing
- Note any modifications
-

Accessibility Compliance Approach

➔ [RECERTIFY]

Accessibility Support and AT Integration Plan

➔ [INITIAL]

508-ELC: Sample Accessibility Test Plan, & Test Results

Criteria

1194.21 (d): Sufficient information about a user interface element including the identity, operation and state of the element shall be available to assistive technology. When an image represents a program element, the information conveyed by the image must also be available in text.

Remarks and Explanations (defining N) or Exception Claimed (defining NA)

Next and Previous buttons along with Submit are not announced with correct names with screen readers

Accommodation Plan (for non-conforming provisions)

None available

Tracking Issue

347

Testing Technical Mechanism To Be Used

JAWS, ZoomText, Dragon

Testing Manual Evaluation Method To Be Used

Focusable, Name label, Tab Order

Testing Remarks and explanations Testing outcomes

Buttons have correct screen text, but are no programmatically labelled correctly. Fails with Jaws and ZoomText. Dragon can locate, but is not sufficient to pass alone, must work with all assistive technology. Fail complete for JAWS and ZoomText. (reading mode plus magnification)

Final Determination ? (Y/N/NA)

N

508-ELC: Test Plan - Requirements

Types of Testing
⚜ Assistive Technology (AT) Testing (JAWS, Dragon, ZoomText)
⚜ Automated Tools (AccVerify, Compliance Sherriff, Deque)
⚜ Manual Test Methods (Manual-Keyboard, Visual Contrasts & Magnification)
⚜ End-User Testing
⚜ Programmer Training for Testing

Testing Classifications
⚜ Conflicts with AT
⚜ Minor Issues (Do Not Affect Primary Functionality)
⚜ Critical Issues (significantly affect time, confusion, and difficulty in completing task)
⚜ Blocker (Cannot complete task)
⚜ Anticipated Release Corrections (with dates)

508-ELC: Test Results - Actions

⌘ Create Summary of Technical 508 Issues
⌘ Give Recommendations for Fix (Helpful Yes, But Keeps in Line with Expectations)
⌘ Final Compliance Must be Free of Critical and Blocker Issues - if Not Then those Issues Must Have a Reasonable Workaround While a Fix is Being Scheduled.

End Of Tutorial

21   508 and WCAG Manual

21.1   Purpose

The purpose of this manual is to provide rules and guidelines for creating accessible content and applications on internal and external websites and other mediums of delivery. This manual is supported and guided by Section 508 of the Rehabilitation Act of 1973 (Section 508), as amended (29 U.S.C. Section 794d) and the World Wide Web Consortium (W3C) Web Content Accessibility Guidelines (WCAG) 2.0. This manual will also incorporate standards and procedures that are useful or necessary to ensure that all people have full access to information resources.

The key to compliance with this guide is adherence to the requirements which can be met usually in many ways.

21.2   Internal Versus External (Public) Environment

Some strict 508 rules can be avoided where you have total control over the environment. For example if you have a company or agency that only uses one browser, one screen reader, one voice control, and provides alternative formats for non-accessible formats, then you can avoid some standards and tests as long as all the disabled get access and equal information. This also means you can require CSS, scripts, JAVA, or anything else, given that it provides equal information. However once you open to the public you have no control on how the users access your content and applications. That means the strict 508 rule comes into effect, meaning everything you put online must work with all assistive technology and be able to produce a format of the users choice if no other method allows access.

21.3   References and Regulations

The accessibility policy originates from:

Section 508 of the Rehabilitation Act:

>   http://www.section508.gov/index.cfm?fuseAction=stdsdoc

WCAG 2.0:

>   http://www.w3.org/TR/WCAG20/

21.4   Requirements for Web Pages, Applications, and Documents

This guide describes the Requirements in detail and provides an explanation for each.

Requirements that Always Apply

These are the generally applied Section 508 Requirements that ensure that the product is capable of usage by the various members of disabled community. The other sections that follow are specific in application.

Section 508 Functional Performance Criteria

Visual

Section 508 1194.31 (a) At least one mode of operation and information retrieval that does not require user vision shall be provided, or support for assistive technology used by people who are blind or visually impaired shall be provided.

Section 508 1194.31 (b) At least one mode of operation and information retrieval that does not require visual acuity greater than 20/70 shall be provided in audio and enlarged print output working together or independently, or support for assistive technology used by people who are visually impaired shall be provided.

Audio

Section 508 1194.31 (c) At least one mode of operation and information retrieval that does not require user hearing shall be provided, or support for Assistive technology used by people who are deaf or hard of hearing shall be provided

Section 508 1194.31 (d) Where audio information is important for the use of a product, at least one mode of operation and information retrieval shall be provided in an enhanced auditory fashion, or support for assistive hearing devices shall be provided.

Speech

Section 508 1194.31 (e) At least one mode of operation and information retrieval that does not require user speech shall be provided, or support for Assistive technology used by people with disabilities shall be provided.

Motor (Physical Abilities)

Section 508 1194.31 (f) At least one mode of operation and information retrieval that does not require fine motor control or simultaneous actions and that is operable with limited reach and strength shall be provided.

Section 508 Information, Documentation, and Support

Alternative Formats

Section 508 1194.41 (a) Product support documentation provided to end-users shall be made available in alternate formats upon request, at no additional charge

Accessibility Page

Section 508 1194.41 (b) End-users shall have access to a description of the accessibility and compatibility features of products in alternate formats or alternate methods upon request, at no additional charge.

Support

Section 508 1194.41 (c) Support services for products shall accommodate the communication needs of end-users with disabilities.

2. WCAG 2.0 Conformance Levels

Level A: The minimum level of conformance, the Web page satisfies all the Level A Success Criteria, or a conforming alternate version is provided.

Level AA: The Web page satisfies all the Level A and Level AA Success Criteria, or a Level AA conforming alternate version is provided.

Level A and AA are required.

Level AAA: The Web page satisfies all the Level A, Level AA and Level AAA Success Criteria, or a Level AAA conforming alternate version is provided.

Level AAA is recommended and strongly encouraged but is not required. Satisfying AAA increases accessibility and usability.

22   Images With Information Must Have Alternative Text.

Description

Any image that contains information such as image text, stylized text such as logos, button image text, math equations, ASCII symbols or art, photographs, image charts, and graphs must have equivalent text. Images that do not contain information or are decorative should be coded in alternative text as an empty string or "NULL" and not be exposed to Assistive technology.

Categories

Images, ALT text, Alternative Text, Charts, Pictures, Photos

Reference

Section 508: 1194.22 (a) A text equivalent for every non-text element shall be provided (for example: via "alt", "longdesc", or in element content).

WCAG 2.0: 1.1.1 (Level A) All non-text content that is presented to the user has a text alternative that serves the equivalent purpose:

> http://www.w3.org/WAI/WCAG20/quickref/20081211/#text-equiv-all

WCAG 2.0: H30: Providing link text that describes the purpose of a link for anchor elements

> http://www.w3.org/TR/2008/NOTE-WCAG20-TECHS-20081211/H30

WCAG 2.0: H2: Combining adjacent image and text links for the same resource.

> http://www.w3.org/TR/WCAG20-TECHS/H2.html

WCAG 2.0: H33: Supplementing link text with the title attribute.

http://www.w3.org/TR/WCAG20-TECHS/H33.html

22.1 ALT Attribute Must Be Present For All Images (While This Attribute Must Be Present, It Can Be An Empty String).

Use: Alt="(text equivalent)". For example:
(Image with newsletter image and image text)
<img src="newsletter.gif" alt="Free newsletter. Get free recipes, news, and more. Learn more."/>

22.2 Use Empty String (A NULL String) For Images With No Information.

Use Null HTML ALT text (empty string – quotes with no space "") and no title attribute on IMG elements for images that Assistive technology should ignore. For example:
(end of section decorative line image) <img="section_end_line.png" alt="">

Figure 2: Decorative paragraph line divider requiring no ALT text.

22.3 Providing For Longer Descriptions For Equivalent Text.

If more than a sentence is required (greater than 100 characters) for a text equivalent and description then use one of the following methods:

- Captions: Captions can also contain links and be styled. Captions must be numbered.
- Adjacent Text: Text directly next to the image. This can be a full paragraph that is directly close in proximity and is visually associated.
- Link to full description: Link to a description located in another location such as the appendix. Supply a return link.
- Link to a file that has data for many charts (include a return link)
- A combination of a short caption description with a link to more complete explanation.

For example:

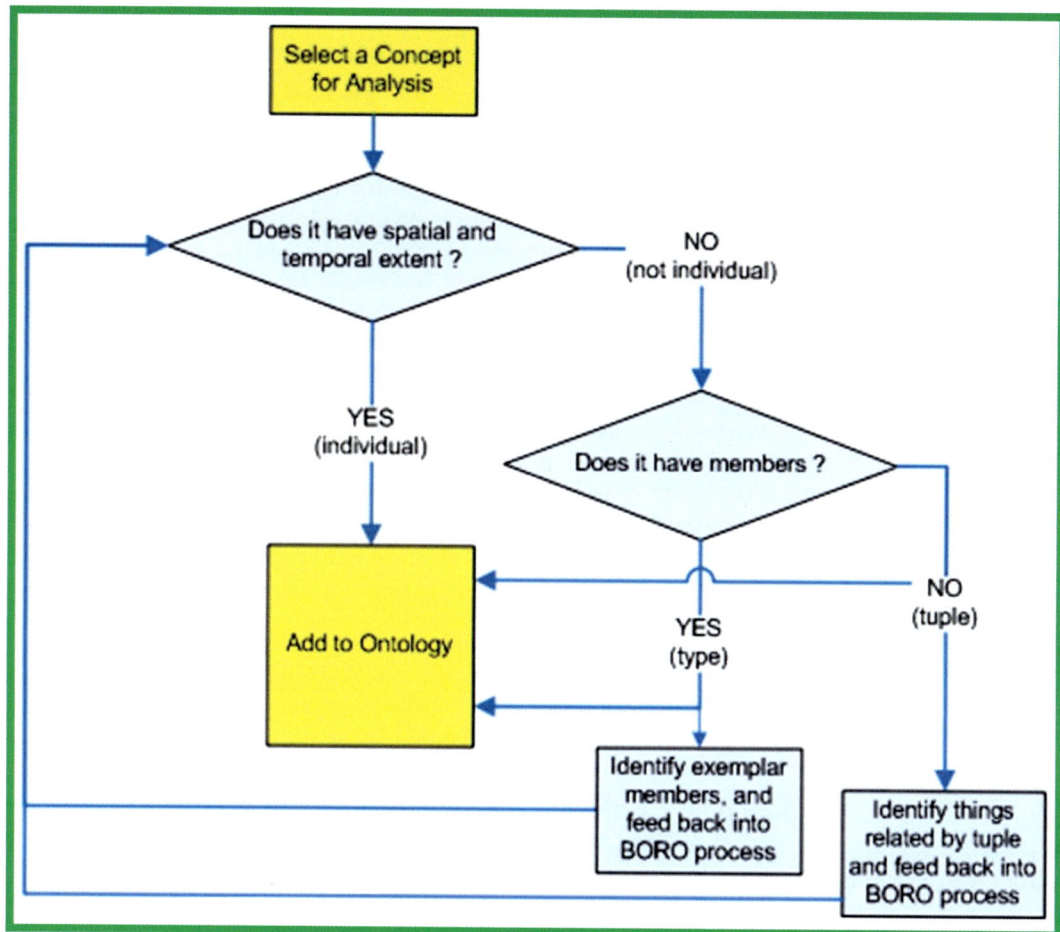

Figure 3: The steps of a process.

Where the caption text "steps of processing facilities procurement" would be a link to the steps described in detail elsewhere in the document, an external file, or website.

22.4   Do Not Duplicate Link Text Surrounding Linked Images.

If a link wraps around an image, do not duplicate the link text with ALT text. Use the null or empty string alt="" when described by the link. For example:

```
<a href="information.html" ><img src="info.png" alt="" >
```

22.5   Icons Indicating Information Or Action Must Have Alternative Text Unless Wrapped In A Descriptive Link.

If a descriptive link text wraps around an icon, do not duplicate the link text with ALT text. If the icon image is not wrapped in a descriptive link then there must be ALT text to describe what the icon is indicating. This information must be specific to the item the icon is related to. If a checkmark indicates status or action needed for a row in a table then the checkmark should indicate what record it refers to and what that status or action required is. When an image is the only content of a link, the description lets a user distinguish this link from other links in the Web page and helps the user determine whether to follow the link. The text alternative for the image describes the unique function of the link.

22.6   Test: Code Check: Every IMG Has ALT With Text Or "".

Any <img> tag must have an alt=. If missing this will result in the image file name being referenced and will trigger failures in automated testing.

22.7   Test: Length Of ALT.

For each IMG element, calculate the length of text within the ALT attribute value. If the ALT text is greater than 100 characters (English) then it must be shortened or the user must confirm that it is the shortest ALT text possible. If ALT text is extensive and cannot be condensed suggest another method such as adding text to the page, or providing a descriptive link in the document.

22.8   Test: Determine If The Image Is Decorative.

"Decorative" is defined as "content that does not provide information, functionality, and sensory experience and is neither multimedia nor time-dependent interactive". ALT text for all IMG elements is the empty string ("") if the image is decorative.

23   Color Cannot be Used As The Only Means Of Conveying Information And This Means: Indicating An Action, Prompting A Response, Or Distinguishing An Object. Information Conveyed By Color Differences Must Be Available In Text.

Description

Examples of information conveyed only by color differences are: "required fields are red", "error is shown in red", and "Mary's sales are in red, Tom's are in blue". Examples of indications of an action include: using color to indicate that a link will open in a new window or that a database entry has been updated successfully. An example of prompting a response would be: using highlighting on form fields to indicate that a required field had been left blank.

Note: This should not in any way discourage the use of color on a page, or even color coding if it is redundant with other visual or textual indication.

Categories

Color

Reference

Section 508: 1194.22 (c) Web pages shall be designed so that all information conveyed with color is also available without color, for example from the context or markup.

WCAG 2.0: Use of Color: Understanding SC 1.4.1 (Level A):

http://www.w3.org/TR/UNDERSTANDING-WCAG20/visual-audio-contrast-without-color.html

WCAG 2.0: G14 (Level A): Ensuring that information conveyed by color differences is also available in text:

http://www.w3.org/TR/2012/NOTE-WCAG20-TECHS-20120103/G14

23.1   Always Include Text With Controls Identified By Color.

Include a text cue for colored form controls where color has meaning. This can in the name and appear directly on the control as text or directly adjacent to the control.

23.2   Disabled Fields Must Not Be Indicated By Color Alone (For Example: Visually Grayed Out But Not Disabled In The Code).

Disabled form elements must be disabled via code markup or script command that make the field both visually grayed out and inactive functionally. The disabled elements do not receive focus. Disabled controls are skipped in tabbing navigation. For example: <input disabled name="address">

23.3   Use Text And Common Symbols For Status Indicators.

Text along with color and commonly know icons can be used to clearly identify the status.

See the following for a list of icons:

http://www.w3.org/TR/WD-wwwicn.html

For Example:

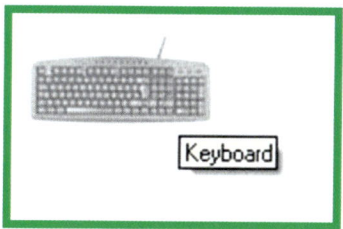

Figure 4: Keyboard Icon with ALT-text "Keyboard".

23.4 Test: Indicate In Text What The Color Is Indicating.

For each item where a color difference is used to convey information: Check that the information conveyed is also available in text. If the color changes due to state, the text must be updated at the same time. Color can be used in conjunction with text to highlight content such as marking an asterisk red for required fields where color alone is not required to indicate the requirement.

24 Tables Must Have SCOPE For Column And Row Headers in Simple Tables.

Description

Header cells without SCOPE cannot be associated with data cells using most Assistive technology (Some new versions can deduce which are which but you cannot rely on that). The objective is to associate header cells with data cells in complex tables using the SCOPE attribute. The SCOPE identifies whether the cell is a header for a row, column, or group of rows or columns. The values ROW, COL, ROWGROUP, and COLGROUP identify these possible scopes respectively.

Categories

Table, Scope, Header, Columns, Rows

Reference

Section 508: 1194.22(g) Row and column headers shall be identified for data tables.

Section 508: 1194.22(h) Markup shall be used to associate data cells and header cells for data tables that have two or more logical levels of row or column headers.)

WCAG 2.0: H63 (Level A): Using the scope attribute to associate header cells and data cells in data tables:

> http://www.w3.org/TR/WCAG-TECHS/H63.html

WCAG 2.0: H43 (Level A): Using ID and HEADERS attributes to associate data cells with header cells in data tables:

> http://www.w3.org/TR/WCAG20-TECHS/H43.html

24.1 Column And Row Headers Must Have SCOPE In All Cases In Simple Tables.

TH is for headers, TD for data, but for cells acting as both use TD

All TH elements must have a scope attribute.

All TD elements that act as headers for must have a scope attribute.

Example usage of TH and SCOPE, in this example both the number and name will read along with the column header to identify the data cell with Assistive technology:

```
<style>
table {font-family: arial;}
table {margin: .9em; border: 2px solid blue; }
th, tr, td { padding: .9em; border: 2px solid blue; }
</style>

<table border="2">
 <caption>Contact Information</caption>
 <tr>
 <th scope="col">Item#</th>
 <th scope="col">Name</th>
 <th scope="col">Phone#</th>
 <th scope="col">Fax#</th>
 <th scope="col">City</th>
 </tr><tr>
 <td>1.</td>
 <th scope="row">Joel Garner</th>
 <td>412-212-5421</td>
 <td>412-212-5400</td>
 <td>Pittsburgh</td>
 </tr><tr>
 <td>2.</td>
 <th scope="row">Clive Lloyd</th>
 <td>410-306-1420</td>
 <td>410-306-5400</td>
 <td>Baltimore</td>
 </tr><tr>
 <td>3.</td>
 <th scope="row">Gordon Greenidge</th>
 <td>281-564-6720</td>
 <td>281-511-6600</td>
 <td>Houston</td>
 </tr>
</table>
```

Contact Information				
Item#	Name	Phone#	Fax#	City
1.	**Joel Garner**	412-212-5421	412-212-5400	Pittsburgh
2.	**Clive Lloyd**	410-306-1420	410-306-5400	Baltimore
3.	**Gordon Greenidge**	281-564-6720	281-511-6600	Houston

Figure 5: Table using SCOPE for row and column headers.

24.2 Complex Tables (Merged Cells, Sub-Headers) Must Have ID And HEADERS in HTML or Tagged as Headers And Associated in PDF And Not Used in Word.

For complex tables use IDs and HEADERS, For example:

```
<table border="3">
<tr>
<th rowspan="2" id="h">Homework</th>
<th colspan="3" id="e">Exams</th>
<th colspan="3" id="p">Projects</th>
</tr>
<tr>
<th id="e1" headers="e">1</th>
<th id="e2" headers="e">2</th>
<th id="ef" headers="e">Final</th>
<th id="p1" headers="p">1</th>
<th id="p2" headers="p">2</th>
<th id="pf" headers="p">Final</th>
</tr>
<tr>
<td headers="h">15%</td>
<td headers="e e1">15%</td>
<td headers="e e2">15%</td>
<td headers="e ef">20%</td>
<td headers="p p1">10%</td>
<td headers="p p2">10%</td>
<td headers="p pf">15%</td>
</tr>
</table>
```

Homework	Exams			Projects		
	1	2	Final	1	2	Final
15%	15%	15%	20%	10%	10%	15%

Figure 6: Table using HEADERS.

24.3   Do Not Format Data Tables With Blank Cells.

Do not use blank rows or columns for visual table spacing. If you need separation, use thicker colored lines or similar.

24.4   Test: Check Column Header Code.

Check table code for presence of SCOPE for headers. Determine whether column or row headers contain SCOPE for the columns or rows that the TH header represents, in particular check for and needed COLGROUP to match correct headers with cells.

Determine whether or not table cell and table header relationships correspond correctly with TH and TD scope attribute content.

The following chart serves as a general guide:

Header Cells with Scope Set to Column and Row			
Column Header 1 (scope set to "col")	Column Header 2 (scope set to "col")	Column Header 3 (scope set to "col")	Column Header 4 (scope set to "col")
Row Header 1 (scope set to "row")	Row 1 Column 2	Row 1 Column 3	Row 1 Column 4
Row Header 2 (scope set to "row")	Row 2 Column 2	Row 2 Column 3	Row 2 Column 4
Row Header 3 (scope set to "row")	Row 3 Column 2	Row 3 Column 3	Row 3 Column 4
Row Header 4 (scope set to "row")	Row 4 Column 2	Row 4 Column 3	Row 4 Column 4

Figure 7: Table showing use of SCOPE set to "col" and "row".

24.5   Test: Check Code For IDs And HEADERS For Complex Tables.

- Check for layout tables: determine whether the content has a relationship with other content in both its column and its row. If "no," the table is a layout table. If "yes," the table is a data table.

- For data tables, check that any cell that is associated with more than one row and/or one column header contains a headers attribute that lists the ID for all headers associated with that cell.

- For data tables that have any cells containing an ID or HEADERS attribute,

  a. Check that each ID listed in the headers attribute of the data cell matches the ID attribute of a cell that is used as a header element

  b. Check that the headers attribute of a data cell contains the ID attribute of all headers associated with the data cell

  c. Check that all IDs are unique (that is, no two elements in the page have the same ID)

24.6 PDF files Must Have Header Tags Cell Associated for Complex Tables.

A simple grid table needs only tags <H1>, <H2>, etc for columns and row headers. For complex tables you must set the cell ID to the headers. This can be done manually or with a program like CommonLook.

24.7 Test: Screen Reader

Screen Read table and determine if column and row headers are voiced from middle of table.

25 Windows, Frames, and Regions Must Have Unique Titles.

Description

Frames and windows without unique titles cause Assistive technology and cognitively disabled users to lose orientation and identification of pages. The title of each web page should identify the subject of the page and make sense when read out of context, for example when read by a screen reader or in a list of search results which uses the window title. These should be concise.

Categories

Windows, Frames, Titles, Regions, Names

Reference
Section 508: 1194.21 (d) Sufficient information about a user interface element including the identity, operation and state of the element shall be available to Assistive technology. When an image represents a program element, the information conveyed by the image must also be available in text.

Section 508: 1194.22 (i) Frames shall be titled with text that facilitates frame identification and navigation

WCAG 2.0: H64 (Level A): Using the TITLE attribute of the frame and IFRAME elements:

25.1   Each Page Must Have A Unique Title.

Pages must have unique titles that describe the content. For example in HTML:
<head><title>
 G88: Providing descriptive titles for web pages | Techniques for WCAG 2.0
</title></head>

25.2   Frames Must Have Unique Titles Correctly Describing Frame Content.

Frames must have unique titles; Use a unique TITLE attribute of the FRAME or IFRAME element to describe the contents of each frame. For example:

```
[Frames.htm]

<head>
 <title>Simple Frameset Page</title>
</head>
 <frameset cols="30%, 70%">
 <frame src="MainMenu.htm" title="Main Menu" />
 <frame src="Documents.htm" title="Documents" />
 <noframes>
 <body>
 <a href="Documents.htm">Select to go to the Documents library</a>
 </body>
 </noframes>
 </frameset>

[MainMenu.htm]

<head>
 <title>Main Menu</title>
<style>
h1 {font-family: arial;}
</style>
</head>

<h1> MainMenu </h1>

[Documents.htm]

<head>
 <title>Documents</title>
```

```
<style>
h1, p {font-family: arial;}
</style>
</head>

<h1> Documents </h1>

<p>

<iframe src="Ad.htm" id="iframe" height="100" width="300" name="iframe" title="Announcements">
</iframe>

</p>

[Ad.htm]

<head>
 <title>Advertisement</title>
<style>
h1 {font-family: arial;}
</style>
</head>

<h3>** Announcements **</h3>
```

25.3　Regions Must Have Unique Names.

```
<div role="region" aria-labelledby="Name">
<form method="post" action="#">

    <input type="text" id="radio1" name="First" />
    <label for="radio1">First Name</label>
    <input type="text" id="radio2" name="Last" />
    <label for="radio2">Last Name</label>

</form>
</div>
```

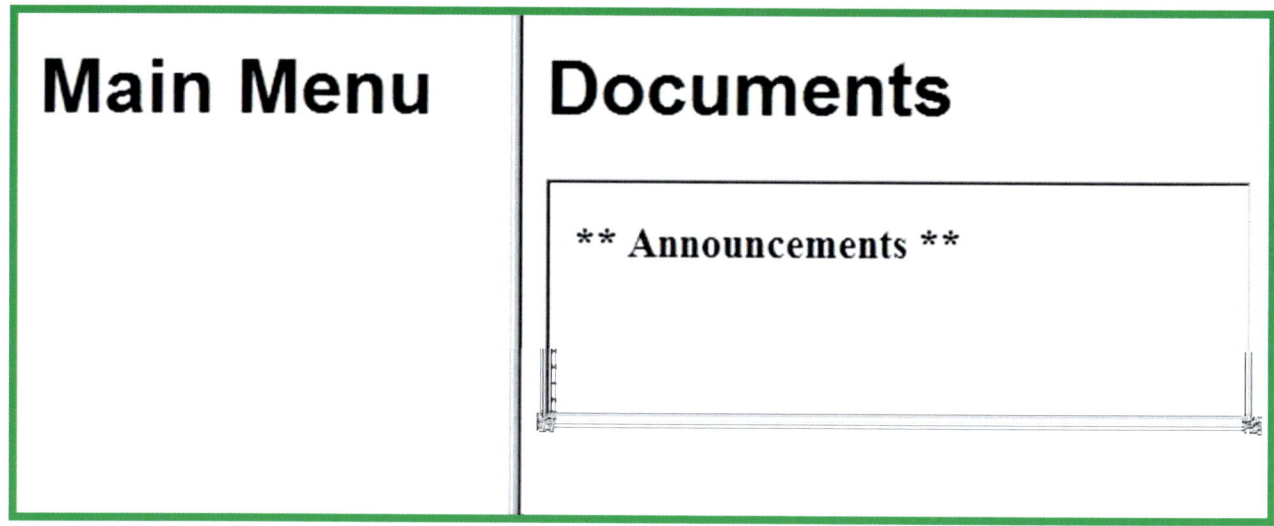

Figure 8: Frames with each frame having a unique title.

25.4   Test: Title Description.

The title must identify the subject of the web page and make sense when read out of context, for example by a screen reader or in a site map or list of search results.

Titles that fail are those which are only meaningful within context. For example:

```
<title>Introduction</title>
```

Or the titles are too long (greater than 100 characters, excluding numbering and main site or volume information)

Titles should list the most important identifying information first

25.5   Test: Unique Frame Title.

Check that while moving from frame to frame each frame has its own unique TITLE.

26 LABEL Element Must Be Associated With The Screen Text Label. Both Are Required For Each Field.

Description

Explicit LABEL must be used or the field will not have an identifier associated with it for Assistive technology. LABEL element must be used to explicitly associate a form control with a LABEL. A LABEL is attached to a specific form control through the use of the FOR attribute. Every form field must have an ID that matches the FOR attribute of exactly one label.

Categories

Fields, Label, Form, Control

Reference

Section 508: 1194.22 (n) When electronic forms are designed to be completed on-line, the form shall allow people using Assistive technology to access the information, field elements, and functionality required for completion and submission of the form, including all directions and cues.

WCAG 2.0: H44 (Level A): Using label elements to associate text labels with form controls:

   http://www.w3.org/TR/WCAG-TECHS/H44.html

26.1   Use LABEL For All User Input And Selection Type Fields.

Use LABEL for INPUT TYPE="TEXT", TYPE="CHECKBOX", TYPE="RADIO", TYPE="FILE", TYPE="PASSWORD", TEXTAREA, and SELECT. For example:

```
<label for="firstname">First name:</label>
<input type="text" name="firstname" id="firstname" /><br/><br/>

Computer Skills:<br/>
<input type="checkbox" id="HTML" name="computerskills" >
<label for="HTML">HTML</label>
<input type="checkbox" id="XML" name="computerskills" >
<label for="XML">XML</label>
<br/><br/>

Flavor:<br/>
<input type="radio" name="flavor" id="choc" value="chocolate" />
 <label for="choc">Chocolate</label><br/>
<input type="radio" name="flavor" id="cream" value="cream"/>
 <label for="cream">Cream Filled</label><br/>
<input type="radio" name="flavor" id="honey" value="honey"/>
 <label for="honey">Honey Glazed</label>
<br/><br/>

<label for="s1">Numbers</label>
 <select id="s1" size="1">
 <option>One</option>
 <option selected="selected">Two</option>
 <option>Three</option>
 </select>
```

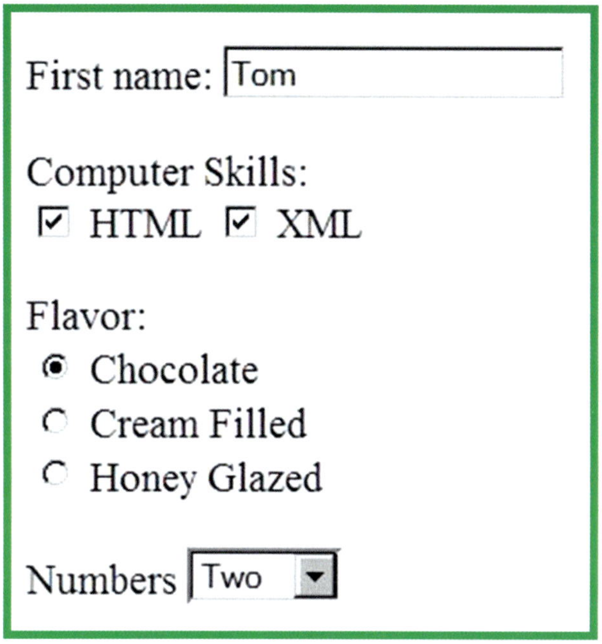

Figure 9: Form fields using LABEL and screen text.

26.2   Do Not Use TITLE Attribute In Place Of LABEL.

TITLE should not be used as a substitute for LABEL. TITLE should also not duplicate the LABEL. The TITLE cannot be activated by keyboard and is not recognized by all screen readers. TITLE may be used for supplementary helpful information but not critical instructions or duplication of field names.

Title may be used when there is no other way to use LABEL. An example would be multiple fields within a table where use of LABEL would distort the visual usage or cause association issues among the cells and fields with the table layout. It is important to note that the form design must allow for correct use of LABEL; however it is noted that last minute changes may necessitate secondary accessibility solutions. Future modifications must correct the layout to allow for correct labeling.

26.3   Test: LABEL

Check that there is a LABEL element that identifies the purpose of the control directly adjacent to the INPUT, TEXTAREA, or SELECT element.

26.4   Test: FOR Matches ID

Check that the FOR attribute of the LABEL element matches the ID of the INPUT, TEXTAREA, or SELECT element.

26.5   Test: LABEL is Visible

Check that the LABEL element is visible on the user screen.

27 FIELDSET must be used for multiple fields that are logically grouped.

Description

Users must understand the relationship of the controls and be able to interact with the form it is when presented in a non-visual format. Provide a semantic grouping for related form controls. A set of radio buttons (or checkboxes) is related if they all submit values for a single named field. They must be grouped semantically so they can be more easily treated as a single control. The border visual effect (FIELDSET box) can be modified in CSS by overriding the BORDER property of the FIELDSET and the POSITION property of the legend.

Categories

Field, Fieldset, Field Group

Reference

Section 508:1194.22 (n) When electronic forms are designed to be completed on-line, the form shall allow people using Assistive technology to access the information, field elements, and functionality required for completion and submission of the form, including all directions and cues.

WCAG 2.0: H71 (Level A): Providing a description for groups of form controls using FIELDSET and LEGEND elements:

http://www.w3.org/TR/2008/NOTE-WCAG20-TECHS-20081211/H71.html

27.1 Provide A LEGEND For The FIELDSET That Is Concise And Related To Each LABEL.

Follow these rules in making a LEGEND:

- LEGEND is between 1 and 6 words.
- Words chosen for the LEGEND make sense when joined to each LABEL

In this example, form fields for residential and postal addresses are distinguished by the value of the legend in each FIELDSET grouping.

```
<form action="http://example.com/adduser" method="post">
 <fieldset>
 <legend>Residential Address</legend>
 <label for="raddress">Address: </label>
 <input type="text" id="raddress" name="raddress" />
 <label for="rzip">Postal/Zip Code: </label>
 <input type="text" id="rzip" name="rzip" />
 <br/>...more Residential Address information...
 </fieldset><br/><br/>

 <fieldset>
 <legend>Postal Address</legend>
 <label for="paddress">Address: </label>
 <input type="text" id="paddress" name="paddress" />
 <label for="pzip">Postal/Zip Code: </label>
 <input type="text" id="pzip" name="pzip" />
 <br/>...more Postal Address information...
 </fieldset>
</form>
```

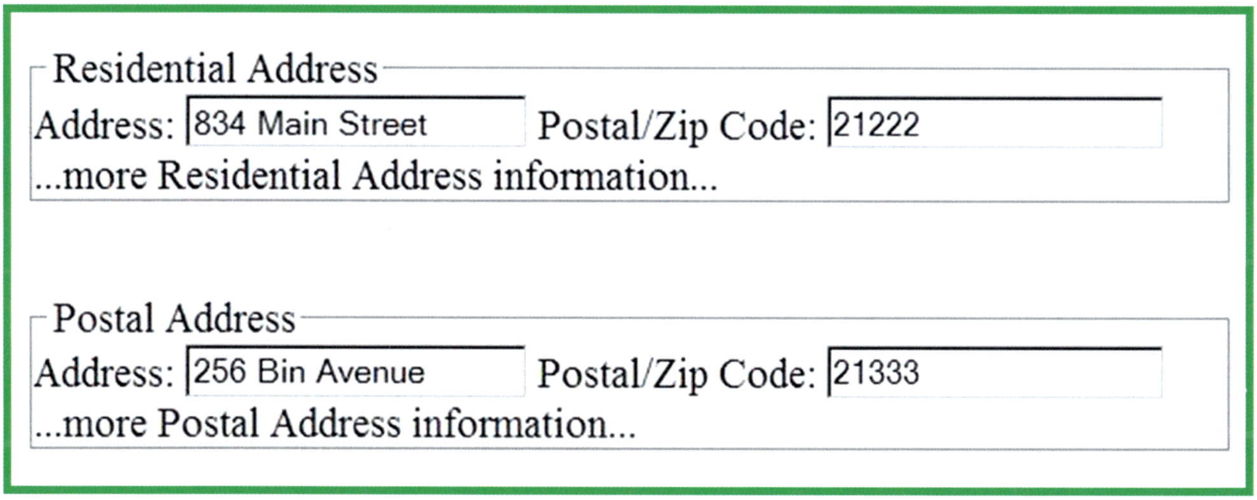

Figure 10: LEGEND and FIELDSET for INPUT fields.

27.2   Use FIELDSET For Related Radio Buttons And Checkboxes.

Grouping controls is most important for related radio buttons and related checkboxes. A set of radio buttons or checkboxes is related if they all submit values for a single named field. They must be grouped semantically so they can be more easily treated as a single control.

```
<fieldset>
 <legend>I am interested in: (Check all that apply):</legend>
 <input type="checkbox" id="photo" name="interests" value="ph">
 <label for="photo">Photography</label><br />
 <input type="checkbox" id="watercol" name="interests" checked="checked" value="wa">
 <label for="watercol">Watercolor</label><br />
 <input type="checkbox" id="acrylic" name="interests" checked="checked" value="ac">
 <label for="acrylic">Acrylic</label>
 …
</fieldset>
```

```
I am interested in: (Check all that apply):
☐ Photography
☑ Watercolor
☑ Acrylic …
```

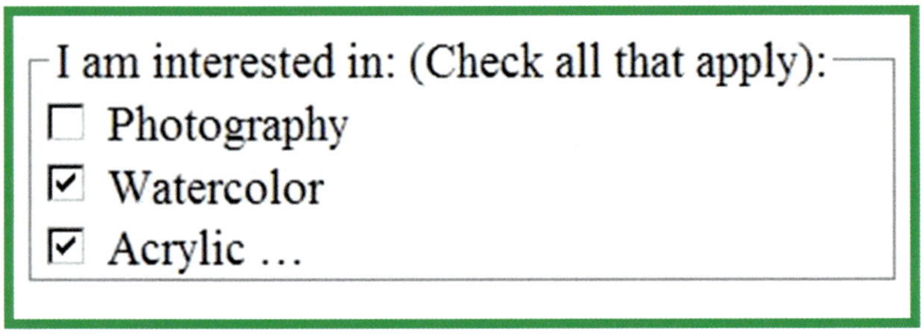

Figure 11: FIELDSET with LEGEND and LABEL.

27.3   Test: Check Grouped Elements.

- Check for groups of related form controls.

- Check that the group of logically related input or select elements are contained within a FIELDSET.

- Check that each FIELDSET has a LEGEND element that includes a description for that group. If there are related form controls, they should be grouped with FIELDSET.

28 Timeouts Must Allow More Time To Complete And Save Progress.

Description

Users with disabilities may require additional time to complete multiple field inputs, especially when they span pages. The time required may exceed the session timeout. Web servers that require user authentication often terminate the session after a set period of time if there is no activity by the user. If the user is unable to input the data quickly enough and the session times out before they submit, the server will require re-authentication before proceeding. When this happens, the server stores the data in a temporary session cache while the user logs in, and when the user has re-authenticated, the data is made available from the cache and the form is processed as if there had never been a session timeout. The server does not keep the cache indefinitely, merely long enough to ensure success after re-authentication in a single user session, such as one day.

Whether the timeout is a local script or a network/server timeout, it is the duty of the developer to catch the timeout with error handling and inform the user of the status and allow more time. If there is no further activity after notification (at least 5 minutes) the session can then finally end, but with notification of the session ending.

Categories

Timeout, Session

Reference

Section 508: 1194.22 (p) When a timed response is required, the user shall be alerted and given sufficient time to indicate more time is required.

WCAG 2.0: G105 (Level AAA): Saving data so that it can be used after a user re-authenticates:

> http://www.w3.org/TR/2012/NOTE-WCAG20-TECHS-20120103/G105

WCAG 2.0: G133 (Level A): Providing a checkbox on the first page of a multipart form that allows users to ask for longer session time limit or no session time limit:

> http://www.w3.org/TR/2007/WD-WCAG20-TECHS-20071211/G133.html

WCAG 2.0: Re-authenticating: Understanding SC 2.2.5 (Level AAA):

> http://www.w3.org/WAI/GL/UNDERSTANDING-WCAG20/time-limits-server-timeout.html

28.1   Session Must Retain User Data.

Provide options to continue without loss of data. Check that the process can continue and be completed without loss of data, including the original data and any changes made after re-authentication.

28.2   Provide For Extra Time At Start Of Session.

Provide a checkbox or link on the first page of a multipart form that allows users to ask for longer session time limit or no session time limit. This technique is used to minimize the risk that users with disabilities will lose their work by providing a checkbox to request additional time to complete multipart forms.

For example, a script timer that allows for more time before a page refresh:

```
<script type="text/javascript">
<!--
function timeControl()
{
        // set timer for 15 minutes , then ask user to confirm.
setTimeout('userCheck()', 900000);
}

function userCheck()
{
        // set page refresh for 5 minutes
var id=setTimeout('pageReload()', 300000);
        // If user selects "OK" the timer is reset
        // else the page will refresh from the server.
if (confirm("This page will refresh in 5 Minutes. Would you like more time?"))
 {clearTimeout(id);timeControl();}
}

function pageReload() { window.location.reload(true);}

timeControl();
-->
</script>
</head>
<body>
<h1>Stock Market Quotes</h1>
...etc...
```

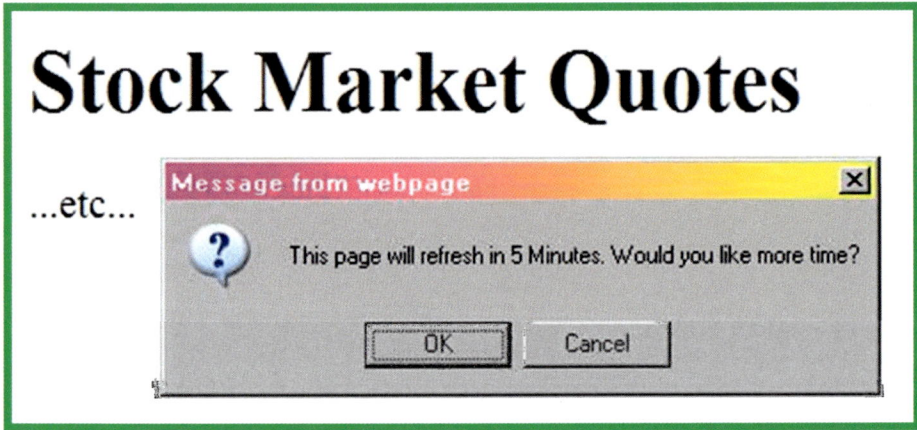

Figure 12: Timeout message allowing for more time option.

28.3   Provide Option To Save Data If Session Cannot Be Continued.

187

A long questionnaire provided within a single web page has information at the beginning that indicates that the user session will time out after 15 minutes. The user is also informed that the questionnaire can be saved at any point and completed at a later time.

28.4   Test: Additional Time Option.

- Check that the web page includes a checkbox to request additional time to complete the form.

- Check that if the checkbox is checked, additional time is provided to complete the form.

- 7.5 Test Additional Time Process Check.

- Log in and begin the timed activity.

- Allow the session to time out.

- Submit the data.

- Re-authenticate.

- Check that the process can continue and be completed without loss of data, including the original data and any changes made after re-authentication.

29 Error Messages Must Be Located At The Top Of Screen With Links To Fields With The Link Text Indicating The Field Name And Error OR Contain The Same Information In A Pop-Up OR Dynamically Indicate Issue At Time Of Error.

Description

Assistive technology users will not know there was an error until they have an indicator to identify an error and provide error correction information to the user, with navigation to correct the error and advance to the next error.

Categories

Error, Message

Reference

Section 508:1194.22 (n) When electronic forms are designed to be completed on-line, the form shall allow people using Assistive technology to access the information, field elements, and functionality required for completion and submission of the form, including all directions and cues.

WCAG 2.0: G139 (Level A): Creating a mechanism that allows users to jump to errors:

http://www.w3.org/TR/WCAG20-TECHS/G139.html

WCAG 2.0: G83 (Level A): Providing text descriptions to identify required fields that were not completed:

http://www.w3.org/TR/2012/NOTE-WCAG20-TECHS-20120103/G83

WCAG 2.0: G85 (Level A): Providing a text description when user input falls outside the required format or values:

http://www.w3.org/TR/WCAG20-TECHS/G85.html

29.1 Provide Text Errors At Top Of Page Linking To Error Location With Instructions Or Provide The Same Information And Function In A Pop-Up Window.

Errors must be identified in text. The error text names the field in which the error occurred, describes the error and the method to make a correction. You can add (in addition to text) a unique character, color, and highlights.

- Indicate clearly in text at the top of the page that there were errors.

- Text describes the nature of the errors.

- Text names the field which is the same as the visible and programmatic label.

- Provide links to the fields that had the problem so the user can navigate to them to fix the problems.

29.2 Indicate In Text Which Fields Are Mandatory.

For mandatory fields, the labels of the fields indicate whether or not they are mandatory. The user tabs to a mandatory field, and tabs out of the field without entering any data or selecting a choice. A client-side script modifies the label of the field or executes a pop-up to indicate that leaving it blank was an error. The key is to put focus to the error message and then return focus to the field to be corrected.

29.3 In All User Error Cases Provide A Text Description, Method To Correct, And Focus Method To Field In Question (Usually a Link or Next Focus).

Correct error handling scenarios:

- The user inputs invalid data in a form field. When the user exits the field, an alert dialog appears that describes the nature of the error so the user can fix it. The focus is then directed back to form field in error.

- The user inputs invalid data in a form field and submits the form. The server returns the form, with the user's data still present, and indicates clearly in text at the top of the page that there were input errors. The text describes the nature of the error(s) and clearly indicates which field had the problem so the user can easily navigate to it to fix the problem.

- The user inputs invalid data in a form field and attempts to submit the form. Client side scripting detects the error, cancels the form submission, and modifies the document to provide a text description after the submit button describing the error, with links to the field(s) with the error. The script also modifies the labels of the fields with the problems to highlight them. Optionally a pop-up can notify the user of the error for that specific field or group of fields. The focus must always return to the field with the error or links for multiple fields so the user can gain focus to fix the selected field from the group. The error links must indicate the field name.

29.4 Alert Or Popup Error Notice Must Direct Focus Back To Field In Error When Done.

Individual validation for fields before submitting can use an alert or popup with focus to the error explanation and then return focus to named field in question. For example:

```
<script>

var numb = '0123456789';
var lwr = 'abcdefghijklmnopqrstuvwxyz';
var upr = 'ABCDEFGHIJKLMNOPQRSTUVWXYZ';

function isValid(parm,val)
{
if (parm == "") return true;
        for (i=0; i<parm.length; i++)
        {
        if (val.indexOf(parm.charAt(i),0) == -1) return false;
        }
return true;
}

function isNumber(parm) {return isValid(parm,numb);}
function isLower(parm) {return isValid(parm,lwr);}
function isUpper(parm) {return isValid(parm,upr);}
function isAlpha(parm) {return isValid(parm,lwr+upr);}
function isAlphaNum(parm) {return isValid(parm,lwr+upr+numb);}
```

```
</script>

<label for="Name">Name:</label>
<input type="text" name="Name" id="Name" tabindex="1"
onblur="if(!isAlpha(Name.value))
{alert('This is not a valid Name. Please use Alphabetic Letters only. (Example: Fred Smith)');
Name.focus();}" ;
 }"/>

<label for="Property">Property Number:</label>
<input type="text" name="Property" id="Property" tabindex="2"
onblur="if(!isNumber(Property.value))
{alert('This is not a valid Property Number. Please use Numbers only (Example: 212378).');
Property.focus();}"/>

<input type="button" value="Save" tabindex="3">
```

Figure 13: Error handling captures incorrect input, notifies user and returns focus to input field with error.

29.5 Test: Error Notifications.

- Fill out a form, deliberately leaving a required (mandatory) field blank, make an input error on another field, and submit the form.

- Check that a text message is provided that identifies the field that is missing required data.

- Check that a text message is provided that identifies the field with the input error.

- Check that there is a link to each field that is missing required data from the missing data message.

191

- Check that there is a link to the list of errors from the error message.

29.6   Test: Error Instructions.

- Fill out a form, deliberately entering user input that falls outside the required format or values

- Check that a text description is provided that identifies the field in error and provides some information about the nature of the invalid entry and how to fix it.

29.7   Test: Individual Errors.

For individual field errors before submit:

- Enter invalid data.

- Determine if an alert describing the error is provided.

29.8   Test: Controls Information.

Determine if each of the form controls provides information about the expected format.

30   Keyboards Can Access All Controls And Navigation.

Description

Permit individuals who rely on a keyboard or keyboard interface to access the functionality of the content. To do this, make sure that all event handlers triggered by non-keyboard events are also associated with a keyboard-based event, or provide redundant keyboard-based mechanisms to accomplish the functionality provided by other device-specific functions. Some assistive technologies rely on keyboard only access and cannot use a mouse; as a result all functionality must work completely with the keyboard as it does with the mouse.

Categories

Keyboard Access, Keyboard Only

Reference

Section 508:1194.21(a) When software is designed to run on a system that has a keyboard, product functions shall be executable from a keyboard where the function itself or the result of performing a function can be discerned textually.

Section 508:1194.22(n) When electronic forms are designed to be completed on-line, the form shall allow people using Assistive technology to access the information, field elements, and functionality required for completion and submission of the form, including all directions and cues.

WCAG 2.0: SCR20 (Level A): Using both keyboard and other device-specific functions:

http://www.w3.org/WAI/GL/WCAG20-TECHS/SCR20.html

30.1   Combine Keyboard Equivalents For Mouse State Detection.

For mouse specific JavaScript use:

- MOUSEDOWN with KEYDOWN

- MOUSEUP with KEYUP

- MOUSEOVER with FOCUS

- MOUSEOUT with BLUR

30.2   Include Keyboard Equivalency For All Mouse Events.

Include a series of buttons to execute, via keyboard, the equivalent mouse-specific functions implemented. This will handle mouse control that cannot be easily scripted to keyboard.

Event handler functions should check first to ensure the ENTER key was pressed before proceeding to handle the event. Check with mouse and then keyboard separately.

30.3   Provide keyboard alternatives for MOUSEOVER

TAB key substitute method for MOUSEOVER with ONFOCUS and ONBLUR. Hidden text is made visible and link is activated either by keyboard or mouse in this example:

```
<script type="text/javascript">

function visible()
{
if(document.getElementById)
 {document.getElementById('foward').style.visibility ="visible";}
else if(document.all)
 {document.all['foward'].style.visibility ="visible";}
else if(document.layers)
 {document.layers['foward'].visibility ="visible";}
}
```

```
function hidden()
{
if(document.getElementById)
 {document.getElementById('foward').style.visibility ="hidden";}
else if(document.all)
 {document.all['foward'].style.visibility ="hidden";}
else if(document.layers)
 {document.layers['foward'].visibility ="hidden";}
}

</script>

<body onload="javascript:hidden();">

<div id="FF">
<a href=# style="font-family: Webdings; color: #FF0000; font-size: 50pt"
onmouseover="visible()"
onfocus="visible()"
onblur="hidden()"
onmouseout="hidden()"
onclick="alert('Link Selected!')"
>8

</a>
</div>
<div id="foward">
<p class="enter">This is more information on the selection, </br>if you want to continue just select
the link.</p>
</div>

</body>
```

This is more information on the selection,
if you want to continue just select the link.

Figure 14: Keyboard can access rollover text that appears by TAB to object – indicated by focus - or mouse hover, When TAB focus is moved text is not visible same as mouse moving away.

30.4   Provide keyboard alternatives for Mouse Highlights

This routine allows for both keyboard and mouse to highlight some text and an image, it also allows the keyboard to make text appear.

```
<body onload="javascript:hide();">
<br/><br/>
<span id="text" style="font-family: arial; color: blue; background-color: yellow; font-weight: bold">
This is some text.<br/>
</span>
<button type="button" onclick="javascript:alert('Button Clicked')"
onfocus="show()"
onblur="hide()"
onmouseover="show()"
onmouseout="hide()">
Text Content</button>
<script>
function hide() { document.getElementById("text").style.visibility = "hidden";}
function show() { document.getElementById("text").style.visibility = "visible";}
</script>

<br/><br/>
<a href= "javascript:alert('Image Clicked')"
onkeypress="on(1)"
onkeyup="on(1)"
onblur="off(1)">
<img id="1" src="1.jpg"
onfocus="on(1)"
onblur="off(1)"
onmouseover="on(1)"
onmouseout="off(1)"
onkeypress="on(1)"
onkeyup="on(1)">
</a>

<script>
function on(imageId)
{document.getElementById(imageId).style.border = "solid yellow";}
function off(imageId)
{document.getElementById(imageId).style.border = "solid white";}
</script>

</body>
```

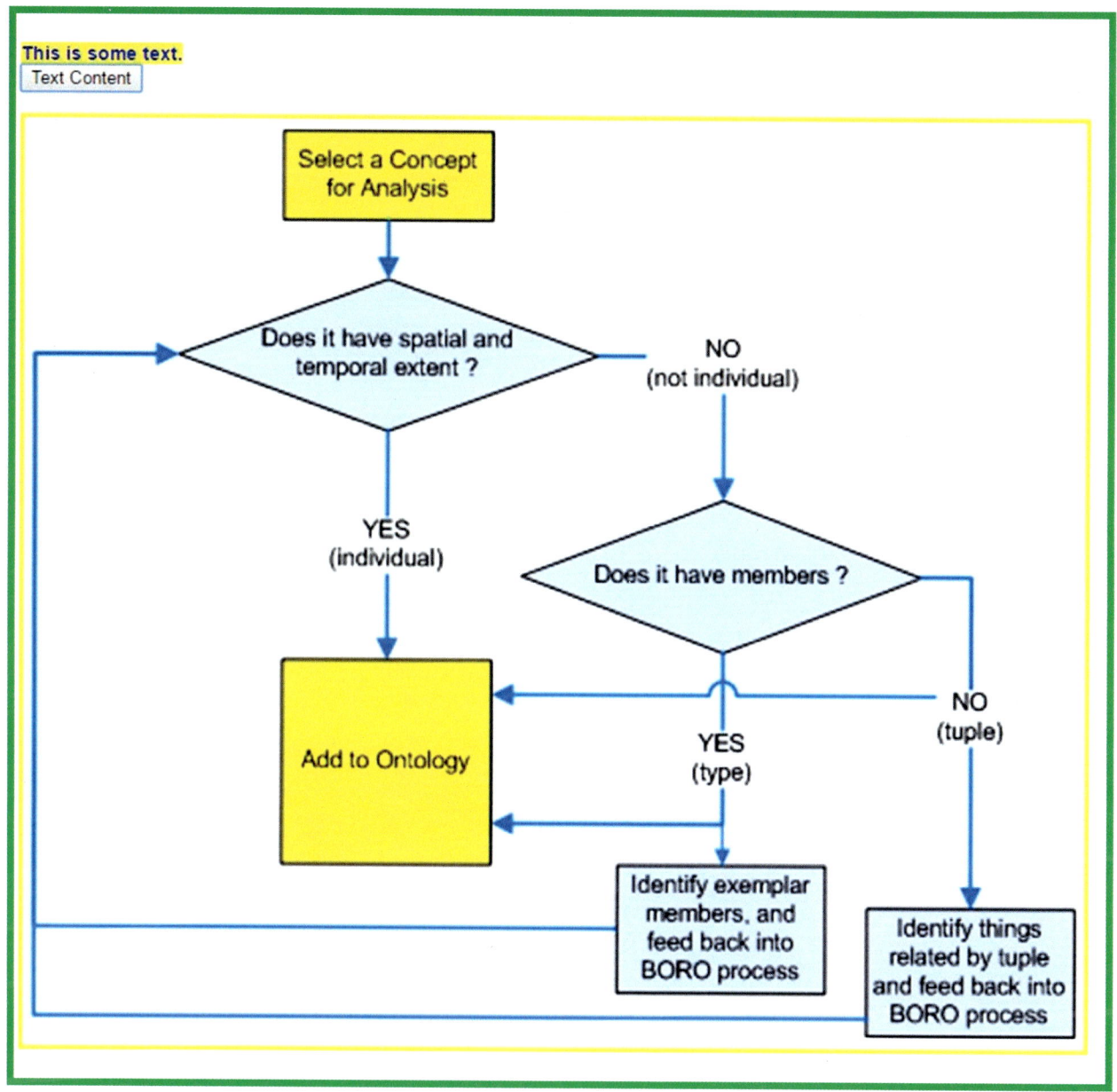

Figure 15: Highlight and text appear by Tab key.

30.5 Provide Keyboard Alternatives For ONCLICK For Non-Script Activation.

This approach can be used to create sites that do not rely on script, only if the navigation target provides the same functionality as the script. HREF is set to a real page, Process_Form htm. Process_Form.htm must provide the same functionality as the script. The "return false;" at the end of the Process_Form () event handling function tells the browser not to navigate to the URI. Without it, the browser would navigate to Process_Form.htm after the script ran.

```
<script>
function Process_Form()
{
//do stuff
return false;
}
</script>
<a href=" Process_Form.htm" onclick="return Process_Form();">Process Form </a>
```

30.6   Test: Keyboard Access.

- Find all interactive functionality.

- Check that all interactive functionality can be accessed using the keyboard alone.

30.7   Test: Keyboard Rollover.

Check keyboard for rollover events:

- Use the keyboard to set focus to the element containing the event handlers. Check that the image changes to the expected image.

- Use the keyboard to remove focus from the element (generally by moving focus to another element). Check that the image changes to the "standard" image.

- Verify that the layout of other elements on the page is not affected when the image is changed.

- Check with mouse and then keyboard separately. Both should execute functions the same.

31   Focus Must Always Be Visible And It Synchronizes With The TAB Key.

Description

Many types of users must track the focus with the visible indicator using the TAB key. The focus must track with the TAB key or orientation will be lost. When text fields receive focus, a vertical bar is displayed in the field, indicating that the user can insert text, or all of the text is highlighted, indicating that the user can type over the text. When a user interface control receives focus, a visible border is displayed around it. CSS can be used to enhance the focus but the focus must be synchronized with the keyboard. The CSS enhancements can never be used alone as indicators, the programmatic focus must be visible even if CSS is disabled and it must track with the TAB key.

Categories

Focus, Keyboard

Reference

Section 508:1194.21(c) A well-defined on-screen indication of the current focus shall be provided that moves among interactive interface elements as the input focus changes. The focus shall be programmatically exposed so that Assistive technology can track focus and focus changes.

WCAG 2.0: Focus Visible: Understanding SC 2.4.7 (Level AA):

http://www.w3.org/TR/UNDERSTANDING-WCAG20/navigation-mechanisms-focus-visible.html

31.1   Provide Enhanced Focus For Navigation And Controls.

Controls and links can be made more visible upon focus with CSS highlighting:

- Highlighting (local text background color difference such as black text with yellow background) a link or control when the mouse hovers over it or it receives focus

- Link text becomes bold and/or different color when it is focused on or active

- Dynamic rollover effects for text and buttons work well when keyboard equivalents are used.

31.2   Use CSS To Control Highlighting Input Fields.

Using CSS to highlight input fields upon focus:

```
<style>

.hform1
{
position: relative;
border: 1px solid blue;
background: Bisque;
color: darkred;
}

.hform2
{
```

```
position: relative;
border: 1px solid red;
background: yellow;
color: black;
}

</style>

</br></br>

<span class="hform1">
<label for="firstname">First Name (Label):</label>

<input class="hform1" id="firstname" type="text" onfocus="this.className='hform2'"
onmouseover="this.className='hform2'" onblur="this.className='hform1'"
onmouseout="this.className='hform1'"/>
Regular Text
</span>

</br></br>

<span class="hform1">
 <input type="radio" name="sex" value="male" id="sm" onfocus="this.className='hform2'"
onmouseover="this.className='hform2'" onblur="this.className='hform1'"
onmouseout="this.className='hform1'"/> <label for="sm"> Male (Label) </label><br/>

 <input type="radio" name="sex" value="female" id="sf" onfocus="this.className='hform2'"
onmouseover="this.className='hform2'" onblur="this.className='hform1'"
onmouseout="this.className='hform1'"/> <label for="sf"> Female (Label) </label>
</span>
```

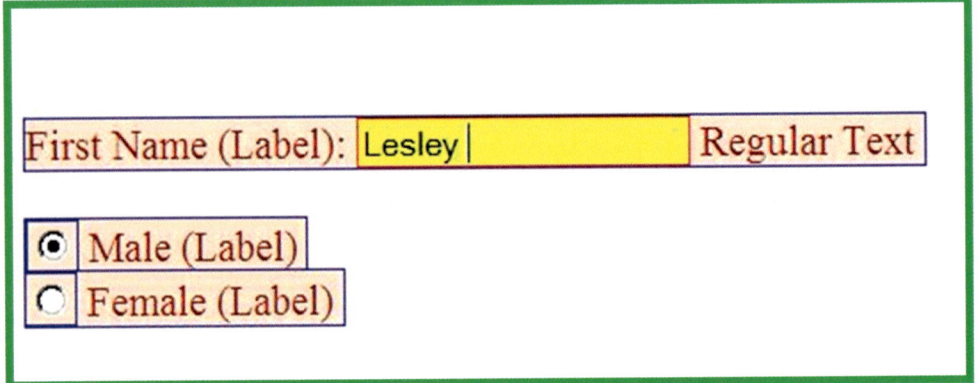

Figure 16: Field "First Name" is highlighted with background yellow upon focus by both keyboard and mouse.

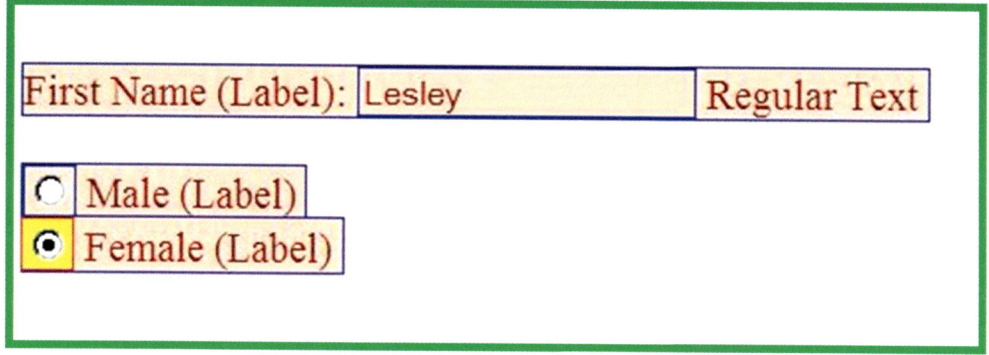

Figure 17: Field "Female" radio button selection is highlighted upon focus by both keyboard and mouse to indicate active selection.

31.3   Use CSS To Control Highlighting Focused Fields.

This CSS changes the background color for the elements in the links when they receive mouse or keyboard focus:

```
<style>

#hlinks a:hover, #hlinks a:active, #hlinks a:focus
{
 background-color: yellow;
 color: black;
}

</style>

<ul id="hlinks">
 <li><a href="#">Home</a></li>
 <li><a href="#">Services</a></li>
 <li><a href="#">Demo</a></li>
</ul>
```

- Home
- Services
- Demo

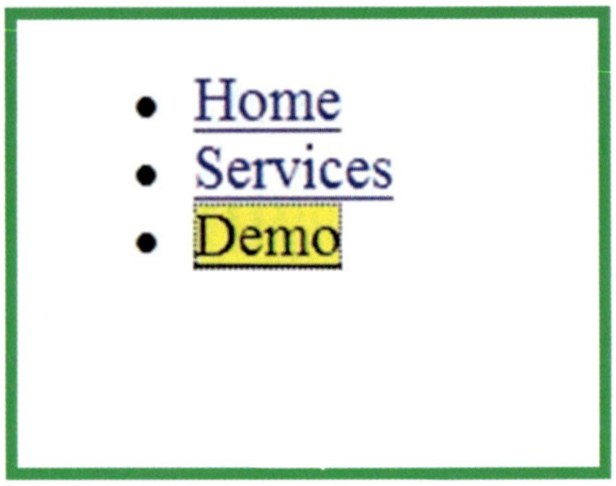

Figure 18: Focused links by keyboard or mouse have background yellow and font color back.

31.4   Test: Visual Focus.

- Verify that when text input fields receive focus, browsers display a blinking vertical bar at the insertion point in the text field.

- Verify that when links receive focus, they are surrounded by a dashed focus highlight rectangle.

31.5   Test: Context Change.

Check that when any component receives focus, it does not initiate a change of context. The content should remain the same and the state should not change by focus alone.

31.6   Test: CSS Highlights.

- Using a mouse, hover over the element.

- Check that the background or border changes color.

- Move the mouse away from the object before attempting keyboard focus.

- Using a keyboard, TAB to the element.

- Check that the background or border changes color.

- Check that the background or border changes in color are removed when the element loses focus.

32   Audio-Only: You Must Create An Alternative.

Description

In an audio-only presentation, information is presented in a variety of ways including dialogue and sounds (both natural and artificial). In order to present the same information in accessible form, create a document that tells the same story and presents the same information as the audio-only content. The document serves as description for the content and includes all of the important

201

dialogue and as well as descriptions of background sounds etc. that are part of the story. You can use closed captioning guides as an example of how to create the transcript of the audio.

Categories

Audio, Recorded Speaking

Reference

Section 508: 1194.31 (c) At least one mode of operation and information retrieval that does not require user hearing shall be provided, or support for Assistive technology used by people who are deaf or hard of hearing shall be provided.

WCAG 2.0: Audio-only and Video-only (Prerecorded) (Level A):

http://www.w3.org/TR/UNDERSTANDING-WCAG20/media-equiv-av-only-alt.html

WCAG 2.0: G158 (Level A): Providing an alternative for time-based media for audio-only content

http://www.w3.org/TR/2012/NOTE-WCAG20-TECHS-20120103/G158

32.1   Provide A Transcript For Audio-Only Media.

A link to a text transcript is provided immediately adjacent to the link to the audio clip. The transcript includes a verbatim record of everything the speakers say. It identifies who is speaking as well as noting other significant sounds that are part of the recording, such as applause, laughter, questions from the audience, and so on. The speaker must describe any visual references (if these are omitted by the speaker, then you must supply them).

32.2   Test: Audio Transcript Checks.

- View the audio-only content while referring to the alternative for time-based media.

- Check that the dialogue in the transcript matches the dialogue and information presented in the audio-only presentation.

- If the audio includes multiple voices, check that the transcript identifies who is speaking for all dialogue.

- Check that the following is absolutely true: The transcript itself can be fully screen reader accessed.

- If the alternate version(s) are on a separate page, check for the availability of link(s) to allow the user to get to the other version(s).

33   Video-Only: An Audio Track and Closed-Captioning Is Provided That Presents Equivalent Information.

Description

The purpose of the transcript is to provide an equivalent to what is presented visually. For video content, authors have the option to provide an audio track. The purpose of the audio alternative is to be an equivalent to the video. This makes it possible for users with and without vision impairment to review content simultaneously. The approach can also make it easier for those with cognitive, language and learning disabilities to understand the content because it would provide parallel presentation.

Categories

Video

Reference

Section 508: 1194.31 (a) At least one mode of operation and information retrieval that does not require user vision shall be provided, or support for Assistive technology used by people who are blind or visually impaired shall be provided.

WCAG 2.0: G159 (Level A): Providing an alternative for time-based media for video-only content:

http://www.w3.org/TR/2012/NOTE-WCAG20-TECHS-20120103/G159

33.1 Provide An Audio Track For Video-Only Media.

Provide an audio track which includes a description of the action in the video. The audio track must be descriptive of all elements in the video that contain information.

33.2 Provide A Text Alternative For Video-Only Media.

A transcript that fully describes all events and informational references is the text alternate. The same information must be available in the text alternative that was available in the video. Any updates must be synchronized.

33.3 Alert The User To Audio Not Available For A Video.

Provide a note saying "No sound is used in this clip" for video-only clips.

33.4 Test: Transcript Checks.

- View the video-only content.

- Check that the information in the transcript includes the same information that is in the video-only presentation.

- If the video includes multiple people or characters, check that the transcript identifies which person or character is associated with each action described.

- Check that the following is absolutely true: The transcript itself can be fully screen reader accessed.

- If the alternate version(s) are on a separate page, check for the availability of link(s) to allow the user to get to the other versions.

34 Movies, Videos, Flash, Animations, And E-Learning With Motion And Sound, Must Provide A Method For Assistive Technology To Access Equivalent Information.

Description

Any non-text content or text that is animated or not rendered as actual text (text that is graphics or is in layers not rendered by the operating system as text) must be either rendered as text in another mode or alternative text is provided. Any alternative must provide a fully equivalent text representation including description of all images and sounds that convey information. If additional information is required to understand logical relationships this must be provided also.

Closed captions provide the part of the content available via the audio track for people who are deaf or hard of hearing users. Captions not only include dialogue, but identify who is speaking and include non-speech information conveyed through sound, including meaningful sound effects. Captions are not needed when the synchronized media is, itself, an alternate presentation of information that is also presented via text on the screen or web page. For example, if information on a page is accompanied by a synchronized media presentation that presents no more information than is already presented in text, but is easier for people with cognitive, language, or learning disabilities to understand, then it would not need to be captioned since the information is already presented on the page in text or in text alternatives (for example: for images).

Categories

Movie, Video, Flash, Animation, E-Learn, Caption

Reference

Section 508:1194.22 (a) A text equivalent for every non-text element shall be provided (for example: via "alt", "longdesc", or in element content).

Section 508: 1194.22 (b) Equivalent alternatives for any multimedia presentation shall be synchronized with the presentation.

Section: 508:1194.21 (f) Textual information shall be provided through operating system functions for displaying text. The minimum information that shall be made available is text content, text input caret location, and text attributes.

Section 508: 1194.21 (h) When animation is displayed, the information shall be displayable in at least one non-animated presentation mode at the option of the user.

WCAG 2.0: Non-text Content: Understanding SC 1.1.1 (Level A):

http://www.w3.org/TR/UNDERSTANDING-WCAG20/text-equiv-all.html

WCAG 2.0: G158 (Level A): Providing an alternative for time-based media for audio-only content:

http://www.w3.org/WAI/PA/WCAG20/WD-WCAG20-TECHS/G158.html

WCAG 2.0: G159 (Level A): Providing an alternative for time-based media for video-only content:

http://www.w3.org/WAI/PA/WCAG20/WD-WCAG20-TECHS/G159.html

WCAG 2.0: G166 (Level A): Providing audio that describes the important video content:

http://www.w3.org/WAI/PA/WCAG20/WD-WCAG20-TECHS/G166.html

WCAG 2.0: G68 (Level A): Providing a descriptive label that describes the purpose of live audio-only and live video-only content:

http://www.w3.org/WAI/PA/WCAG20/WD-WCAG20-TECHS/G68.html

WCAG 2.0: G150 (Level AAA): Providing text based alternatives for live audio-only content:

http://www.w3.org/WAI/PA/WCAG20/WD-WCAG20-TECHS/G150.html

WCAG 2.0: G173 (Level A): Providing a version of a movie with audio descriptions:

http://www.w3.org/WAI/PA/WCAG20/WD-WCAG20-TECHS/G173.html

WCAG 2.0: G8 (Level A): Providing a movie with extended audio descriptions:

http://www.w3.org/WAI/PA/WCAG20/WD-WCAG20-TECHS/G8.html

WCAG 2.0: Captions (Prerecorded): Understanding SC 1.2.2 (Level A):

http://www.w3.org/TR/UNDERSTANDING-WCAG20/media-equiv-captions.html

WCAG 2.0: G160 (Level AAA): Providing sign language versions of information, ideas, and processes that must be understood in order to use the content:

http://www.w3.org/TR/WCAG20-TECHS/G160.html

34.1 Provide Closed Captioning For All Types Of Video, Animated, Or Dynamic Presentations.

Provide closed captions (closed captions allow for user control, open captions are fixed) for any type of video, movies, clips, flash videos, or animations that have no accessible text (text that is exposed to Assistive technology). If the type of video or animation cannot have captions incorporated, then provide a full transcript that describes all audio, video, images, and any visual relationships that convey information.

34.2   Provide An Accessible Format Of The Media.

Provide a link to an accessible format that contains equivalent information as in the presentation. If a presentation such as online learning has inaccessible quizzes and animated diagrams then provide a link to an HTML or other version containing text. The format must contain the same information as the original presentation. Conversion to any other format must be checked for localized accessibility issues inherent in PDF or MS Word. Plain text files can be made inaccessible if they are not organized in a manner that they can be navigated or if they represent information that cannot be interpreted in plain text (such as tables).

34.3   Describe Dynamic Information In Text.

Information conveyed through variations in the formatting of text, shapes, colors, or sizes of objects must also be conveyed in text. For example:

- Background changing to red indicates an action that is not allowed, indicate this also in text. If part of a video, include this as part of the description.

- An expanding or glowing box in an organization chart indicates that this is the person to contact for the issues being discussed. Indicate this also in text.

- Arrows appear and indicate the path for processing. This must also be in text format.

Note: Charts, images, symbols, math, and diagrams can be very helpful with explaining complex issues and in some cases they should be added to text that is difficult to understand. The issue is non-text items that convey information and understanding do not have text equivalents. The non-text items cannot stand alone and require text descriptions.

34.4   Provide Accessible Structure In Alternative Formats.

The alternative format must have structure so users can determine headings, paragraphs, lists, and navigate the contents. For HTML, MS Word, PDF, the structural markup must indicate the types of text and orientation.

Plain text should only be used as a last resort and for simple formatted text only. For plain text techniques, see:

http://www.w3.org/TR/WCAG-TECHS/text.html

34.5   Captions Must Be Synchronized, Equivalent, And Readable.

Captions must be:

- Synchronized and appear at approximately the same time as the audio is delivered.

- Equivalent and equal in content to that of the audio, including speaker identification and sound effects.

- Readable using sans-serif font with strong foreground/background contrast.

34.6   Provide Sign Language For Those Needing It.

For people who are deaf or hard of hearing and who are fluent in a sign language provide sign language interpretation to understand the content of the audio track. Some individuals may not be able to read and comprehend the captions and thus require a sign language interpretation. Both human and digital versions are available.

34.7   Provide Keyboard Accessible Controls And Options For All Media And Alternatives.

Provide users with control over stopping, starting, and advance and replay. For all formats, users must have complete control over delivery. Alternative formats must be associated with presentation (For example: a directly adjacent link).

34.8   Test: Information Is Available.

Check that information, structure, and relationships conveyed through presentation can be programmatically determined (screen reader test) or are available in text.

34.9   Test: Reading Order.

Check that when the sequence in which content is presented that affects its meaning, a correct reading sequence can be programmatically determined. That order is the order in which the author intended.

34.10 Test: Sense Dependency.

Check that the presentation and any instructions provided for understanding and operating content do not rely solely on sensory characteristics of components such as shape, size, visual location, orientation, or sound.

34.11 Test: Same Information.

Check that any alternative format provides the same information as the original presentation including descriptions of non-text items and relationships.

34.12 Test: Caption Information & Operation.

- Check that the captions include all of the dialogue (either verbatim or in essence) and informational sounds.
- Check that the captions work in all modes.

34.13 Test: That Text Captures All Dialogue During Portions Of The Material.

- View the material with captioning turned on.

- Check that all dialogue is accompanied by a caption.

- Check that all important sounds are captioned.

35 Audio Automatically Playing For More Than 3 Seconds Must Have A Mechanism Available To Pause Or Stop The Audio, Or To Control Audio Volume Independently From The System Volume Level.

Description

Individuals who use screen reading software can find it hard to hear the speech output if there is other audio playing at the same time. This difficulty is exacerbated when the screen reader's speech output is software based and is controlled via the same volume control as the sound. Therefore, it is important that the user be able to turn off the background sound. Note: Having control of the volume includes being able to reduce its volume to zero.

Note: Playing audio automatically when landing on a page may affect a screen reader user's ability to find the mechanism to stop it because they navigate by listening and automatically started sounds might interfere with that navigation. Do not automatically start sounds (especially if they last more than 3 seconds), and encourage that the sound be started by an action initiated by the user after they reach the page, rather than requiring that the sound be stopped by an action of the user after they land on the page.

Categories

Audio, Auto-play

Reference

Section 508: 1194.21 (b) Applications shall not disrupt or disable activated features of other products that are identified as accessibility features, where those features are developed and documented according to industry standards. Applications also shall not disrupt or disable activated features of any operating system that are identified as accessibility features where the application programming interface for those accessibility features has been documented by the manufacturer of the operating system and is available to the product developer.

WCAG 2.0: Audio Control: Understanding SC 1.4.2 (Level A):

http://www.w3.org/TR/UNDERSTANDING-WCAG20/visual-audio-contrast-dis-audio.html

35.1   Provide A Mechanism To Stop Audio.

If an audio file begins playing automatically when a page is opened, ensure that the audio can be stopped by the user by selecting a "silent", "stop", "cancel", or similar link at the top of the page.

For example: A splash page with sound plays automatically includes a control at the top that allows users to turn the sound off.

35.2   Test: For A Site-Wide Preference To Turn Off Audio.

35.3   Test: For A Control Near The Top Of The Web Page That Turns Off Sounds That Play Automatically.

35.4   Test: For A Mechanism Is Available To Control Audio Volume Independently From The Overall System Volume Level.

36   Text And Images Of Text Has A Contrast Ratio Of At Least 4.5:1. Large-Scale Text And Images Of Large-Scale Text Have A Contrast Ratio Of At Least 3:1. Use A Tool To Measure It.

Description

The intent of this is to provide enough contrast between text and its background so that it can be read by people with moderately low vision (who do not use contrast-enhancing Assistive technology). For people without color deficiencies, hue and saturation have minimal or no effect on legibility as assessed by reading performance. Contrast is calculated in such a way that color is not a key factor so that people who have a color vision deficit will also have adequate contrast between the text and the background.

Categories

Text, Contrast, Color

Reference

Section 508: 1194.31 (b) At least one mode of operation and information retrieval that does not require visual acuity greater than 20/70 shall be provided in audio and enlarged print output, working together or independently, or support for Assistive technology used by people who are visually impaired shall be provided.

WCAG 2.0: Contrast (Minimum): Understanding SC 1.4.3 (Level AA):

http://www.w3.org/TR/UNDERSTANDING-WCAG20/visual-audio-contrast-contrast.html

WCAG 2.0: Contrast (Enhanced): Understanding SC 1.4.6 (Level AA):

http://www.w3.org/TR/UNDERSTANDING-WCAG20/visual-audio-contrast7.html

36.1   Provide A Contrast Ratio Of 4.5:1.

Provide enough contrast between text and its background so that it can be read by people with moderately low vision (who do not use contrast-enhancing Assistive technology). Use a contrast ratio of 4.5:1. Use a Contrast Tool such as this:

Contrast Analyzer for Windows and Mac:

http://www.paciellogroup.com/resources/contrast-analyser.html

Figure 19: Sample of color contrast ratios that meet the requirement of 4.5, CR=Contrast Ratio.

See the Color Contrast Chart for Text and Background in this manual for more samples that meet the specification.

36.2   Provide An Option Of High Contrast As An Alternative.

As an option you can provide a control with a sufficient contrast ratio that allows users to switch to a presentation that uses sufficient contrast.

36.3   Test: For Overlays And Contrast.

- Check if any text overlays an image or background with lines. The lines cross behind the letters making F's look like E's etc.

- Check that if any text overlays an image with dark areas. Wherever the text crosses a dark area, the contrast is so bad that the text cannot be read.

- Check that a contrast ratio of at least 4.5:1 exists between text (and images of text) and background behind the text. If the background or the letters vary in relative luminance (or are patterned) then the background around the letters can be chosen or shaded so that the letters maintain a 4.5:1 contrast ratio with the background behind them even if they do not have that contrast ratio with the entire background. A number of tools exist to assist with the analysis including extensions to browsers. See:

  http://www.w3.org/WAI/GL/WCAG20-TECHS/general.html#G18

36.4 Test: To See If The Contrast In Image Text Meets Or Exceeds A Contrast Ratio Of 1.4.3 Or 1.4.5.

See 15.3 to apply same test to image text. Remember to have real text somewhere that can be read by screen readers.

37 Text Can Be Resized, Without Assistive Technology, Up To 200 Percent Without Loss Of Content Or Functionality Except For Captions And Images Of Text.

Description

The intent is to ensure that visually rendered text, including text-based controls (text characters that have been displayed so that they can be seen - vs. text characters that are still in data form such as ASCII) can be scaled successfully so that they can be read directly by people with mild visual disabilities, without requiring the use of Assistive technology such as a screen magnifier. Users may benefit from scaling all content on the web page, but text is most critical.

The scaling of content is primarily a browser's responsibility. The author's responsibility is to create web content that does not prevent the browser from scaling the content effectively. Authors may satisfy this by verifying that content does not interfere with the browser support for resizing text, including text-based controls, or by providing direct support for resizing text or changing the layout. An example of direct support might be via server-side script that can be used to assign different style sheets.

One method is to use HTML5 and not legacy HTML as this is more device independent. Be sure to check browser display for your types of browsers and audience. You may need to add information on your accessibility page informing users how best to display your content such as "Best displayed for accessibility with Internet Explorer version 8 and above or Firefox version 42 and above"

Categories

Text, Size

Reference

Section 508: 1194.31 (b) At least one mode of operation and information retrieval that does not require visual acuity greater than 20/70 shall be provided in audio and enlarged print output working together or independently, or support for Assistive technology used by people who are visually impaired shall be provided.

WCAG 2.0: Resize text: Understanding SC 1.4.4 (Level AA):

http://www.w3.org/TR/UNDERSTANDING-WCAG20/visual-audio-contrast-scale.html

37.1 Text Resizing Does Not Interfere With Assistive Technology Or Prevent Access To All Information On The Page.

User can increases the text size on a web page in a browser. All the information on the page is still displayed when the larger font is used for the text. Magnification software can retain focus on text being read and logical order is maintained (generally top-to-bottom, left-to-right or the steps, process, or hierarchy indicated by the content or author's intent).

37.2 Where Page Control Of Text Sizing Is Needed, Provide A Control Option To The User.

A web page contains a control on the page for changing the scale of the page. Selecting different settings changes the layout of the page to use the best design for that scale. This is to provide an easy method for those without magnification software, have difficulty with browser or system settings or those with cognitive disabilities and older users. CSS can be used to provide alternative versions of the page.

37.3 Text Resizing Must Be Provided For All Text Contained In Objects.

User can increase the size of text in different areas of the page (for example: in a floating box or an updating dashboard). This requires that the text when resized preserves all spatial relationships on the page and that all functionality continues to be available.

- Increase the text size of the content by 200% or 10x.

- Check that no text is clipped, truncated, or obscured.

- Check that text is not moved out of order.

- Check that all menus and controls still operate and are labeled.

37.4 Test: Text Size Options.

Check that if a web page contains a control for changing the scale of the page or increases the text size, the page is still readable and usable as it was in the un-resized state.

38 Navigation Is Consistent And Provides Option To Skip If Navigation Is Repeated.

Description

This requirement is to provide consistent presentation and layout for users who interact with repeated content within a set of web pages and need to locate specific information or functionality more than once. Individuals with low vision who use screen magnification to display a small portion of the screen at a time often use visual cues and page boundaries to quickly locate repeated content. Presenting repeated content in the same order is also important for visual users who use spatial memory or visual cues within the design to locate repeated content.

A "skip navigation" or "skip to main content" link is consistently located at the beginning of each page so that keyboard users can easily locate it when needed. This allows a screen reader to jump to the main content and bypass multiple repetitive links on each page.

Categories

Navigation, Skip Repetitive Links, Skip to Main Content, Skip Navigation

Reference

Section 508: 1194.22 (o) A method shall be provided that permits users to skip repetitive navigation links.

WCAG 2.0: Consistent Navigation: Understanding SC 3.2.3 (Level AA):

http://www.w3.org/TR/UNDERSTANDING-WCAG20/consistent-behavior-consistent-locations.html

WCAG 2.0: G123 (Level A): Adding a link at the beginning of a block of repeated content to go to the end of the block:

http://www.w3.org/TR/2008/NOTE-WCAG20-TECHS-20081211/G123

38.1 Keep Navigation Controls In Same Location.

Navigation must be consistently located at the same position on each page in a set of web pages. Controls such as Search, Home, Contact Us, and Help must be in their same position across pages.

38.2 Navigational Controls Must Be Consistently Named.

Give unique non-duplicative names to navigational controls.

38.3 Do Not Change Appearance Of The Navigation.

Navigational controls must have consistent styling of size, color, and text.

38.4　Navigational Controls Must Remain In The Same Order.

Do not switch controls around in the order as dynamic updates occur, you may disable or enable but the order must be maintained.

38.5　Skip Navigation Must Be The First Focused Item On The Page.

A link at the top of the page, first in the tab order, must allow for skipping repetitive links. This link need not be visible or have visible width beyond 1 pixel but must be exposed programmatically to screen readers. The first interactive item in the web page is a link to the beginning of the main content.

The following example uses the technique of making the link the same color as the background so that it will be detected by screen readers but not interfere with the page design. Selection of the link allows the focus be shifted to the main content bypassing the navigational links:

```
<a href="#Skip_Text" style="color: white;">Skip to Main Content</a>

<ul id="hlinks">
 <li><a href="#">Home</a></li>
 <li><a href="#">Services</a></li>
 <li><a href="#">Demo</a></li>
</ul>

<h1><a name="Skip_Text">

Skip Navigation to Main Content

</a></h1>

<p>

For users with screen readers, hearing the same list of links at
the beginning of each page is time consuming.
Therefore a skip navigation strategy must be included to allow users of
screen readers to skip over a block of navigational links.

</p>
```

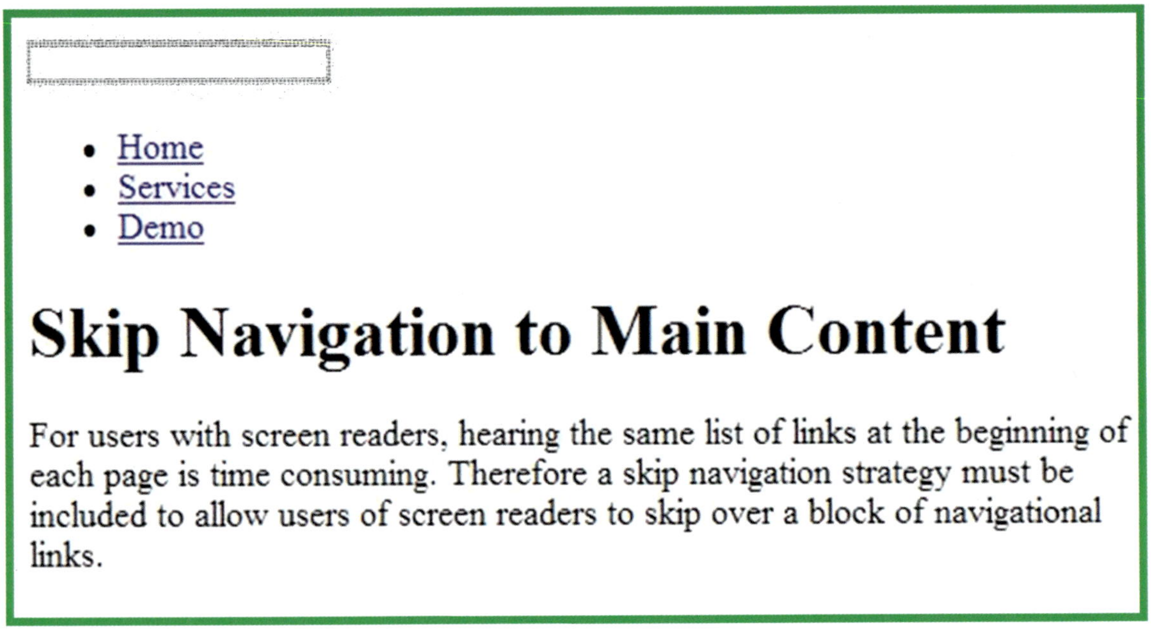

Skip Navigation to Main Content

For users with screen readers, hearing the same list of links at the beginning of each page is time consuming. Therefore a skip navigation strategy must be included to allow users of screen readers to skip over a block of navigational links.

Figure 20: Skip navigation link is not visible on page in this option except when the focus rectangle is active on the link as above.

38.6   Test: Navigation Order.

- Check to see if a navigation mechanism is being used on more than one web page.

- Check the default presentation of the navigation mechanism on each page to see if the list of links is in the same relative order on each web page.

Note: "Same relative order" means that secondary navigation items may be in between the link items on some pages. They can be present without affecting the outcome of this test.

38.7   Test: Link Logical Flow.

- Check that a link is the last focusable control before the block of repeated content or the first link in the block.

- Check that the description of the link communicates that it skips the block.

- Check that the link does not change its visibility state; It is either always visible or not visible, or is visible upon tabbing focus. If the link is invisible as is common practice, it should remain not visible everywhere.

- Check that activating the link moves the focus to the content immediately after the block.

- Check that after activating the link, the keyboard focus has moved to the content immediately after the block.

39 Tab Order (Keyboard Focus Order) Must Preserve The Logical Meaning That The Form Components Or Controls Require To Follow The Steps Of Completion.

Description

When users navigate sequentially through content, they encounter information in an order that is consistent with the meaning of the content and can be operated from the keyboard. This reduces confusion by helping users form a consistent mental model of the content. There may be different orders that reflect logical relationships in the content. For example, moving through components in a table one row at a time or one column at a time both reflect the logical relationships in the content.

HTML defines sequential navigation via the notion of tabbing order. Dynamic HTML may modify the navigation sequence using scripting along with the addition of a TABINDEX attribute to allow focus to additional elements. If no scripting or TABINDEX attributes are used, the navigation order is the order that components appear in the content stream or the order of the elements in the code.

Categories

Tab Order, Focus Order, Keyboard Focus

Reference

Section 508: 1194.22 (c) A well-defined on-screen indication of the current focus shall be provided that moves among interactive interface elements as the input focus changes. The focus shall be programmatically exposed so that Assistive technology can track focus and focus changes.

Section 508: 1194.22 (l) When electronic forms are used, the form shall allow people using Assistive technology to access the information, field elements, and functionality required for completion and submission of the form, including all directions and cues.

WCAG 2.0: Focus Order: Understanding SC 2.4.3 (Level A):

http://www.w3.org/TR/UNDERSTANDING-WCAG20/navigation-mechanisms-focus-order.html

WCAG 2.0: H4 (Level A): Creating a logical tab order through links, form controls, and objects:

http://www.w3.org/TR/2012/NOTE-WCAG20-TECHS-20120103/H4

39.1   Set Tab/Focus Order To Logical Form Completion.

If a form is completed from top to bottom, left to right, and fields may be grouped, then the focus order must follow the exact field by field steps for completion as the visual form.

When the interactive elements are navigated using the TAB key, the elements are given focus in increasing order of the value of their TABINDEX attribute. Elements that have a TABINDEX value higher than zero will receive focus before elements without a TABINDEX or a TABINDEX of 0. After all of the elements with a TABINDEX higher than 0 have received focus, the rest of the interactive elements are given focus in the order in which they appear in the web page.

Column by column logical filling out of form:

```
<form action="#" method="post">
<table summary="the first column contains the search criteria
of the groom, the second column the search criteria of
of the bride">
<caption>Search for Marriage Records</caption>
<tr>
<th>Search criteria</th>
<th>Groom</th>
<th>Bride</th>
</tr>
<tr>
<th scope="row">First name</td>
<td><input type="text" size="30" value="" name="groomfirst" id="groomfirst"
title="First name of the groom" tabindex="1"></td>
<td><input type="text" size="30" value="" name="bridefirst" id="bridefirst"
title="First name of the bride" tabindex="4"></td>
</tr>
<tr>
<th scope="row">Last name</td>
<td><input type="text" size="30" value="" name="groomlast"
title="Last name of the groom" tabindex="2"></td>
<td><input type="text" size="30" value="" name="bridelast"
title="Last name of the bride" tabindex="5"></td>
</tr>
<tr>
<th scope="row">Place of birth</td>
<td><input type="text" size="30" value="" name="groombirth"
title="Place of birth of the groom" tabindex="3"></td>
<td><input type="text" size="30" value="" name="bridebirth"
title="Place of birth of the bride" tabindex="6"></td>
</tr>
</table>
</form>
```

39.2 Use TABINDEX To Control Focus In Paragraphs And Headings.

The TABINDEX can be used to order the focus to paragraphs and headings in addition to form input. This allows for placement options and design while keeping content in the order in which it was intended to be read.

```
<style>
h2, p, div {font-family: arial;}
</style>

<h2 p tabindex="0">Using TABINDEX to Set Focus on headings and paragraphs</h2>

<p tabindex="1">
Tabindex can also be used as a means to allow focus to be sent to components such as dialogs and menus, whose location in the DOM is not adjacent to their respective trigger controls. In such cases, focus can be sent via scripting to the relevant component, where that component's container element, or one of its child elements, has a tabindex value. This will allow the logical tab order to be maintained, while also dynamically correcting the reading order of the page.
</p>

<p tabindex="2">
Three behaviors are defined for the tabindex attribute. If the value is a negative integer, the element can be focused, but is not reached using sequential focus navigation. If the value is 0, the element will be included in sequential focus navigation without being given special preference in the tab order. If the value is a positive integer, the element will be included in sequential focus navigation and have a tab order preference relative to its value.
</p>

<p tabindex="3">
Note: Explicitly setting the tab order with the tabindex attribute will usually not correct the programmatically determined reading order. Success criterion 1.3.2 requires that the reading order be correct regardless of the tab order. This technique only allows authors to set a tab order which will aid keyboard users to navigate the page in a preferred sequence. In addition to a logical tab order, authors must make sure that the programmatically determined reading order is maintained. See Example 3 below for a proper implementation of reading order. </p>
```

Using TABINDEX to Set Focus on headings and paragraphs

Tabindex can also be used as a means to allow focus to be sent to components such as dialogs and menus, whose location in the DOM is not adjacent to their respective trigger controls. In such cases, focus can be sent via scripting to the relevant component, where that component's container element, or one of its child elements, has a tabindex value. This will allow the logical tab order to be maintained, while also dynamically correcting the reading order of the page.

Three behaviors are defined for the tabindex attribute. If the value is a negative integer, the element can be focused, but is not reached using sequential focus navigation. If the value is 0, the element will be included in sequential focus navigation without being given special preference in the tab order. If the value is a positive integer, the element will be included in sequential focus navigation and have a tab order preference relative to its value.

Note: Explicitly setting the tab order with the tabindex attribute will usually not correct the programmatically determined reading order. Success criterion 1.3.2 requires that the reading order be correct regardless of the tab order. This technique only allows authors to set a tab order which will aid keyboard users to navigate the page in a preferred sequence. In addition to a logical tab order, authors must make sure that the programmatically determined reading order is maintained. See Example 3 below for a proper implementation of reading order.

Figure 22: Focus is shown on second paragraph while tabbing.

39.3 Provide Script To Force Focus When TABINDEX Will Not Work.

When the TABINDEX attribute has the value 0, the element can be focused on via the keyboard and is included in the tab order of the document. When the TABINDEX attribute has the value -1, the element cannot be tabbed to, but focus can be set programmatically, using ELEMENT.FOCUS().

39.4 Test: TABINDEX.

- Check if TABINDEX is used.

- If TABINDEX is used, check that the tab order specified by the TABINDEX attributes follows relationships in the content.

39.5   Test: Element Order.

- Determine the order of interactive elements in the content.

- Determine the logical order of interactive elements.

- Check that the order of the interactive elements in the content is the same as the logical order.

39.6   Test: Scripting.

- Click on the control with the mouse.

- Check that the scripting action executes properly.

- Check that it is possible to navigate to and give focus to the control via the keyboard.

- Set keyboard focus to the control.

- Check that pressing ENTER invokes the scripting action.

40   Name, Role, State, And Value For All User Interface Components, Can Be Programmatically Determined.

Description

Programmatically determined means provided in a way that different browsers, including assistive technologies, can extract and present this information to users in different modes.

When standard controls from accessible technologies are used, this process is straightforward. If the user interface elements are used according to specifications then the conditions of this requirement will be met. States, properties, and values that can be set by the user can be programmatically set; and notification of changes to these items is exposed to assistive technologies.

If custom controls are created, however, or interface elements are programmed (in code or script) to have a different role and/or function than usual, then additional measures need to be taken to ensure that the controls provide important information to assistive technologies and allow themselves to be controlled by assistive technologies.

A particularly important state of a user interface control is whether or not it has focus. The focus state of a control can be programmatically determined, and notifications about change of focus are sent to interfaces and assistive technology. Other examples of user interface control state are whether or not a checkbox or radio button has been selected, or whether or not a collapsible tree or list node is expanded or collapsed.

Providing role, state, and value information on all user interface components enables compatibility with assistive technology, such as screen readers, screen magnifiers, and speech recognition software, used by people with disabilities.

Note: This requires a programmatically determinable name for all user interface components. Names may be visible or invisible. Occasionally, the name must be visible, in which case it is identified as a label.

Categories

Name, Role, Value

Reference

Section 508: 1194.21 (l) When electronic forms are used, the form shall allow people using Assistive technology to access the information, field elements, and functionality required for completion and submission of the form, including all directions and cues.

WCAG 2.0: G108 (Level A): Using markup features to expose the name and role, allow user-settable properties to be directly set, and provide notification of changes:

> http://www.w3.org/TR/2012/NOTE-WCAG20-TECHS-20120103/G108

WCAG 2.0: H44 (Level A): Using label elements to associate text labels with form controls:

> http://www.w3.org/TR/2012/NOTE-WCAG20-TECHS-20120103/H44

40.1   Use Standard HTML And Use It According To HTML Specification.

Use only features that are defined in the specification HTML defines sets of elements, attributes, and attribute values that may be used on web pages. These features have specific semantic meanings and are intended to be processed by interfaces in particular ways. Sometimes, however, additional features come into common authoring practice. These are usually initially supported by only one interface. When features not in the specification are used, many interfaces may not support the feature in the future. Furthermore, lacking standard specifications for the use of these features, different interfaces may provide varying support. This impacts accessibility because assistive technologies developed with fewer resources than mainstream interfaces, may take a long time if ever to add useful support. Therefore, authors should avoid features not defined in HTML and XHTML to prevent unexpected accessibility problems.

Using features in the manner prescribed by the specification. The HTML specification provides specific guidance about how particular elements, attributes, and attribute values are to be processed and understood semantically. Sometimes, however, authors use features in a manner that is not supported by the specification, for example, using semantic elements to achieve visual effects without intending the underlying semantic message to be conveyed. This leads to confusion for interfaces and assistive technologies that rely on correct semantic information to present a coherent representation of the page. It is important to use HTML features only as prescribed by the HTML specification.

Exceptions to this would be a controlled environment with only one browser with secure configurations. This would still have to meet other Requirements such as non-interference with Assistive technology and keyboard access.

For more detail see the section on "Methods for Coding to HTML Standards"

40.2 Use LABEL To Programmatically Associated Names With Fields.

Use the LABEL element to explicitly associate a form control with a LABEL. A LABEL is attached to a specific form control through the use of the FOR attribute. The value of the FOR attribute must be the same as the value of the ID attribute of the form control.

The ID attribute may have the same value as the NAME attribute, but both must be provided, and the ID must be unique in the web page.

Elements that use explicitly associated labels are:

- input type="text"

- input type="checkbox"

- input type="radio"

- input type="file"

- input type="password"

- textarea

- select

For example:

```html
<label for="fullname">Name:</label>
<input id="fullname" type="text" name="fullname"/><br/><br/>


<label for="address">Enter Your Address:</label><br/>
<textarea id="address" name="address"></textarea><br/><br/>

<label for="pass">Password:</label>
<input id="pass" type="password" name="password"/><br/><br/>

<fieldset>
<legend>Select your department:</legend>

<input id="department1" type="checkbox" name="department" value="D1"/>
<label for="department1">Department 1</label><br/>

<input id="department2" type="checkbox" name="department" value="D2"/>
<label for="department2">Department2</label><br/>

</fieldset><br/><br/>


<fieldset>
<legend>Choose an Archive Method:</legend>

<input id="proccess1" type="radio" name="method" value="p1"/>
<label for="proccess1">Proccess 1</label><br/>

<input id="proccess2" type="radio" name="method" value="p2"/>
<label for="proccess2">Proccess 2</label><br/>

</fieldset><br/><br/>


<label for="amount">Choose Your Purchase Amount</label><br/>
<select id="amount" name="Select">

<option value="1">Less than $1,000</option>
<option value="2">Greater than $1,000 but less than $50,000</option>
<option value="3">Greater than $50,000</option>

</select><br/><br/>

<label for="upload">Upload file:</label>
<input type="file" name="data" id="upload"/>
```

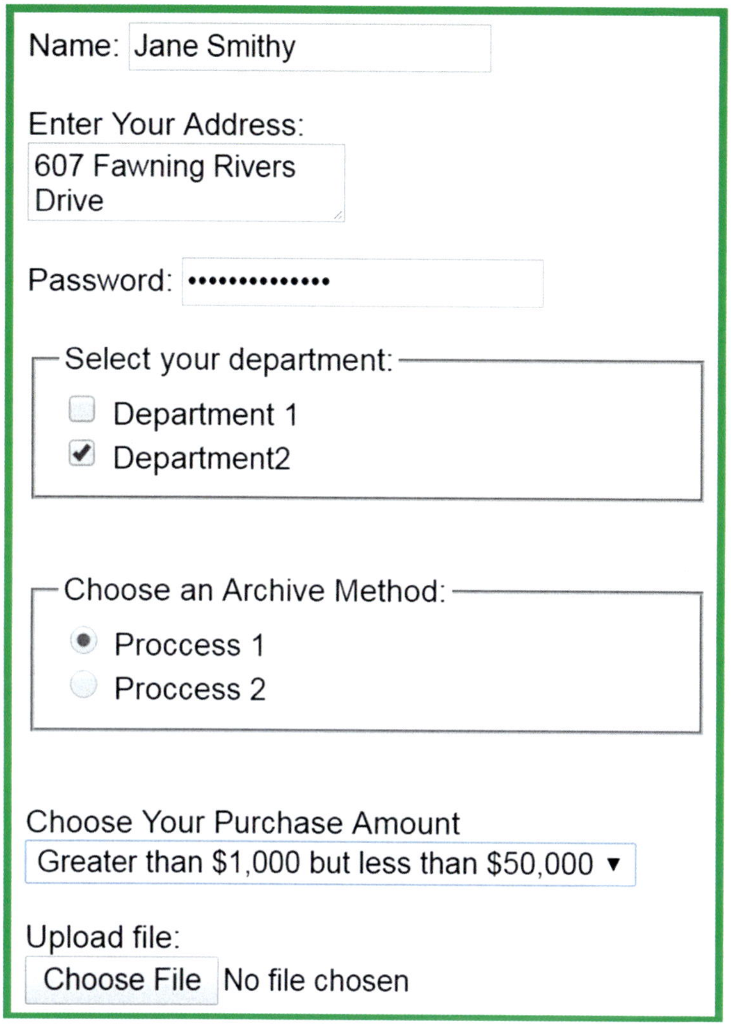

Figure 23: Use of LABEL to provide programmatic field name identification.

The LABEL element is **not used for the following** because labels for these elements are provided via the VALUE attribute (for SUBMIT and RESET buttons), the ALT attribute (for image buttons), or element content itself (button):

- SUBMIT and RESET buttons (input type="submit" or input type="reset")

- IMAGE buttons (input type="image")

- HIDDEN input fields (input type="hidden")

- Script buttons (BUTTON elements or <input type="button">)

40.3   Name Buttons As A Label For The INPUT Fields They Are Associated With.

When a button invokes a function on an INPUT field, has a clear text label, and is rendered adjacent to the INPUT field, the button also acts as a label for the INPUT field. This label helps users understand the purpose of the field without introducing repetitive text on the web page. Buttons that label single text fields typically follow the INPUT field.

Note: The field must also have a programmatically determined name.

For example: A web page contains a text field where the user can enter search terms and a button labeled "Search" for performing the search. The button is positioned right after the text field so that it is clear to the user that the text field is where to enter the search term.

40.4   Text Must Be Exposed Through The Operating System With All Attributes.

Text is available to operating system and provides text content, attributes, location and text input cursor. Assistive technology must be able to access information about text through the operating system. Hardware, software, and manual usage rely on text being exposed through the operating system with its text characteristics and information about that text retained. The text is not only viewable but can be accessed via keyboard except for disabled text which is marked up as such.

40.5   Test: Code For Markup.

- Check that proper markup is used so that the name and role, for each user interface component can be determined.

- Check that proper markup is used so that the user interface components that accept user input can all be operated from assistive technology.

40.6   Test: for LABEL.

- Check that there is a label element that identifies the purpose of the control before the INPUT, TEXTAREA, or SELECT element

- Check that the for attribute of the LABEL element matches the id of the INPUT, TEXTAREA, or SELECT element

- Check that the LABEL element is visible.

40.7   Test: for Proximity.

- Check that the field and button are adjacent to one another in the programmatically determined reading sequence.

- Check that the field and button are visually rendered adjacent to one another.

41 Abbreviations And Acronyms Require A Method For Identifying The Expanded Form Or Meaning.

Description

Some abbreviations do not look like normal words and cannot be pronounced according to the usual rules of the language. For example, the English word "room" is abbreviated as "rm," which does not correspond to any English word or phoneme. The user has to know that "rm" is an abbreviation for the word "room" in order to say it correctly.

Sometimes, the same abbreviation means different things in different contexts. For example, in the English sentence "Dr. Johnson lives on Boswell Dr.," the first "Dr." is an abbreviation for "Doctor" and the second instance is an abbreviation for the word "Drive" (a word that means "street"). Users must be able to understand the context in order to know what the abbreviations mean.

Some acronyms spell common words but are used in different ways. For example, "JAWS" is an acronym for a screen reader whose full name is "Job Access with Speech." It is also a common English word referring to the part of the mouth that holds the teeth, and of course a famous movie. The acronym is used differently than the common word.

Some acronyms sound like common words but are spelled differently. For example, the acronym for Synchronized Multimedia Integration Language, SMIL, is pronounced like the English word "smile."

Categories

Abbreviation, Acronym

Reference

Section 508: 1194.21 (l) When electronic forms are used, the form shall allow people using assistive technology to access the information, field elements, and functionality required for completion and submission of the form, including all directions and cues.

Section 508: 1194.22 (n) When electronic forms are designed to be completed on-line, the form shall allow people using assistive technology to access the information, field elements, and functionality required for completion and submission of the form, including all directions and cues.

WCAG 2.0: Guideline 3.1 (Level A) Make text content readable and understandable:

http://www.w3.org/TR/UNDERSTANDING-WCAG20/meaning.html

WCAG 2.0: G102 (Level AAA): Providing the expansion or explanation of an abbreviation:

http://www.w3.org/TR/2012/NOTE-WCAG20-TECHS-20120103/G102

WCAG 2.0: Abbreviations: Understanding SC 3.1.4 (Level AAA):

http://www.w3.org/TR/UNDERSTANDING-WCAG20/meaning-located.html

WCAG 2.0: H28 (Level AAA): Providing definitions for abbreviations by using the abbr and acronym elements:

http://www.w3.org/TR/2012/NOTE-WCAG20-TECHS-20120103/H28

41.1   Provide Information Necessary To Understand An Abbreviation.

Any of these methods can be used:

- Links or pop-ups to definitions

- Provide a glossary

- Provide a function to search an online dictionary

- Provide the first use of an abbreviation immediately before or after following the expanded form

- Provide definitions for abbreviations by using the ABBR element

- Provide a legend

If the abbreviation has no expanded form, an explanation is provided.

Using ABBR element to expand abbreviations:

```
Sugar is commonly sold in 5 <abbr title="pound">lb.<abbr> bags. <br/>
```

Using ABBR element to define abbreviations:

```
Tasini <abbr title="and others">et al.</abbr> <abbr title="versus">v.</abbr> <br/>
The New York Times <abbr title="and others">et al.</abbr> is the landmark lawsuit
brought by members of the National Writers Union against.
```

Using the ABBR to expand acronyms:

Note: The ACRONYM element is not supported in HTML 5 and ABBR must be used for both acronyms and abbreviations:

Enter that into <abbr title="IBM - Rational RequisitePro">ReqPro </abbr> today if possible
The<abbr title="World Wide Web Consortium"> W3C </abbr> is the main international standards organization for the World Wide Web.

41.2 Provide Meaning Of Abbreviation/Acronym In First Sentence Following Headings.

Any abbreviation or acronym must be spelled out or be provided a definition link when it is shown the first time, even in the heading.

However it is possible to not provide the definition in the heading if you provide the expansion of the letters in the first sentence following the heading or otherwise directly adjacent so it is visually connected.

In addition, if you have an application where the user cannot land on the page out of linear sequence (for example: forced navigation for steps) then the previous page that expands the abbreviation or acronym will accomplish the task. However be aware that a large number of these can be difficult to remember.

For example:

    About W3C

The World Wide Web Consortium (W3C) is an international community where Member organizations, a full-time staff, and the public work

41.3 Test: That An Expansion Or Definition Is Provided For Each Abbreviation Via:

- ABBR

- Link to definition

- Adjacent expansion of definition or explanation

- Glossary is available

42 Link Target And Purpose Can Be Determined From The Link Text Alone Or From The Link Text Together With Its Programmatically Determined Link Context.

Description

The purpose is to help users understand the purpose of each link so they can decide whether they want to follow the link. Provide link text that identifies the purpose of the link without needing additional context. Assistive technology has the ability to provide users with a list of links that are on the web page. Link text that is as meaningful as possible will aid users who want to choose from this list of links. Meaningful link text also helps those who wish to TAB from link to link. Meaningful links help users choose which links to follow without requiring complicated strategies to understand the page.

In some situations, authors may want to provide part of the description of the link in logically related text that provides the context for the link. In this case the user should be able to identify the purpose of the link without moving focus from the link. In other words, they can arrive on a link and find out more about it without losing their place. This can be achieved by putting the description of the link in the same sentence, paragraph, list item, the heading immediately preceding the link, or table cell as the link, or in the table header cell for a link in a data table, because these are directly associated with the link itself.

Categories

Link

Reference

Section 508: 1194.21 (d) Sufficient information about a user interface element including the identity, operation and state of the element shall be available to assistive technology. When an image represents a program element, the information conveyed by the image must also be available in text.

WCAG 2.0: G91 (Level A): Providing link text that describes the purpose of a link:

http://www.w3.org/TR/2012/NOTE-WCAG20-TECHS-20120103/G91

WCAG 2.0: Link Purpose (In Context): Understanding SC 2.4.4 (Level A):

http://www.w3.org/TR/UNDERSTANDING-WCAG20/navigation-mechanisms-refs.html

42.1   Provide An Accurate Concise Description Of The Link Target.

Provide a link that contains text giving a description of the information at that destination URI.

Links with the same destination should have the same descriptions but links with different purposes and destinations should have different descriptions.

42.2   Indicate File Type In Link Text Or Adjacent Text.

Users should know the file type (non-HTML) when opening a file that results in opening a new application to view the file include this additional information.

```
<a href="2009mycorp_report.pdf">MyCorp 2009 Annual Report (PDF)</a><br />
<a href="2009mycorp_budget.xls">MyCorp 2009 Annual Budget (Excel)</a>
```

An exception would be when all files on the page are of the same type and the information is provided at the top of page.

42.3 Visually Distinguish Different Types Of Links With Color And Line Styles In CSS.

To visually show different types of links such as help or definitions use CSS as this will prevent relying on color only for making items appear different. You can still use color, this method allows for black/white/gray to show for all color visual levels.

For example: You can do dotted or dashed if you choose this setting in the style:

```
<style>

a.dot { text-decoration: none; border-bottom:1px dotted; }
a.dash { text-decoration: none; border-bottom:1px dashed; }

</style>

<ul>
 <li><a class="dot" href="#">Dotted Underline Link</a></li><br/><br/>
 <li><a class="dash" href="#">Dashed Underline Link</a></li><br/><br/>
 <li><a href="#">Standard Solid underline Link</a></li>
</ul>
```

- Dotted Underline Link

- Dashed Underline Link

- Standard Solid underline Link

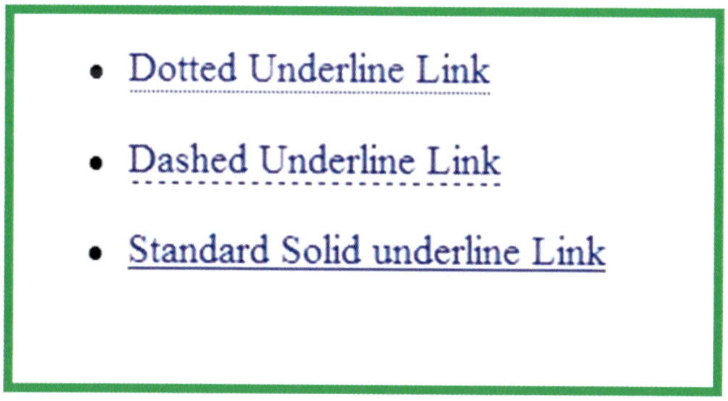

Figure 24: Links with dotted, dashed and solid underline styling.

Using CSS faux underlines to distinguish and highlight links:

230

```
<style>
a
{
 text-decoration: none;
 font-size: 1.2em;
 line-height: 2em;
 color: blue;
 font-family: arial, sans-serif;
}

.thick1
{
 border-bottom: 6px solid blue;
}

.thick2
{
 border-bottom: 3px solid blue;
}
</style>


<ul>
 <li><a class="thick1" href="#">Very Thick Faux Underline Link</a></li><br/><br/>
 <li><a class="thick2" href="#">Medium Thick Faux Underline Link</a></li><br/><br/>

</ul>
```

- <u>Very Thick Faux Underline Link</u>

- <u>Medium Thick Faux Underline Link</u>

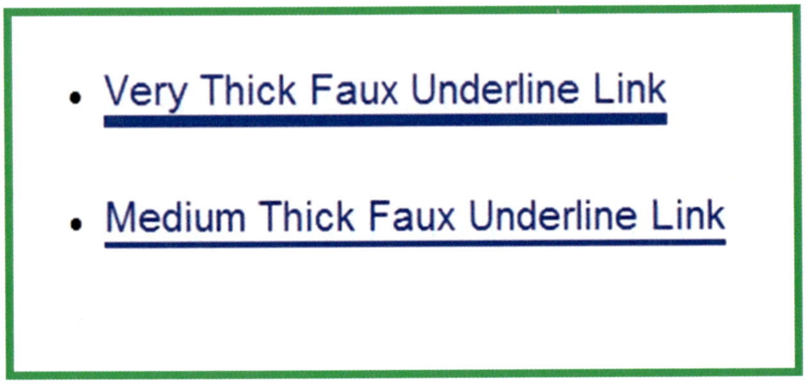

Figure 25: CSS Faux underlines to create emphasis and bold distinct lines.

See: W3 technique: Faux underlines using border-bottom:

http://www.w3.org/wiki/Styling_lists_and_links#Faux_underlines_using_border-bottom

42.4   Do Not Use Underlines Except For Links.

While underlines are a standard font attribute, they can easily be confused with the underline link, particularly in context of web pages and documents. In this context underlines should be reserved for links as color alone (standard blue) is not enough an indicator of a link.

42.5   Test: Link Information.

- Check that text of the link text describes the purpose of the link.
- Check that different types of links are distinguishable.
- Check that file types are indicated when non-HTML is the target.

42.6   Test: For Screen Text With Images With No Alternative Text.

If the a element contains one or more IMG element(s) and the text alternative of the IMG element(s) is empty, check that the text of the link describes the purpose of the link

43   Scripting Must Include Keyboard Support, And Not Be Device Dependent.

Description

Developers should consider whether they genuinely need to use script in certain situations, or whether they can augment an HTML-based solution with script so that users with script turned off may still use the document. It is always important to adopt the least restrictive set of technologies possible when authoring web content.

Categories

Script, JavaScript

Reference

Section 508: 1194.22 (l) When pages utilize scripting languages to display content, or to create interface elements, the information provided by the script shall be identified with functional text that can be read by assistive technology.

WCAG 2.0: Client-side Scripting Techniques for WCAG 2.0 (Level AA):

http://www.w3.org/TR/2005/WD-WCAG20-SCRIPT-TECHS-20050630/

WCAG 2.0: F42: Failure of Success Criterion 1.3.1 and 2.1.1 (Level A): due to using scripting events to emulate links in a way that is not programmatically determinable:

http://www.w3.org/TR/WCAG20-TECHS/F42.html

WCAG 2.0: SCR29 (Level A): Adding keyboard-accessible actions to static HTML elements:

http://www.w3.org/TR/WCAG20-TECHS/SCR29

43.1   Do Not Use Device-Dependent Events.

Combine both keyboard and mouse-based functions.

- TAB key substitutes for MOUSEOVER:

- Button allows text to appear and highlight with keyboard and mouse

- Image allows focus to highlight border with keyboard and mouse

- Both are also clickable events with keyboard and mouse

```
<body onload="javascript:hide();">
<br/><br/>

<span id="text" style="font-family: arial; color: blue; background-color: yellow; font-weight: bold">
This is some text.<br/>
</span>

<button type="button" onclick="javascript:alert('Button Clicked')"
onfocus="show()"
onblur="hide()"
onmouseover="show()"
onmouseout="hide()">
Text Content</button>

<script>
function hide() {    document.getElementById("text").style.visibility = "hidden";}
function show() {    document.getElementById("text").style.visibility = "visible";}
</script>

<br/><br/>

<a href= "javascript:alert('Image Clicked')"
onkeypress="on(1)"
onkeyup="on(1)"
onblur="off(1)">

<img id="1" src="1.jpg"
onfocus="on(1)"
onblur="off(1)"
onmouseover="on(1)"
onmouseout="off(1)"
onkeypress="on(1)"
onkeyup="on(1)">
</a>

<script>
function on(imageId)
{document.getElementById(imageId).style.border = "solid yellow";}
function off(imageId)
```

```
{document.getElementById(imageId).style.border = "solid white";}
</script>

</body>
```

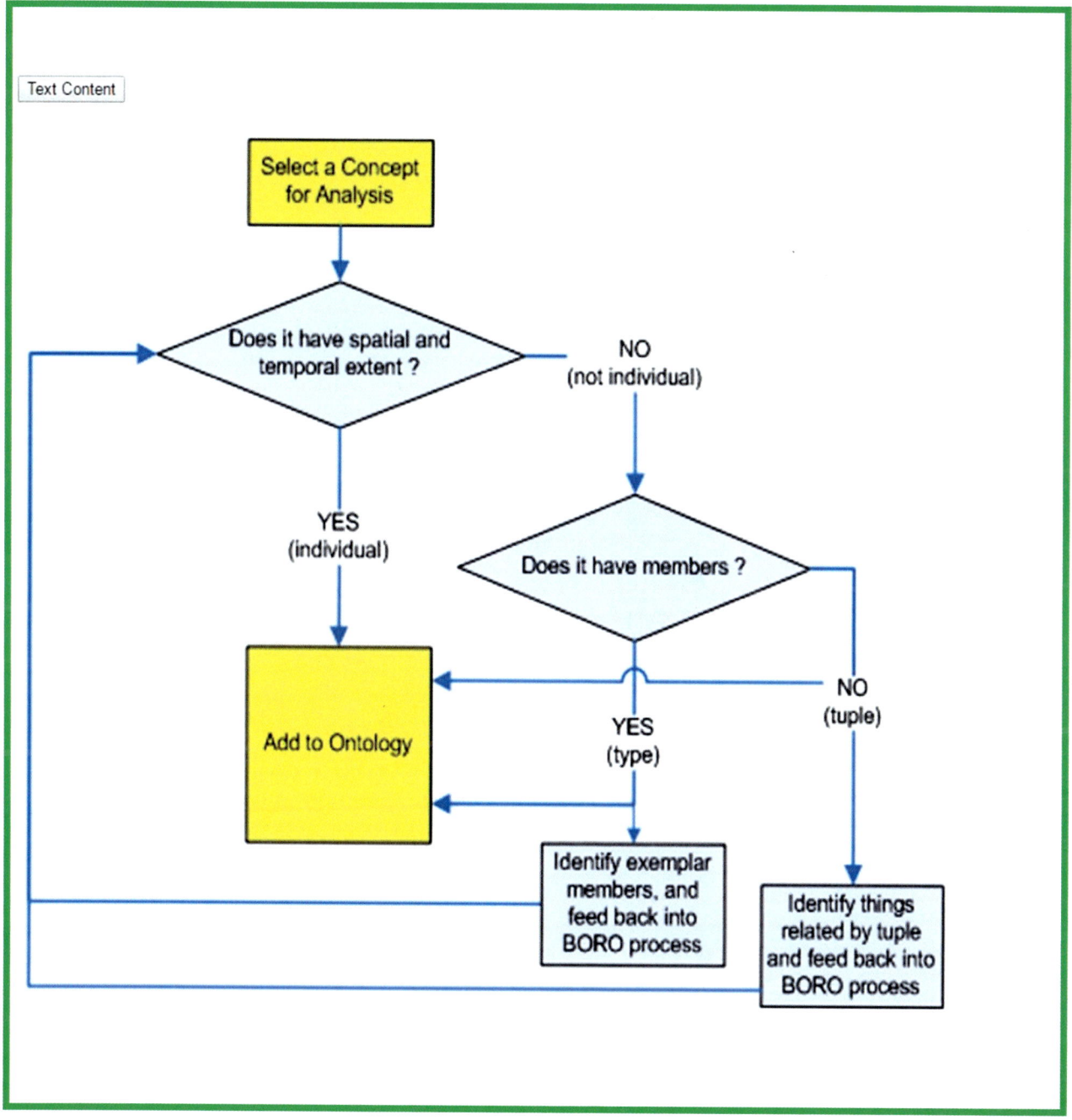

This is some text.
Text Content

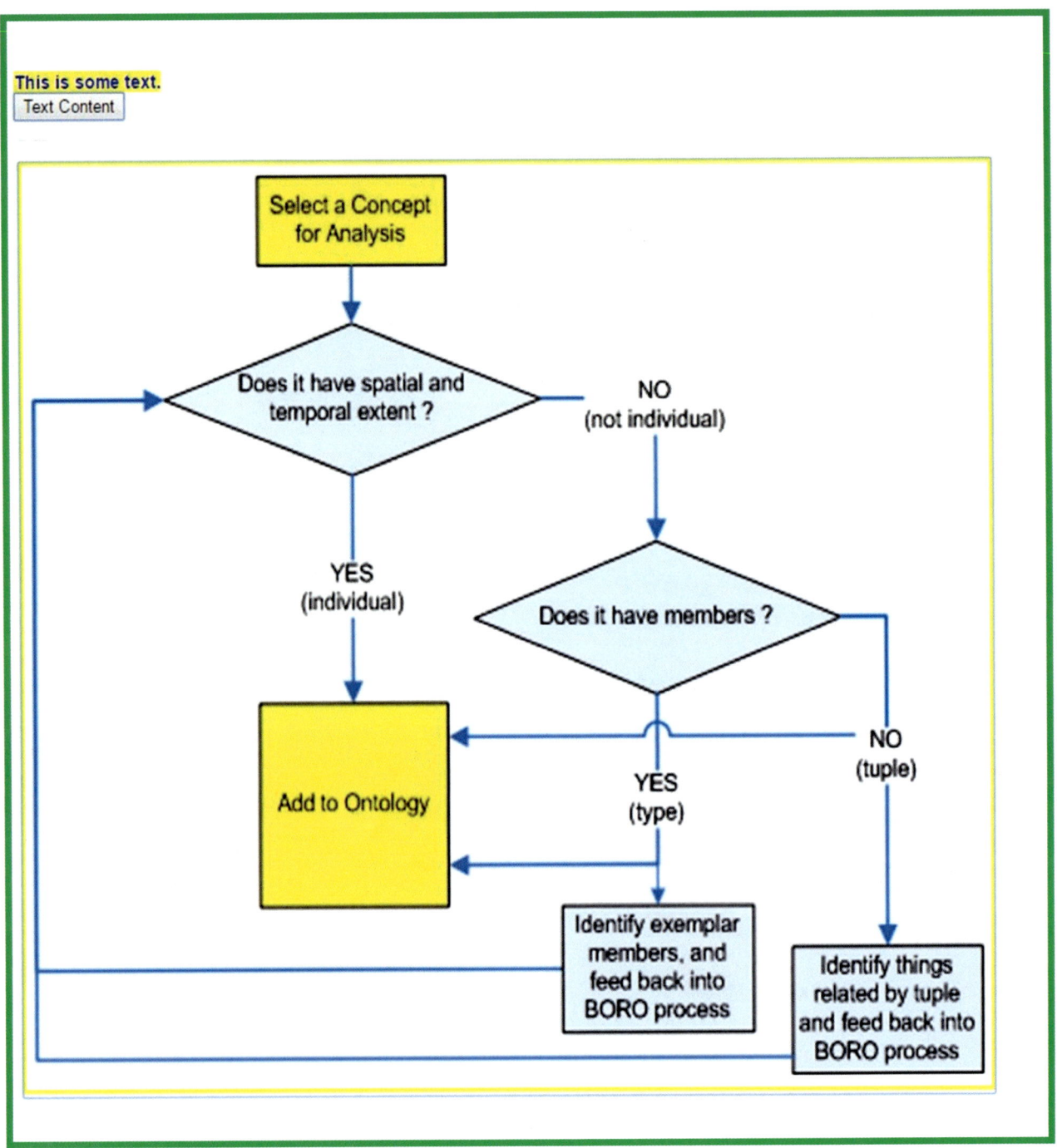

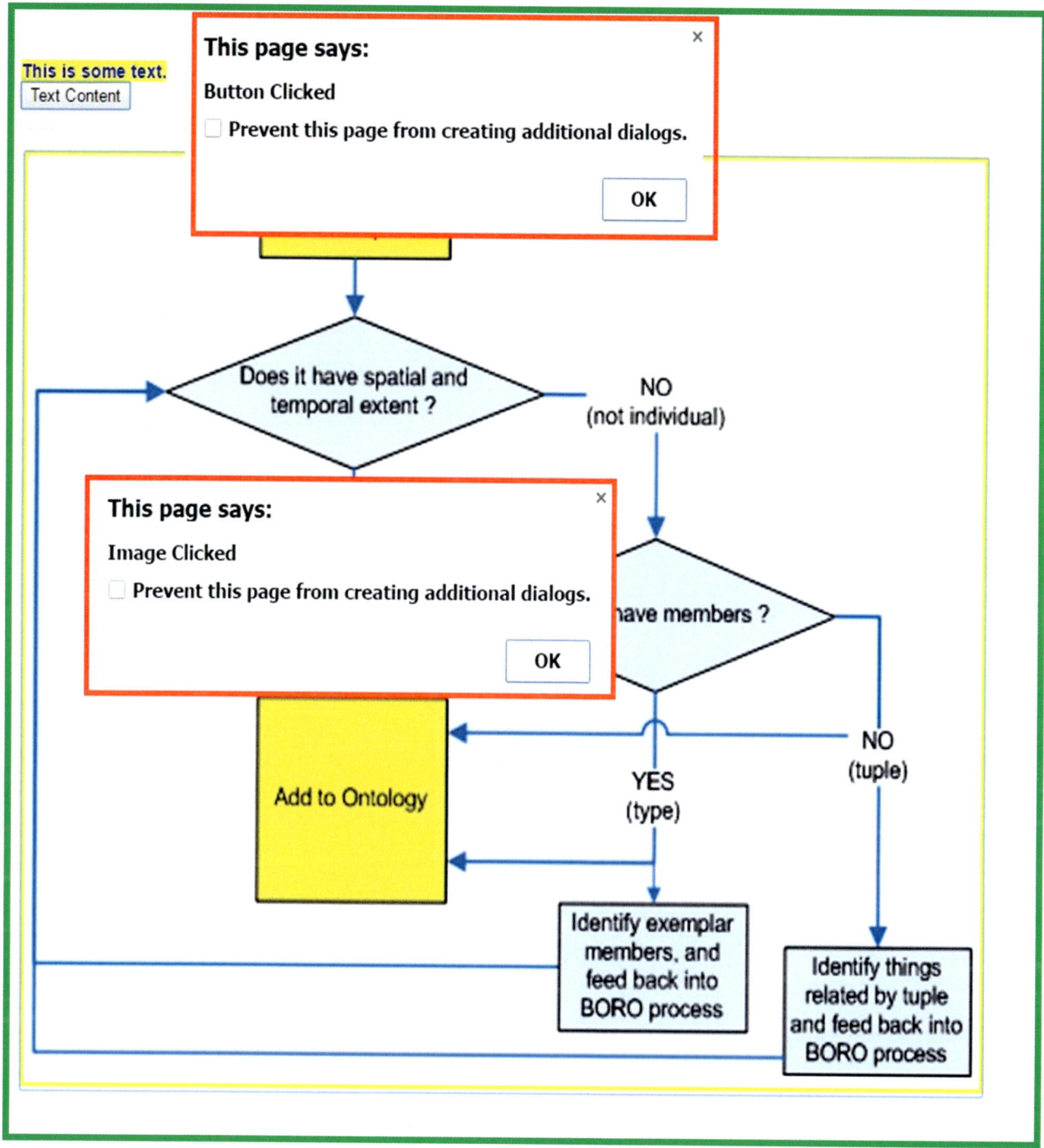

Figure 26: Highlight focus on button and image by mouse and TAB key.

43.2   Provide Support For Scripting Turned Off.

Provide an alternative for those who cannot use scripting at all if scripting is required. If an HTML only option cannot be made available provide a TTY capable phone number or support service to allow another mode to complete a task offered on the web page.

Interfaces that do not support client-side scripts must render this element's contents.

Using NOSCRIPT:

In the following example, an interface that executes the SCRIPT will include some dynamically created data in the document. If the interface doesn't support scripts, the user may still retrieve the data through a link.

```
<script>

var x=window.open('', 'newWin', "width=200,height=200");
var txt='';

txt+='<head><title>Javascript WIndow</title></head>';
txt+='Javascript Window';

x.document.write(txt);
x.focus();

</script>

<noscript>
<p>To access the data, <a href="#">Select This Data Link .</a>
</noscript>
```

To access the data, Select This Data Link .

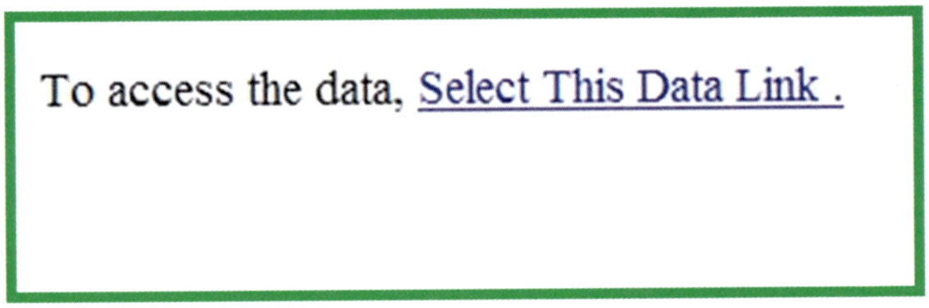

Figure 27: Noscript option appears when JavaScript is not available or turned off.

43.3   Use ONSUBMIT To Capture Errors.

Use the ONSUBMIT event. In this example the validate function would return true if there are form errors, stopping the submission of the form:

```
<script>
function validate()
{
alert("** " + document.forms["frm1"]["fname"].value + " ** "+ " Will be validated before submission")
}
</script>

What is your name?<br>
<form name="frm1" action="#" onsubmit="validate()">
<input type="text" name="fname">
<input type="submit" value="Submit">
</form>
```

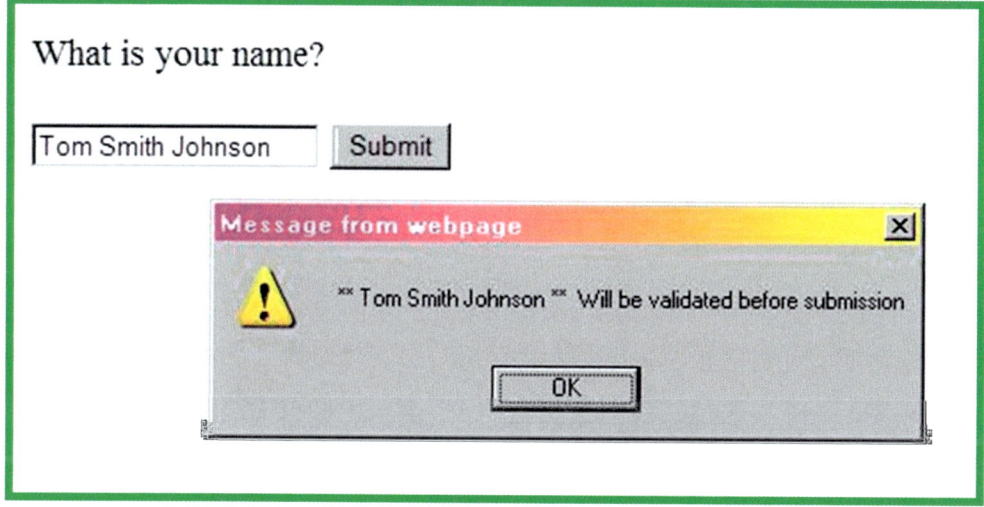

Figure 28: onsubmit will run user input through validation scripts before submission.

43.4 Use ONBLUR, ONKEUP Or ONCHANGE To Validate Current Field Upon Exit.

When a user attempts to leave the required field, the ONBLUR, ONKEYUP or ONCHANGE event calls a JavaScript function to confirm that the number field has an acceptable value.

```
ONBLUR, ONKEYUP Method:
<script>

var numb = '0123456789';

function check(parm,val)
{
if (parm == "") return true;
 for (i=0; i<parm.length; i++)
         {if (val.indexOf(parm.charAt(i),0) == -1) return false;}
return true;
}

function isNumber(parm) {return check(parm,numb);}

</script>

Enter the Number (onblur):
<input type="text" name="num1" id="num1"
onblur="if (!isNumber(num1.value))
{alert('This is not a Number. Please use Numbers only (Example:534).');num1.focus();}
"/>

<br/><br/>
Or this method
<br/><br/>

Enter the Number (onkeyup):
<input type="text" name="num2" id="num2"
onkeyup="if (!isNumber(num2.value))
{alert('This is not a Number. Please use Numbers only (Example:534).');num2.focus();}
"/>
```

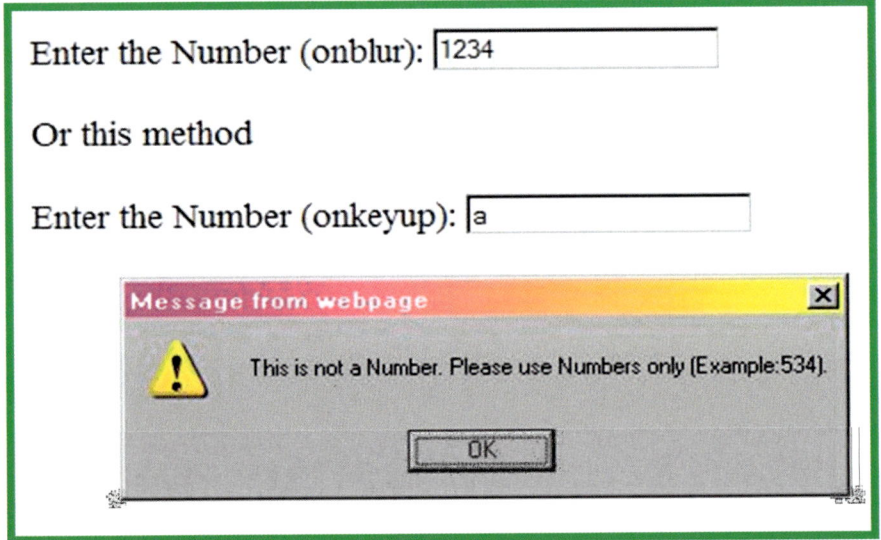

Figure 29: Using onblur and onkeyup to capture errors and return focus to field with both keyboard and mouse.

ONCHANGE Method:

```
Note: ONCHANGE with ALERT() does not return focus to field with the error with FOCUS alone. If an
ONCHANGE is used add SELECT() and RETURN FALSE
<script>

var numb = '0123456789';

function check(parm,val)
{
if (parm == "") return true;
 for (i=0; i<parm.length; i++)
         {if (val.indexOf(parm.charAt(i),0) == -1) return false;}
return true;
}

function isNumber(parm) {return check(parm,numb);}

</script>

Enter the Number ():
<input type="text" name="num2" id="num2"

onchange="if (!isNumber(num2.value))
 {alert('This is not a Number. Please use Numbers only (Example:534).');
 num2.select(); num2.focus(); return false;}"/>
```

Figure 30: ONCHANGE with SELECT() and FOCUS() with ALERT() to force focus back to field with the error with mouse or TAB key.

240

43.5   Give Focus And Keyboard Access To DIV.

If you use DIVs for structuring complex interactions, for example, parent-child DIVs for menus and sub-menus and expanding collapsing menus within multiple DIV containers. Keep interactions within a DIV as simple as possible to reduce the repositioning of focus and to increase access to a larger array of assistive technology devices. DIVs can also effectively be used for static page content and has a wide level of best practices available, for example using CSS to create columns or informational boxes that have conditional visibility.

Adding a JavaScript action to a DIV element

The DIV element on the page is given a unique id attribute and a TABINDEX attribute with value 0. A script uses the Document Object Model (DOM) to find the DIV element by its ID and add the ONCLICK handler and the ONKEYUP handler. The ONKEYUP handler will invoke the action when the ENTER key is pressed. Note that the DIV element must be loaded into the DOM before it can be found and modified. This is usually accomplished by calling the script from the ONLOAD event of the body element. The script to add the event handlers will only execute if the interface supports it and has JavaScript enabled.

```
<style>
#active
{
border:solid;
font-size: 1.1em;
font-family: arial, sans-serif;
}

#message
{
border:solid;
background-color: yellow;
color: blue;
font-size: 1.3em;
font-family: arial, sans-serif;
}

</style>

 <script>

function doSomething(event) {
var msg=document.getElementById("message");
msg.style.display = msg.style.display=="none" ? "" : "none";
return false;
}

function doSomethingOnEnter(event)
```

```
{
 var key = 0;
 if (window.event) {key = window.event.keyCode;}
 else if (event) {key = event.keyCode;}
 if (key == 13) {return doSomething(event);} //enter

 if (key == 9) {return doSomething(event);} //tab
 return true;
}

 function setUpActions()
{
 var active=document.getElementById("active");
 active.onclick=doSomething;
 active.onkeyup=doSomethingOnEnter;
}

 </script>

 <body onload="setUpActions();">
 <br/><br/>
 <div>
 <span id="active" tabindex="0">Do Something</span>
 </div>
<br/><br/>

 <div id="message" style="display:none">Div activated with focus by TAB or ENTER</div>
 </body>
 </html>
```

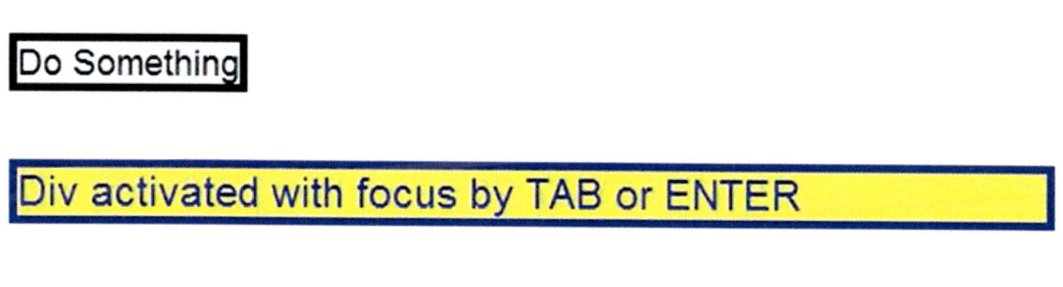

Figure 31: Key capture routine within first DIV out focus on second DIV via keyboard or mouse.

43.6   Test: Scripting.

- Check that the scripting action executes properly

- Check that it is possible to navigate to and give focus to the control via the keyboard

- Set keyboard focus to the control

- Check that pressing ENTER invokes the scripting action.

43.7 Test: Element Roles.

- Examine the source code for elements which have event handlers assigned within the markup or via scripting.

- If those elements are acting as user interface controls, check that the role of the control is defined.

44 Symbols And Text In Charts And Tables Must Have Direct Meaning To The Data, Status, Or Results, So That They Do Not Require Explanation.

Description

Symbols and text in tables and charts can have meaning that may be different from the intention of the table presentation. Any ambiguity can result in confusion over what the actual meaning is or the content of the cell. Data, results, status, or indicators, must all be clearly understood based on the cell contents in the table, legend, or chart alone, no further explanation should be necessary.

Categories

Symbols, Text, Charts, Tables

Reference

Section 508: 1194.22 (l) Sufficient information about a user interface element including the identity, operation and state of the element shall be available to assistive technology. When an image represents a program element, the information conveyed by the image must also be available in text.

WCAG 2.0: Non-text Content: Understanding SC 1.1.1(Level A):

http://www.w3.org/TR/UNDERSTANDING-WCAG20/text-equiv-all.html

WCAG 2.0: HTML Techniques 12.1 Markup and style sheets rather than images: the example of math [G1.3](Level A):

http://www.w3.org/TR/2005/WD-WCAG20-HTML-TECHS-20050630/#markupnotimage

44.1 Use Text Or Image With Text For Status.

The best practice is to use text so the meaning is clear. Commonly understood individual characters can be used such as "Y" or "N" for Yes/No and "N/A" for Not Applicable. A simple legend for special letters or abbreviations before the table or chart will associate better with related characters such as "C" or "Cov" for Covered. Do not use a image X or checkmark unless using an image with ALT text that is descriptive. Common expected usage is important for comprehension, for example asterisks are widely used to mean required fields. Though asterisks can be used for emphasis and special notation, they should not be used in that context adjacent to a field or on a form

44.2   Use Text Instead Of Symbols, If Symbols Are Needed Use Text Symbols.

Cells may be empty (an empty cell means it contains no data, do not use for spacing or formatting).

These are considered common knowledge, use of any other symbols must be spelled out on the page:

> "-"(dash) can be used if consistent in usage for 'data not available'. Best is em-dash (long dash).
>
> "x" or "*" (asterisk) can be used but must be defined, before usage.
>
> ".." (2 periods) means 'data not available',
>
> "-" (dash) means an exact value of zero.
>
> "0.0" means that the value is zero when rounded to the precision used.

- Notations must be explained.

- Explanations of any kind must precede the table.

- Priority is given to text words or common letters such as Y/N or Yes/No as less explanation is required for meaning. This is particularly true in context where a status, indicator, or result is used.

  The values in this table need no explanation:

Additional Features	Accessibility Valet Demonstrator	Acc Monitor Online	Cynthia Says	TAW	Torquemada	Wave 3.5	WebXact
Checks searchability and page content	No	Yes	No	No	No	No	Yes
Checks webpage data collection information	Yes	Yes	No	No	No	Yes	Yes

44.3 Use ALT Text With Graphic Symbols Or Icons.

Using graphic symbols with ALT text will work for small tables but creates unnecessary processing for a screen reader with large tables. When the symbols are numerous, this content will result in a delay in reading – the best use of these is sparingly where appropriate. An example would be an occasional image of an up arrow image with ALT text of "Increase" and a down arrow image with ALT text "Decrease". However even in that example, if the arrows are numerous they can become a burden as the reading delay will add up. For all large tables use text alphabetic characters (A-to-Z, a-to-z) with direct reference to words instead of symbols to make for equivalent reading by a screen reader, and to also make it clear for cognitive users (for example: Y for Yes instead of a symbol).

If a symbol serves a different purpose, different text or text alternative must be used to make it understand. The best practice is to be consistent throughout.

For example:

```
<style>
table { margin: 1.1em; border: 2px solid brown; font-family: arial, sans-serif;}
th, tr, td { padding: .6em; border: 2px solid black; }
</style>

<table >
 <caption>Services Sales Amount</caption>
 <thead>
 <tr>
 <th>Software</th>
 <th>Server</th>
 <th>Compared Last Year </th>
 </tr>
 </thead>
 <tbody>
 <tr>
 <td>$10.8K</td>
 <td>$50.6K</td>
 <td><img src="Green-Up-Arrow-Small.JPG" width="40" height="90" alt="Total Profits
Increased"</td>
 </tr>
 <tr>
 <td>$5.8K</td>
 <td>$47.6K</td>
 <td><img src="Red-Down-Arrow-Small.JPG" width="40" height="90" alt="Total Profits
Decreased"</td>
 </tr>
 </tbody>
 </table>
```

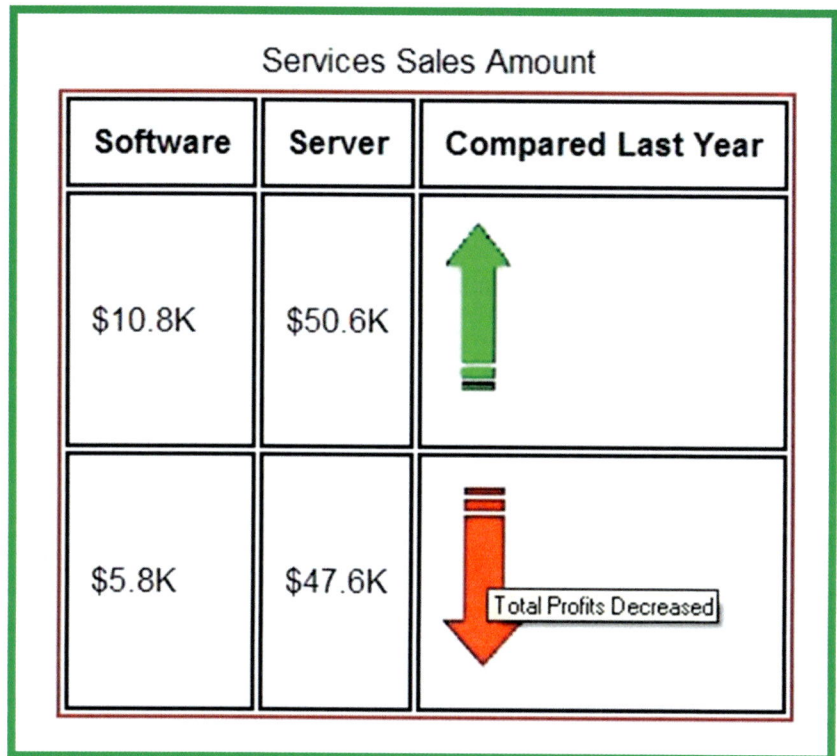

Figure 32: Table with images containing ALT text.

44.4   Do Not Use Empty Columns Or Rows For Formatting.

Do not use empty table cells for spacing or layout as these are all read by a screen reader and also can cause disorientation with a magnifier. Use CSS for layout. The rule is never to use any structural markup to create visual formatting as structural markup is exposed to a screen reader.

44.5   Using CSS For Empty/Blank Cells.

The EMPTY-CELLS property allows users to leave table cells empty and still give them proper borders on the screen or on paper. A data cell that is meant to be empty should not be filled with white space or a non-breaking space just to achieve a visual effect. !DOCTYPE must be declared. This has no effect on screen readers and is for visual considerations only.

```
<!DOCTYPE html>

<style>
table, th, tr, td
{
margin: 0em;
border: 2px solid blue;
padding: 1em;
font-size: 1.1em;
color: brown;
font-family: arial, sans-serif;

empty-cells: show;
}

</style>

<table border="1">
 <tr>
 <td><b>Column 1</b></td>
 <td><b>Column 2</b></td>
 </tr>
 <tr>
 <td>Row 1 Cell 1</td>
 <td>Row 1 Cell 2</td>
 </tr>
 <tr>
 <td>Row 2 Cell 1</td>
 <td>Row 2 Cell 2</td>
 </tr>
 <tr>
 <td>Row 3 Cell 1</td>
 <td>Row 3 Cell 2</td>
 </tr>
 <tr>
 <td></td>
 <td>Row 4 Cell 2</td>
 </tr>
</table>
```

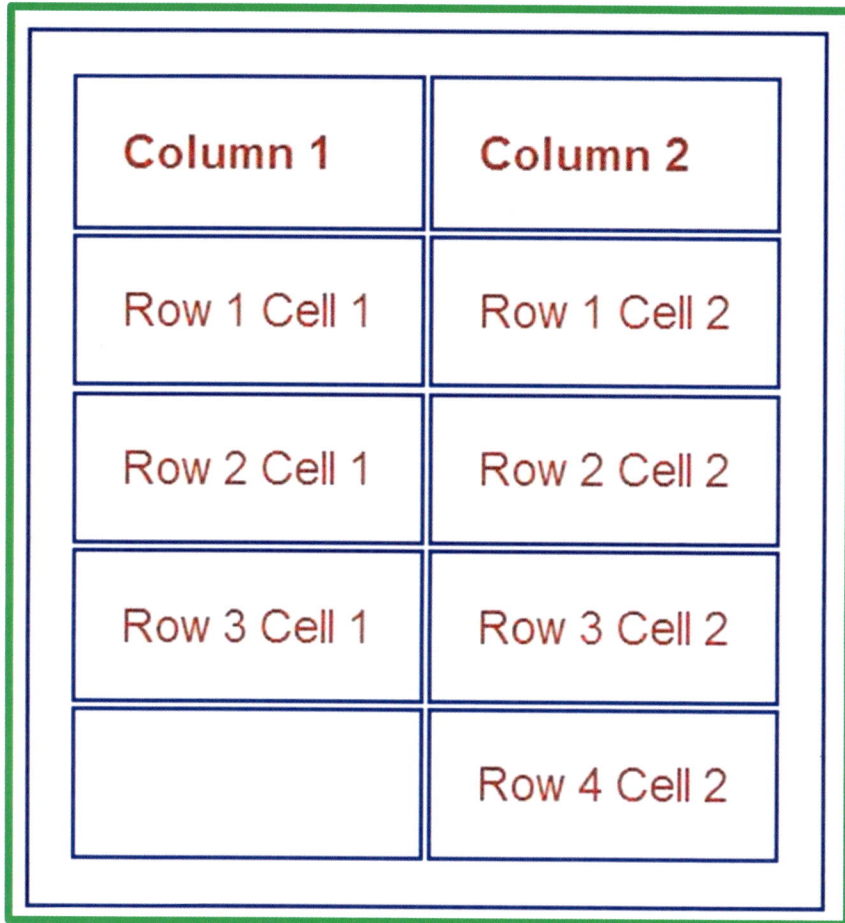

44.6 Use Text For Simple X+Y Equations But Use Mathml For Complex Math.

- Users must know what variables represent, for example, in the equation "F = m * a", indicate that F= Force, m = mass, a = acceleration.

- Use straightforward equations, use characters, as in "x + y = z"

- For more complex equations, mark them up with MathML [MATHML] or TeX. Note. MathML can be used to create very accessible documents but currently is not as widely supported or used as TeX.

- Provide a text description of the equation and, where possible, use character entity references to create the mathematical symbols. A text alternative must be provided if the equation is represented by one or more images.

Note: Internet Explorer 7, 8, and 9 will require a plug-in such as MathPlayer:

http://www.dessci.com/en/products/mathplayer/ .

To meet the 508 requirement for plug-ins place a notice about viewing MathMl on the page.

```
<!DOCTYPE html PUBLIC "-//W3C//DTD XHTML 1.0 Transitional//EN"
"http://www.w3.org/TR/xhtml1/DTD/xhtml1-transitional.dtd">
<html xmlns="http://www.w3.org/1999/xhtml" >
<math xmlns="http://www.w3.org/1998/Math/MathML">
<math xmlns="&mathml;">

<mlongdiv longdivstyle="lefttop">
 <mn> 3 </mn>
 <mn> 435.3</mn>
 <mn> 1306</mn>

 <msgroup position="2" shift="-1">
 <msgroup>
 <mn> 12</mn>
 <msline length="2"/>
 </msgroup>
 <msgroup>
 <mn> 10</mn>
 <mn> 9</mn>
 <msline length="2"/>
 </msgroup>
 <msgroup>
 <mn> 16</mn>
 <mn> 15</mn>
 <msline length="2"/>
 <mn> 1.0</mn>
 </msgroup>
 <msgroup position='-1'>
 <mn> 9</mn>
 <msline length="3"/>
 <mn> 1</mn>
 </msgroup>
 </msgroup>
</mlongdiv>

<mo linebreak='newline'> </mo>
<mo linebreak='newline'> </mo>

<mroot>
<mrow>
<mn>1</mn>
<mo>-</mo>
<mfrac>
<mi>x</mi>
```

```
<mn>2</mn>
</mfrac>
</mrow>
<mn>3</mn>
</mroot>

<mo linebreak='newline'> </mo>
<mo linebreak='newline'> </mo>
<mo linebreak='newline'> </mo>

<mrow>
 <mi>A</mi>
 <mo>=</mo>
 <mfenced open="[" close="]">
 <mtable>
 <mtr>
 <mtd><mi>x</mi></mtd>
 <mtd><mi>y</mi></mtd>
 </mtr>
 <mtr>
 <mtd><mi>z</mi></mtd>
 <mtd><mi>w</mi></mtd>
 </mtr>
 </mtable>
 </mfenced>
</mrow>

<mo> . </mo>

<mo linebreak='newline'> </mo>
<mo linebreak='newline'> </mo>

</html>
```

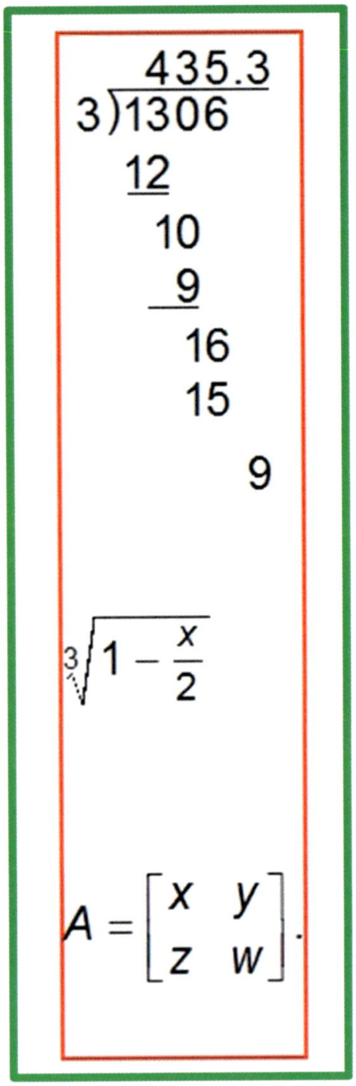

$$\begin{array}{r} 435.3 \\ 3\overline{)1306} \\ \underline{12} \\ 10 \\ \underline{9} \\ 16 \\ 15 \\ \\ 9 \end{array}$$

$$\sqrt[3]{1 - \frac{x}{2}}$$

$$A = \begin{bmatrix} x & y \\ z & w \end{bmatrix}.$$

Figure 34: MathML displayed in Internet Explorer 9 with plug-in MathPlayer enabled.

44.7   Test: Math Conveyed.

- Examine the page for non-text marks that convey information.

- Check whether there are other means to determine the information conveyed by the non-text marks such as text or abbreviated known text for example: Y or N, N/A

44.8   Test: Text Description.

If Text is used, is the text self-explanatory?

An "X" can mean yes/no, included/not-included, etc., in this respect the ambiguity of "X" can be equal and function similar to that of a checkmark symbol.

- Land the focus in the middle of the table and see if the value in the table cell can be understood without further reference.

- If the cell is blank, can that be understood?

45 Image Maps Must Have Text Alternatives. Client-Side Image Maps Must Be Used Instead Of Server-Side Image Maps.

Description

Text alternatives must serve the same purpose as the selectable regions of an image map. An image map is an image divided into selectable regions defined by area elements. Each area is a link to another web page or another part of the current web page. The ALT attribute of each area element serves the same purpose as the selectable area of the image.

Image maps are created with the MAP element. HTML allows two types of image maps: client-side (the user's browser processes a URI) and server-side (the server processes click coordinates). Use only the client-side. For all image maps, developers must supply a text alternative.

Categories

Image Map

Reference

Section 508: 1194.22 (e) Redundant text links shall be provided for each active region of a server-side image map.

Section 508: 1194.22 (f) Client-side image maps shall be provided instead of server-side image maps except where the regions cannot be defined with an available geometric shape.

WCAG 2.0: H24 (Level A): Providing text alternatives for the area elements of image maps:

http://www.w3.org/WAI/GL/WCAG20-TECHS/H24.html

45.1 Provide Text Alternatives For The Area Elements Of Image Maps.

Use the ALT attribute of the area element to provide text that describes the purpose of the image map areas.

Images with ALT describing map sections:

```
<img src="welcome.gif" usemap="#map1"
 alt="Areas in the library. Select an area for
more information on that area." />
<map id="map1" name="map1">
 <area shape="rect" coords="0,0,30,30"
 href="reference.html" alt="Reference" />
 <area shape="rect" coords="34,34,100,100"
 href="media.html" alt="Audio visual lab" />
</map>
```

45.2   Test: ALT.

- Check that the area element has an ALT attribute.

- Check that the text alternative specified by the ALT attribute serves the same purpose as the part of image map image referenced by the AREA element of the image map.

46   User Selected Contrast And Color Cannot Be Overridden By Applications. When The Products Permits Users To Adjust Color/Contrast, A Variety Of Color Selections With A Range Of Contrast Levels Must Be Provided.

Description

When an application disables these system-wide contrast/color settings, accessibility is reduced or eliminated. Users must be allowed to select personalized settings which cannot be disabled by software programs.

Categories

Display, Color, Contrast

Reference

Section 508: 1194.21 (g) Applications shall not override user selected color and contrast selections and other individual display attributes.

WCAG 2.0: User Agent Accessibility Guidelines 7. Contrast and Color Selections:

http://www.w3.org/WAI/UA/sect508-UAAG.html#color-selections

46.1   Revert To System Settings Or Provide High Contrast Viewing.

If custom display settings are used then provide an option (e.g. link or button) that lets the user revert to the system settings: "Use System Display Setting." Optionally if the page is complex with multiple CSS color, and background settings, then offer a high contrast setting for the whole application or website.

46.2   Test: User Color Setting.

- Attempt to change basic accessibility color settings such as high contrast.

- Use the OS color contrast settings and then load a user style sheet.

- Both methods should allow the user color settings.

47   Links To Plug-Ins Must Be Provided To When Required To View Files Or Media That Cannot Otherwise Be Viewed In The Browser.

Description

Plug-ins, add-ons, and other programs that help in retrieving, rendering, and interacting with web content not native to the browser must have a link to obtain the viewer. The download and installation process must also be accessible.

Categories

Plug-in, Viewer, Add-on

Reference

Section 508: 1194.22 (m) When a web page requires that an applet, plug-in or other application be present on the client system to interpret page content, the page must provide a link to a plug-in or applet that complies with §1194.21(a) through (l).

WCAG 2.0: Techniques, 12.10 Plug-in viewers (Level A) [G4.2 L1 SC1]:

   http://www.w3.org/TR/2004/WD-WCAG20-HTML-TECHS-20041119/#download-viewer

WCAG 2.0: Guideline 4.2 (Level A) Ensure that user interfaces are accessible or provide an accessible alternative(s):

   http://www.w3.org/TR/2004/WD-WCAG20-20041119/#technology-supports-access

WCAG 2.0: Techniques, 12 (Level A) [G1.3 L1 SC1]. Programmatic objects and applets:

   http://www.w3.org/TR/2004/WD-WCAG20-HTML-TECHS-20041119/#programmaticobjects

47.1   Provide A Link To Download An Accessible Plug-In.

It is important for the public facing web pages to link to an accessible plug-in. While it may render content to average users, it may not render content to users with disabilities. If required plug-ins are not accessible, an alternative solution must be provided.

For internal users who cannot download or install executables add this statement instead of the link to the plug-in: "If you do not have the required viewer for the file, open a ticket to request it"

47.2   Plug-Ins or Add-Ons Cannot Trap Keyboard Users.

Plug-ins are user agents that render content inside the interface host window and respond to all user actions that takes place while the plug-in has the focus. If the plug-in does not provide a keyboard mechanism to return focus to the parent window, users who must use the keyboard may become trapped in the plug-in content.

- Ensuring that the keyboard function for advancing focus within content (commonly the TAB key) exits the subset of the content after it reaches the final navigation location.

- Providing a keyboard function to move the focus out of the subset of the content. Be sure to document the feature in an accessible manner within the subset.

- If the technology used in the subset of the content natively provides a "move to parent" keyboard command, documenting that command before the user enters the plug-in so they know how to get out again.

47.3   Test: Methods of Accessing Content.

- Check that the web page includes a list of the technologies that user agents must support in order for its content to work as intended.

- If the plug-in is not accessible, locate an alternative method or remedy via an accessibility page.

47.4   Test: Link Description.

Check that the link to the plug-in or player follows the requirements for links in this manual (Link target and purpose can be determined from the link text alone or from the link text together with its programmatically determined link context). In addition, the link text must describe the function and the target, for example: "Download form viewer from Downloads folder"

47.5   Test: Keyboard With Content.

- TAB through content from start to finish.

- Check to see if keyboard focus is trapped in any of the content so that the person cannot move out of any part of the content and continue through the rest of the content.

48 Blinking, Flickering Or Flashing With A Frequency Greater Than 2 Hz (Flashes Per Second) And Less Than 55 Hz Cannot Occur.

Description

There are two major groups affected by the on/off blinking or strobe effect of objects on a page. One is epileptics whose seizures can be triggered by such an event. The other is those with visual and/or brain disorders that cannot assimilate flashing information being flashed on and off. Some objects flash on their own; some are activated by the user or are conditional upon other chains of events. Look for anything that flashes and eliminate the flashing mode.

Categories

Flicker, Flash, Blink

Reference

Section 508: 1194.22 (j) Pages shall be designed to avoid causing the screen to flicker with a frequency greater than 2 Hz and lower than 55 Hz (per second)

WCAG 2.0: Guideline 2.3 (Level A) Seizures: Do not design content in a way that is known to cause seizures:

> http://www.w3.org/TR/2008/REC-WCAG20-20081211/#seizure-does-not-violate

WCAG 2.0: Three Flashes or Below Threshold: Understanding SC 2.3.1 (Level A):

> http://www.w3.org/TR/UNDERSTANDING-WCAG20/seizure-does-not-violate.html

48.1 No Page Elements Can Blink Out Of Range.

Do not allow any object on a web page to flicker, flash, or blink. Mouse rollovers can result in flashing if coded with opposing images, background or interference. HTML alone cannot control the frequency rate of blinking.

48.2 Test: Blinking.

Fail any interface element that blinks or scrolls out of the allowed parameters. Web HTML tags that render flickering interface elements cannot control frequency of flicker. If there is a control with software that can control flashing or blinking text, objects, or other interface elements flickering, then recommend the standard (not between 2 Hz and 55 H.

49 Style Sheets Must Not Be Required For Basic Content. Users Must Be Able To Load Local Style Sheets And

Obtain All Page Information And Controls. Information Required To Understand And Operate Content Does Not Rely On Shape, Size, Visual Location, Or Orientation Of Components.

Description

Information and relationships conveyed through CSS presentation can be programmatically determined, and notification of presentation changes to is available to assistive technologies. The information itself cannot be controlled by CSS, only the presentation of the information (the appearance).

Categories

Style Sheet, CSS, Presentation

Reference

Section 508: 1194.22 (d) Documents shall be organized so they are readable without requiring an associated style sheet.

WCAG 2.0: Guideline 1.3 (Level A) Ensure that information and structure can be separated from presentation:

http://www.w3.org/TR/2006/WD-WCAG20-20060427/guidelines.html#content-structure-separation

49.1   All Information Is Available Without Style Sheets.

Information must be available without the style sheets. If information or control is not available without the style sheet then an alternative format must be available. Positioning can render text unreadable when layered DIVs and blocks are displayed without CSS. Use the compliance check below to guarantee readable text.

49.2   Visual Cues Must Be Retained With Style Sheets.

Visual Cues must not be lost when CSS is turned off. Visual cues, for example:

- Headings are often in a larger, bold font separated from paragraphs by blank lines

- List items are preceded by a bullet and perhaps indented

- Paragraphs are separated by a blank line

- Items that share a common characteristic are organized into tabular rows and columns

- Form fields may be positioned as groups that share text labels

- A different background color may be used to indicate that several items are related to each other

- Words that have special status are indicated by changing the font family and /or bolding, italicizing, or changing the color of them.

Any of these and other cues needed for comprehension and completing forms must either be maintained, presented in another way or an alternative format is offered.

49.3   Visual Cues Must Be An Enhancement Only To Correct Structural Markup.

Headings cannot only be in a larger, bold font, the must have markup (H1 to H6). List items that are preceded by a bullet must have markup in the code to represent this to assistive technology (UL). List with numbers must have the tag OL in addition to indented with numbers.

49.4   Test: Page Information/Controls Without CSS.

- Load page without CSS references. If page was previously loaded the current display may be in the cache, clear cache, close window, reload page.

- All text and controls must be readable.

49.5   Test: Non-CSS Functionality.

- Load page without CSS.

- All controls and form elements must receive focus.

- Form elements must allow interaction specific to that element.

49.6   Test: Non-CSS Reading Order.

- Load page without CSS.

- Logical order must be maintained. Check order of reading.

- Check for parts of text blocked by other text or elements.

49.7   Test: User CSS.

- Load page with local user settings CSS.

- Check all items on page are readable and controls identified.

50 Text-Only Versions Must Be Provided When No Other Method Will Expose All Content Programmatically. This Method Should Not Be Used If The Original Content Can Be Remediated To Be Made Accessible.

Description

Programmatically determined means that the text must be able to be read and used by the assistive technologies (and the accessibility features in browsers) that people with disabilities use.

This technique is not recommended as it removes accessibility features that are available in correctly marked up text that exposes structure. In particular, tables require structure to be understood.

It must also be possible for people using assistive technologies to access text alternatives when they encounter non-text content that they cannot use. To accomplish this, the text must be programmatically associated with the non-text content. This means that the user must be able to use their assistive technology to find the alternative text (that they can use) when they land on the non-text content (that they can't use).

Current production of materials can use document markup to render content accessible, see the section on documents in this manual. However it is recognized that some legacy publications, poorly scanned images of text, or inability to remediate the publication may necessitate a pure text version.

Categories

Text, Alternative

Reference

Section 508: 1194.22 (k) A text-only page, with equivalent information or functionality, shall be provided to make a web site comply with the provisions of this part, when compliance cannot be accomplished in any other way. The content of the text-only page shall be updated whenever the primary page changes.

WCAG 2.0: Plain Text Techniques for WCAG 2.0 [SC 1.3.1] (Level A):

> http://www.w3.org/WAI/GL/WCAG20-TECHS/text.html

WCAG 1.0 (Not directly addressed in WCAG 2.0): 8. Why don't the guidelines recommend using text-only pages?:

> http://www.w3.org/1999/05/WCAG-REC-fact#text

WebAIM: Design Considerations Text-only Versions:

http://webaim.org/articles/design/textonly

50.1 Text Only Version Must Contain All Information As The Original And That Information Must Be Equivalent.

The text only version must be equivalent to the information presented in the inaccessible format. Any charts, processes, statistics, math and equations, animations, videos, dashboards, must all be described in the same detail as presented in the original.

For example: if a chart shows data representing 2.8% of a budget, a text version of "almost 3 percent" is not equivalent, "2.8 percent" is (I actually saw this in a budget that was in the millions of dollars).This is why in the case of charts that data points should be represented as actual text on the bar or line graph points. Even if the chart were a pure image, the image text would indicate the exact number to reflect in the text description and provides accuracy to visual users.

50.2 Text Only Version Must Be Synchronized With The Original.

The text-only version must be identical in content and requires synchronization with the original content to keep text and data consistent. This process of matching multiple versions is the reason why any substantial amount of content made accessible in its native form is the best practice, both from an accessibility standpoint but also resources.

50.3 Test: Content Matches Text-Only Version.

Text-only version must represent all content presented in the original.

- Check that charts used for detail data are represented in text with the same level of data detail.

- Check that organization or flow charts must represent all relationships.

50.4 Test: Reading Order.

- Check for logical, steps, or process order.

- Check for jumbled or merged text that is unreadable.

51 No Disruption Of Assistive Technology Or Accessibility Features Of The Operating System, Browser, Or Media Player Can Occur.

Description

Accessibility features examples include:

- Reversing the color scheme (to assist people with low vision)

- Showing a visual prompt when an error tone is sounded (to assist persons who are deaf or hard of hearing)

- Providing "sticky keys" that allow a user to press key combinations (such as CTRL+C) sequentially rather than simultaneously (to assist persons with dexterity disabilities).

This requirement prohibits applications from disabling these features when they have been activated prior to running the application.

Categories

Disrupt, Interfere, Obstruct, Disable

Reference

Section 508: 1194.21 (b) Applications shall not disrupt or disable activated features of other products that are identified as accessibility features, where those features are developed and documented according to industry standards. Applications also shall not disrupt or disable activated features of any operating system that are identified as accessibility features where the application programming interface for those accessibility features has been documented by the manufacturer of the operating system and is available to the product developer.

WCAG 2.0: Conformance Requirements 5 (Level A). Non-Interference:

http://www.w3.org/TR/2008/REC-WCAG20-20081211/#cc5

51.1 Provide Methods To Avoid Disruption Of AT Or Provide Alternatives.

To avoid disruption of AT or accessibility features provide:

- Audio control

- No Keyboard Trap (keyboard can navigate to all content and out of all content)

- Pause, Stop, Resume, or Hide control (for any object that can disrupt AT)

51.2 Provide Methods To Access Content If Primary Method Is Inaccessible.

If technologies are used in a way that is not accessibility supported, or if they are used in a non-conforming way they must not block the ability of users to access the rest of the page. An accessible method of control or alternative delivery of information must be provided.

51.3   Test: That AT Is Not Disrupted; The List Below Gives A General Range Of Types Of AT.

Assistive technologies that must not be interrupted include the following:

- Screen magnifiers, and other visual reading assistants, which are used to change text font, size, spacing, color, synchronization with speech, etc.

- Screen readers, which are used to read textual information through synthesized speech or Braille.

- Text-to-speech software, which is used by to convert text into synthetic speech;

- Speech recognition software, for voice screen control and voice input.

- Alternative keyboards, which are used to simulate the keyboard (including alternate keyboards that use head pointers, single switches, sip/puff and other special input devices).

- Alternative pointing devices, which are used to simulate mouse pointing and button activations.

If interference is present, check to see if the technology is user controllable. If it is turned off, can the information still be accessed or accessed in another manner.

51.4   Test: OS Accessibility.

- Check that the operating system accessibility features are not disrupted.

  - In Microsoft Windows check the magnifier and speech.

  - In Apple iOS check magnifier, speech, and voice control.

- Check both for Mouse Keys, Slow Keys, and Sticky Keys.

52   Input, Editing & Authoring Mode And Views Must Be Operable With Assistive Technology.

Description

The purpose of this requirement is to ensure that editing modes and authoring tool user interfaces that are fully or partially web-based are more accessible to those with disabilities.

Even when a web-based user interface has met the requirements of 508 and WCAG 2.0, many factors will determine the accessibility of any particular end-user's ability to complete an editing task. This includes the features and settings of the end-user's browser platform, and assistive technology (if any). Developers of web-based authoring tools must be familiar with these accessibility guidelines.

In general edit modes or authoring tools or forms have more controls and options. These can take the form of buttons, panels, sliders, selectors, drag and drop, or mouse lasso. Any edit option must be available to the keyboard or provide an alternative method of operation.

Categories

Edit, Author, View, Input

Reference

Section 508:1194.21(a) When software is designed to run on a system that has a keyboard, product functions shall be executable from a keyboard where the function itself or the result of performing a function can be discerned textually.

Section 508:1194.21(l) When electronic forms are used, the form shall allow people using assistive technology to access the information, field elements, and functionality required for completion and submission of the form, including all directions and cues.

Section 508: 1194.22(n) When electronic forms are designed to be completed on-line, the form shall allow people using assistive technology to access the information, field elements, and functionality required for completion and submission of the form, including all directions and cues.

WCAG 2.0: Authoring Tool Accessibility Guidelines 2.0 Guideline A.2.2: Editing-view presentation can be programmatically determined. Guideline A.3.1: Provide keyboard access to authoring features (Level A):

http://www.w3.org/TR/ATAG20/

52.1   Editing And Input Views Provide Status Information And Help.

Provide flexible and informative editing views, navigation aids and access to display properties to users for editing or inputting. Editing or inputting triggers that changes state or options must indicate that in an accessible manner in the form of an alert or message with focus to allow the user to resume at the last editing position. Help should be available on every editing or input page. Repeated instructions must be given in the same order each time. The order of editing or inputting steps must follow a logical sequence.

52.2   Expose Accessible Markup To Assistive Technology.

Editors cannot introduce inaccessible markup or remove accessibility content, particularly when a edit mode hides the markup changes from the author's view. An option can be provided to "reveal codes". The essential requirement is to indicate status of the markup to authors or users inputting an automated or user-implemented change in the markup of content and allow for modifications of that markup. The user also must get an updated markup status upon request (for example: show formatting, reveal codes, and highlight styles).

52.3   Put Accessibility Mode Option Settings On First Or Primary Edit Page.

Allow efficient and fast access to accessibility-related settings with as few steps needed as possible to make any changes that will generate accessible content.

52.4   All Edit Options Must Be Programmatically Exposed.

Authoring mode must also ensure that the author can navigate a document efficiently while editing, regardless of disability. Authors who use screen readers, refreshable Braille displays, or screen magnifiers can make limited use (if any) of graphical artifacts that communicate the structure of the document and act as signposts when traversing it. As a result the authoring options must be exposed visually and programmatically.

One method is to make available optional methods of control. This can be achieved by having panels with multiple icons for quick visual selection, these panel selections are replicated in the main menus (link lists). The panels must be able to be loaded or unloaded so as not to disrupt menu usage by assistive technology.

52.5   Provide Overall Structure View And Navigation.

Edit mode must provide an editing view that conveys a sense of the overall structure and allows structured navigation.

52.6   Test Keyboard Access:

- Check for keyboard access to all functions.

- Check logical navigation order for the keyboard interface.

- Check for repetitive use of special keys for basic editing. This may also involve multi-key strikes with three keys and even four at once.

- Check for both keyboard & mouse access for functions.

52.7   Test: That Related Controls Are Grouped.

52.8   Test: That Viewing Content (I.E., Moving The Focus To A New Point) Should Not Cause Unexpected Events Or Results.

52.9   Test: Options Instructions.

If the editing environment has options beyond the simple HTML TEXTAREA or INPUT, then instructions should be provided for those options – a check on the page, via a link, or help.

53 Live Presentations, Webinars, Conferencing, And Shared Media Must Be Made Available In An Accessible Format.

Description

Depending on the live format in use, an alternate version such as a transcript may be required for an audience member. Ideally the accessibility would either be built-in to the software or hardware or live interpreters or live transcribers would be used. Since this is not always possible, efforts must be made to make any information available in an accessible format after the event is over. Depending on resources and availability, many options are possible including virtual sign language and automatic software transcription.

Categories

Live Presentation, Webinar, Conference, Shared Media

Reference

Section 508: 1194.22 (a) A text equivalent for every non-text element shall be provided (e.g., via "alt", "longdesc", or in element content).

Section 508: 1194.22 (b) Equivalent alternatives for any multimedia presentation shall be synchronized with the presentation.

Section 508: 1194.21 (a) When software is designed to run on a system that has a keyboard, product functions shall be executable from a keyboard where the function itself or the result of performing a function can be discerned textually.

Section 508: 1194.21 (c) A well-defined on-screen indication of the current focus shall be provided that moves among interactive interface elements as the input focus changes. The focus shall be programmatically exposed so that assistive technology can track focus and focus changes.

Note: Due to the wide array of software and systems to deliver presentations in rooms or virtual setups, many other standards may apply to your specific presentation. Refer to the other sections to see which may affect the presentation.

WCAG 2.0 Guideline 1.1 (Level A):

> http://www.w3.org/TR/2008/REC-WCAG20-20081211/#text-equiv

W3C: How to Make Presentations Accessible to All:

> http://www.w3.org/WAI/training/accessible

W3C: Making Presentations Accessible Notes:

> http://www.w3.org/WAI/EO/wiki/Making_Presentations_Accessible_Notes

W3C: Multimedia Accessibility FAQ:

http://www.w3.org/2008/06/video-notes

W3C: Best practices:

http://www.uiaccess.com/transcripts/transcripts_on_the_web.html#bests

53.1 Provide Copy Of Presentation Beforehand.

Provide copies of the presentation ahead of the event. This will solve a lot of the accessibility issues and will promote notification from any users that require different formats. However do not rely on this alone; ask if anyone will need an alternative format, assistance or special needs beforehand. The copy of the presentation should have as much detail as possible. A clean and professional look can be preserved with an appendix or additional notes.

53.2 Provide Transcripts Of Live Events.

Provide a fully descriptive transcript of the live event. The transcript must include all speaking parties' text in addition to any charts and diagrams, which must also be accessible. In addition, there are often messaging, and notes. Some webinar and conferencing services can provide this as captured in a transcript, however you must ensure it is accurate and accessible.

Sample transcript: Note identification of speakers when changed and reference to all items on slide 4, giving orientation to which slide and which topic on the slide:

....

M. Templeman: Now, on slide four I'd just like to very quickly go over a brief timeline of the progression. As I mentioned at the onset, there was a continuation from the last fiscal year when we started this to right now where we are working toward the final report. But before we do that, Rhonda is going to tell you a little bit about the overall objectives of the project.

R. Migdail: As Monika just indicated, 401(k) plans are the most prevalent type of retirement plan in the United States and a key focus has been in ensuring compliance with these plans and we've worked diligently to provide guidance and tools to try to foster that compliance....

We're also trying to educate ourselves as to how to optimize our outreach and compliance efforts going forward. Are there areas or issues where we need to provide further guidance and tools? So, with that, I'm going to turn it back to Monika.

M. Templeman: Thank you, Rhonda. So, now let's take a quick look at that timeline on slide four. Now, when we say 2009, 2010, we're referring to fiscal years and for the Service the years begin in October and end the end of September, so just keep that in mind.

(Transcript excerpt: Text illustrates identification of speakers, slide, and slide contents)

Figure 35: Transcript showing speaker identification and orientation to slides and information.

53.3 Media Information Must Be Described.

Media such as video and audio that are part of the presentation must also be made accessible. For short clips and last minute additions of graphics, explain in detail what is being presented and follow-up with descriptive notes. Any media used in the presentation that contains information must also be fully described in any resulting transcript.

53.4 Projected Media Must Be Viewable From All Points; Audio Must Be Clearly Heard Throughout Room.

Projected media must be visible and readable from the back of the room. Though not always easy to implement, check your audience for different seating and projection options. In a classroom with adjustable height monitors, lowering the monitors to the lowest height allows people in back to get a more unobstructed view. In a similar manner, check for ability to interpret audio from various points of the room. Close doors and try to eliminate other sounds that can mask the presentation audio.

53.5 Provide Full Description Of Visual Aids During Presentation.

Describe graphics, videos, and other visual content in detail. This will assist in providing an accurate transcript, in addition to those with visual disabilities or who are in the back of the room. The description will also help those attending remotely to follow what is going on.

53.6 Provide Extended And Alternate Descriptions And Explanations To Interpreters And Transcriptionists.

If sign language or other interpreters are used, provide the content of the presentation beforehand so they can prepare and plan accordingly. Provide for pauses and breaks, as interpreters normally will switch to a backup interpreter for long sessions. Not all concepts can easily be represented on the fly with interpreters. Allow time for the presenter to explain concepts in a different way to make a point clear to the audience and to the interpreter so that the interpreter can understand the concept better and communicate the idea. Be ready with multiple synonyms and alternative descriptions for technical words or little known jargon as this will facilitate translations. Also allow time for the transcriptionist, or note takers to ask questions for clarity so they can record information accurately.

If automated software transcriptions are used these must be edited to ensure they capture equivalent information that was presented.

53.7 Provide Structured Alternate Formats That Represent The Presentation Accurately.

Provide alternative formats that represent the presentation accurately and completely. If you are requested to provide this in Braille format be aware that charts, tables, and images will not be accessible unless they already have fully descriptive text. Complex tables – tables with sub-headers and merged cells cannot be represented in Braille. Very small simple tables – a simple grid with fewer than 5 rows and 5 columns can still be a challenge. If a table is critical and must be converted to Braille, the solution is to provide descriptive text of the values with association to the headers. Another alternative is to provide multiple formats, such as tables in a spreadsheet, or an accessible PDF file in addition to the Braille. The best practice is to provide accessible digital format, from which other formats can be generated.

53.8   Test: Keyboard Full Functionality.

Conduct a test of the keyboard to control functions and read content, navigate, and perform any edit capabilities. For movies and slide shows the user should be able to select Next, Previous, and Home/Table of Contents at any time. In addition the user should have capability to Pause or Stop any video or animation with the option to Continue or Resume. Despite the wide array of media, the basic requirement is that the user must be able to access all controls both by keyboard and mouse equally.

53.9   Test: Alternative Formats.

For live presentations via the internet or projected, check that the materials are presented beforehand in an accessible format. After the event, check to make sure that any transcript, detailed minutes, or log of conversations has been provided to the list of attendees and any late arrivals. Disabled attendees may require more setup time and alternative formats, have methods available to accommodate.

53.10   Test: Accessible Webinar.

If a live event such as a webinar allows for real time user interaction (such as sending message questions or taking pop quizzes) check that the keyboard users can access these features. If these features are not accessible to the keyboard, check that phone access along with alternative formats to the event is available and that any on-the-fly content or quizzes introduced are distributed during the event or directly after. Plan ahead for inclusiveness, alternative access provides participation methods for all users when they have a sudden physical, travel, or communication issue. Provide a transcript of all spoken and images along with image descriptions (captions are best) presented.

53.11   Test: Verbal Descriptions.

Check that visual elements presented are described verbally. Any images charts and notes written by the presenter should be verbalized fully and these descriptions captured in the transcript.

54   Moving, Scrolling, Or Auto-Updated Information Lasting More Than 5 Seconds Must Provide Controls To Stop, Cancel, Hide, Or Restart.

Description

Users must be able to complete tasks without unexpected changes in content or context (such as screen updates or status indicators) that are a result of a time limit. There are three groups affected by these directly, one is assistive technology, the others are cognitive, and visual. All groups must be able to set focus on the task at hand. Users focus can be disrupted by moving, scrolling information or auto updates on the page. This does not prevent dashboard updates or similar auto-filled data fields, in those cases the user will want the focus to be onto the new information. However, they should still be able to move from the auto-updated fields to another part of the page they may be working on and visa-versa, the same as a mouse user could. The user should have the option of where to keyboard focus and what to turn off and on.

Categories

Move, Scroll, Auto, Update

Reference

Section 508: 1194.21 (b) Applications shall not disrupt or disable activated features of other products that are identified as accessibility features, where those features are developed and documented according to industry standards. Applications also shall not disrupt or disable activated features of any operating system that are identified as accessibility features where the application programming interface for those accessibility features has been documented by the manufacturer of the operating system and is available to the product developer.

Section 508: 1194.21 (l) When electronic forms are used, the form shall allow people using assistive technology to access the information, field elements, and functionality required for completion and submission of the form, including all directions and cues.

Section 508: 1194.22 (n) When electronic forms are designed to be completed on-line, the form shall allow people using assistive technology to access the information, field elements, and functionality required for completion and submission of the form, including all directions and cues.

WCAG 2.0: Guideline 2.2 (Level A) Enough Time: Provide users enough time to read and use content. 2.2.2 Pause, Stop, Hide:

http://www.w3.org/TR/WCAG/#time-limits

WCAG 2.0: G4 (Level A): Allowing the content to be paused and restarted from where it was paused:

http://www.w3.org/TR/2012/NOTE-WCAG20-TECHS-20120103/G4.html

WCAG 2.0: G75 (Level AAA): Providing a mechanism to postpone any updating of content:

http://www.w3.org/TR/2012/NOTE-WCAG20-TECHS-20120103/G75.html

54.1 Provide A Mechanism To Pause, Stop, Or Hide Moving, Scrolling, Or Auto-Updating Content.

Moving, scrolling, or auto-updated content must be able to not only be paused, but also resumed if required information is part of the dynamic content. Allow the content to be paused and restarted from the point where it was paused.

Example showing method to allow display of entire scrolled content:

```
</style>

<script>

var tid;

function init()
{
var st = document.getElementById('scrollingText');
st.style.top = '0px';
initScrolling();
}

function initScrolling ()
{
tid = setInterval('scrollText()', 300);
}

function scrollText ()
{
var st = document.getElementById('scrollingText');
 if (parseInt(st.style.top) > (st.offsetHeight*(-1) + 8))
 {
 st.style.top = (parseInt(st.style.top) - 5) + 'px';
 }
 else
 {
 var sc = document.getElementById('scrollContainer');
 st.style.top = parseInt(sc.offsetHeight) + 8 + 'px';
 }
}

function toggle()
{
var scr = document.getElementById('scrollContainer');
 if (scr.className == 'scrolling')
 {
 scr.className = 'notscrolling';
 clearInterval(tid);
 document.getElementById('scrollButton').value="Shrink";
 }
 else
 {
 scr.className = 'scrolling';
```

```
    initScrolling();
    document.getElementById('scrollButton').value="Expand";
    }
}

</script>

<body onload="init()">

<input type="button" id="scrollButton" value="Expand" onclick="toggle()" />
 <div id="scrollContainer" class="scrolling">
 <div id="scrollingText" class="on">
.... Text to be scrolled ...

</div></div></body>
```

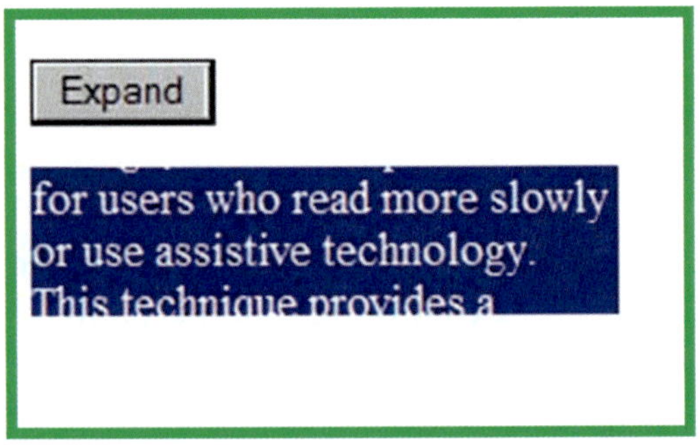

Expand

for users who read more slowly
or use assistive technology.
This technique provides a

Figure 36: Scrolling text in scrolling mode with button option to display all text at once.

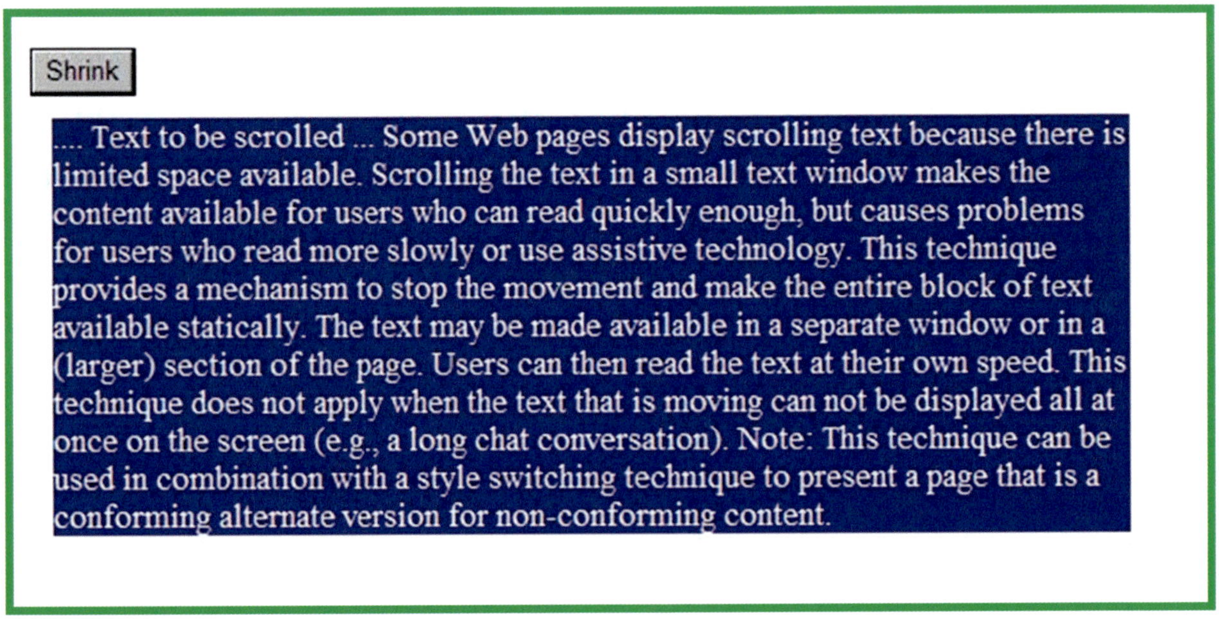

Shrink

.... Text to be scrolled ... Some Web pages display scrolling text because there is limited space available. Scrolling the text in a small text window makes the content available for users who can read quickly enough, but causes problems for users who read more slowly or use assistive technology. This technique provides a mechanism to stop the movement and make the entire block of text available statically. The text may be made available in a separate window or in a (larger) section of the page. Users can then read the text at their own speed. This technique does not apply when the text that is moving can not be displayed all at once on the screen (e.g., a long chat conversation). Note: This technique can be used in combination with a style switching technique to present a page that is a conforming alternate version for non-conforming content.

Figure 37: Scrolling text display all at once with button option to return to scrolling mode.

Some Web pages display scrolling text because there is limited space available. Scrolling the text in a small text window makes the content available for users who can read quickly enough, but causes problems for users who read more slowly or use assistive technology. This technique provides a mechanism to stop the movement and make the entire block of text available statically. The text may be made available in a separate window or in a (larger) section of the page. Users can then read the text at their own speed.

This technique does not apply when the text that is moving cannot be displayed all at once on the screen (for example: a long chat conversation).

Note: This technique can be used in combination with a style switching technique to present a page that is a conforming alternate version for non-conforming content.

Some Web pages display scrolling text because there is limited space available. Scrolling the text in a small text window makes the content available for users who can read quickly enough, but causes problems for users who read more slowly or use assistive technology. This technique provides a mechanism to stop the movement and make the entire block of text available statically. The text may be made available in a separate window or in a (larger) section of the page. Users can then read the text at their own speed.

This technique does not apply when the text that is moving cannot be displayed all at once on the screen (for example: a long chat conversation).

Note: This technique can be used in combination with a style switching technique to present a page that is a conforming alternate version for non-conforming content.

54.2 Providing A Mechanism To Postpone Any Updating Of Content And Allow Request Of Update Or Restart.

Ensure that users can postpone automatic updates of content, or other non-emergency interruptions. This can be accomplished either through a preference or by alerting users of an imminent update and allowing them to suppress it. If a preference is provided, automatic content update can be disabled by default and users can specify the frequency of automatic content updates if they choose to enable the setting.

```
<a href="news.jsp">Update this page</a>
```

The ability to control the content must be available. If text is displayed from start to finish and only the final part is left on the screen then the user must be able to restart the display of the text.

54.3 Test: Controls.

272

- Check for controls to pause, stop, hide, or restart any moving, scrolling or auto-updating content.

- Check for ability to move keyboard focus to the content and out of it, repeatedly. Check that the moving or scrolling will stop and does not restart by itself.

54.4   Test: User Update Control.

- For each automatic update, check for a mechanism to adjust the timing of the updates. If there is no adjustment, check for stop/restart controls.

- Check for a mechanism that allows the user to request an update of the content only as needed.

55 Web Pages, Sections, And Sub-Sections Must Have Headings.

Description

Scanning content is difficult for everyone without section headings. These can be used as identification, and orientation. The main title of each web page should: Identify the subject of the page and make sense when read out of context, for example by a screen reader or in a list of search results. These should be concise.

Categories

Titles, Sections, Headings

Reference

Section 508: 1194.21 (d) Sufficient information about a user interface element including the identity, operation and state of the element shall be available to assistive technology. When an image represents a program element, the information conveyed by the image must also be available in text.

WCAG 2.0: G88 (Level A): Providing descriptive titles for web pages:

> http://www.w3.org/TR/WCAG20-TECHS/G88

WCAG 2.0: G141 (Level A): Organizing a page using headings:

> http://www.w3.org/TR/WCAG-TECHS/G141.html

55.1   Provide Section Headings Or Sub-Headings With Unique Titles

Section headings should be concise, unique, and descriptive. Headings must be marked so they can be programmatically identified using the HTML heading elements H1, H2, H3, H4, H5, and H6).

```
<style>

h1 { text-indent: 0em; font-family: arial; }
h2 { text-indent: 1.2em; font-family: arial; }
h3 { text-indent: 3em; font-family: arial;}
p { text-indent: 2em; font-family: arial; }
</style>

<h1>Cooking techniques (H1)</h1>
 <p> Paragraph text </p>
 <h2>Cooking with oil (H2)</h2>
 <p> Paragraph text </p>
 <h3>Sautéing (H3)</h3>
 <p> Paragraph text </p>
 <h3>Deep frying (H3)</h3>
 <p> Paragraph text </p>
 <h2>Cooking with butter (H2)</h2>
 <p> Paragraph text </p>

<br/><br/>

<h1>Plant Foods that Humans Eat (H1)</h1>
 <p>There are an abundant number of plants that humans eat...</p>
 <h2>Fruit (H2)</h2>
 <p> A fruit is a structure of a plant that contains its seeds...</p>
 <h3>Apple (H3)</h3>
 <p>The apple is the pomaceous fruit of the apple tree...</p>
 <h3>Orange (H3)</h3>
 <p>The orange is a hybrid of ancient cultivated origin...</p>
 <h3>Banana (H3)</h3>
 <p>Banana is the common name for herbaceous plants ...</p>
 <h2>Vegetables (H2)</h2>
 <p>A vegetable is an edible plant or part of a plant other than a sweet fruit ...</p>
 <h3>Broccoli (H3)</h3>
 <p>Broccoli is a plant of the mustard/cabbage family ... </p>
 <h3>Brussels sprouts (H3)</h3>
 <p>The Brussels sprout of the Brassicaceae family, is a Cultivar group of wild cabbage ...</p>
 <h3>Green beans (H3)</h3>
 <p>Green beans have been bred for the fleshiness, flavor, or sweetness of their pods...</p>
```

Cooking techniques (H1)

Paragraph text

Cooking with oil (H2)

Paragraph text

   Sautéing (H3)

Paragraph text

   Deep frying (H3)

Paragraph text

Cooking with butter (H2)

Paragraph text

Plant Foods that Humans Eat (H1)

There are an abundant number of plants that humans eat...

Fruit (H2)

A fruit is a structure of a plant that contains its seeds...

   Apple (H3)

The apple is the pomaceous fruit of the apple tree...

   Orange (H3)

Figure 38: Heading levels.

55.2   Test: Headings.

- Check that each heading identifies its section of the content with descriptive text that is representative.

- Check for pages with text that does not have headings for the sections.

- Check for pages without a main title or heading.

56 Adobe PDF Files Must Be Tagged And Expose All Information And Elements In Logical Order To Assistive Technology.

Description

PDF files (Adobe PDF format) can be very simple with plain text or highly complex with multiple layers of content and can even include applications within them. PDF fillable forms must allow keyboard access to all fields and expose all labels, states, values, and instructions to assistive technology (AT). Tables must have cells associated to headers. Images with information must have text descriptions.

Many requirements apply to PDF files, critical ones are:

- The file is tagged (see below: 35.1)

- Text can be accessed by AT

- Navigation and orientation is logical and consistent, content can be located and current location can be determined

- Forms can be read and filled out by keyboard and AT

- Information in images and charts must have alternative text available

Categories

PDF

Reference

Section 508: 1194.22 (a) A text equivalent for every non-text element shall be provided (for example: via "alt", "longdesc", or in element content).

Section 508: 1194.22 (b) Equivalent alternatives for any multimedia presentation shall be synchronized with the presentation.

Section 508:1194.21(l) When electronic forms are used, the form shall allow people using assistive technology to access the information, field elements, and functionality required for completion and submission of the form, including all directions and cues.

Section 508: 1194.22 (n) When electronic forms are designed to be completed on-line, the form shall allow people using assistive technology to access the information, field elements, and functionality required for completion and submission of the form, including all directions and cues.

WCAG 2.0: PDF Techniques for WCAG 2.0:

http://www.w3.org/WAI/GL/WCAG20-TECHS/pdf.html

Adobe 2.0: Accessing PDF Documents with assistive technology:

http://www.adobe.com/accessibility/pdfs/accessing-pdf-sr.pdf

Adobe 2.0: Using Adobe tools to make accessible content:

http://www.adobe.com/accessibility/best_practices.html#acrobat9

WebAIM: PDF Accessibility Defining PDF Accessibility:

http://webaim.org/techniques/acrobat/

56.1   PDF Files Must Be Tagged With Tags That Represent Visual Structure.

The adobe acrobat plug-in for Microsoft Office products offers an accessibility conversion option to produce tagged files. Make sure this option is turned on. If a file does not have tags it can be tagged within Acrobat Professional, but not the Acrobat Reader.

Tags are roughly similar to HTML tags. They define the structure of the content. The H1 tag in PDF serves the same function as HTML to make as Heading Level 1. The difference is that the tags in a PDF are formatted as tree branches whereas HTML has a start and stop tag. If the document being converted is MS Word and it is structured properly with correct styles (such as Heading levels 1-6 {Heading levels 7-9 are not support in conversions}) and built-in markup, then the PDF for the most part will be accessible. However this depends on how complex and large the original document is.

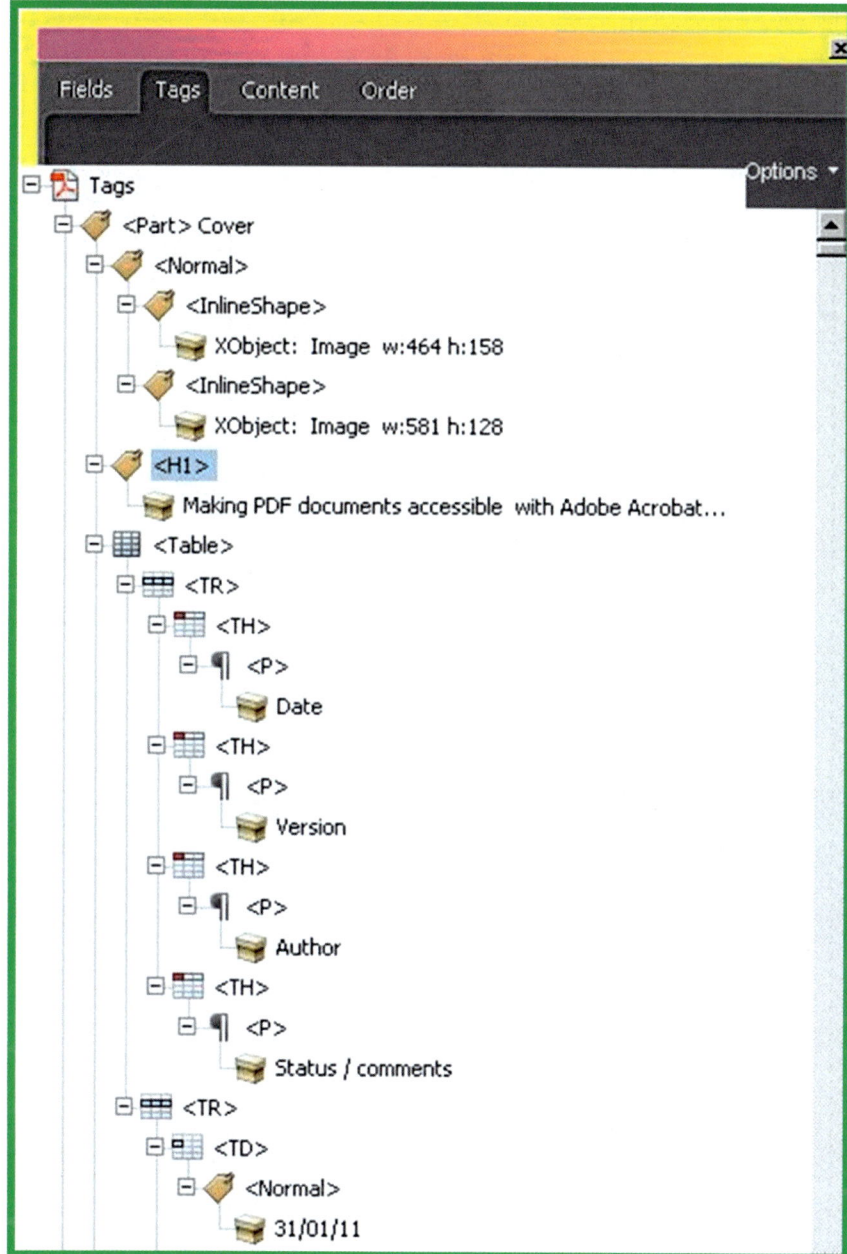

Figure 39: Example of tags in a PDF file viewed with Acrobat Professional.

Known items that **must be checked** for correct tagging:

Tables

If constructed in MS Word, tables cannot support markup to represent merged cells or sub-headers. If a simple table grid cannot be maintained then editing of the table will be necessary in the PDF.

Tables when structured correctly still may not end up with tags that represent the original structure. The conversion to PDF is not 100% as Adobe does not support every type of markup in Microsoft products. Even when the markup is supported the conversion often scatters content into incorrect tags as the conversion process is highly complex and prone to error. This is why tags must be manually examined, tested, and run with an accessibility check (built-in with Acrobat Professional or NetCentric CommonLook). All these efforts together will result in a correctly tagged file.

Images

if images are to have alternative text (alt-text), then the tag must have the alternative text . Each tag has a property and this can be manually set. Also the TouchUp Reading Order tool can be used. See references for tagging instructions. If the images do not contain information or the information is adjacent to the image or accessed via a link, then there should be no alt-text in the tag for the image (Figure tag in PDF). This can be deleted manually or removed via the TouchUp tool.

Alt-text should be less than 100 characters if used. A preferred method is to use a caption instead of alt-text. A caption:

- Is available to visual users

- Can be assigned a figure number

- A list of figures (index of images linked and numbered) can be generated

- Can contain a link placed in the caption for more detail

    o This method provides navigation and orientation in addition to content information

- Reads faster than an image

56.2 Provide Concise Alt-Text, Caption, Adjacent Text, Or A Full Description Via A Link.

Images, charts, scanned pages, and screen captures: must all have text descriptions. The descriptions must communicate the same amount of information provided visually. The information must be equivalent. There are several methods to achieve this goal in Acrobat Professional.

If the information is less than 100 characters, add this information either by the inserting alternative text in the properties of the tag or by use of the TouchUp tool. This description can also be placed in the caption alone. Do not use both a caption and alternative text both as the description will be read twice by a screen reader.

If the description is more than 100 characters use one of the following methods apply:

- Place the description directly adjacent to the image.

- Provide a link to a description in another location (e.g. appendix)

- Provide a link to a file (and a return link).

56.3   Provide OCR For Any Scanned Documents.

Images of document pages are inaccessible unless they have accurate OCR performed. Even with major software the end result must still be edited for accuracy. If an image is a screen shot or highly stylized image of difficult to capture image text then a text description of that image must be provided. This can be accomplished with alt-text (if it is less than 100 characters), in a caption, adjacent text, or a link to a description elsewhere with a return link.

PDF files allow for indexing of images of document pages, this cannot be used alone as equivalent text contained in the image is required.

56.4   Tags Must Be Structured To Be Readable, Eliminating Nonfunctioning Tags And Using Default Style Names Before Conversion.

- Empty tags must be deleted. These make editing difficult and use up screen reader processing.

- Section <Sect> and other lesser used division tags (<Art>, <Div>, <Part>, <Document>) must move content into a simple reduced structure of no more than one section per page (all tags for that page fall under that <Sect> tag). Multiple tags can be easily moved. The section and division tags are not needed and can be completely eliminated if document does not require tags to be divided into sections for tag readability purposes. Except for chapter designations, the less clutter the easier it is to read and correct the tags.

- Examine the Role Map to determine if tags are correctly converted. If not edit the tags to change them to the correct type, For example a heading is incorrectly mapped to <P> which is regular paragraph text and should be <H1> instead. The Role Map is the result of conversion and cannot be changed for the current document. You can change items in it for future conversions to another format such as HTML. For your purposes it is just informational.

- <Figure> tags that do not represent a valid image must be deleted. <Figure> tags often pick up tables lines, beginning or ending paragraph symbols or mistake other objects as images. In the [Tags] panel view turn on the option of [Highlight Content] select a starting tag and use the ARROW keys to scroll quickly through the tags to determine what the tag represents.

- The order of the tags is the reading order for the screen reader. The [Order] panel in Acrobat can cause issues with both the correct order and the placement of tags. Do not use the [Order] panel to rearrange items on the page. Reorder tags by moving the tags around the [Tags] panel.

- Repetitive header and footer information. This is usually left out of the tags. Depending on the nature of the document converted they are sometimes picked up and inserted in the tags. These can be deleted if there is no essential information that must be forced read for every page. Preserve footnotes and any other text in the footer region that is a reference.

Note: The TouchUp tool (TouchUp Reading Order) generates new tags and modifies others when parts of the page are lassoed and a tag type selected. As a result the tags must be examined when the TouchUp tool editing is completed. If a screen reader is being used, save the file first as the screen reader actually loads the file into memory not what is on the screen. Reloading the file will create a fresh start with the screen reader.

56.5   Test: Tag Availability.

- View Tags in Acrobat professional.

- Tags must be available.

- If tags are not available, use the add tags option to add tags to the document and conduct the additional Tests.

56.6   Test: Image Information Alternatives.

Images with information must have a text description in either:

- Alternative text

- Caption

- Adjacent text

- Link to text in another location

Images with no information should not have alternative text. This includes:

- Mood setting

- Decoration

- Background

- Non-informational symbols and icons

56.7   Test: With Accessibility Checker.

- Run the Acrobat Accessibility Checker.

- Determine if each error points to valid content in the file.

    - An indicator of an invalid error is if the link to it does not work

- Determine if any image errors are pointing to orphaned image components.

- Depending on the nature of the errors and any false positives, remediation should be conducted to eliminate the valid errors. Deleting tags for orphaned image parts will remove image errors.

56.8   Test: With Screen Reader.

Screen Reader Essential Checks

Unlike HTML the underlying code cannot be read in a PDF file. While the tags can be deciphered, certain combinations of complex formatting – large tables - cannot be evaluated for accessibility without an actual screen reader interpretation of the tags. To alleviate the need for time consuming screen reader testing it is important to check that the tags are clean and easy to read. See section on tag format.

Logical Reading Order

Read the first few words of each paragraph and skip to the next paragraph or section and repeat on each page or sample of pages to determine order. Pay close attention to:

- Columns

- Indented text

- Boxed text

- Vertical text

Remediation: Rearrange tags to rearrange order. Note that the order panel in Acrobat does not always reflect actual tag order. If the order panel is used then carefully retest and also check the tags.

Note 1: When making any changes to a PDF file, you must resave it to have the screen recognize the changes. Otherwise it reads the older PDF you have loaded in memory.

Note 2: Tag changes cannot be undone, so you must save the file frequently if you need to backtrack to a safe version.

Table Cell Association

Move to a few cells in the middle of a table and check the column header and row header (if any) are identified. Check that any row header must not be identified if it is not an actual row header, not just a regular data cell.

Remediation: For many tables you can simply change TD tags to TH if needed or move tags around and create new ones. The table inspector in Acrobat can be used but will not work properly on all tables. For complex tables PDF accessibility products like NetCentric CommonLook can manipulate cell to header association easily.

Forms

The order of the fields must logically represent how they would be filled out and grouped. The fields themselves must have labels. In addition instructions should be associated with the field and exposed to assistive technology. PDF files allow for hidden fields and these are often used for additional instructions for screen readers. TAB key or a screen reader hot key for fields (F for JAWS and Window-Eyes) will locate all fields. Inputting text should keep focus in the field and move to next logical field when completed.

Structure

Headings should be noted as such and the heading level should be hierarchical. They must be in alignment with the level of the section or sub-section. A hierarchical manner means structuring with 1st degree headings (<H1>) being the most important (usually page titles or section heading), then 2nd degree headings (<H2> - usually major section headings), down to 3rd degree headings (sub-sections of the <H2>), and so on. Lower degree headings should be contained within headings of the next highest degree. The following outline shows the hierarchy of what a page might contain:

Heading Level 1
    Heading Level 2
    Heading Level 2
    Heading Level 2
Heading Level 1
Heading Level 1
    Heading Level 2
        Heading Level 3
        Heading Level 3
        Heading Level 3
        Heading Level 3

Links must describe the target. Document links should move the focus to the correct location. Note: In a PDF this can include a zoom level change. Multiple links on page must be unique and easily identified. Footnotes must be numbered. Do not use symbols.

Lists must be identified as lists. Sometimes bullets get separated in the tags from the line text. If the screen reader reflects the list on the screen and reads only "bullet" before the text, it passes. But if the bullet is read as "image" then it fails. Editing of these tags may be needed.

Images

See the requirement for images above. For the screen reader, images with no information should be skipped; images with information must relay that information in text that is exposed to the screen reader. The order of reading the image should follow the logical reading order of the page.

56.9   Test: Corruption.

If the file is structured correctly with the right tags in the right order and still cannot be read successfully with a screen reader, it is most likely corrupted. Be sure to reload the file and re-test using different approaches to confirm this.

Corruption

PDF files can get easily get corrupted. There are known errors in conversions of structures and styles, especially in complex or large documents. These corrupt files can appear to work correctly until they are tested with assistive technology. There may be no direct relation to the tags and the content. There can also be tags that represent non-existing content. The tags may even extend beyond display panel boundaries.

Remediation: This can be very complex to correct but in some cases these methods may work:

- Delete and re-tagging can often solve issues – Note this will delete any alternative text

- Reconvert the file but without the accessibility option to include tags – then add tags in Acrobat

   o You can also convert a file from within Acrobat itself using it own conversion instead of a plug-in.

   o NetCentric CommonLook also converts to PDF.

- Simplifying the structure with the TouchUp Reading Order Tool can reduce the number of tags and complexity.

- Simplifying the original document may eliminate the errors. Reducing the number of styles and different structures can also help. Tables within tables with complex cell content can cause issues.

   o A Word file can contain hidden markup without content associated from repeated cut & paste, Reveal Codes may not show all markup. Cleaning whitespace and areas between paragraphs can help. Use Paragraph Spacing to create spacing in all areas.

- Conversion to another format (e.g. RTF) and conversion back can sometimes clean a document.

- Breaking the file into pieces (Extraction) can often correct issues. In many cases it is a single page that is corrupted and needs to be rebuilt and then inserted back into the PDF.

Testing with a screen reader may help narrow down the page. You may need to extract a few pages before and after the corrupt section, or even divide the document in half to narrow down the issue.

Check for basic screen reader identification with the essential tests listed above to confirm the file is fixed.

57 Microsoft Word Documents Must Contain Structural Markup Set By Built-In Functions.

Description

Microsoft Word has built-in functions for setting headings, column, lists, links, and the first header row of a table. These are necessary for both assistive technology and for conversion to other formats such as PDF or HTML. If structured correctly, the accessibility will travel with the document.

Categories

Word

Reference

Section 508: 1194.22 (m)

WCAG 2.0:

> http://www.w3.org/WAI/GL/WCAG20-TECHS/pdf.html

- WCAG 2.0: In Word

- Alternative text see: PDF1

- Table header row see: PDF6

- Headings see: PDF9

- Links see: PDF11

WebAIM:

> http://webaim.org/techniques/word/

Microsoft:

> http://office.microsoft.com/en-us/word-help/creating-accessible-word-documents-HA101999993.aspx

57.1   Use Built-In Formatting To Structure Document.

MS Word structural formatting must be set with built-in functions. Formatting cannot be set visually only; it must exist in the markup.

Tables

- Tables must be created with the Table Insert. Do not use Draw Table or simulate a table with lines, tabs, or spaces.

- Tables Cells must be associated with column headers. In Word the only option is to set the first row as Repeat Header Row, this adds a Table Header markup in addition to repeating headers across pages if large enough.

- For all versions of Word you cannot create accessible complex tables. These are tables with sub-headers and merged cells. In addition these will often cause further issues if converted to another format such as PDF and require remediation in that format. If possible, keep the table to a simple grid where each column and row represents a single cell. If you must merge cells or add sub-headers, then the table must be tested and remediated if necessary in the PDF version (this will not affect the file visually).

Headings

- Headings must be in markup by the styles with heading level 1-6. Do not use levels 7-9 as it is not recognized in conversions. You can modify the style visually any way you wish use the current visual style but the "Heading 1-6" styles put a code with the text that will work with assistive technology as opposed to bold and font size changes alone which will not recognized as heading text by the AT.

- Heading levels should not be used for visual effect only because they have accessibility meaning for hierarchical levels of content and define sections and are used for orientation and navigation.

- Headings must be as concise as possible and unique because they serve as the title for each section and its level.

Images

Alternative text should not be added to images that contain no information. Do not use alternative text if you have a text description elsewhere such as the caption, adjacent text, or a link to a description. Otherwise use alternative text if it is less than 100 characters in [Format Picture].

57.2   Links Must Indicate The Target.

In Word:

- Set the link text; use this to clearly indicate the target by an easily readable name.

- Links for footnotes, appendix, references, and endnotes must be numbered. Do not use symbols.

- Table of Contents must be links and not plain text.

- Use bookmarks to set links for internal reference and navigation.

- List of Figures and Index must be links.

Do not use underlines except for links. If emphasis is needed, use bold, color or another font styling. You can also use a limited number of text symbols for emphasis such as asterisks *, brackets [], braces {}, bars |. dash -. There are many Unicode symbols available that are recognized by assistive technology. Before using any of these symbols consult a chart such as one in this appendix (Character Recognition by Screen Reader JAWS) to see what is recognized. Keep in mind that not all screen readers can read all the symbols that another screen reader can. If extensive use of symbols is needed then testing with a wider range of tools will be required.

57.3 Use Sans-Serif Fonts Such As Arial, Calibri, Verdana, Corbel, And Tahoma.

- See: Sans-Serif list at end of manual. There are wide varieties with many that come close to matching Serif fonts. Serif fonts have little hooks on the end of the character strokes such as Times Roman, Ariel does not.

- Provide an expansion of the acronym or abbreviation on first use.

- Use Styles to set appearance.

- Headings levels must use different font sizes and are set by the styles. Adding a color difference will increase ability to distinguish difference for visual users.

57.4 Test: Styles and Formats.

- View the Styles and Formatting panel in Word. Select sample text of each section.

- Check Heading is using Heading 1-6.

- Lists are true built-in formatted lists and not constructed from TAB or SPACE.

57.5 Test: Columns.

Check that columns are actual built-in Word marked-up columns by selecting groups of text within the column. The block of text selected will stay within the column boundaries if using the column structure.

57.6 Test: Table Headings.

- Check that Heading Rows Repeat is active for the first row.

- Check that cells are not merged and that there are no sub-headers. Inform the author that these will not be accessible in Word. Notify the author that the document can be made accessible if converted to HTML or PDF but additional remediation and testing is required. Also indicate that in some cases the effort required may be extensive.

57.7   Test: Images.

- Check that images with information have either: alternative text, caption text, adjacent text or links to text. It is also possible to have a brief description with a link to a detail description elsewhere.

- Flow charts or diagrams must retain the hierarchical order and process flow in the text description.

57.8   Test: Word Hidden Code Formats.

- Turn on Reveal Codes and examine the document..

- Determine if Paragraph (noted as a reverse stylized "P" ¶) sections are stopped and started to encase only the section grouped in a style. Soft-Returns (ENTER symbol – hooked left arrow) are used to create space without using styles. If a lot of these are used a paragraph adjustment must be used instead to create the space for the Paragraph section.

- Check that page breaks are Page-Break instead of ENTER.

57.9   Test: Text Contrast And Clarity.

- Check contrast for foreground text to background color.

- Check that text does not overlay with any type of lines or grid.

57.10 Test: Access To All Text.

- Check that you can access any text in a box or floating text via keyboard or a screen reader. If it cannot be accessed see if a text alternative is available.

- Note: Accessibility may differ depending on both the version of Word and the version of the screen reader. For most cases, text boxes and floating text will fail.

57.11 Test: Indents.

Check that there are no indents of text except for use with lists, numbered, bulleted, or quotes.

57.12 Test: Number Of Headings.

Each page should generally have at least 3 or more headings (from the styles panel) depending on the nature of the content. Check that a full page of text with paragraphs has headings. A manual such as the one you are reading will have many headings and sections.

57.13 Test: Charts.

Check for visual users that all Charts have:

- Legends.

- Definitions.

- Abbreviations and acronyms are spelled out somewhere adjacent if first occurrence.

- Clear and distinct objects or lines. Each shape or line can easily be distinguished from the other.

- Each data bar or line data also has the data at the data point in addition to the axis.

- Color alone is not used to indicate data lines or points

  - Unique symbols used with lines and points can distinguish them from other data nearby such as asterisks, dashed lines, thicker solid lines and so on.

  - The peaks on a graph should have the data points in text if there are referenced and not rely on the axis alone. This also ensures accurate representation of the data.

58 Microsoft PowerPoint Contains Accessible Text Or Equivalent Text Descriptions For All Information Presented.

Description

When PowerPoint is formatted correctly, the file can be made accessible. However, it is easy to render a presentation unreadable by assistive technology. It is also not as easy to convert to other formats as Word or PDF is. As a result it is very important to get it right the first time. Reducing the number of container objects like text boxes and images on a single page will make that task easier. Logical reading order is top to bottom, left to right. The objects on a PowerPoint page can lose logical reading order very easily due to editing. The order is critical to assistive technology to render the content so it is understood and is presented as the author intended.

Categories

PowerPoint, Presentation, Slide

Reference

Section 508: 1194.22 (a) A text equivalent for every non-text element shall be provided (for example: via "alt", "longdesc", or in element content).

Section 508: 1194.21 (a) When software is designed to run on a system that has a keyboard, product functions shall be executable from a keyboard where the function itself or the result of performing a function can be discerned textually.

Section 508: 1194.21 (c) A well-defined on-screen indication of the current focus shall be provided that moves among interactive interface elements as the input focus changes. The focus shall be programmatically exposed so that assistive technology can track focus and focus changes.

WCAG 2.0: Web Accessibility Presentations and Tutorials:

http://www.w3.org/WAI/train.html

WebAIM: PowerPoint Accessibility:

http://webaim.org/techniques/powerpoint/

58.1   Use Templates With Few Text Boxes.

Create a template or slide to copy from that contains a simple structure. This structure should look like a Title text box and a main content text box. It is crucial to keep the number of text boxes small due to issues with logical reading order.

58.2   Provide A Printed And A Digital Copy Before The Presentation.

- The printed and electronic copy will also allow users to request any special versions needed.

- To format an easier-to-read printout than the built-in PowerPoint print layouts, move the final version to MS Word. There you can increase the page size and use more of the borders. This option is only in MS 2007 and higher. To package the Word-formatted version for a print service, convert it to PDF. You can convert directly to PDF from PowerPoint, but you will not have as many edit options to control size and margins.

58.3   Use Fonts And Charts That Can Be Read From The Back Of The Room.

- Use Sans-Serif fonts such as Arial, Calibri, Verdana, Corbel, and Tahoma (See Sans-Serif list at end of manual).

- Provide strong contrast between foreground text and objects and background (See contrast examples at end of manual).

58.4   Provide Large And Clear Projections.

- Provide the largest projection possible with clear edge definition. Many projectors have an adjustable setting; use it to increase edge definition to make text more readable.

- Pay attention to obstacles that prevent a clear view of the presentation. Tables, chairs, and height of computers monitors may need to be adjusted.

- Be prepared to provide extra descriptions of slides, if some people in the audience are not able to fully understand the visual information.

- If possible, reduce any background noise as this can interfere with many who rely on hearing for comprehension.

58.5   Add Verbal, Printed, Or Whiteboard Material To Slides.

Do not rely solely on the slide presentation. Give equal time to strong verbal explanations and handouts. Providing further reading and extended guides via printouts and links gives additional options for comprehension.

58.6   Control Logical Order With Settings.

Set TAB order by moving objects to the front and back (Send to Back, Bring to Front). This can be difficult to perform if there are many text boxes and objects. Keep the number of text boxes small, 3 or less if possible, to make the logical order easier to control.

58.7   Test: Text Descriptions.

- Ensure images and audio are described in text.

- Verify all images and charts with information have text descriptions.

- Verify any audio or video clips have text descriptions.

- Check when verbal descriptions of images, charts, or relationships are provided that they are in text somewhere (slide, notes, link) or are captured by a someone taking notes and made available.

58.8   Test: Additional Materials.

- Check that slides and any additional material covers any verbal material given. If additional verbal material is given there must be a follow-up with additional links or documents.

- Check that a contact is given for additional information and presentation copies and format alternatives.

58.9   Test: Tables.

Check that tables have column headers and if applicable, row headers. The table headers should be visually distinguished with sharp contrast.

58.10 Test: Contrast And Fonts.

- Check for sufficient contrast.

- Check for Sans-Serif fonts such as Arial, Calibri, Verdana, Corbel, and Tahoma (See Sans-Serif list at end).

- Check for largest fonts possible for the individual slides. If text is packed too tightly for reading at a distance, recommend breaking into multiple slides.

58.11 Test: Handouts, Downloads.

Check that all handout and additional resource material formats are accessible, refer to other manual checks that are applicable to Word, PDF, Excel, and web content.

58.12 Test: TAB Order.

Check the TAB order is the logical order of the process or reading order.

59 Microsoft Excel Must Associate Cells To Headers. Tab Pages Must Have Unique And Descriptive Titles.

Description

Any

Categories

Excel, Spreadsheet, Table, Row, Column, Cell

Reference

Section 508: 1194.22(g) Row and column headers shall be identified for data tables.

Section 508: 1194.22(h) Markup shall be used to associate data cells and header cells for data tables that have two or more logical levels of row or column headers.)

Microsoft: Creating accessible Excel workbooks:

http://office.microsoft.com/en-us/excel-help/creating-accessible-excel-workbooks-HA102013545.aspx

WCAG 2.0: Guideline 1.3 (Level A) Adaptable: Create content that can be presented in different ways (for example simpler layout) without losing information or structure:

http://www.w3.org/TR/WCAG/#content-structure-separation

WCAG 2.0: Guideline 2.1 (Level A) Keyboard Accessible: Make all functionality available from a keyboard:

http://www.w3.org/TR/WCAG/#keyboard-operation

59.1   Do Not Merge Cells. Do Not Use Sub-Headers.

Keep single rows and single columns.

59.2   Provide Unique Descriptive Titles For Tabs.

Provide titles, descriptions, legends, and definitions for tables. Do not use symbols. Use text or known single characters such as "Y" and "N" for "Yes" and "No" and N/A for "Not Applicable" instead. Provide expansion of other characters in a legend. Combining color and text can make cells easier to read that indicate status.

59.3   Set Column Headers.

- For Excel 2007 and up: [Table Tools Design] tab > [Table Style Options] group > [Header Row] check box. Add header information.

- To specify a header row in a new block of cells to be marked as table:
  Highlight the cells you want to include in the table
  On the [Insert] tab, in the [Tables] group, select [Table] > [My Table Has Headers] check box.

- For Excel 2003 and higher, cells can be named in the Name Box. This should not be used as the primary cell name nor can it be used as replacement for column header. The only valid column header occurs in the table first row. So it is directly available to screen readers and visual users including those using magnification.

- Complex tables should be avoided – those with merged cells and sub-headers as they are not accessible to most assistive technology. Often a table can be rendered accessible by breaking out merged cells and repeating Primary cell names in the second level sub-headers:

For example:

	A	B	C	D
1	Fy2011		Fy2012	
2	Paper	Toner	Paper	Toner
3	400	500	600	700
4				
5	Becomes:			
6				
7	Fy2011 Paper	Fy2011 Toner	Fy2012 Paper	Fy2012 Toner
8	400	500	600	700

Figure 40: Excel table showing sub-headers combined into a single header.

59.4   Associate Cells To Headers.

If complex tables must be used – merged cells and sub-headers, then an alternative format must be provided, especially if the table exceeds 5 rows. The solution is to associate cells with row and column headers at any level is to convert the file to HTML and use the HTML Headers and ID to relate the individual cells to the correct headers. See the section on Tables for details. For a single row header follow settings below:

Settings for Excel to associate headers:

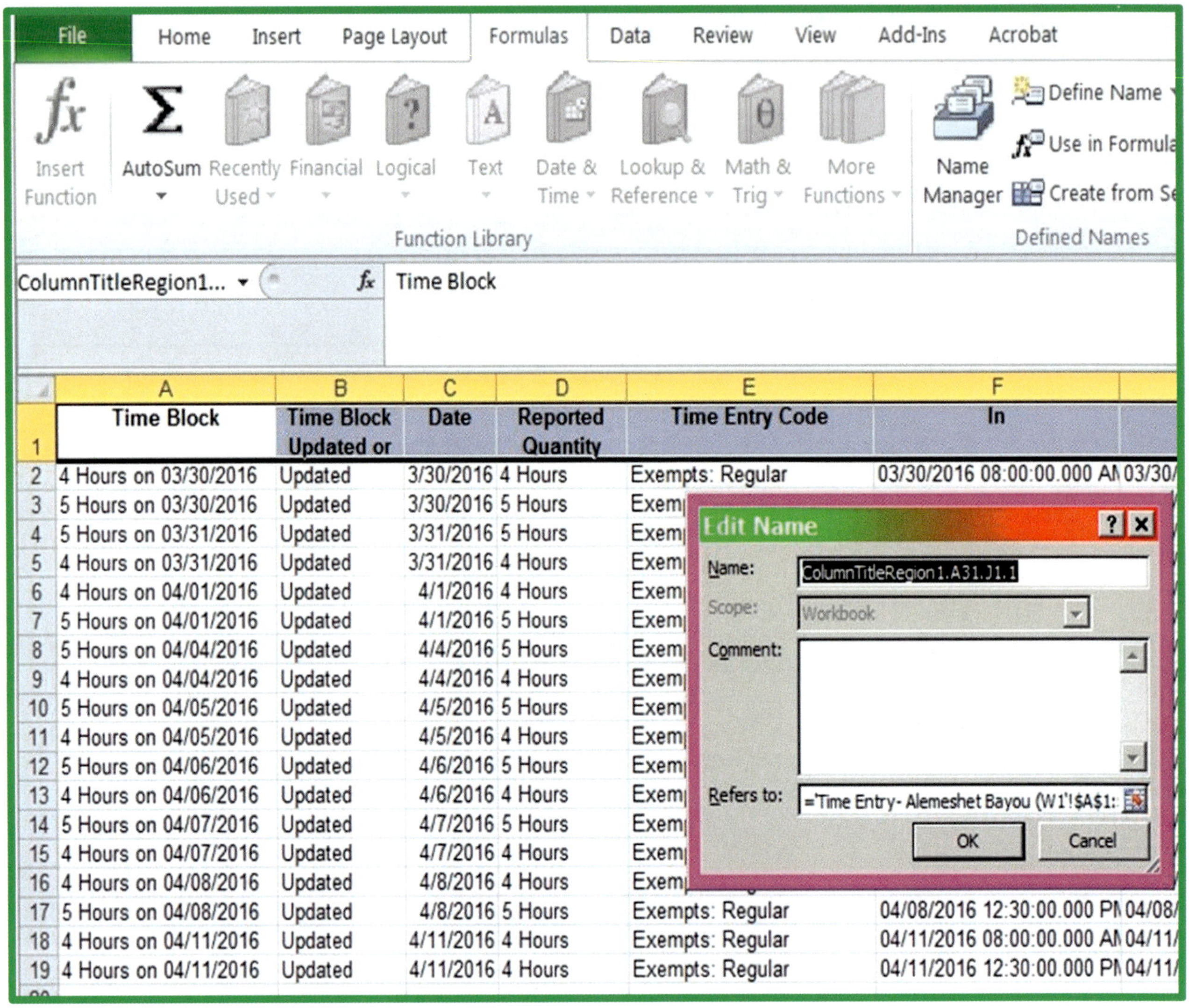

| | File | Home | Insert | Page Layout | Formulas | Data | Review | View | Add-Ins | Acrobat |

Function Library — Insert Function, AutoSum, Recently Used, Financial, Logical, Text, Date & Time, Lookup & Reference, Math & Trig, More Functions

Defined Names — Name Manager, Define Name, Use in Formula, Create from Se...

ColumnTitleRegion1... ▼ f_x Time Block

	A	B	C	D	E	F
1	**Time Block**	**Time Block Updated or**	**Date**	**Reported Quantity**	**Time Entry Code**	**In**
2	4 Hours on 03/30/2016	Updated	3/30/2016	4 Hours	Exempts: Regular	03/30/2016 08:00:00.000 AM 03/30/
3	5 Hours on 03/30/2016	Updated	3/30/2016	5 Hours	Exemp	
4	5 Hours on 03/31/2016	Updated	3/31/2016	5 Hours	Exemp	
5	4 Hours on 03/31/2016	Updated	3/31/2016	4 Hours	Exemp	
6	4 Hours on 04/01/2016	Updated	4/1/2016	4 Hours	Exemp	
7	5 Hours on 04/01/2016	Updated	4/1/2016	5 Hours	Exemp	
8	5 Hours on 04/04/2016	Updated	4/4/2016	5 Hours	Exemp	
9	4 Hours on 04/04/2016	Updated	4/4/2016	4 Hours	Exemp	
10	5 Hours on 04/05/2016	Updated	4/5/2016	5 Hours	Exemp	
11	4 Hours on 04/05/2016	Updated	4/5/2016	4 Hours	Exemp	
12	5 Hours on 04/06/2016	Updated	4/6/2016	5 Hours	Exemp	
13	4 Hours on 04/06/2016	Updated	4/6/2016	4 Hours	Exemp	
14	5 Hours on 04/07/2016	Updated	4/7/2016	5 Hours	Exemp	
15	4 Hours on 04/07/2016	Updated	4/7/2016	4 Hours	Exemp	
16	4 Hours on 04/08/2016	Updated	4/8/2016	4 Hours	Exemp	
17	5 Hours on 04/08/2016	Updated	4/8/2016	5 Hours	Exempts: Regular	04/08/2016 12:30:00.000 PM 04/08/
18	4 Hours on 04/11/2016	Updated	4/11/2016	4 Hours	Exempts: Regular	04/11/2016 08:00:00.000 AM 04/11/
19	4 Hours on 04/11/2016	Updated	4/11/2016	4 Hours	Exempts: Regular	04/11/2016 12:30:00.000 PM 04/11/

Edit Name

Name: ColumnTitleRegion1.A31.J1.1

Scope: Workbook

Comment:

Refers to: ='Time Entry- Alemeshet Bayou (W1'!A1:

OK   Cancel

ColumnTitleRegion1.A31.J1.1

Workbook

Inform those who use JAWS screen reader to make these settings:

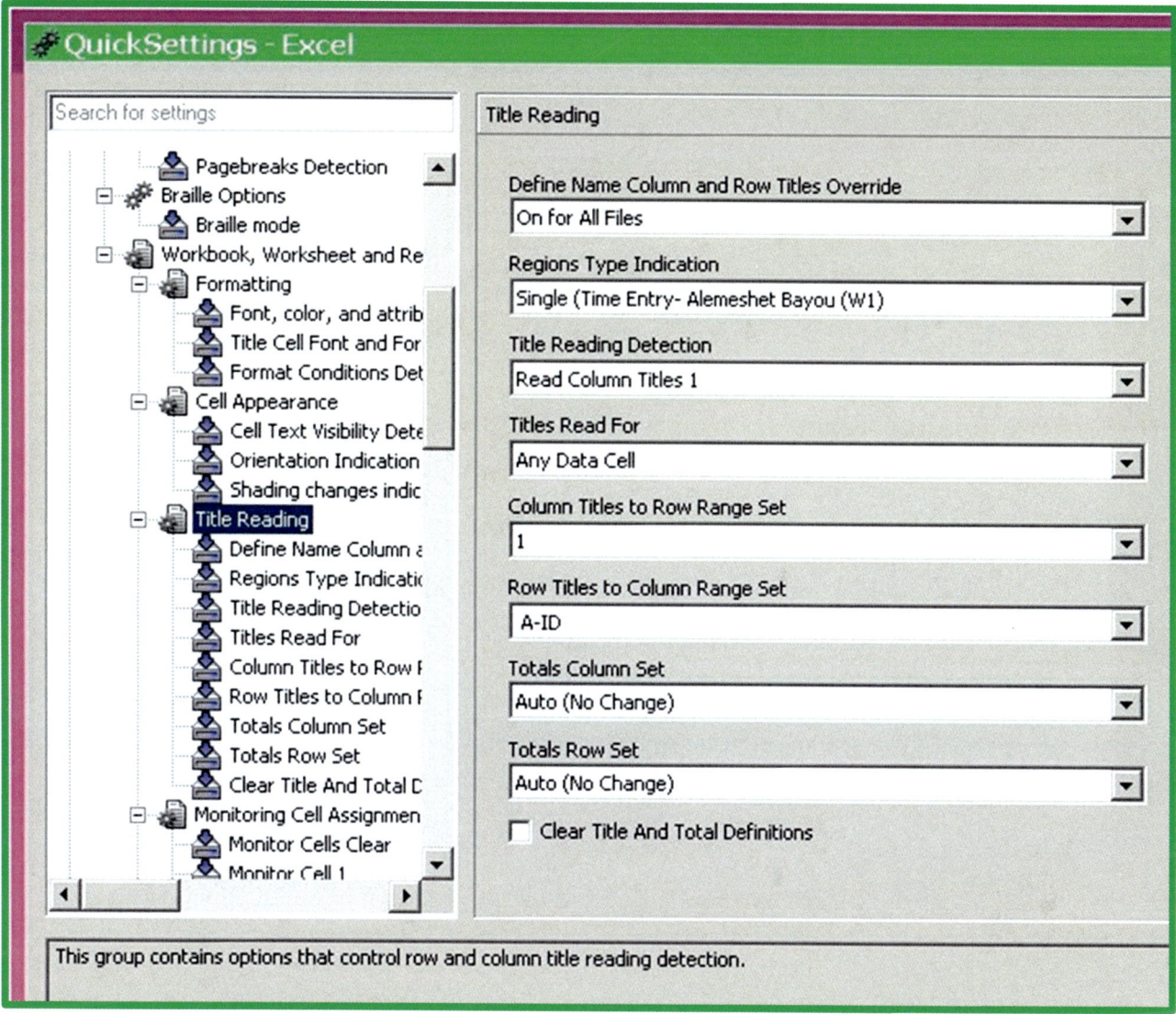

59.5 Show Source Data For Charts.

Provide the actual table from which the data was used to generate a chart. If space permits, this can be adjacent to the chart or a link to another location can be provided. The table must have cells associated with headers; have a title, and a description. You may find many able-bodied users will also like to see where the data came from.

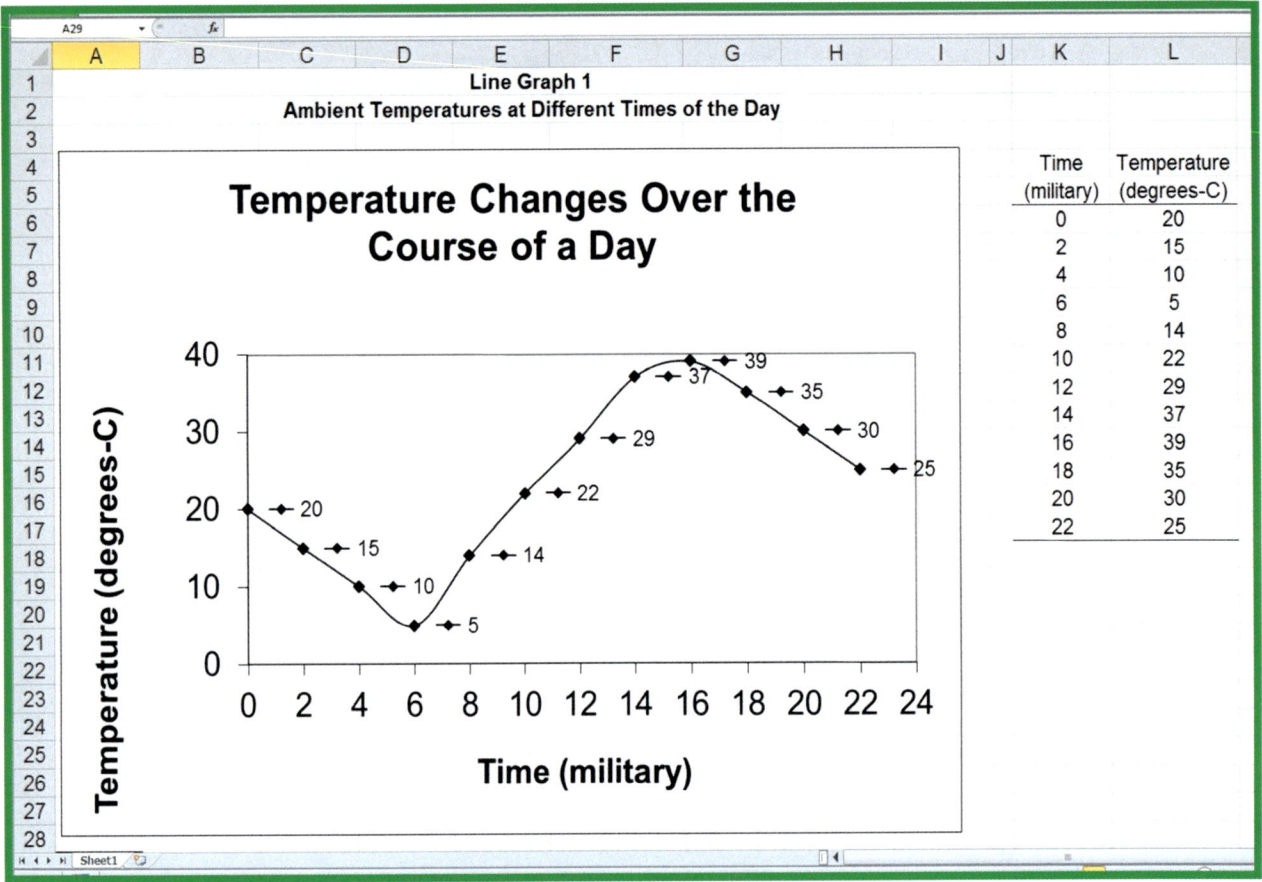

Figure 41: Excel chart with data labels and source table.

59.6   Test: Data Cells

Check for programmatic exposure to data cells and column headers using a screen reader. If testing with JAWS use the setting of [Use Column Titles] (instead of Row/Column Numbers).

59.7   Test: Blank Cells

- Check for formatting with blank cells. Blank cells must only be used for blank data.

- Check if there are lots of blank data cells such as an entire row or column. Recommend to author to make clear why row or column is empty with either a text description note or N/A or text character(s) that will communicate the status of data. For example a dash "-", indicates no data available. Better is to use em dash "—". This works better with screen readers and is more visible..

59.8   Test: Chart Components

Check that charts have all descriptive components:

- Legend

- Data Point Text

- Descriptive Axis

- Clearly distinguished lines, bars, or compared objects

- Chart caption and number if more than 1

60 Application Generated Reports And Documents From Inaccessible Or Difficult To Read Sources Must Be Made Accessible Or Offered In Alternative Formats.

Description

Many scanning, testing, tracking, monitoring, and database applications can generate reports. Often these reports are tables with little formatting. Most major software has options to save in specific formats. The most accessible format must be used or available for generation of an accessible report when requested.

Categories

Conversion, Document, Format, Report

Reference

Section 508: 1194.22(g) Row and column headers shall be identified for data tables.

Section 508: 1194.22(h) Markup shall be used to associate data cells and header cells for data tables that have two or more logical levels of row or column headers.)

Microsoft: Creating accessible Excel workbooks:

http://office.microsoft.com/en-us/excel-help/creating-accessible-excel-workbooks-HA102013545.aspx

WCAG 2.0: Guideline 1.3 (Level A) Adaptable: Create content that can be presented in different ways (for example simpler layout) without losing information or structure:

http://www.w3.org/TR/WCAG/#content-structure-separation

WCAG 2.0: Guideline 2.1 (Level A) Keyboard Accessible: Make all functionality available from a keyboard:

http://www.w3.org/TR/WCAG/#keyboard-operation

WCAG 2.0: Guideline 3.1 (Level A) Make text content readable and understandable:

http://www.w3.org/WAI/WCAG20/quickref/Overview.php#meaning

WCAG 2.0: 8.4 Tables for layout, Linear reading order of tables:

http://www.w3.org/TR/2004/WD-WCAG20-HTML-TECHS-20041119/Overview.html#layouttables_linearize

60.1 Provide Large Print, Braille, Accessible Structured Files, Or Formatted Text On Request.

There are numerous disabilities that are affected when documents are involved and providing all possible formats all the time is not practical. This is why the source document should be marked up with correct structural codes. This will reduce the number of special requests and make any conversions more accurate. Some formats are not conducive for modification such as PowerPoint. That is why sending the PowerPoint content to Word and manipulating size and spacing in the Word document is very effective. See the section on PowerPoint for more details. Unless you compensate for increased spacing and margins, large print could be rendered as unreadable. Columns, text blocks, indented text can all cause issues and may need to be reformatted for the large print to be readable. Consider maximum allowable margins for your printer to accommodate any large print.

Tables

Be aware that converting structures such as tables to Braille will usually render them unreadable because everything is converted to plain text. Tables with many columns or multiple merged cells may not be readable in large print either. If no other method is available and the table is not readable once converted, it may be necessary to write out the associations of the cells to headers in text. The method for this is the same as if you were reading the table to someone over the phone. The person on the phone cannot see the table and you must describe the data or information in the table including what column or row header is associated with it. For example: "In Year 2016, Team A generated $20,000 in Sales"

Braille

Braille may not represent content in the original format correctly as noted above with tables. Braille must be tested to make sure content is represented accurately. This is especially true in any document area that has multiple complex elements. Keep in mind, you simply cannot convert a training course to Braille without describing images, charts with information, and formatting quizzes.

Large Print

Spacing and justification can cause significant reading issues. Text that is in the format of an indented column can wrap portions of words out of alignment. You may need to move text to the left and eliminate any large blocks of space. Be aware that page numbers that traveled with the report as text may not have meaning in this format. Column headings may not be in align the rest of the column, try to correct by getting the text in the heading and the cells to be the same width. This may involve breaking up words – however this is prefer able to scattered text that is not associated.

Word and PDF

Follow the manual on structure of these file types. If a report is output in this format it must be checked for accessibility for both visual and structural markup. Complex tables (merged cells and sub-headers) can cause issues in both file types. There is no way to make them work in Word, and effort is required for PDF.

HTML

The primary issue is table headers and cell association. In addition section headings are needed for multi-page reports. An advantage of output in this format is that all aspects can be edited and a script could be run to modify entire files to be made accessible.

All File Types

It is recommended that a report or conversion output settings be saved in a filter or saved settings file, or the settings for generating the accessible output documented can serve as a templated procedure once optimal accessibility settings are known.

60.2   Export To Spreadsheets From Report Generating Software If Available.

Most major project, defect, and testing software have an option for exporting reports to spreadsheets (or commas separated values CSV – which can be uploaded into a spreadsheet). If the export filter has heading fields, titles, and number orientation, it should generally be accessible. However a check is required to make sure enough data and information was captured to make the report intelligible. Be aware that order can be important to accessibility as many assistive devices read in a linear method (top-to-bottom, left-to-right). How the first column is used (the name of the item or is an ID number) can determine how effective use is depending on what is required for lookup in that environment.

Planning For Conversions

Note that some characters can make conversions more difficult, especially from CSV files. Some of these characters include: commas, quotes (single, double, and smart quotes), control characters, spaces, and symbols (learn about en-dash and em-dash). Using a unique delimiter may solve this issue.

60.3   Create Accessible Forms, Input Screens, And Reports In Configurable Enterprise Software.

Software such as:

- Business Objects

- Informatica

- Oracle

- SharePoint

- Documentum

Allow for numerous methods of creating form input, report generation. The report generating software may have additional add-on modules that create user forms and report options aside from the built-in modules. These types of software are usually tailored to the project with unique forms and reports. Both the forms and reports must meet Section 508. To meet these requirements, follow the guide for reports above and the section on forms.

60.4   Test: Tabular Headers

Tabular Report:

- Check that tables have column headers, and row headers if any.

- Check that the headers are associated to the cells.

- Check that the table does not have merged cells or sub-headers unless it is correctly associated to data cells in HTML or PDF.

60.5   Test: Fields

Report Forms:

- Check that all fields are uniquely labeled visually and programmatically.

- Check that keyboard has access to all input and controls.

- Check that error handling provides focus to primary error message and links to errors, with instructions for corrections.

61 Reference Character Recognition By Screen Reader JAWS And Window-Eyes

Some Commonly Used Characters

Description	Character	Entity Reference	Numeric Reference	JAWS Output	Window-Eyes Output Reading Letter
no-break space = non-breaking space				NOT SPOKEN	NOT SPOKEN
cent sign	¢	&cent;	&#162;	cents	cents
broken bar = broken vertical bar	¦	&brvbar;	&#166;	broken bar	vertical bar
section sign	§	&sect;	&#167;	section	section
diaeresis = spacing diaeresis	¨	&uml;	&#168;	dyaeresis	umlaut
copyright sign	©	&copy;	&#169;	copyright	copyright
registered sign = registered trade mark sign	®	&reg;	&#174;	registered	registered
degree sign	°	&deg;	&#176;	degrees	degrees
plus-minus sign = plus-or-minus sign	±	&plusmn;	&#177;	plus or minus	plus or minus
pilcrow sign = paragraph sign	¶	&para;	&#182;	paragraph	paragraph
middle dot = Georgian comma = Greek middle dot	·	&middot;	&#183;	dot	bullet
multiplication sign	×	&times;	&#215;	times	times
division sign	÷	&divide;	&#247;	divided by	divides
bullet = black small circle	•	&bull;	&#8226;	bullet	bullet
horizontal ellipsis = three	…	&hellip;	&#8230;	ellipsis	ellipsis

dot leader					
prime = minutes = feet	′	&prime;	&#8242;	NOT SPOKEN	apostrophe
double prime = seconds = inches	″	&Prime;	&#8243;	NOT SPOKEN	question
overline = spacing overscore	‾	&oline;	&#8254;	NOT SPOKEN	question
fraction slash	⁄	&frasl;	&#8260;	slash	slash
trade mark sign	TM	&trade;	&#8482;	trademark	trademark
minus sign	−	&minus;	&#8722;	NOT SPOKEN	dash
asterisk operator	∗	&lowast;	&#8727;	asterisk	star
tilde operator = varies with = similar to	□	&sim;	&#8764;	tilda	tilda
almost equal to = asymptotic to	≈	&asymp;	&#8776;	tilda	tilda
not equal to	≠	&ne;	&#8800;	NOT SPOKEN	question
identical to	≡	&equiv;	&#8801;	equals	equals
less-than or equal to	≤	&le;	&#8804;	equals	equals
greater-than or equal to	≥	&ge;	&#8805;	equals	equals
left-pointing angle bracket = bra	⟨	&lang;	&#9001;	less than	less than
right-pointing angle bracket = ket	⟩	&rang;	&#9002;	greater than	greater than
quotation mark = APL quote	"	&quot;	&#34;	quote	quote
ampersand	&	&amp;	&#38;	and	and

303

less-than sign	**<**	&lt;	&#60;	less	less than
greater-than sign	**>**	&gt;	&#62;	greater	greater than
modifier letter circumflex accent	^	&circ;	&#710;	NOT SPOKEN	circumflex
small tilde	~	&tilde;	&#732;	tilda	tilda
en space				NOT SPOKEN	NOT SPOKEN
em space				NOT SPOKEN	NOT SPOKEN
thin space				NOT SPOKEN	question
en dash	—	&ndash;	&#8211;	en dash	en dash
em dash	—	&mdash;	&#8212;	em dash	em dash
left single quotation mark	'	&lsquo;	&#8216;	apostrophe	single open quote
right single quotation mark	'	&rsquo;	&#8217;	apostrophe	apostrophe
single low-9 quotation mark	,	&sbquo;	&#8218;	NOT SPOKEN	single open quote
left double quotation mark	"	&ldquo;	&#8220;	quote	double open quote
right double quotation mark	"	&rdquo;	&#8221;	quote	double close quote
double low-9 quotation mark	„	&bdquo;	&#8222;	NOT SPOKEN	double open quote
dagger	†	&dagger;	&#8224;	single dagger	dagger
double dagger	‡	&Dagger;	&#8225;	double dagger	double dagger

62   Sans-Serif Fonts

Sans-Serif fonts common in MS Word:

- Arial
- Berlin Sans FB
- Calibri
- Candara
- Century Gothic
- Consolas
- Corbel
- Eras Light ITC
- Estrangelo
- Franklin Gothic Book
- Gautami
- Gill Sans MT
- Haettenschweiler
- Latha
- Lucida Sans
- Mangal
- Microsoft Sans Serif
- MS Reference Sans Serif
- MV Boli
- Raavi
- Shruti
- Tahoma
- Trebuchet MS
- Tunga
- Tw Cen MT
- Verdana

Font Example:

Arial

Arial Black

Bell Gothic

Berlin Sans

Calibri

Candara

Comic Sans

Consolas

Eras

Franklin Gothic

Gill Sans

Kozuka Gothic

Lucinda Sans

Myriad Pro

Tahoma

Trebuchet

TW Cent MT

Verdana

Figure 42: Sans-serif fonts illustrated with the name of the font.

63 Methods For Coding To HTML Standard

In addition to being technically correct in coding to the standard, a major advantage to standard HTML is:

- Device independence

- Providing markup that provides both visual and programmatic information

- Cross browser

The purpose of this section is to note HTML issues that directly affect accessibility and must be coded correctly.

63.1   Emphasis

To emphasize something, use the <STRONG> tag instead of <BOLD> and the <EM> tag instead of <I>. Bold and italics (<I>) both connote visual emphasis, whereas strong and emphasis (<EM>) suggest *semantic* emphasis. Visually, <B> and <STRONG>, and <EM> and <I> look exactly the same, but developers must use the correct HTML tags.

63.2   Titles

Every HTML document must have a TITLE element in the HEAD section. Every page must have a unique TITLE. The TITLE must be context-rich so it can be understood out of context.

63.3   Paragraphs

The <P> element represents a paragraph, not a line break. It is a container of a block of content.
 is a line break. <P> is used by some assistive technology to navigate within pages. The   entity prevents a line break from occurring between two words.

63.4   Lists

Use lists <OL> <UL> to indicate a formatted list. Do not use the option of Roman Numerals. Lower Roman such as: i, ii, iii, etc. or upper Roman such as: I, II, III, etc., can cause issues for many types of assistive technology. Do not use them in titles or headings for the same reason as they cannot be distinguished from words.

Definition Lists <DL>are recognized by most assistive technology and browsers, for example:

```
<style> dl {font-family: arial;} </style>
<dl>
 <dt>Coffee</dt>
 <dd>Black hot drink</dd>
 <dt>Milk</dt>
 <dd>White cold drink</dd>
 </dl>
```

Coffee
        Black hot drink
Milk
        White cold drink

Figure 43: Definition list, programmatically structures content and visually indents for each definition.

63.5   Tables Use Scope And Headers (If Applicable)

Use SCOPE to indicate programmatically which cells are represented for columns and rows:

```
<table border="1">
 <tr>
 <td>Monthly Savings</td>
 <th scope="col">Month</th>
 <th scope="col">Savings</th>
 </tr>
 <tr>
 <th scope="row">Item 1</th>
 <td>January</td>
 <td>$100</td>
 </tr>
 <tr>
 <th scope="row">Item 2</th>
 <td>February</td>
 <td>$80</td>
 </tr>
</table>
```

Figure 44: Table with row and column scope.

Use HEADERS and ID for complex tables (merged cells and sub-headers):

```
<style>
table {font-family: arial;}
table {margin: .9em; border: 2px solid blue; }
th, tr, td { padding: .9em; border: 2px solid blue; }
</style>

<table border="4">
<caption>Headers & ID: Cell Association R=Row C=Column</caption>

<tr>
 <th id="R1C1">                          Budget </br> R1C1 (TH) </th>
 <th id="R1C2">                          Type </br> R1C2 (TH) </th>
 <th id="R1C3">                          List A </br> R1C3 (TH) </th>
 <th id="R1C4">                          List B </br> R1C4 (TH) </th>
</tr>

<tr>
 <th rowspan="2" id="R2R3C1">            Employees </br> R2R3C1 (TH) </th>
 <th id="R2C2">                          Male </br> R2C2 (TH) </th>
 <td headers="R2R3C1 R2C2 R1C3">         Jim </br> R2C3 </br> headers="R2R3C1 R2C2 R1C3"</td>
 <td headers="R2R3C1 R2C2 R1C3">         Bob </br> R2C4 </br> headers="R2R3C1 R2C2 R1C3"</td>
</tr>

<tr>
 <th id="R3C2">                          Female </br> R3C2 (TH) </th>
 <td headers="R2R3C1 R3C2">                 Sally </br> R3C3 </br> headers="R2R3C1
R3C2"</td>
 <td headers="R2R3C1 R3C2 R1C4">         Jen </br> R3C4 </br> headers="R2R3C1 R3C2 R1C4"</td>
</tr>

<tr>
 <th id="R4C1">                          Resources </br> R4C1 (TH) </th>
 <th id="R4C2">                          Equipment </br> R4C2 (TH) </th>
 <td headers="R4C1 R4C2 R1C3">           Servers </br> R4C3 </br> headers="R4C1 R4C2
R1C3"</td>
 <td headers="R4C1 R4C2 R1C4">           Laptops </br> R4C4 </br> headers="R4C1 R4C2
R1C4"</td>
</tr>

</table>
```

Headers & ID: Cell Association R=Row C=Column			
Budget **R1C1 (TH)**	**Type** **R1C2 (TH)**	**List A** **R1C3 (TH)**	**List B** **R1C4 (TH)**
Employees **R2R3C1 (TH)**	**Male** **R2C2 (TH)**	Jim R2C3 headers="R2R3C1 R2C2 R1C3"	Bob R2C4 headers="R2R3C1 R2C2 R1C3"
	Female **R3C2 (TH)**	Sally R3C3 headers="R2R3C1 R3C2"	Jen R3C4 headers="R2R3C1 R3C2 R1C4"
Resources **R4C1 (TH)**	**Equipment** **R4C2 (TH)**	Servers R4C3 headers="R4C1 R4C2 R1C3"	Laptops R4C4 headers="R4C1 R4C2 R1C4"

Figure 45: Table using HEADERS and ID for complex table (sub-headers and merged cells.

63.6   TITLE Attribute

The TITLE attribute can be used for:

- <ABBR> and <ACRONYM>

- Supplementary information (clarification or further information) but not primary information for fields, except when LABEL cannot be used effectively.

  - It is important not to use both LABEL and TITLE at the same time as assistive technology can voice both and this can be confusing and disorienting.

- Additional information for a link, this should not replace the link text which much describe the target. If the information is critical then the title should not be used as it cannot be triggered by the keyboard.

  - A better method for important information that does not need to be available until the link is focused is to make information visible and hidden with CSS. Using a tooltip constructed from a DIV works well and can be made to work with both keyboard and mouse. See the example under the section on "Keyboards can access all controls and navigation".

Note: The TITLE attribute can be applied to many elements but code should be tailored to common expectations such as ALT text should be used instead of TITLE for an image. Both can functionally be added but do not add or substitute TITLE for alternative text.

63.7   Forms: Radio Buttons And Checkboxes

Radio buttons often cause issues with accessibility due to modification from expected behavior. Radio buttons are meant to have only one selection among several – mutual exclusion. However these can be made to act like checkboxes and allow multiple choices. To add to the confusion checkboxes can be set to act like radio buttons. You can even make the square or circle indicator field be switched. Often JavaScripts, VBScripts, and scripting module libraries can have routines that affect the accessible operation of the radio buttons and checkboxes. An easy check is to make all selections function with keyboard only, if that test is passed, they will most likely be accessible. For complex forms a screen reader and voice recognition test should always be conducted.

Keep radio buttons in a group for one selection only and maintain the style of a circle field filled input. Create a different group of radio buttons for a different single selection. Use checkboxes for multiple selections and maintain the style of a square input border design for the field check input.

There is no reason styling cannot be added to make radio buttons or checkboxes have 3D effects, highlight upon focus, shaded boxes, lines of varying thickness, texture, and color. The key is expected standard HTML behavior for mouse, keyboard, and voice users.

For example this styling allows for various colors and sizing without affecting normal operation of the radio buttons:

```
<style>
p, li, input {font-family: arial;}

.b {width: 40px; height: 40px; background : blue;}

.b2
{
border: 3px solid red;
font-family: Arial;
font-size: 30px;
height: 30px;
width: 30px;
text-decoration: none;
text-indent: 9px;
background : yellow;
margin: 7;
}

</style>

<p>
<label for="radio"> Radio Selection </label><input type="radio" class="b" id="radio" name="radiob"/>

<ul>
 <li><label for="radio1">Radio 1 </label><input type="radio" class="b2" id="radio1" name="radiob2"
checked="checked"/></li>
 <li><label for="radio2">Radio 2 </label><input type="radio" class="b2" id="radio2"
```

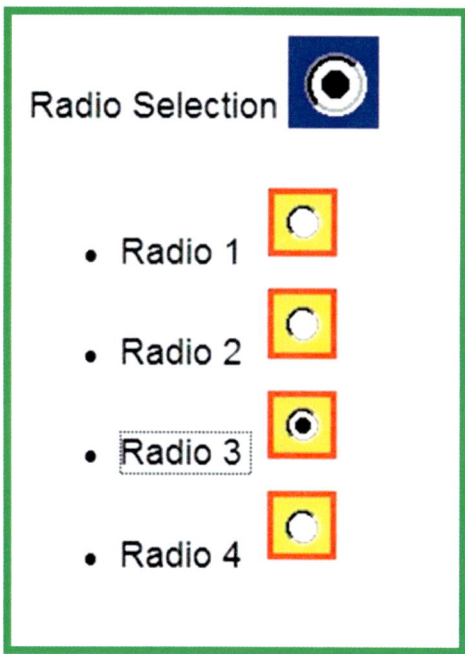

Figure 46: Radio buttons visually altered in color and size without affecting operation or operation with assistive technology.

63.8   Forms: Keyboard Focus And Maintaining TABINDEX In Error Handling

Forms that contain multiple sections and fields must keep the focus directed to the logical step in the process of completing and editing the form. TAB and SHIFT-TAB is the standard keyboard keys to move from HTML controls, links, and fields in a form along with ENTER for activation. Once a message, error handling, or dynamic form change occurs the focus may be lost, particularly with scripting.

When the TABINDEX attribute has the value 0, the element can be focused via the keyboard and is included in the tab order of the document. When the TABINDEX attribute has the value -1, the element cannot be tabbed to, but focus can be set programmatically, using ELEMENT.FOCUS(). Scripts that generate events on forms can easily lose focus

To keep focus in the logical usage of the form or edit/correction input location, focus may need to be set after it is interrupted. A simple test is to use the keyboard to generate the form action and then attempt to complete the form from the last position or position indicated by a form message or instruction without starting from the top of the page.

For example: A function to place focus to the form field in error:

```
<!DOCTYPE HTML PUBLIC "-//W3C//DTD HTML 4.01//EN" "http://www.w3.org/TR/html4/strict.dtd">
<html><head>
 <title>ECMAScript Form Validation</title>
<style> body, form {font-family: arial;} </style>

<script>
window.onload = initialise;
function initialise()
{
        // Ensure we're working with a relatively standards compliant interface
 if (!document.getElementById || !document.createElement || !document.createTextNode)
 return;

        // Add an event handler for the number form
 var objForm = document.getElementById('numberform');
 objForm.onsubmit= function(){return validateNumbers(this);};
}

function validateNumbers(objForm)
{
        // Test whether fields are valid
 var bFirst = isNumber(document.getElementById('num1').value);
 var bSecond = isNumber(document.getElementById('num2').value);
        // If not valid, display errors
 if (!bFirst || !bSecond)
 {
 var objExisting = document.getElementById('validationerrors');
 var objNew = document.createElement('div');
 var objTitle = document.createElement('h2');
 var objParagraph = document.createElement('p');
 var objList = document.createElement('ol');
 var objAnchor = document.createElement('a');
 var strID = 'firsterror';
 var strError;
                // The heading element will contain a link so that screen readers
                // can use it to place focus - the destination for the link is
                // the first error contained in a list
 objAnchor.appendChild(document.createTextNode('Errors in Submission'));
 objAnchor.setAttribute('href', '#firsterror');
 objTitle.appendChild(objAnchor);
 objParagraph.appendChild(document.createTextNode('Please review the following'));
 objNew.setAttribute('id', 'validationerrors');
 objNew.appendChild(objTitle);
 objNew.appendChild(objParagraph);
                // Add each error found to the list of errors
```

313

```
        if (!bFirst)
{
strError = 'Please provide a numeric value for the first number';
objList.appendChild(addError(strError, '#num1', objForm, strID));
strID = '';
}
if (!bSecond)
{
strError = 'Please provide a numeric value for the second number';
objList.appendChild(addError(strError, '#num2', objForm, strID));
strID = '';
}
        // Add the list to the error information
objNew.appendChild(objList);
        // If there were existing errors, replace them with the new lot,
        // otherwise add the new errors to the start of the form
if (objExisting)
objExisting.parentNode.replaceChild(objNew, objExisting);
else
{
var objPosition = objForm.firstChild;
objForm.insertBefore(objNew, objPosition);
}
        // Place focus on the anchor in the heading to alert
        // screen readers that the submission is in error
objAnchor.focus();
        // Do not submit the form
objForm.submitAllowed = false;
return false;
}
return true;
}


        // Function to validate a number
function isNumber(strValue)
{
return (!isNaN(strValue) && strValue.replace(/^\s+|\s+$/, '') !== '');
}



        // Function to create a list item containing a link describing the error
        // that points to the appropriate form field
function addError(strError, strFragment, objForm, strID)
{
var objAnchor = document.createElement('a');
var objListItem = document.createElement('li');
objAnchor.appendChild(document.createTextNode(strError));
objAnchor.setAttribute('href', strFragment);
objAnchor.onclick = function(event){return focusFormField(this, event, objForm);};
objAnchor.onkeypress = function(event){return focusFormField(this, event, objForm);};
// If strID has a value, this is the first error in the list
```

```
if (strID.length > 0)
objAnchor.setAttribute('id', strID);
objListItem.appendChild(objAnchor);
return objListItem;
}

        // Function to place focus to the form field in error
function focusFormField(objAnchor, objEvent, objForm)
{
        // Allow keyboard navigation over links
if (objEvent && objEvent.type == 'keypress')
if (objEvent.keyCode != 13 && objEvent.keyCode != 32)
return true;
        // set focus to the form control
var strFormField = objAnchor.href.match(/[^#]\w*$/);
objForm[strFormField].focus();
return false;
}
</script>
</head><body>

<h1>Form Validation</h1>
<form id="numberform" method="post" action="form.php">
<fieldset>
<legend>Numeric Fields</legend>
<p>
<label for="num1">Enter first number</label>
<input type="text" size="20" name="num1" id="num1">
</p>
<p>
<label for="num2">Enter second number</label>
<input type="text" size="20" name="num2" id="num2">
</p>
</fieldset>
<p>
<input type="submit" name="submit" value="Submit Form">
</p>

</form></body></html>
```

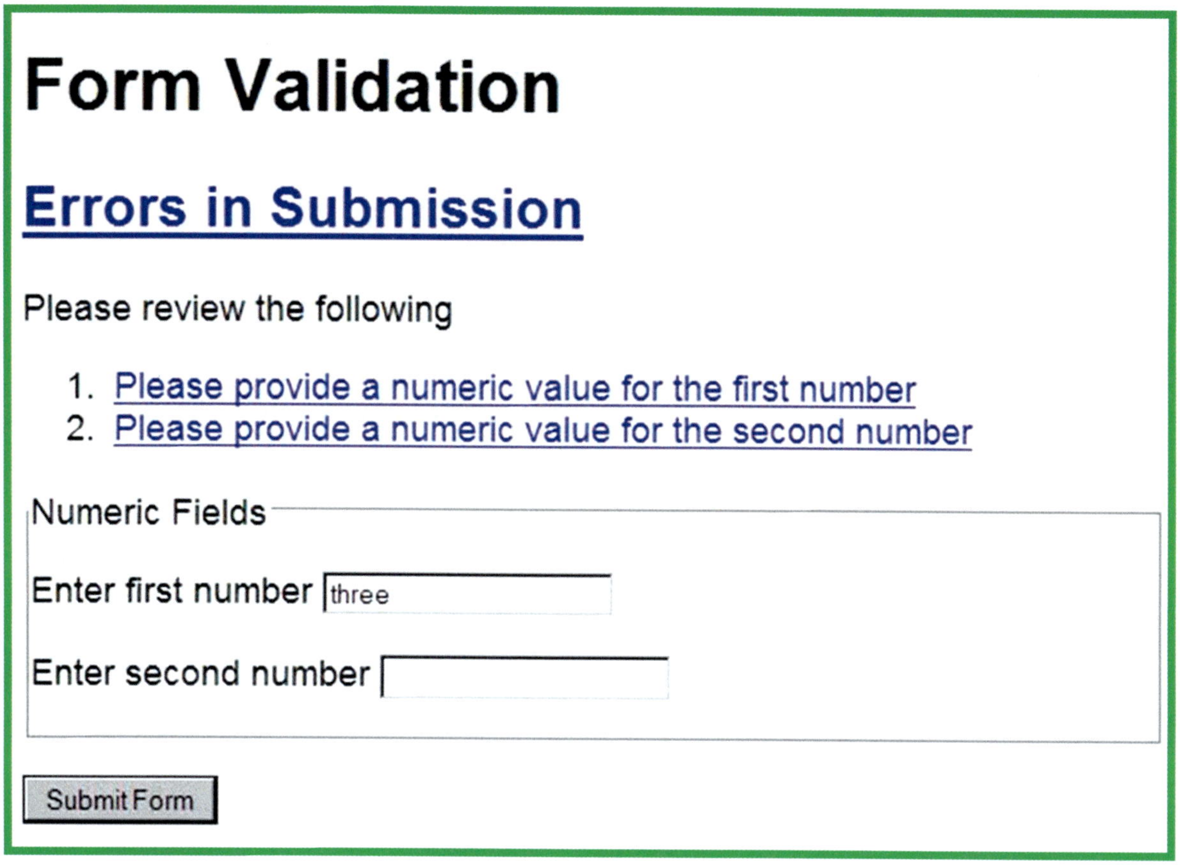

Form Validation

Errors in Submission

Please review the following

1. Please provide a numeric value for the first number
2. Please provide a numeric value for the second number

Numeric Fields

Enter first number [three]

Enter second number [   ]

[Submit Form]

Figure 47: Focus is set back to the field(s) in error by user selection of links with status and instruction.

Note: This is an area where accessibility issues usually arise, so testing of all form functions is critical.

ACCESSKEY is one method to allow the user to trigger focus to another part of the form, such as a sort function, editor, or spell check. The focus should be returned to the last visited location before the invocation of the ACCESSKEY once the action is completed unless the nature of the action is to move to another location or shift form modes (for example: modify or edit entire form as opposed to a single field). Even with shifting to full form edit mode the focus should be placed in the first field and not to the top of page above the menus and window controls.

63.9   Flash

Flash can be embedded in and also made interactive with HTML. When coded correctly Flash can be accessible. Primarily the issue is setting focus to objects the user should either be reading or interacting with. In addition content displayed in different panels, boxes, or layers must be programmatically exposed – made available to assistive technology. For details of Flash methods see:

http://www.w3.org/TR/WCAG20-TECHS/FLASH17 .

63.10 CSS: Hide Text Visually But Make Available To Screen Readers

These techniques provide a method of hiding supplementary text from the visual page that are helpful and additional for screen readers to understand context. These are cross-browser techniques that also follow the code standards for correct implementation.

Text "Washington stimulates economic growth" is hidden from visual page but exposed to screen readers.
Do not duplicate the text with a TITLE as this will be read twice. Use TITLE alone if you want both users to see helpful text. Keep in mind not all screen readers can access TITLE, check for your environment.

```
<head><style>
.Hide
{
 position: absolute;
 height: 1px; width: 1px;
 overflow: hidden;
 clip: rect(1px 1px 1px 1px);
}
</style></head>

</br></br>
 <a href="#"> <span class="Hide"> Washington stimulates economic growth </span> Full Story</a>
</br></br>
```

Figure 48: Text "Washington stimulates economic growth" is not shown visually but is read by screen readers.

63.11 CSS: Highlighting Links

Highlighting links is useful to help visual focus for cognitive and limited vision disabilities.

317

```
<style>

#hlinks a:hover, #hlinks a:active, #hlinks a:focus
{
 background-color: yellow;
 color: black;
}

</style>

<ul id="hlinks">
 <li><a href="#">Home</a></li>
 <li><a href="#">Services</a></li>
</ul>
```

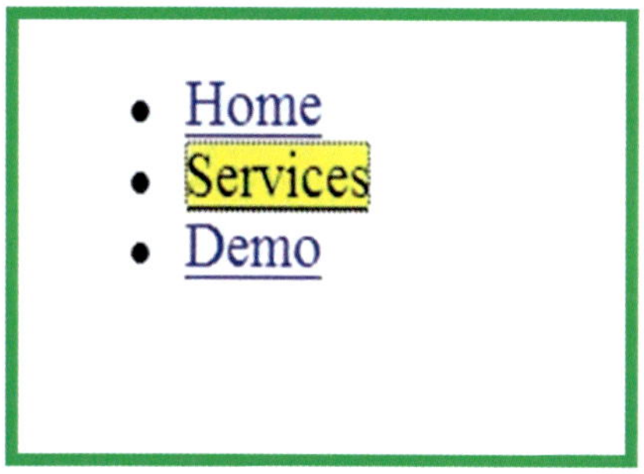

- Home
- Services
- Demo

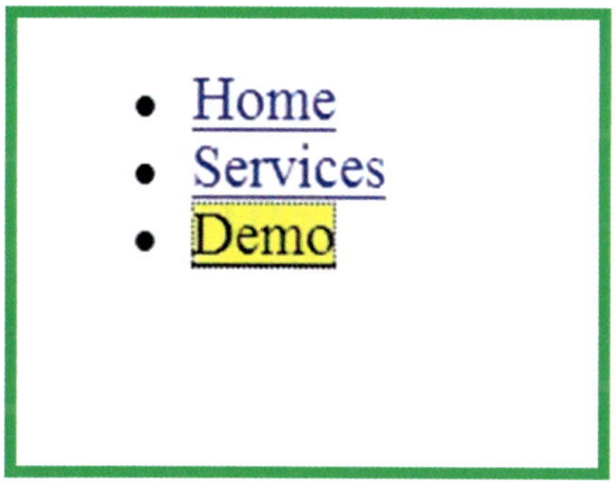

- Home
- Services
- Demo

Figure 49: Link is highlighted when active by keyboard or mouse.

63.12 CSS: Highlighting Active Input Fields

Highlighting input fields servers the same purpose as highlighting links which is to make clear what is active and to guide focus of the user. The technique can also be used to indicate what has been completed by leaving completed fields in a different color or helping to indicating errors. However the form should completely function without need of any of the highlighting effects, and all indicators of errors must be in text also. If this highlighting technique is used it must be noted that pure CSS methods alone are not cross-browser or legacy-browser when certain input fields are

318

used. The following method adding short JavaScript will work with all browsers and earlier versions of those browsers. For keyboard users and assistive technology, the highlighting effect can be equally triggered by the keyboard as well as the mouse.

For example: A text input field and radio buttons that are highlighted when either mouse or keyboard enters field, highlight is removed upon exit from the field.

```
<style>

.hform1
{
position: relative;
border: 1px solid blue;
background: Bisque;
color: darkred;
}

.hform2
{
position: relative;
border: 1px solid red;
background: yellow;
color: black;
}

</style>

</br></br>

<span class="hform1">
<label for="firstname">First Name (Label):</label>

<input class="hform1" id="firstname" type="text" onfocus="this.className='hform2'"
onmouseover="this.className='hform2'" onblur="this.className='hform1'"
onmouseout="this.className='hform1'"/>
Regular Text
</span>

</br></br>

<span class="hform1">
 <input type="radio" name="sex" value="male" id="sm" onfocus="this.className='hform2'"
onmouseover="this.className='hform2'" onblur="this.className='hform1'"
onmouseout="this.className='hform1'"/> <label for="sm"> Male (Label) </label><br/>

 <input type="radio" name="sex" value="female" id="sf" onfocus="this.className='hform2'"
onmouseover="this.className='hform2'" onblur="this.className='hform1'"
onmouseout="this.className='hform1'"/> <label for="sf"> Female (Label) </label>
</span>
```

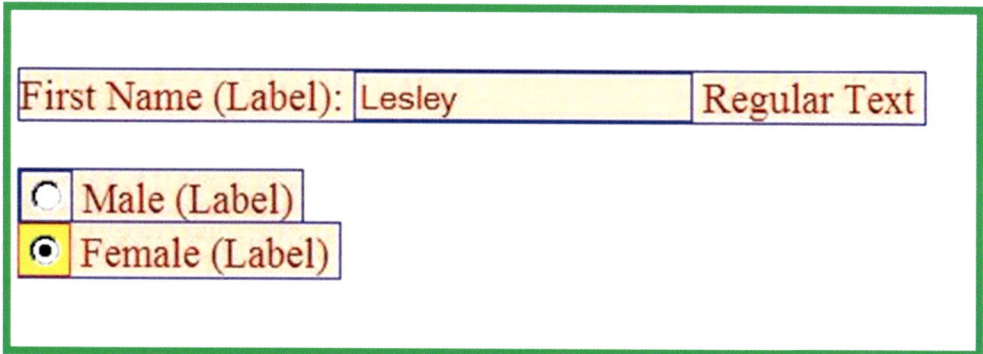

Figure 50: First Name field is highlighted when active with keyboard or mouse.

Figure 51: Female radio button is highlighted when active with keyboard or mouse.

63.13 CSS: Use Border And Visibility Settings Instead Of Spacer Images Or Empty Table Cells For Layout.

There is no need to use spacer images, empty table cells or complete empty table rows and columns to create spacing in the layout design. When empty or blank cells are used assistive technology picks this up and counts them as valid cells. To use them for entire rows and columns makes understanding of the table content very difficult by screen readers. There are two main issues, one is the number of rows and columns are announced and this is a guide to the user to be oriented to the table, the other is the blank cells each of which will be announced by a screen reader.

Note: To keep the scrolling from jumping too fast across rows and columns with assistive technology, do not make individual cells more than 25% of the un-scrolled page. Try to manage cells so they break with the page if possible. If a table is across pages, remember to repeat headers and make sure they are associated with the cells.

The following techniques show how to create empty cells that will work with assistive technology. Both the bold wide red line and the empty cells are ignored by screen readers.

```
<style>

.hide
{
visibility:hidden;
}

.hideall
{
visibility:hidden;
border: none;
}

.right
{
border-right: 20px solid red;
}

table
{
border-collapse:collapse;
}

</style>
```

This example produces a red border line along-side blank cells.

```
<table border>
 <caption>Books Part 1 (Red Line With Empty Cells)</caption>
 <thead>
 <tr>
 <th class="right"> Title </th>
         <th class="hide">      </th>
 <th> Author </th>
 <th> Date </th>
 </tr>
 </thead>
 <tbody>
 <tr>
 <td class="right"> Web Standards 1</td>
         <td class="hide">      </td>
 <td> GEF Foundation 1 </td>
 <td> Jan 01 2012 1 </td>
 </tr>
 </tbody>
</table>
```

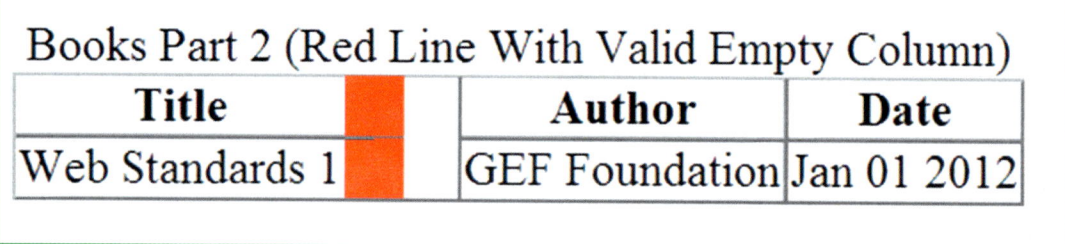

Books Part 1 (Red Line With Empty Cells)

Title		Author	Date
Web Standards 1		GEF Foundation 1	Jan 01 2012 1

Figure 52: Red line with empty cells not read by assistive technology.

```
<br/></br>

This example produces a red border line along-side a blank column.

<table border>
 <caption>Books Part 2 (Red Line With Valid Empty Column)</caption>
 <thead>
 <tr>
 <th class="right"> Title </th>
        <th class="hideall" >      </th>
 <th> Author </th>
 <th> Date </th>
 </tr>
 </thead>
 <tbody>
 <tr>
 <td class="right"> Web Standards 1</td>
        <td class="hideall">      </td>
 <td> GEF Foundation </td>
 <td> Jan 01 2012 </td>
 </tr>
 </tbody>
</table>
```

Books Part 2 (Red Line With Valid Empty Column)

Title		Author	Date
Web Standards 1		GEF Foundation	Jan 01 2012

Figure 53: Red line with empty column not read by assistive technology.

```
<br/></br>

This example produces a red border line with no blank cells.

<table border>
 <caption>Books Part 3 (Red Line With No Blank Cells or Column)</caption>
 <thead>
 <tr>
 <th class="right"> Title </th>
 <th> Author </th>
 <th> Date </th>
 </tr>
 </thead>
 <tbody>
 <tr>
 <td class="right"> Web Standards </td>
 <td> GEF Foundation </td>
 <td> Jan 01 2012 </td>
 </tr>
 </tbody>
</table>
```

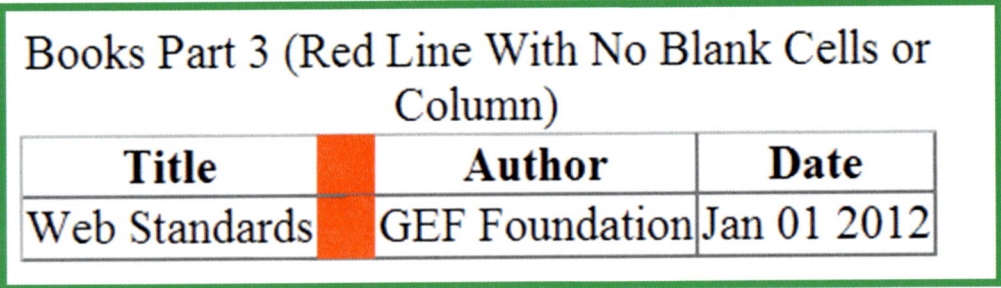

Figure 54: Red line not read by assistive technology.

This example produces a red border line in red bordered table with no blank cells.

```
<br/></br>
<table border bordercolor="red">
 <caption>Books Part 4 (Red Line with Red Borders)</caption>
 <thead>
 <tr>
 <th class="right"> Title </th>
 <th> Author </th>
 <th> Date </th>
 </tr>
 </thead>
 <tbody>
```

```
<tr>
<td class="right"> Web Standards </td>
<td> GEF Foundation </td>
<td> Jan 01 2012 </td>
</tr>
</tbody>
</table>
```

Books Part 4 (Red Line with Red Borders)

Title		Author	Date
Web Standards		GEF Foundation	Jan 01 2012

Figure 55: Red line with borders not read by assistive technology.

63.14 CSS: Use Cross-Browser Outline To Make Light Fonts Easy To See On Light Background And Vice Versa

Use CSS instead of images to get the shadow/outline effect on text, the text is scalable to the page since it is regular text with styled effects. Using an outline allows font colors that would not produce enough contrast in relation to the background to be readable to the visually disabled and accessible to assistive technology.

For example, the word "TEXT" is a yellow font with a shadow/outline style on a white background. This works in all the major browsers.

```
<style>

.s
{
height: 3em;
filter: Shadow
(Color=black,
Direction=135,
Strength=5);

text-shadow:
 1px 1px 0px #000,
 1px -1px 0px #000,
 -1px 1px 0px #000,
 -1px -1px 0px #000;
}
```

324

```
.f {font: 3em Verdana, Arial, Helvetica, sans-serif; font-weight: bold; color: yellow;}

</style>

<div class="s">
 <span class="f">TEXT</span>
</div>
```

Figure 56: CSS shadow/outline.

63.15 CSS: Drop Down Select Lists Menus

CSS can be used in traditional HTML SELECT lists for enhancements without any interference with assistive technology. CSS can also be used in to functionally replace the SELECT input type. This method will allow additional types of visual design. Using the methods below pure CSS drop down menus will be cross-browser and cross-assistive technology.

The first method uses SELECT with styling to color and enhance the traditional functionality of the SELECT lists. Note: DOCTYPE is required:

```
<!DOCTYPE html PUBLIC "-//W3C//DTD XHTML 1.0 Transitional//EN"
"http://www.w3.org/TR/xhtml1/DTD/xhtml1-transitional.dtd">

<style>
form, h4 {font-family: arial;}

.Blue
{
background-color: blue;
font-weight: bold;
font-size: 12px; color: white;
}

</style>
```

```
<script>

function on()
{

len = document.Nav.Menu.length;
i = 0;
chosen = "none";

for (i = 0; i < len; i++)
 {
 if (document.Nav.Menu[i].selected)
 {
 chosen = document.Nav.Menu[i].value
 }
 }

alert(chosen);
//document.location.href="http://google.com";

}

</script>

<h4>HTML Select List Enhanced with CSS - Mouse & Keyboard Accessible</h4>

<form name="Nav">
 <select class="Blue" id="Menu" size="1" onchange="on();">

 <option tabindex="1" selected > Top Navigation Category</option>

 <option value="Link 1 Navigation"> Link 1</option>

 <option value="Link 2 Navigation"> Link 2</option>

 <option value="Link 3 Navigation"> Link 3</option>

 <option value="Link 4 Navigation"> Link 4</option>
 </select>
</form>
```

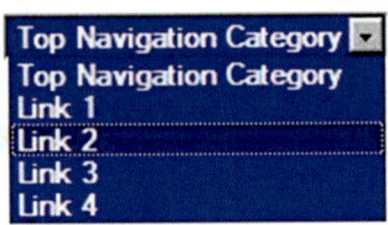

HTML Select List Enhanced with CSS - Mouse & Keyboard Accessible

Top Navigation Category
Top Navigation Category
Link 1
Link 2
Link 3
Link 4

Figure 57: Conventional SELECT list with CSS enhancement.

The next method has many more options for design. Follow the basic coding techniques below and the final design will be accessible. Note: DOCTYPE is required.

```
<!DOCTYPE html PUBLIC "-//W3C//DTD XHTML 1.0 Transitional//EN"
"http://www.w3.org/TR/xhtml1/DTD/xhtml1-transitional.dtd">

<script> location.hash = ''; </script>


<style>

body
{
 font-family: arial, sans-serif;
 font-size: 1em;
 color: black;
 background-color: #fff;
 margin-left: 20px;
 margin-top: 50px;
 margin-right: 20px;
 margin-bottom: 20px;
}

a, a:hover, a:active, a:focus
{
 outline: 0;
 direction: ltr;
}

.wrapper
{
 position: relative;
 height: 25px;
}
```

327

```css
.mainmenu
{
 position: absolute;
 z-index: 100;
 font-family: arial, sans-serif;
 font-weight: normal;
 font-size: 1em;
 line-height: 25px;
 left: 50%;
 margin-left: -303px;
 width: 606px;

-moz-box-shadow: 3px 3px 4px #000;
-webkit-box-shadow: 3px 3px 4px #000;
box-shadow: 3px 3px 4px #000;
/* For IE 8 */
-ms-filter: "progid:DXImageTransform.Microsoft.Shadow(Strength=6, Direction=135,
Color='#000000')";
/* For IE 5.5 - 7 */
filter: progid:DXImageTransform.Microsoft.Shadow(Strength=6, Direction=135, Color='#000000');
}

ul.menu
{
 padding: 0;
 margin: 0;
 list-style: none;
 width: 100px;
 overflow: hidden;
 float: left;
 margin-right: 1px;
}

ul.menu a
{
 background: #369;
 text-decoration: none;
 color: #fff;
 padding-left: 5px;
}

ul.menu li.list
{
 float: left;
 width: 250px;
 margin: -32767px -125px 0px 0px;
 background: purple;
 font-weight: bold;
}

ul.menu li.list a.category
```

```css
{
 position: relative;
 z-index: 50;
 display: block;
 float: left;
 width: 120px;
 margin-top: 32767px;
 background: transparent;
}

ul.menu li.list a.category:hover,
ul.menu li.list a.category:focus,
ul.menu li.list a.category:active
{
 margin-right: 1px;
 background: black;
}

ul.submenu
{
 float: left;
 padding: 25px 0px 0px 0px;
 margin: 0;
 list-style: none;
 background: blue;
 margin: -25px 0px 0px 0px;
}

ul.submenu li a
{
 float: left;
 width: 120px;
 background: blue;
 clear: left;
 color: #fff;
 font-size: .75em;
}

ul.submenu a:hover,
ul.submenu a:focus,
ul.submenu a:active
{
 background: #900;
 margin-right: 1px;
 color: #fff;
}

</style>

<h4 tabindex="0">CSS Only Drop Down Menu - Mouse & Keyboard Accessible</h4>
```

```html
<div class="wrapper">
 <div class="mainmenu">

 <ul class="menu">
 <li class="list">
 <a class="category" href="#A">Category A</a>
 <ul class="submenu">
 <li><a href="#A1"> Submenu Link 1 </a></li>
 <li><a href="#A2"> Submenu Link 2 </a></li>
 </ul>
 </li>
 </ul>


 <ul class="menu">
 <li class="list">
 <a class="category" href="#B">Category B</a>
 <ul class="submenu">
 <li><a href="#B1"> Submenu Link 1 </a></li>
 <li><a href="#B2"> Submenu Link 2 </a></li>
 <li><a href="#B3"> Submenu Link 3 </a></li>
 <li><a href="#B4"> Submenu Link 4 </a></li>
 <li><a href="#B5"> Submenu Link 5 </a></li>
 <li><a href="#B4"> Submenu Link 6 </a></li>
 <li><a href="#B5"> Submenu Link 7 </a></li>
 </ul>
 </li>
 </ul>


 <ul class="menu">
 <li class="list">
 <a class="category" href="#C">Category C</a>
 <ul class="submenu">
 <li><a href="#C1"> Submenu Link 1 </a></li>
 <li><a href="#C2"> Submenu Link 2 </a></li>
 <li><a href="#C3"> Submenu Link 3 </a></li>
 </ul>
 </li>
 </ul>


 </div>
</div>
```

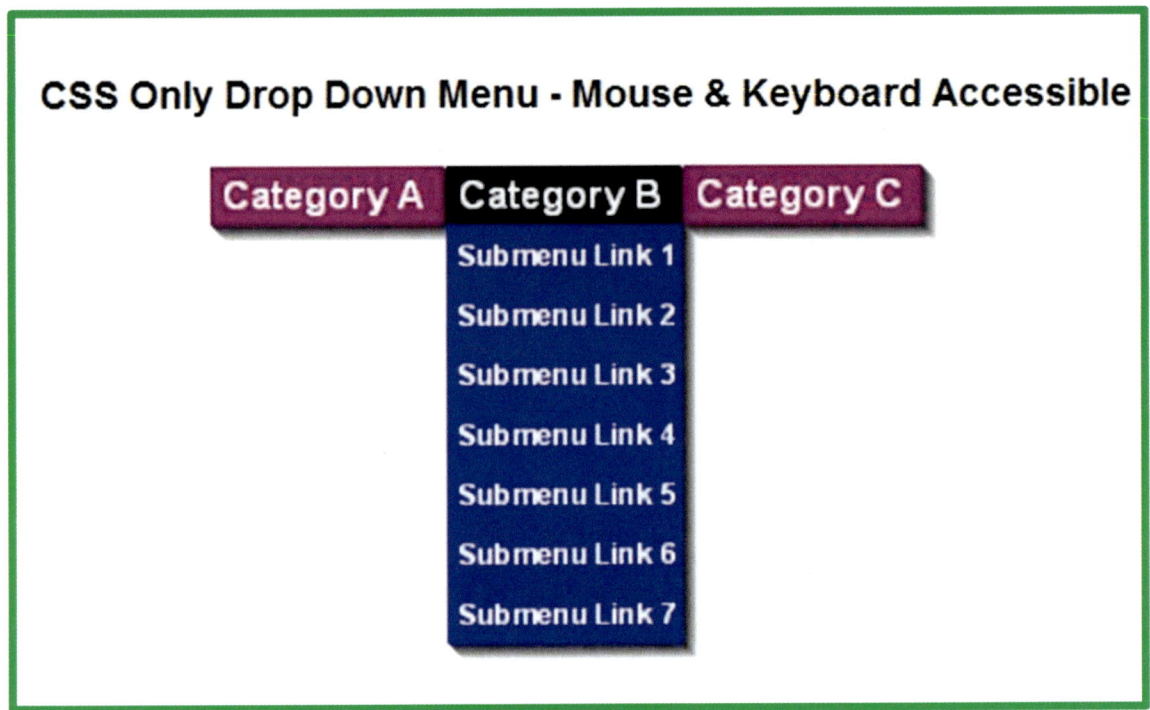

Figure 58: Drop down list composed of CSS and UL.

63.16 Abbreviations And Acronyms

The content of the ABBR (The ACRONYM element is not supported in HTML 5 and ABBR must be used for both acronyms and abbreviations) elements specifies the abbreviated expression itself, as it would normally appear in running text. The TITLE attribute of these elements may be used to provide the full or expanded form of the expression. For example:

```
<abbr title="Abbreviation"> abbr. </abbr>
```

63.17 Color Contrast Chart For Text And Background

The following chart illustrates nine common colors displayed as text and background both as bold and then as regular font weight.

Note: There are many factors that can affect the ability to read text against a background. A review should include the page as a whole and how text appears when the page changes due to interaction. Factors in addition to color of the text and background that affect readability of text include:

- The font itself (such as sans-serif which is more readable)

- Font-weight, line spacing, characters spacing, and font effects

- Proximity of other text, colors, lines, and objects

- Layered text

- Layout and design

Colors used in this chart include the following with the associated Hex value:

Red:	FF0000
Orange:	FFA500
Yellow:	FFFF00
Green:	008000
Blue:	0000FF
Purple:	800080
Black:	000000
White:	FFFFFF
Gray:	808080

The word "Yes" next to the color name indicates the color combination adheres to the W3C color contrast specifications. "No" indicates that the color contrast does not meet that specification. No text visible in the table cell indicates a color background and text color that is the same; this indicates a "No".

Meeting the color contrast requirement for text/background combination for some non-complying color combinations can met by adjusting the lightness of either the text or background. For example, making the gray background darker can allow usage of orange and yellow which would not be allowed as currently shown in the chart at this lightness level. See the W3C WCAG list of tools to test and select specific color combinations:

http://www.w3.org/TR/UNDERSTANDING-WCAG20/visual-audio-contrast-contrast.html#visual-audio-contrast-contrast-resources-head

Note: While some color combinations may appear to have high contrast to a user with normal vision but are marked as not acceptable for use this is because they are not visible to many users with color deficiencies which can render the foreground text color unreadable due to blending in with the background color. Other users need a high degree of edge definition and may have combinations of optical and neural issues; this necessitates the usage of those color combinations with the highest contrast.

	Red:No	Red:No	Red:No	Red:No	Red:No	Red:Yes	Red:Yes	Red:No
Orange:No		Orange:No	Orange:No	Orange:No	Orange:No	Orange:Yes	Orange:No	Orange:No
Yellow:Yes	Yellow:No		Yellow:Yes	Yellow:Yes	Yellow:Yes	Yellow:Yes	Yellow:No	Yellow:No
Green:No	Green:No	Green:Yes		Green:Yes	Green:No	Green:No	Green:Yes	Green:No
Blue:No	Blue:Yes	Blue:Yes	Blue:Yes		Blue:No	Blue:No	Blue:Yes	Blue:No
Purple:No	Purple:No	Purple:Yes	Purple:No	Purple:No		Purple:No	Purple:Yes	Purple:No
Black:No	Black:Yes	Black:Yes	Black:Yes	Black:No	Black:Yes		Black:Yes	Black:Yes
White:Yes	White:No	White:No	White:No	White:Yes	White:Yes	White:Yes		White:No
Gray:No	Gray:No	Gray:No	Gray:No	Gray:No	Gray:No	Gray:Yes	Gray:No	

	Red:No	Red:No	Red:No	Red:No	Red:No	Red:Yes	Red:Yes	Red:No
Orange:No		Orange:No	Orange:No	Orange:No	Orange:No	Orange:Yes	Orange:No	Orange:No
Yellow:Yes	Yellow:No		Yellow:Yes	Yellow:Yes	Yellow:Yes	Yellow:Yes	Yellow:No	Yellow:No
Green:No	Green:No	Green:Yes		Green:Yes	Green:No	Green:No	Green:Yes	Green:No
Blue:No	Blue:Yes	Blue:Yes	Blue:Yes		Blue:No	Blue:No	Blue:Yes	Blue:No
Purple:No	Purple:No	Purple:Yes	Purple:No			Purple:No	Purple:Yes	Purple:No
Black:No	Black:Yes	Black:Yes	Black:Yes	Black:No	Black:Yes		Black:Yes	Black:Yes
White:Yes	White:No	White:No	White:No	White:Yes	White:Yes	White:Yes		White:No
Gray:No	Gray:No	Gray:No	Gray:No	Gray:No	Gray:No	Gray:Yes	Gray:No	

Figure 59: Chart indicating which color combinations meet contrast requirements in first bolded font and then normal font.

63.18 CSS & Field ID/Name Naming Conventions

Names used for identifiers in general must:

- Have Uniqueness

- Be easy to understand

- Have concise wording

- Avoid using names that rely on location (position) or visual aspects of the particular element that can be confusing outside the context of that layout

- Use names that are intuitive

- Determine from the name what information it holds

- Have a name that states it's function, within the context of the occurrence

- Avoid abbreviations

CSS class name examples:

MainNav
SubNav
Nav
Menu
Sidebar
GlobalNav
SitenNav
NavigationPrimary
Breadcrumb

Content
MainContent
SideBar
Header
SecondaryContent

Footer
Masthead
Banner

SubCol
SideCol
MainCol

img.posA
img.posB

Uploading_Panel
Alert_Dialog
Video_Player
Link_Popup
Confirm_Dialog

Field names and IDs

- Use full descriptors that accurately describe the variable, field, or ID

- Use easy to recognize names like:

    - CellPhoneNumber

    - PaymentType

    - AccountID

    - FirstName

    - GrandTotal,

    - Customer

- Use terminology applicable to the environment

- If your users refer to their clients as customers, then use the term Customer

- Use mixed case to make names readable such LastName

    - Capitalize the first letter of class names and interface names, and compound words

- Avoid abbreviations if possible, if not then:

    - Maintain a list of standard abbreviations

- Avoid long names

    - Pick a maximum length

- Avoid names that are too similar, plural, or that differ only in upper or lower case

64   Types Of Assistive Technologies.

Alternative input devices allow individuals to control their computers through means other than a standard keyboard or pointing device. Due to the wide variety of devices it becomes critical to code to the standards: HTML, 508, and WCAG, to ensure that all devices can function properly and function without disruption.

Braille Embossers: Transfer computer-generated text into embossed Braille output. Braille translation programs convert text scanned-in or generated via standard word processing programs into Braille, which can be printed on the embosser.

An impact printer is used that embosses Braille on paper and other materials. Braille embossers are available that produce single-side or double-sided documents, as well as magazine formats and plates (plastic and metal) for signage. A Braille conversion application is generally required to convert text and images to Braille and tactile graphics for embossing.

Electronic Pointing Devices: Used to control the cursor on the screen without use of hands. Devices used include ultrasound, infrared beams, eye movements, nerve signals, muscle tension, and brain waves.

For example, Brain-Machine Interfaces (BMI) or Brain-Computer Interfaces (BCI), also referred to as Neuro-Prostheses, are implemented as technological interfaces between a machine (usually a computer) and the brain of a user. They should permit the use to perform a certain task, usually without implementing any motor action. This implies that neural impulses generated by the user's brain are detected, elaborated and utilized by the machine, approximately in real-time, to perform definite tasks. As an example, information can be processed and employed to control mechanical systems

Eye and Head Tracking: Eye-tracking systems serve as a replacement for common input devices such as mouse, keyboard or remote control. Using such systems, users with complex physical disabilities can operate computers and other connected devices simply by moving their eyes. An eye-tracking system consists of a camera that continuously scans one of the user's eyes and of software that analyses the picture captured by the camera to determine the exact point on the screen the user is looking at.

For example, one type of head tracker uses a color vision algorithm that tracks the head based on flesh colored pixels. It uses algorithms that are tolerant to low resolution web cams. The system can be used on low-end PCs and webcams. In addition, some trackers are tolerant of image noise, and hand movements. The tracker is able to find the face if the user moves his or her head out of the view of the camera, occludes the face, or otherwise moves the head out of view.

Fusers and Swell Tactile Paper: Fusers are used to produce tactile printed materials, such as diagrams and maps, on especially designed swell paper.

For example, a partially-automated method prints computer generated graphics onto capsule or swell paper, which causes the lines to rise when the paper is sent through a special heating device. In this process, the black portions of the copy swell outward to form a raised line tactile graphic. Tactile diagrams are proofread in a two-step process. First, a Braille transcriber examines the drawing for labeling accuracy. In the second step, an illustrator checks for graphic content and clarity.

Joysticks: Manipulated by hand, feet, chin, etc., used to control the cursor on screen.

For example, joystick and switch combinations enable an individual lacking sufficient mobility to use a full keyboard to access a computer through an on-screen keyboard or other "virtual" substitute.

Keyboards, Alternative: Featuring larger or smaller-than-standard keys or keyboards, alternative key configurations (such as split or ergonomic shapes), and keyboards for use with one hand.

For example, a mouth stick keyboard can be operated using a mouth-stick or other pointing device and the touch sensitivity can be adjusted as needed. Computer key locking ability allows one-hand or mouth stick users to depress two or more keys of a computer simultaneously.

Keyboard Filters: Typing aids such as word prediction utilities and add-on spelling checkers that reduce the required number of keystrokes. Keyboard filters enable users to quickly access the letters they need and to avoid inadvertently selecting keys they don't want.

Light Signaler: Monitors computer sounds and alert the computer user with light signals. This is useful when a computer user cannot hear computer sounds or is not directly in front of the computer screen. For example, a light can flash alerting the user when a new e-mail message has arrived or a computer command has completed.

Optical Character Recognition (OCR) and Scanners: Take scanned text and converts the scanned image into to an electronic text file, which can be saved and edited. Some are very intelligent and can handle tables and unusual formats.

On-Screen Keyboards: Provide an image of a standard or modified keyboard on the computer screen that allows the user to select keys with a mouse, touch screen, trackball, joystick, switch, or electronic pointing device. On-screen keyboards often have a scanning option that highlights individual keys that can be selected by the user. On-screen keyboards are helpful for individuals who are not able to use a standard keyboard due to dexterity or mobility difficulties.

Reading Tools and Learning Disabilities Programs: Include software and hardware designed to make text-based materials more accessible for people who have difficulty with reading. Options can include scanning, reformatting, navigating, or speaking text out loud. These programs are helpful for those who have difficulty seeing or manipulating conventional print materials; people who are developing new literacy skills; or who are learning English as a foreign language, and people who comprehend better when they hear and see with text highlighted simultaneously.

Refreshable Braille Displays: Provide tactile output of information represented on the computer screen – think Braille keyboard. A Braille "cell" is composed of a series of dots. The pattern of the dots and various combinations of the cells are used in place of letters. Refreshable Braille displays mechanically lift small rounded plastic or metal pins as needed to form Braille characters. The user reads the Braille letters with his or her fingers, and then, after a line is read, can refresh the display to read the next line.

Screen Magnifiers or Enlargers: Function like a zoom magnification for the computer by enlarging a portion of the screen to increase legibility and make it easier to see items on the computer. Some screen enlargers allow a person to zoom in and out on a particular area of the screen and have multiple portions displayed.

Screen Readers: Are used to verbalize, or "speak," everything on the screen including text, graphics, control buttons, and menus into a computerized voice that is spoken aloud. In essence, a screen reader transforms a graphic user interface (GUI) into an audio interface. Screen readers are essential for computer users who are blind or have limited vision. Cognitive users who have tracking or focus issues also find these helpful.

Single-Switch Access: A switch is placed to the side of the head that allows the person to click it with head movements. This clicking action is interpreted by special software on the computer, allowing the user to navigate through the operating system, web pages, other software and environments. Some software facilitates the typing of words by using an auto-complete feature that guesses what the person is typing, and allowing the person to choose between the words that it guessed.

Sip-and-Puff Systems: Activated by inhaling or exhaling.

Speech or Voice Recognition Programs: Allow people to give commands and enter data using their voices rather than a mouse or keyboard. Voice recognition systems use a microphone attached to the computer, which can be used to create text documents such as letters or e-mail messages, browse the Internet, and navigate among applications and menus by voice.

Talking and Large-Print Word Processors: Are software programs that use speech synthesizers to provide auditory feedback of what is typed. Large-print word processors allow the user to view everything in large text without added screen enlargement.

Text-to-Speech (TTS) or Speech Synthesizers: Receive information going to the screen in the form of letters, numbers, and punctuation marks, and then "speak" it out loud in a computerized voice. Using speech synthesizers allows computer users who are blind or who have learning difficulties to hear what they are typing and also provide a spoken voice for individuals who cannot communicate orally, but can communicate their thoughts through typing.

Touch Screens: Allow direct selection or activation of the computer by touching the screen, making it easier to select an option directly rather than through a mouse movement or keyboard. Touch screens are either built into the computer monitor or can be added onto a computer monitor.

Trackballs: Movable balls, on top of a base, can be used to move the cursor on screen. There are many variations for people with limited mobility.

TTY/TDD Conversion Modems: Are connected between computers and telephones to allow an individual to type a message on a computer and send it to a TTY/TDD telephone or other Baudot equipped device.

Wands and Sticks: Worn on the head, held in the mouth or strapped to the chin and used to press keys on the keyboard.

See below for illustrations of some of the devices:

http://webaim.org/articles/motor/assistive

65   Glossary

65.1   Accessible

The content and interaction, and functionality must be able to be used by people regardless of disability. The US Census counts 56.7 million in the US as disabled.

Examples of people who require accessible content:

- They may not be able to see, hear, move, or may not be able to process some types of information easily or at all.

- They may have difficulty reading or comprehending text.

- They may not have or be able to use a keyboard or mouse.

One group with millions of people with different variations is those with visual disability. Some of the visual limitations include:

- Poor visual perception

- Near or far-sightedness

- Extreme sensitivity to light and/or glare

- Color distortions

- Visual field defects

- Spots before the eyes

- Central vision loss

Another group is cognitive and neurological disabilities; this group has a larger range of sub-groups, each of which has its own list of sub-groups:

- Dyslexia, Dyscalculia

- Attention Deficit Disorder, or ADD

- Attention Deficit Hyperactive Disorder, or ADHD

- Impairments of Intelligence, or Learning Disabilities

- Memory Impairments

- Mental Health Disabilities

- Seizure Disorders

Accessibility Usage

It is very important to note that many people do not rely on one type of assistive technology. Due to multiple disabilities or a condition that requires different approaches to understand content many people use several types of software and hardware at the same time to assist them. For example, someone with visual issues may use a magnifier and screen reader. Others may add highlighter reading (highlights sections of text at a user pace to aid in focus). I worked with a typical multi-assistive technology user who used a screen magnifier, screen reader, large monitor, and a desk magnifier – the person would print out the screen or document and place it on the physical magnifier with a TV like high contrast display.

65.2   Alternative Text

Since rendered content in some forms is not always accessible to users with disabilities, authors must supply alternative equivalents for content. In the context of this document, the equivalent must fulfill essentially the same information for the person with a disability as the informational content does for the person without any disability.

Equivalent information focuses on providing information for the disabled user. For example, if the image is part of a link and understanding the image is crucial to guessing the link target, an equivalent must also give users an idea of the link target. Interfaces must make the alternative equivalent content available to users or software that requires it (in place of and/or in addition to the informational content). Alternative representations include text equivalents (long and short, synchronized and unsynchronized) and non-text equivalents (for example: captions, auditory descriptions, a visual track that shows sign language translation of a written text, etc.).

Equivalent Alternative Information

Content is "equivalent" to other content when both provide fulfill essentially the same (equal) information and purpose upon presentation to the user. Certain types of content may not be accessible to all users (for example: video, images, audio, etc.) unless a text description is provided.

65.3   Assistive Technology

Assistive technology is hardware and/or software that acts as an interface, or works with a mainstream interface (any software that retrieves and presents web content, applications, or documents for users). This includes:

- Assistive web browsers

- Applications

- Media players

- Plug-ins

- Add-Ons

And any other programs that help in retrieving, rendering, and interacting with web content., to provide functionality to meet the requirements of users with disabilities that go beyond those offered by mainstream interfaces. Functionality provided by assistive technology includes:

- Alternative presentations (for example: as synthesized speech or magnified content)

- Alternative input methods (for example: voice)

- Additional navigation or orientation mechanisms

- Content transformations (for example: to make tables more accessible)

The distinction between mainstream interfaces and assistive technologies is not absolute. Many mainstream browsers provide some features to assist individuals with disabilities. The basic difference is that mainstream interfaces target broad and diverse audiences that usually include people with and without disabilities.

Assistive technologies target narrowly defined populations of users with specific disabilities. The assistance provided by an assistive technology is more specific and appropriate to the needs of its target users. The mainstream interface may provide important functionality to assistive technologies like retrieving web content from program objects or parsing markup into identifiable bundles. Some are quite expensive due to the nature of interpreting all the main applications and browsers we use.

Examples of Assistive Technologies:

- Screen magnifiers, and other visual reading assistants, which are used by people with visual, perceptual and physical print disabilities to change text font, size, spacing, color, synchronization with speech, etc. in order to improve the visual readability of rendered text and images;

- Screen readers, which are used by people who are blind to read textual information through synthesized speech or Braille;

- Text-to-speech software, which is used by some people with cognitive, language, and learning disabilities to convert text into synthetic speech;

- Speech recognition software, which may be used by people who have some physical disabilities;

- Alternative keyboards, which are used by people with certain physical disabilities to simulate the keyboard (including alternate keyboards that use head pointers, single switches, sip/puff and other special input devices.). There are also many different keyboard configurations where the arrangement is physically altered to accommodate different abilities and reduce physical requirements. Keyboards are available to suit almost any type of situation. Keyboards can have illumination, large bright keys, special stickers for the keys, Braille keys, be reprogrammable, and switches for multiple keyboards.

- Alternative pointing devices, which are used by people with certain physical disabilities to simulate mouse pointing and button activations.

See the section "Types of Assistive Technologies" for a more comprehensive and descriptive list.

65.4   Audio Description

Narration added to the soundtrack to describe important visual details that cannot be understood from the main soundtrack alone. Audio description of video provides information about actions, characters, scene changes, on-screen text, and other visual content. In standard audio description, narration is added during existing pauses in dialogue.

Extended audio description is an audio description that is added to an audiovisual presentation by pausing the video so that there is time to add additional description. This technique is only used when the sense of the video would be lost without the additional audio description and the pauses between dialogue/narration are too short.

65.5   Captions

Synchronized visual and/or text alternatives for both speech and non-speech audio information needed to understand the media content. Captions are similar to dialogue-only subtitles except captions convey not only the content of spoken dialogue, but also equivalents for non-dialogue audio information needed to understand the program content, including sound effects, music, laughter, speaker identification and location. Captions should not obscure or obstruct relevant information in the video.

Closed Captions are equivalents that can be turned on and off with some players.

Open Captions are any captions that cannot be turned off. For example, if the captions are visual equivalent images of text embedded in video.

65.6   Contrast Ratio

(L1 + 0.05) / (L2 + 0.05), where

- L1 is the relative luminance of the lighter of the colors, and

- L2 is the relative luminance of the darker of the colors.

Contrast ratios can range from 1 to 21 (commonly written 1:1 to 21:1).

Contrast is measured with respect to the specified background over which the text is rendered in normal usage. If no background color is specified, then white is assumed.

Background color is the specified color of content over which the text is to be rendered in normal usage. It is a failure if no background color is specified when the text color is specified, because the user's default background color is unknown and cannot be evaluated for sufficient contrast. When there is a border around the letter, the border can add contrast and would be used in calculating the contrast between the letter and its background. A narrow border around the letter would be used as the letter. A wide border around the letter that fills in the inner details of the letters acts as a halo and would be considered background.

65.7   Device Independent

Users must be able to interact with the application, form, or web page (and the document it renders) using the supported input and output devices of their choice and according to their needs. Input devices may include:

- Pointing devices

- Keyboards

- Braille devices

- Head wands

- Microphones

Output devices may include:

- Monitor

- Speech synthesizers

- Braille devices

"Device-independent support" does not mean that every input or output device must be supported. Interfaces should offer redundant input and output mechanisms for all the devices that are supported.

For example: If keyboard and mouse input are supported, users should be able to interact with all features using either the keyboard or the mouse.

65.8   Keyboard Interface

Interface used by software to obtain keystroke input. A keyboard interface allows users to provide keystroke input to programs.

Operation of the application (or parts of the application) through a keyboard-operated mouse emulator, such as MouseKeys, does not qualify as operation through a keyboard interface because operation of the program is using its pointing device interface, not through its keyboard interface.

65.9   Linearized Table

A table rendering process where the contents of the cells become a series of paragraphs (for example: down the page) one after another. The paragraphs will occur in the same order as the cells are defined in the document source. Cells should make sense when read in order and should include structural elements (that create paragraphs, headers, lists, etc.) so the page makes sense after linearization.

65.10 Programmatically Determined

Determined by software from author-supplied data provided in a way that different interfaces, including assistive technologies, can extract and present this information to users in different modalities

For example:

- Determined in a markup language from elements and attributes that are accessed directly by commonly available assistive technology.

- Determined from technology-specific data structures in a non-markup language and exposed to assistive technology via an accessibility API that is supported by commonly available assistive technology.

Programmatically Determined Link Context

Additional information that can be programmatically determined from relationships with a link or combined with the link text, and presented to users in different modalities

Programmatically Determined Text

Sequence of characters that can be programmatically determined when the sequence is expressing something in human language.

Programmatically Determined Alternative Text

This is text that is programmatically associated with non-text content or referred to from text that is programmatically associated with non-text content. Programmatically associated text is text whose location can be programmatically determined from the non-text content.

65.11 Synchronized Media

Audio or video synchronized with another format for presenting information and/or with time-based interactive components, unless the media is a media alternative for text and is clearly labeled as such.

65.12 Usability and Accessibility

Usability = Refers to **Ease of use**. Note: poor usability can create inaccessibility.

Accessibility (specifically Section 508) = Refers to **Federal Law** providing equal access (barrier free) to content and functionality with information technology.

Usability is the art and science of designing systems or products that are effective, efficient, engaging, error tolerant and easy to learn. Usability and accessibility are often confused. Usability means intuitive and easy to use. Accessibility means as barrier-free as possible. Accessibility and usability are closely related, as they both improve satisfaction, effectiveness, and efficiency of the generic user population. But while accessibility is aimed at making systems or products open to a much wider user population, usability is aimed at making the target population more efficient, more effective, and productive.

Many aspects of usability reinforce and provide solutions for Section 508 issues. The people with cognitive issues especially benefit because making content easy to read, easy to navigate, easy to orient, and easy to edit provides the basis for a framework to make content accessible. In addition easy to use design makes it accessible to the aging population.

Types of usability solutions that solve accessibility issues for many types of disabilities:

- Keeping the display of information uncluttered and the layout consistent from one page to the next.

- Minimizing and making clear references to spatial information and/or directions in text-based material.

- Utilizing search databases that allow for spelling errors, either by accommodating spelling approximations and/or suggesting alternative or intended spellings.

- Providing extended time on timed steps, file uploads, selections, or quizzes.

- Defining organization as a course outline, with clear directions and marked navigational links and menu.

- Offering alternative formats.

- Study aides and review sheets covering key concepts.

- Highly visible keyboard focus and highly visible interactive elements

- Multiple levels of help, quick hints, examples, links to full explanations and tutorials within context sensitive help system.

Many accessibility standards increase usability and make the website easier and faster to use. Some of these are:

- Clear and simple language as appropriate

- Styled text instead of bitmap images of text to convey information

- Separating content from presentation

- Clear and consistent design, navigation, and links

66   WCAG 2.0 Core Requirements

The following is a condensed list of the WCAG 2.0 core requirements for HTML. These are the Level A and Level AA conformance guidelines. This manual is based on Section 508 and these WCAG 2.0 guidelines.

66.1 Text Alternatives: Guideline 1.1

Provide text alternatives for any non-text content so that it can be changed into other forms people need, such as large print, Braille, speech, symbols or simpler language.

Non-text Content: 1.1.1: All non-text content that is presented to the user has a text alternative that serves the equivalent purpose, except for the situations listed below.

- **Controls; Input:** If non-text content is a control or accepts user input, then it has a name that describes its purpose. (Refer to Guideline 4.1 for additional requirements for controls and content that accepts user input.)

- **Time-Based Media:** If non-text content is time-based media, then text alternatives at least provide descriptive identification of the non-text content. (Refer to Guideline 1.2 for additional requirements for media.)

- **Test:** If non-text content is a test or exercise that would be invalid if presented in text, then text alternatives at least provide descriptive identification of the non-text content.

- **Sensory:** If non-text content is primarily intended to create a specific sensory experience, then text alternatives at least provide descriptive identification of the non-text content.

- **CAPTCHA:** If the purpose of non-text content is to confirm that content is being accessed by a person rather than a computer, then text alternatives that identify and describe the purpose of the non-text content are provided, and alternative forms of CAPTCHA using output modes for different types of sensory perception are provided to accommodate different disabilities.

- **Decoration, Formatting, Invisible:** If non-text content is pure decoration, is used only for visual formatting, or is not presented to users, then it is implemented in a way that it can be ignored by assistive technology.

66.2 Time-based Media: Guideline 1.2

Provide alternatives for time-based media.

Audio-only and Video-only (Prerecorded): 1.2.1: For prerecorded audio-only and prerecorded video-only media, the following are true, except when the audio or video is a media alternative for text and is clearly labeled as such:

- **Prerecorded Audio-only:** An alternative for time-based media is provided that presents equivalent information for prerecorded audio-only content.

- **Prerecorded Video-only:** Either an alternative for time-based media or an audio track is provided that presents equivalent information for prerecorded video-only content.

Captions (Prerecorded): 1.2.2: Captions are provided for all prerecorded audio content in synchronized media, except when the media is a media alternative for text and is clearly labeled as such.

Audio Description or Media Alternative (Prerecorded): 1.2.3: An alternative for time-based media or audio description of the prerecorded video content is provided for synchronized media, except when the media is a media alternative for text and is clearly labeled as such.

Captions (Live): 1.2.4: Captions are provided for all live audio content in synchronized media.

Audio Description (Prerecorded):1.2.5: Audio description is provided for all prerecorded video content in synchronized media.

66.3   Adaptable: Guideline 1.3

Create content that can be presented in different ways (for example simpler layout) without losing information or structure.

Info and Relationships: 1.3.1: Information, structure, and relationships conveyed through presentation can be programmatically determined or are available in text.

Meaningful Sequence: 1.3.2: When the sequence in which content is presented affects its meaning, a correct reading sequence can be programmatically determined.

Sensory Characteristics: 1.3.3: Instructions provided for understanding and operating content do not rely solely on sensory characteristics of components such as shape, size, visual location, orientation, or sound.

66.4   Distinguishable: Guideline 1.4

Make it easier for users to see and hear content including separating foreground from background.

Use of Color: 1.4.1: Color is not used as the only visual means of conveying information, indicating an action, prompting a response, or distinguishing a visual element.

Audio Control: 1.4.2: If any audio on a Web page plays automatically for more than 3 seconds, either a mechanism is available to pause or stop the audio, or a mechanism is available to control audio volume independently from the overall system volume level.

Contrast (Minimum): 1.4.3: The visual presentation of text and images of text has a contrast ratio of at least 4.5:1, except for the following:

- **Large Text:** Large-scale text and images of large-scale text have a contrast ratio of at least 3:1;

- **Incidental:** Text or images of text that are part of an inactive user interface component, that are pure decoration, that are not visible to anyone, or that are part of a picture that contains significant other visual content, have no contrast requirement.

- **Logotypes:** Text that is part of a logo or brand name has no minimum contrast requirement.

Resize text: 1.4.4: Except for captions and images of text, text can be resized without assistive technology up to 200 percent without loss of content or functionality.

Images of Text: 1.4.5 If the technologies being used can achieve the visual presentation, text is used to convey information rather than images of text except for the following:

- **Customizable:** The image of text can be visually customized to the user's requirements;

- **Essential:** A particular presentation of text is essential to the information being conveyed.

Note: Logotypes (text that is part of a logo or brand name) are considered essential.

66.5   Keyboard Accessible: Guideline 2.1

Make all functionality available from a keyboard.

Keyboard: 2.1.1: All functionality of the content is operable through a keyboard interface without requiring specific timings for individual keystrokes, except where the underlying function requires input that depends on the path of the user's movement and not just the endpoints.

No Keyboard Trap: 2.1.2: If keyboard focus can be moved to a component of the page using a keyboard interface, then focus can be moved away from that component using only a keyboard interface, and, if it requires more than unmodified arrow or tab keys or other standard exit methods, the user is advised of the method for moving focus away.

66.6   Enough Time: Guideline 2.2

Provide users enough time to read and use content.

Timing Adjustable: 2.2.1: For each time limit that is set by the content, at least one of the following is true:

- Turn off: The user is allowed to turn off the time limit before encountering it; or

- Adjust: The user is allowed to adjust the time limit before encountering it over a wide range that is at least ten times the length of the default setting; or

- Extend: The user is warned before time expires and given at least 20 seconds to extend the time limit with a simple action (for example, "press the space bar"), and the user is allowed to extend the time limit at least ten times; or

- Real-time Exception: The time limit is a required part of a real-time event (for example, an auction), and no alternative to the time limit is possible; or

- Essential Exception: The time limit is essential and extending it would invalidate the activity; or

- 20 Hour Exception: The time limit is longer than 20 hours.

Pause, Stop, Hide: 2.2.2: For moving, blinking, scrolling, or auto-updating information, all of the following are true:

- **Moving, blinking, scrolling:** For any moving, blinking or scrolling information that (1) starts automatically, (2) lasts more than five seconds, and (3) is presented in parallel with other content, there is a mechanism for the user to pause, stop, or hide it unless the movement, blinking, or scrolling is part of an activity where it is essential; and

- **Auto-updating:** For any auto-updating information that (1) starts automatically and (2) is presented in parallel with other content, there is a mechanism for the user to pause, stop, or hide it or to control the frequency of the update unless the auto-updating is part of an activity where it is essential.

Notes:

- Content that is updated periodically by software or that is streamed to the interface is not required to preserve or present information that is generated or received between the initiation of the pause and resuming presentation, as this may not be technically possible, and in many situations could be misleading to do so.

- An animation that occurs as part of a preload phase or similar situation can be considered essential if interaction cannot occur during that phase for all users and if not indicating progress could confuse users or cause them to think that content was frozen or broken.

66.7   Seizures: Guideline 2.3

Do not design content in a way that is known to cause seizures.

Three Flashes or Below Threshold: 2.3.1 Web pages do not contain anything that flashes more than three times in any one second period, or the flash is below the general flash and red flash thresholds.

66.8   Navigable: Guideline 2.4

Provide ways to help users navigate, find content, and determine where they are.

Bypass Blocks: 2.4.1: A mechanism is available to bypass blocks of content that are repeated on multiple Web pages.

Page Titled: 2.4.2: Web pages have titles that describe topic or purpose.

Focus Order: 2.4.3: If a Web page can be navigated sequentially and the navigation sequences affect meaning or operation, focusable components receive focus in an order that preserves meaning and operability.

Link Purpose (In Context): 2.4.4: The purpose of each link can be determined from the link text alone or from the link text together with its programmatically determined link context, except where the purpose of the link would be ambiguous to users in general.

Multiple Ways: 2.4.5: More than one way is available to locate a Web page within a set of Web pages except where the Web Page is the result of, or a step in, a process.

Headings and Labels: 2.4.6: Headings and labels describe topic or purpose.

Focus Visible: 2.4.7: Any keyboard operable user interface has a mode of operation where the keyboard focus indicator is visible.

66.9   Readable: Guideline 3.1

Make text content readable and understandable.

Language of Page: 3.1.1: The default human language of each Web page can be programmatically determined.

Language of Parts: 3.1.2: The human language of each passage or phrase in the content can be programmatically determined except for proper names, technical terms, words of indeterminate language, and words or phrases that have become part of the vernacular of the immediately surrounding text.

66.10 Predictable: Guideline 3.2

Make Web pages appear and operate in predictable ways.

On Focus: 3.2.1: When any component receives focus, it does not initiate a change of context

On Input: 3.2.2: Changing the setting of any user interface component does not automatically cause a change of context unless the user has been advised of the behavior before using the component.

Consistent Navigation: 3.2.3: Navigational mechanisms that are repeated on multiple Web pages within a set of Web pages occur in the same relative order each time they are repeated, unless a change is initiated by the user.

Consistent Identification: 3.2.4: Components that have the same functionality within a set of Web pages are identified consistently.

66.11 Input Assistance: Guideline 3.3

Help users avoid and correct mistakes.

Error Identification: 3.3.1: If an input error is automatically detected, the item that is in error is identified and the error is described to the user in text.

Labels or Instructions: 3.3.2: Labels or instructions are provided when content requires user input.

Error Suggestion: 3.3.3: If an input error is automatically detected and suggestions for correction are known, then the suggestions are provided to the user, unless it would jeopardize the security or purpose of the content.

Error Prevention (Legal, Financial, Data): 3.3.4: For Web pages that cause legal commitments or financial transactions for the user to occur, that modify or delete user-controllable data in data storage systems, or that submit user test responses, at least one of the following is true:

1. Reversible: Submissions are reversible.

2. Checked: Data entered by the user is checked for input errors and the user is provided an opportunity to correct them.

3. Confirmed: A mechanism is available for reviewing, confirming, and correcting information before finalizing the submission.

66.12 Compatible: Guideline 4.1

Maximize compatibility with current and future interfaces, including assistive technologies.

Parsing: 4.1.1: In content implemented using markup languages, elements have complete start and end tags, elements are nested according to their specifications, elements do not contain duplicate attributes, and any IDs are unique, except where the specifications allow these features.

Note: Start and end tags that are missing a critical character in their formation, such as a closing angle bracket or a mismatched attribute value quotation mark are not complete.

Name, Role, Value: 4.1.2: For all user interface components (including but not limited to: form elements, links and components generated by scripts), the name and role can be programmatically determined; states, properties, and values that can be set by the user can be programmatically set; and notification of changes to these items is available to interfaces, including assistive technologies.

Note: This success criterion is primarily for Web authors who develop or script their own user interface components. For example, standard HTML controls already meet this success criterion when used according to specification.

67   Developer Pass/Fail Checks

Primary Checks
Images
Images, animations, graphs, and audio files must have equivalent text descriptions.
Images must be used consistently throughout the application.

Images with Information must have text in some format such as ALT text, captions or adjacent text.

Section 508: 1194.22 (a)

To Pass

Every image, Java applet, Flash file, video file, audio file, plug-in, etc. has an ALT or text description.
Complex graphics (graphs, charts, etc.) are accompanied by detailed text descriptions. These can be links to text elsewhere.
Note: ALT descriptions for images used as links are descriptive of the link destination.
Decorative graphics with no other function have empty ALT descriptions (alt= "")｛no space in quotes｝, but they never have missing ALT. ALT either contains text or the empty string.
All the meanings of bit map images must be consistent throughout the application.

To Fail

A non-text element with information or is a control has no ALT description.
Complex graphics have no alternative text, or the alternative does not fully convey the meaning of the graphic.

Inconsistent meanings for image controls/icons.

Test Method

Reveal ALT content on images. Description must be equal to image information.
TITLE should not be used in place of ALT unless there is no other way. WCAG allows this for secondary or helpful methods after ALT or captions or adjacent or linked descriptions are used.
Mouse over graphics to check for an equivalent text description. If it is a decorative element it should not have any text.
If the Alt text is greater than 100 characters (English) then it must be shortened or else move text to the page adjacent or as a link.
http://www.w3.org/TR/html401/struct/objects.html#h-13.8
http://www.w3.org/TR/WCAG20-TECHS/H36.html
http://www.w3.org/TR/WCAG20-TECHS/H37.html
http://www.w3.org/WAI/GL/WCAG20/tests/test3.html

Color Dependence & Contrast

Color cannot be the only method of conveying information.
Section 508: 1194.22 (c)

To Pass

If color is used to convey important information, an alternative indicator is used, such as Text (preferred and requires no explanation). Use of any symbols (e.g. asterisk "*" for required form fields) must be described on first use.
As long as there is a text alternative to color, it does not mean that color can't be used. Color and highlights increase accessibility when used in addition to primary methods.

Other Examples: http://www.w3.org/TR/UNDERSTANDING-WCAG20/visual-audio-contrast-without-color.html

The use of a color monitor is required.
Anything unreadable in black and white or grayscale.

Test Method

Check Color: Take a screenshot of the page and print it in black and white. All items should be easily readable. Any text too light against the background will fail.
Use one of the public tools listed in section 7.
To get accurate contrast combinations see: http://www.dasplankton.de/ContrastA/
For color and contrast in images see:
http://webaim.org/techniques/images/color

Tables

Row and column headers must be identified for data tables.
Associate data cells and header cells for data tables that have two or more row or column headers.
Section 508: 1194.22 (c)

To Pass

Determine if a data table is simple or complex.

Note: Simple Tables use:

SCOPE (works only with 1 or 2 level headers)
Example:
<TH SCOPE="col">Name</TH>
<TD SCOPE="row">Joe Smith</TD>;
Additional Information http://www.w3.org/TR/WCAG-TECHS/H63.html
Table cells must be associated with the appropriate headers.
Note: Complex Tables – Header and ID (works with all data tables but most often used for complex data tables)
Example:
<TR><TH id="fullname" colspan="2"> Name </TH></TR>
<TR><TH headers="fullname" id="fname"> First </TH>
<TH headers="fullname" id="lname" >Last </TH></TR>
<TR><TD headers="fullname fname"> John </TD>
<TD headers="fullname lname"> Smith </TD></TR>
http://www.w3.org/TR/WCAG20-TECHS/H43.html

To Fail

Data tables have no column headers or row headers (in rows with header text in first row cell).

Tables used for layout use the header attribute (TH) when there is no true header.

Columns and rows are not associated with column and row headers, or they are associated incorrectly.

Each column must have column header TH and each row a row header TH if applicable.

Inspect each row and column header for SCOPE or ID.

Look for the option of HEADERS to associate any cell to any header for merged cells or sub-headers.

Using AT such as a screen reader can be helpful in determining if cells in a table are associated with headers.

Windows and Frames must be titled with text that uniquely identifies them and provides for orientation.

Each frame and window is given a unique title that helps the user understand the frame's or windows purpose.

The title also helps indicate its location among other pages or a process.

See:
http://www.w3.org/TR/WCAG-TECHS/H64.html

http://www.w3.org/TR/UNDERSTANDING-WCAG20/navigation-mechanisms-title.html

Frames/Windows have no titles.

Titles that are not descriptive and do not indicate purpose.

Titles that are not unique and can be confused with one another based on title.

Landing on a page does not indicate what it is and what it is part of.

Test Method

Move focus through each window and frame.

Note: Window and frame Titles must be descriptive so the content of the frame is obvious to aid screen reader and voice control navigation and operate with other AT.

Here we know what page and part of what application:
<title>Discovery Directory Usage Disclaimer</title>

Simple indicator for a frame:
<frame src="nav.html" TITLE="left navigation">

Window and frame titles by themselves must have a unique description and an indication of position among other pages.

Forms & Fields

All form elements must be exposed to assistive technology (AT), including:

- Name
- Value
- State
- Directions
- Cues

Fields must be uniquely labeled visually and with LABEL.

Multiple fields are logically grouped with FIELDSET.

Do not use ALT text for fields.

Section 508: 1194.22 (i)

To Pass

All form controls have unique text labels visually adjacent to them and in code with LABEL.

Form elements have labels associated with them in the markup (i.e. the ID and Label FOR).T

Dynamic HTML scripting of the form does not interfere with assistive technologies.

INPUT TYPE="HIDDEN" do not need labels.

Note: LABELs must be identical and match case:
FOR="T" and ID="T"

Inspect each field for an ID and a corresponding LABEL:

Radio Buttons:

Age Range:

◯ under 18

⦿ 18 to 25

Using TITLE
<input type="radio"
TITLE="Age range 18 to 25">

Using FIELDSET/LEGEND and LABEL/ID
<FIELDSET><LEGEND>Age Range</LEGEND>
…
<INPUT TYPE="radio" ID="range2">
<LABERL FOR="range2">18 to 25</LABEL>
</FIELDSET>

Labels: http://www.w3.org/TR/WCAG-TECHS/H44.html

Fieldsets: http://www.w3.org/TR/2008/NOTE-WCAG20-TECHS-20081211/H71.html

Error messages: http://www.w3.org/TR/WCAG20-TECHS/G139.html

http://www.w3.org/TR/2012/NOTE-WCAG20-TECHS-20120103/G83

To Fail

Form controls have no visible labels, or the labels are not adjacent to the controls.

There is no linking of the form element and its LABEL in the HTML.

Either the visible label or the programmatic LABEL is missing.

Groups of fields that logically should be together are not using FIELDSET.

ALT text is used for field labels.

TITLE is used for field labels when LABEL could be used.

The first entry is a SELECT list that is used for the field label (pseudo label).

Look for form field structure in the code.

Locate FIELDSET for logical groups of fields.

Locate on screen adjacent text labels and LABEL in code for each field.

Each Label must be unique and correctly describe or name the field.

AT can be used to assist in indicating field labels. To account for widest accessibility confirm LABEL is in code and visible label.

Error Messages

Error messages must be located at top of screen or focus to a pop-up window with links to fields requiring correction.

Specific input format required must be indicated. Best is an example of the required format.

Section 508: 1194.22 (n)

To Pass

Errors must be identified in text.

Describing the error and method required to correct.

You can add (in addition to text - required) a unique text character or asterisk, color, and highlights.

Indicate clearly in text at the top of the page that there were errors.

Text describes the nature of the errors.

Provide links to the fields that had the problem so the user can navigate to it to fix the problem.

See:

http://www.w3.org/TR/WCAG20-TECHS/G139.html

http://www.w3.org/TR/2012/NOTE-WCAG20-TECHS-20120103/G83

To Fail

Error messages are scattered about the page. If a screen reader were used, you would have to be in read mode and scan the entire page.

Instructions on how to correct the error are not provided.

Errors are at top of page but are not links to fields needing correction.

Vague instructions:

"Enter a Correct Number"

"Enter Valid Date"

Instructions to correct error must be specific, the best way is to give a range and/or provide an example entry or format.

Test Method

Generate an error by entering an invalid entry and submitting. You should have focus to the top of screen with error information and links to those errors. Attempt to follow with keyboard only.

If available, attempt to locate and correct errors with a screen reader and voice control.

Timed Response

Notification that a timeout is about to occur must be given.

Section 508: 1194.22 (p)

To Pass

Includes notices about server and security timeouts.

The user must be alerted that time is about to expire AND is allowed to request more time.

User must be able to save progress if there are timeouts for long forms that take 20 minutes or more.

See:
http://www.w3.org/TR/2012/NOTE-WCAG20-TECHS-20120103/G105

http://www.w3.org/TR/2007/WD-WCAG20-TECHS-20071211/G133.html

To Fail

If the time out occurs without notification or option to request more time.

If the timeout occurs after 20 minutes of data entry and there is no option to save.

Test Method

Leave the application open and inactive. Check for notification of a pending time out and opportunity to request more time.

Attempt to save progress and restore session later after closing session.

Keyboard and Focus

Keyboard access and Visual focus always apply.

Keyboards must access all controls and navigation.

Section 508: 1194.21 (c)

Section 508: 1194.22 (n)

To Pass

Select the windows keyboard short cuts (Tab, [Shift+Tab to reverse order], Alt, Arrow, Space bar, Enter, and the application's custom keystrokes) to move the focus and activate all menus, links, controls, and functions.

Must be able to navigate through all form fields via keyboard only. Enter text, ARROW to different options from drop down lists, select and unselect (SPACEBAR and ARROW keys) checkboxes and radio buttons.

See for techniques:
http://www.w3.org/WAI/WCAG20/quickref/#qr-navigation-mechanisms-focus-visible

Ensure that visual focus moves with keyboard navigation.

TAB order:

http://www.w3.org/TR/2012/NOTE-WCAG20-TECHS-20120103/H4

To Fail

If any interactive element or function cannot be accessed by keyboard alone.

If there are any instances that interface elements or function can't be accessed by keyboard.

If visual focus is lost at any time and there is no indication of where the visual focus is located.

The focus in not synchronized with the keyboard action.

Test Method

Check whether interface elements can be accessed with keyboard only.

Ensure that the name, role, and state are exposed and are correct.

TAB to each field and link. The logical order must be correct and the visible focus must track to element with keyboard activity.

Using multiple types of AT will be helpful in tracking correct focus. Screen readers and magnifiers are very useful.

CSS

Pages are readable without requiring CSS.

Custom style sheets must not interfere with accessibility.

Custom style sheets cannot eliminate functionality when removed.

Section 508: 1194.22 (d)

To Pass

Style sheets may be used for color, positioning, lines, shadows, and other presentation effects, but the document is still understandable (even if less visually appealing) when the style sheet is turned off.

See:
http://www.w3.org/TR/WCAG10-TECHS/#tech-order-style-sheets

To Fail

The document is jumbled, confusing or information is missing when the style sheet is turned off.

Disable CSS. Clear cache, reload page.

Ensure there is no loss of information or directions without the style sheet.

Note: Some browsers do not support all CSS. Some browsers may not Correctly turn off all CSS depending on version and type. Test in another browser to confirm issues.

You may need to reenter the URL to actually force a full refresh of the page.

Skip Navigation

Provide a method to skip past the repetitive navigation links.

Section 508: 1194.22 (o)

To Pass

A link is provided to skip over lists of navigational menus or other lengthy lists of links or controls.

Note: Skip Navigation: Does not have to be visible and Is only required on pages where repetitive navigation links exist.

See:
http://www.w3.org/TR/2008/NOTE-WCAG20-TECHS-20081211/G1

To Fail

If there is no skip function, or the link target is not after the repetitive links.

Test Method

View internal links via the code.

The anchor targets are marked (usually with "#") and must be after the repetitive links.

The skip link must move focus to the main content.

TAB to the skip navigation function and activate the link, observe the visible focus. Using a screen reader can help determine if there is an issue.

When scripting languages display content, or create interface elements, the information provided by the script must be identified with programmatically exposed text.

Section 508: 1194.22 (l)

To Pass

Information within the scripts is text-based, or a text alternative is provided within the script itself.

All scripts (e.g. JavaScript pop-ups, menus, controls, dashboards) are either exposed to AT or an alternative method of accessing equivalent functionality is provided (e.g. a standard HTML link).

See for techniques:
http://www.w3.org/WAI/GL/WCAG20/WD-WCAG20-SCRIPT-TECHS-20040910/

If JavaScript is required then announce that upfront on the landing page. Provide a contact or accessibility page with solutions for non-script users.

To Fail

Scripts only work with a mouse, and there is no keyboard-accessible alternative either within or outside of the script.

Information for non-script users is not provided.

Test Method

Locate script items.

Display information when triggered by a mouse event (mouse over, mouse click, etc.). Check if keyboard has access to the same information.

Determine if functional text is provided.

For scripts attached to a HREF, the name of the link is the functional text.

Determine if functional text is an adequate description for the script.

Using AT to help determine issues will require screen readers, voice control and magnification since scripts can affect operation of all types of AT.

Use of the application must not interrupt user's accessibility functions and must adopt operating system appearance attributes.

Do no disrupt magnification, narration, or high contrast.

Section 508: 1194.21 (b)

To Pass

Ensure that none of the Accessibility Options are disabled.

Windows OS:

- Narrator
- High Contrast
- Magnifier
- Change Fonts, Sizes, Colors
- Sticky Keys, MouseKeys
- OS & Application Sounds

See requirement 5:
http://www.w3.org/TR/UNDERSTANDING-WCAG20/conformance.html

To Fail

If the application does not inherit all of the accessibility settings in the OS.

Test Method

Close the application.

Windows:

Enable each accessibility feature and check for functionality.

If unsure of feature issues use a plain vanilla web page as a control to set baseline operation of accessibility features.

Secondary Checks

Plug-ins

To view file types that will not display in the browser, links must be provided to download plug-ins required.

Provide a link to a page with the download information for the required plug-ins.

Internal site: If all required plug-ins are available via a standard computer image then a plug-in link is not required.

Section 508: 1194.22 (m)

To Pass

Web: A link is provided to a accessible page where the plug-in can be downloaded.

All Java applets, scripts and plug-ins (including Acrobat PDF files and PowerPoint files, etc.) and the content within them are accessible to assistive technologies, or else an alternative means of accessing equivalent content is provided.

See:
http://www.w3.org/WAI/GL/WCAG20/WD-WCAG20-HTML-TECHS-20050211/#download-viewer

To Fail

No link is provided to a page where the plug-in can be downloaded and/or the download page is not accessible.

Test Method

Locate links to download plug-ins required to view file types that will not display in the browser.

Link page must also be accessible.

Blinking

Pages must avoid causing the screen to blink with a frequency greater than 2 Hz and less than 55 Hz.

Section 508: 1194.22 (j)

To Pass

Users can stop, pause, or step through animations or media that can cause flickering or flashing.

Static highlights are used instead of flashing notifications.

An alternative page is available for any media with flashing or strobe issues.

See:
http://www.w3.org/TR/WCAG10-CORE-TECHS/#flicker

To Fail

Manual Inspection: Any interface element that blinks or scrolls. Web HTML tags that render flickering interface elements cannot control frequency of flicker.

Software elements that flicker at a rate of 2 to 55 cycles per second.

Test Method

For web pages, fail any interface element that blinks or scrolls

Software must not use flashing or blinking text, objects, or other interface elements between 2 Hz and 55 Hz.

Free tools to assist analysis include:

Trace Center Photosensitive Epilepsy Analysis Tool
http://trace.wisc.edu/peat/

Web Accessibility Toolbar For IE
http://www.paciellogroup.com/resources/wat-ie-about.html

Image Maps

Redundant text links must be provided for server-side image maps.

Client-side image maps must be provided instead of server-side image maps except where the regions cannot be defined with an available geometric shape.

Section 508: 1194.22 (e)

Section 508: 1194.22 (f)

Separate text links are provided outside of the server-side image map to access the same content that the image map hot spots access.

An alternative page provides the same information.

Standard HTML client-side image maps are used, and appropriate alt text is provided for the image as well as the hot spots.

Providing text alternatives for image maps:
http://www.w3.org/TR/2010/NOTE-WCAG20-TECHS-20101014/H24

To Fail

The only way to access the links of a server-side image map is through the image map hot spots, which usually means that a mouse is required and that the links are unavailable to assistive technologies.

Server-side image maps are used when a client-side image map would suffice.

Test Method

Ensure that all the text links are keyboard accessible.

TAB to each hotspot - If the map regions are not keyboard accessible, check for alternative methods to provide access to the map links (e.g.: drop down list or text links on page).

See:

http://www.w3.org/WAI/GL/WCAG20/tests/test13.html

Multimedia

Equivalent alternatives for any multimedia must be synchronized with the presentation.

Transcripts must be provided for any webinar or audio/visual presentation.

Section 508: 1194.22 (b)

To Pass

Multimedia files have synchronized captions and audio descriptions.

Techniques:
http://www.w3.org/2008/06/video-notes

To Fail

Multimedia files do not have captions, or captions are not synchronized.

There is no text for a webinar or presentation.

Test Method

Multimedia must include synchronized captions and audio descriptions. Look for any delay between the captions and audio.

The visual caption text must track with the audio or screen events.

Any transcript must be complete in capturing information and representing the presentation.

68　Making Special Cases Work

68.1　Making Nested Tables Work With Aria

Tables must eventually be fully accessible directly on the screen by a screen reader of other assistive technology without any workarounds.

When you insert a table section within a larger table (that is static) as long as you keep the IDs from the parent and use aria-labelledby in the child added/updated section, A screen reader such as JAWS will read the entire association of all cells.

The trick is to not use the <TABLE> within the existing table (so technically not nesting) but just add more <Th> and <Td> that are associated by ID to the parent in which you are inserting updated cells with dynamic fields and text.

This example works well, just follow **id="track1"** in the code to see how cells are associated.

So there are 2 solutions:

- One is simply to not nest tables at all, and generate your entire table as one each time there is an update.
- The other is to insert only sub-headers and rows that are associated to the parent columns and row headers.

This citation for this code also describes methods. But just using the code as an example for the Conference table is good enough. JAWS is able to identify every cell through all the headers it is associated with (CTRL+ALT+5 within a cell). Keep in mind this does not work with all browsers or screen readers. This worked with JAWS 16 and IE 11.

```
<table id="wbt" border="1">
<tr>
 <td rowspan="2"></td>
 <th colspan="2" scope="colgroup">Thursday</th>
 <th colspan="2" scope="colgroup">Friday</th>
</tr>

<tr>
 <th scope="col">9 to 12 AM</th>
 <th scope="col">2 to 5 PM</th>
 <th scope="col">9 to 12 AM</th>
 <th scope="col">2 to 5 PM</th>
</tr>

<tr>
 <th id="track1" scope="row">track 1</th>
```

```
  <td>
    <h2 id="title-TM1"><label for="TM1">Workshop 1, Memoirs of a justified coder <span
class="markup">
(<code>label</code> inside <code>h2</code>, with the <code>id</code> referenced by <code>aria-
labelledby</code> on
<code>h2</code>, "Attend" in <code>p</code> element, with an <code>id</code> also referenced
by <code>aria-
labelledby</code>)</span> <span class="hide">by</span>
    <em>Maud McRae</em></label></h2>
    <p>2 places left</p>
    <p id="TM1-att"><input type="checkbox" id="TM1" aria-labelledby="track1 title-TM1 TM1-
att">Attend</p>
  </td>


  <td>
    <h2><label for="TA1" id="title-TA1">Workshop 2, Pride and Vendor Prefixes <span
class="markup">
    (<code>label</code> inside <code>h2</code>, this time with the <code>id</code> referenced by
<code>aria-
labelledby</code> on <code>label</code>, "Attend" in separate <code>label</code> element with
another <code>id</code>
also referenced by <code>aria-labelledby</code>)</span> <span class="hide">by</span>
    <em>Cassandra Barnave</em></label></h2>
    <p>2 places left</p>
    <label id="TA1-att"><input type="checkbox" id="TA1" aria-labelledby="track1 title-TA1 TA1-att">
Attend</label>
  </td>


  <td>
    <h2><label id="title-FM1">Workshop 3, Cutting corners with code: Crime and Punishment
    <span class="markup">(<code>label</code> inside <code>h2</code> without any referenced
<code>
input</code>, <code>id</code> referenced by <code>aria-labelledby</code> on
<code>label</code>)</span><span
class="hide">by</span>
    <em>Chuck Myers</em></label></h2>
    <p id="FM1-booked-out" aria-labelledby="track1 title-FM1 FM1-booked-out" tabindex="0">Sorry,
workshop
booked out!</p>
  </td>


  <td>
    <h2 id="title-FA1"><label>Workshop 4, Dead souls: The perils of memory leaks
    <span class="markup">(<code>h2</code> without native label, <code>id</code> referenced by
<code>aria-
labelledby</code> on <code>h2</code>)</span> <span class="hide">by</span>
    <em>Guntram von Westerndorff</em></label></h2>
    <p aria-labelledby="track1 title-FA1" tabindex="0">Sorry, workshop booked out!</p>
  </td>
</tr>
```

```
<tr>
  <th id="track2" scope="row">track 2</th>
  <td>
    <h2><label for="TM2">Workshop 5, Carrots and Sticks: The impact of Mandate 376
    <span class="markup">(no use of <code>aria-labelledby</code>, native <code>label</code>
inside <code>
h2</code>, "Attend" in <code>label</code> element, both labels referencing the same
<code>input</code> in their <code>
for</code> attribute)</span> <span class="hide">by</span>
    <em>Jacqueline Carnet</em></label></h2>
    <p>17 places left</p>
    <input type="checkbox" id="TM2"><label for="TM2">Attend</label>

  </td>

  <td>
    <h2><label for="TA2">Workshop 6, Far from the madding Flash: native Video in HTML5
    <span class="markup">(no use of <code>aria-labelledby</code>, just native <code>label</code>
inside
<code>h2</code> referencing <code>input</code> in <code>for</code> attribute, "Attend" in
<code>p</code> element)</span>
<span class="hide">by</span>
    <em lang="ru">Sergej Leontiev</em></label></h2>
    <p>2 places left</p>
    <p><input type="checkbox" id="TA2">Attend</p>
  </td>

  <td>
    <h2 id="title-FM2">Workshop 7, Of mice and pen: the battle for smart input
    <span class="markup">(no native <code>label</code> inside <code>h2</code>,
<code>id</code> referenced by
<code>aria-labelledby</code> on <code>h2</code>, "Attend" in <code>p</code> element with
<code>id</code> also referenced
by <code>aria-labelledby</code>)</span> <span class="hide">by</span>
    <em>Jake Ziegler</em></h2>
    <p>2 places left</p>
    <p id="FM2-att"><input type="checkbox" id="FM2" aria-labelledby="track2 title-FM2 FM2-
att">Attend</p>
  </td>

  <td>
    <h2><label for="FA2">Workshop 8, A hitchhiker's guide to conformance
    <span class="markup">(native <code>label</code> inside <code>h2</code> and referencing
<code>
input</code> in <code>for</code> attribute, "Attend" in <code>p</code> element, <code>aria-
labelledby</code> just
referencing "Attend")</span> <span class="hide">by</span><em>Emily Chan</em></label></h2>
    <p>19 places left</p>
    <p id="FA2-att"><input type="checkbox" id="FA2" aria-labelledby="FA2-att">Attend</p>
  </td>
```

		Thursday		Friday	
		9 to 12 AM	2 to 5 PM	9 to 12 AM	2 to 5 PM
track 1		Workshop 1, Memoirs of a justified coder (`label` inside h2, with the id referenced by `aria-labelledby` on h2, "Attend" in p element, with an id also referenced by `aria-labelledby`) by *Maud McRae* 2 places left ☐ Attend	Workshop 2, Pride and Vendor Prefixes (`label` inside h2, this time with the id referenced by `aria-labelledby` on `label`, "Attend" in separate `label` element with another id also referenced by `aria-labelledby`) by *Cassandra Barnave* 2 places left ☑ Attend	Workshop 3, Cutting corners with code: Crime and Punishment (`label` inside h2 without any referenced `input`, id referenced by `aria-labelledby` on `label`) by *Chuck Myers* Sorry, workshop booked out!	Workshop 4, Dead souls: The perils of memory leaks (h2 without native label, id referenced by `aria- labelledby` on h2) by *Guntram von Westerndorff* Sorry, workshop booked out!
track 2		Workshop 5, Carrots and Sticks: The impact of Mandate 376 (no use of `aria-labelledby`, native `label` inside h2, "Attend" in `label` element, both labels referencing the same `input` in their `for` attribute) by *Jacqueline Carnet* 17 places left ☐ Attend	Workshop 6, Far from the madding Flash: native Video in HTML5 (no use of `aria-labelledby`, just native `label` inside h2 referencing `input` in `for` attribute, "Attend" in p element) by *Sergej Leontiev* 2 places left ☐ Attend	Workshop 7, Of mice and pen: the battle for smart `input` (no native `label` inside h2, id referenced by `aria-labelledby` on h2, "Attend" in p element with id also referenced by `aria-labelledby`) by *Jake Ziegler* 2 places left ☐ Attend	Workshop 8, A hitchhiker's guide to conformance (native `label` inside h2 and referencing `input` in `for` attribute, "Attend" in p element, `aria-labelledby` just referencing "Attend") by *Emily Chan* 19 places left ☐ Attend

Figure 60: Adding a table of dynamic fields and text within a static table

68.2   Alternative Output For Dynamic Screens

There are several options available, some are better than others, depending on the complexity of your data and text.

Tables

The usual gremlin, tables cause again the most issues. There are 2 outputs that will meet the requirement of 508 as an alternative, if executed correctly.

- Excel = This must be kept as a simple grid, if there are sub-headers, then they must be repeated to each cell can refer back to the column of row sub header. If possible it is best to put the column headers on the first row. There are also Excel settings that make the spreadsheet automatically accessible, see in this document (Section D39).

- PDF = It is actually easy to output into a PDF, but usually most routines are setup for visual and printing purposes. Use iText software to add on for dynamic output of tagged and table cell associated PDF files. If simply converting a document to PDF see the tutorial B3.

69 List of Figures

Index

70 Last Minute Notes

70.1   Captivate 9

With JAWS 16 and IE in the best possible configuration, the videos are not reliable for accessibility. While closed caption works well, screen reader access is not stable and becomes too verbose and un-navigable with many elements on the screen. This is particularly true when a table of content and buttons are added to the page.

The solution is to add the close captioning for the video for hearing impaired. Then create a transcript for the vision impaired – or those who prefer a file they can control. If the original video started as a PowerPoint you can edit out the images that contain no information and convert to a PDF – remember to clean up the PDF file. If there are charts or screen shots, they must be described.

If this is a simulation with lots of animated mouse clicking and screen elements changing – you will need to capture screens when they are different and describe them. You can do this in Word or PowerPoint. Give a Heading to each page or section, sub-headings if long sections. Breaking into chunks with titles helps a great deal. Numbering (like this book) helps with orientation.

Note: Anything you convert to PDF that has bullet or number lists, especially those that are either more than one line per bullet or have other text or images in-between the bullets will require tag editing as this is a very common conversion error. You may need to move List tags around to make full tag tree branch. If you leave them separated they are read by screen readers incorrectly. See the PDF tutor within this book or for more detail my other book "Fix PDF Files For Accessibility" from Amazon.

70.2   Accessible Training Software

Elucidat is the best HTML5 based training software I have tested among 50 applications. This is the most customizable for any training situation and it can still be totally accessible. This includes both static and dynamic (simulations) with hot spots, quizzes, all types of buttons and pop-ups. All the dynamic elements can be made keyboard and screen reader accessible. Another feature is easy ability to resize for browser, mobile and tablets, and still retains reading order and correct organization of the content. There are other similar products, I just found Elucidat to be the most flexible and the company support go well beyond any other I have dealt with.

https://www.elucidat.com/

71 Contact Me

If you have any comments or suggestions please feel free to send them to my blog. If you run into any issues or solutions that may also help others, feel free to share.

http://accessibilityeveryone.blogspot.com/

72 About the Author

Ed Thrush has 13 years in Section 508, accessibility and 18 years in IT. In both fields he has generated a wealth of guides and training material. Starting with a background in libraries, Ed found out early on that materials had to be understandable to the public at large. People need to have easy access, and search capabilities with options for how people view information differently. The accessibility field requires creativity and communication. It also requires some technical knowledge to help provide solutions. Ed has mastered these over the years by leading teams to fix applications and documents with creative programming and to offer knowledge bases and accessibility websites.

Previous Publishing:

- Fix PDF Files For Accessibility (Amazon)
- SSA Advanced Guide for Accessible PDF Documents (federal government book)
- Probe (free science fiction novella - Smashwords)
- Wormhole Theater (free science fiction short story - Smashwords)
- Tutorials within government: JAWS, MAGic, Word Accessibility, PDF Accessibility, Section 508 Introduction, 508 Procurement, 508 in the SDLC, 508 for Programmers

Experience - Ed Thrush Provided Accessibility For The Following:

- Maryland State Government, IRS, SSA, CMS, VA, Prince Georges County Government MD, Maryland Judiciary.
- 508 Legal: SSA technical adviser to benefits 508 lawsuit

Yes But Did You Apply Accessibility To Anything Big?

- $250M Interface contract for the ACA
- $32M support for MS Office
- Entire IRS support center redesign all IT for Verizon
- HR & Timekeeping cloud system for all Maryland state employees

Made in the USA
Columbia, SC
19 September 2021